SALOONS

— OF THE —

OLD WEST

Related titles from Random House Value Publishing, Inc.,

James Horan's *Authentic Wild West* series
The Gunfighters
The Lawmen
The Outlaws

***

The West That Was
by Tom Lowles and Joe Lansdale

The American West Year by Year
by John S. Bowman

Tales of the Wild West
by The National Cowboy Hall of Fame

The Oregon Trail
by Frances Parkman

Ranch Life and the Hunting Trail
by Theodore Roosevelt and
illustrated by Frederic Remington

History of Western Railroads
by Jane Eliot

SALOONS

— OF THE —

OLD WEST

RICHARD ERDOES

GRAMERCY BOOKS

New York • Avenel

This 1997 edition is published by Gramercy Books,
a division of Random House Value Publishing, Inc.,
40 Engelhard Avenue, Avenel, New Jersey 07001,
by arrangement with Alfred A Knopf, Inc.

Gramercy Books and colophon are trademarks of
Random House Value Publishing, Inc.

Random House
New York · Toronto · London · Sydney · Auckland
http://www.randomhouse.com/

Printed and bound in the United States of America

A CIP catalog record for this book is available from the Library of Congress.

Saloons of the Old West
ISBN 0-517-1873-8
8 7 6 5 4 3 2 1

For Jean,
my wife and favorite drinking companion

CONTENTS

———◆-◆———

1   The Cock-a-Doodle-Do of Democracy 3

2   In the Name of the Great Jehovah and the Continental
        Congress 12

3   Westward the Tanglefoot 28

4   Walnut, Glass, and Brass 37

5   The Mixologist 55

6   Painting One's Nose 68

7   The Stuff They Drank 84

8   "Acomidation fer Man and Hoss" 103

9   The Saddle of Faith, the Bridle of Salvation, and the Six-Gun
        of Righteousness 119

10   His Honor (the Saloon Keeper) on His Bench (the Bar), or
        Saloon Law 131

11   Bucking the Tiger 141

12   Tipsy Thespis 166

13   "Wimmin," or Only a Bird in A Gilded Cage, or Women,
        Good and Bad 182

14   Death in the Barroom, or Likker and Lead 205

15   Death and Transfiguration, or "A Long Time Between Drinks,"
        or "Lips That Touch Liquor . . ." 231

Notes 255

Bibliography 266

Acknowledgments 271

Index 273

SALOONS

— OF THE —

OLD WEST

CHAPTER 1

THE COCK-A-DOODLE-DO OF DEMOCRACY

SALON (Fr. - Hall) an apartment for the reception of guests; 2. a periodic gathering, usually at the home of a distinguished woman, of persons of note in artistic, literary, or political circles. 3. a hall in which works of art are displayed.

SALOON (Americanism) misspelling of the above. A public house, a barroom, a drinking place.

—Consolidated Webster 1957

The *image:* A smoke-filled room, men sitting at tables with either wide-brimmed or high-crowned hats on, playing cards while painted cats in rustling silk or velvet, their hair adorned with ostrich feathers, are gadding about. To the left the bar with the busy mixologist, to the right the swinging doors. Cowboys, resting their spurred, high-heeled boots on brass rails. The blond, blue-eyed hero emerges on the upstairs landing with guns blazing. The neatly drilled, black-visaged villain hurtles through the splintering railing, crashing with a heavy thud to the floor below, and bites the dust—the sawdust covering the floor. The hero jumps from the landing onto the chandelier fashioned from a wagon wheel. He swings himself, orangutan fashion, over onto the bar, his belly hardware still sputtering with an inexhaustible stream of bullets. The mustachioed bardog bobs up and down from behind the bar like a freaked-out yo-yo. Fanning his hogleg, the blond hero severs the rope by which the chandelier is suspended. It crashes heavily down upon the heads of a half-dozen more swarthy villains, burying them for good. The sawdust is covered with broken glass and blood. The blond hero nonchalantly blows away the smoke from the muzzle of his six-shooter—an absolute must serving no discernible purpose. Silence. The bit players stand transfixed like Lot's wife turned into a pillar of salt. The blond demigod backs out defiantly through the swinging doors. His faithful steed whinnies joyfully. The barkeeper rises from behind the counter, his sonorous voice ringing out: "Belly up to the bar, gents, the drinks are on the house!"

Thus the image created by legend and Hollywood which comes invariably to the American mind whenever the word "saloon"—meaning *western* saloon—is mentioned. The saloon is the dream palace of countless Walter Mittys, the fortress of Anglo machismo where masculinity extends its hide, the castle of male chauvinism with hair on its chest, the "rooster crow of democracy," at least in fantasy. It was more often the peaceful refuge of heavy, dull, skirt-scared men watching the flies crawl up the window screen.

And yet the stereotyped, rip-roaring whiskey mill that launched a thousand horse operas existed once, at a certain time and in certain places. Its life was short. In 1930 one out of every two states had been saloonless for over fifty years. Half of the continental United States had been bone dry since the 1880s, turned into a hardshell-Baptist schoolmarm's desert. Hardly anybody but a few living fossils in their nineties has ever beheld the inside of the proverbial den of iniquity of the past.

The saloon, the old-time Indian, the mountain man, the trail-driving cowboy made up the Old West of the novelists and painters. All four shared the same fate. They were misrepresented and their life was short. The West's history was like an accordion, compressing the development of generations into a single lifetime. Around the turn of the century a proud saloon owner conducted an English visitor through his barroom. "This is the oldest, most historic drinking establishment in the state," he explained. "It goes back all the way to the times of the first prospectors, almost fifty years." "My dear fellow," said the Englishman, "where I come from it takes that long to break in a new bartender." The word "saloon" did not replace the older "tavern," "alehouse," or "taproom" until the 1840s, and the typical western saloon with its false front, swinging doors, and carved bar did not make its appearance until the mid-1850s. In an incredibly short time the saloon developed from a single barrel of home brew placed in front of a covered wagon upon whose side the word WHISKEY had been painted, to the ornate drinking place with shining mirrors and gilt-framed nudes; and just as swiftly it decayed and vanished—or metamorphosed into another form. And vanish, too, did the old-type, red-likker-drinking westerner.

A young man, hardly old enough to raise a beard, set out in 1830 from St. Louis to go west and trap the beaver that were already then becoming extinct. Mounted on muleback, he penetrated the Indian Territory with a flintlock muzzleloader, a strike-a-light, and a Green River knife. He was, technologically speaking, still a creature of the colonial, preindustrial age. After surviving his first winter on the prairie, he proudly called himself a mountain man. Ten years later the beaver were gone, and so was the mountain man. The ex-trapper became a guide, an army scout, a rancher, a saloon keeper. He might organize buffalo hunts for Russian archdukes or English aristocrats until, in no time at all, there were no buffalo left. In his old age the former beaver trapper sat down to a dinner at Delmonico's with his New York biographer, rode the elevated, and made telephone calls by the light of Edison's invention, the light bulb.

The Plains Indians whom the trapper in his youth had fought, fraternized, and shacked up with had, in the meantime, with equal suddenness made the step from the neolithic to the industrial age. When the trapper had first met them, they had faced him with flint-tipped spears and arrows or stone-headed clubs. Some had not yet acquired weapons and tools of steel, heard the report of a gun, or encountered a white man. Some still remembered the day when their father or grandfather had brought the first horse to the tribe. The glorious days of the free-roaming "Red Knights of the Prairie," hunting and raiding on horseback, the long tails of their war bonnets trailing behind them in the wind, lasted a mere hundred years. Plains Indian life, as imagined by moviegoers, came into being with the horse, the gun, trade cloth, and glass beads anywhere between 1725 and 1800. For some tribes it ended in the 1850s, for the luckier ones in the 1880s. By the time our ex-mountain man was being interviewed at Delmonico's, most native Americans had been herded onto reservations, and warriors who had fought Custer had become members of Buffalo Bill's Wild West show performing in London before Queen Victoria and the Prince of Wales. Some of these warriors survived into the 1940s, the age of radio, the airplane, and the tourist.

Men and women who had crossed the Plains in covered wagons lived to experience the thrill of a

"The image created by legend and Hollywood." John Wayne and Marlene Dietrich in *The Spoilers*, 1942.

5

ride in a horseless carriage. As for the cowboy, many serious historians insist that the real cowboy went out of existence with the first barbed-wire fence.

Thus the West became a vast Disneyland where history is something that happened just a moment ago, where the thrilled tourist sips his margarita at the very bar whose wood has been worn away by the elbows of Wild Bill Hickok, Buffalo Bill, or Bat Masterson, onetime saloon keeper, gambler, and gunfighter who ended his life as a sportswriter and editor for a New York newspaper.

As it was with people, so it was with the western saloon. It came into being, reached its height, and died with dramatic suddenness, undergoing dazzling changes during its short life, going on living long after its death. Americans, as a whole, never appreciated the frontier until it was gone. Then they promptly resurrected it. The mountain men and scouts became the subjects of penny-dreadfuls, the Indians and gunfighters circus performers as well as subjects for the photographer's lens. The hard-working, grubby cowboy became the singing Roy Rogers or Gene Autry, the saloon a museum. Only the bartenders remained essentially the same.

According to the habitués of yore who watched the saloon's decline and fall, Prohibition did not spell the end of the western saloon. It died, so they say, when the first respectable woman (the others did not count) stepped up to a bar and ordered a fancy cocktail, thereby destroying a myth as well as a vital piece of American folklore. It was at the heart of the old western saloon that it was woman-less, with the exception of the "nymphs of the prairie" or the "pretty waiter girls" who did not interfere with the business of maleness, but rather enhanced it. The ancient barrelhouse was a place for men only, a place where a fellow could get away from the little woman and lay his marital

problems on good old Ned or Vic or Otto (if it happened to be a beer joint). In the true sense McSorley's in New York was the last real saloon; and when it finally bowed to the law in 1970 and admitted women into its Holy of Holies, the old and fabled institution gave up its ghost for good.

If during Prohibition the saloon, like Sleeping Beauty, had merely slumbered, waiting for Prince Charming, then he appeared after repeal in tourist garb, a seeker of the good old times, a lover of aged polished walnut and Tiffany lamps. He and a few old-timers who yearned to hook their boot heels around a brass rail once more reawakened the saloon, but only as a pale shadow of its former self. In most places it was not even allowed to call itself "saloon." Except in certain western tourist spots, for reasons hard to fathom, it was even legally deprived of its hallmark, the swinging doors. Even out in John Wayne's West, the old water hole was never the same again, saloon signs and swinging doors notwithstanding. Ye Aulde Tavern, Le Bistro, the Monkey Bar, La Dolce Vita Café, the Beachcomber Inn, the High Noon Lounge, the Schnitzelbank Bierstube are not the real McCoy. "Them cute kinds ain't saloons,"* explained an old-timer still working in the Homestake mine near Deadwood a few years back. "Them places full of dudes in chartreuse and pink cowboy hats with pointed glo-color, jigsaw boots sitting there with those tangle-haired chicks with see-through blouses and cut-down frazzled Levis so short you can see the whole works, but with two thousand dollars' worth of silver and turquoise around their necks, drinking Harvey Wallbangers, Sunrise Tequilas, and Virgin Coladas—they are no saloons, they are *just bars*."

Nor did this man, who had been around, have a particular liking for what he called Mickey Mouse saloons—not for Lamy's Legal Tender, in

---

*Quotations and factual information are referenced, and often amplified, in the Notes section beginning on page 255.

spite of its old fittings, antique bar, and superb cocktails; nor for Nevada's Bucket of Blood, though the waitresses are prettily gotten up in Gay Nineties outfits; nor for Deadwood's own Old Style Saloon, though it boasts the self-same chair in which Wild Bill got his and stages a "mellerdrama"—*The Trial and Hanging of Cash McCall*—during the tourist season. "Them's painted whores," the old-timer said. "Right purty, but not honest wimmin."

He likewise took a dim view of the two dozen or so "one and only" Faces on the Barroom Floor spread all the way from New Mexico to the Canadian border, and he equally detested the several Silver Dollars, Nuggets, Alamos, and Lone Stars, all claiming, or at least hinting, that they represented the original whiskey mill of that name. It reminded him, he said, of a story once told him of

two monasteries whose pride was that each of them possessed the entire preserved body of St. Martin, or possibly St. Bernard of Clairvaux—he was not sure which. Both cloisters were powerful and rich with donations of pilgrims come to worship the sacred bones. A fierce rivalry rose between the competing abbeys, and they appealed to Rome for a decision as to which one of them possessed the genuine article. Not wanting to offend either, the Curia finally rendered its Solomonic verdict that both were genuine, as nothing was impossible for a saint.

"That may be all right for a saint," said the old man, "but it won't do for a saloon." He admitted that there were still a few places hidden away here and there that *looked* like saloons, served straight drinks, and had customers sitting at the bar who *resembled* their sires of a generation or two ago,

Tiffany's—New Mexico's "oldest" saloon.

but, he concluded his long sermon, "by and large we have no more saloons, just bars *masquerading* as saloons. It ain't what it used to be."

The story of the western saloon, as well as the people who frequented it, is so encrusted with fancy embroideries of a later epoch that truth is hard to come by. Even those with firsthand experience were among the sinners. The writers for *Ballou's, Harper's, Leslie's,* the *Century Graphic,* and the old *Police Gazette* sometimes abandoned themselves to wild exaggeration in order to tickle the fancy of their readers. Some of the main actors themselves—the gunslingers, sheriffs, prospectors, and gamblers—told outrageous lies when their wells of memory were primed with the red essence, or when ego or money was involved. Five hundred books were written about Billy the Kid alone. Whole bookcases can be filled with biographies of Wild Bill Hickok, Bat Masterson, Buffalo Bill, or Silver King Tabor. Fictitious stories have been reprinted again and again, each time improved upon, until they became accepted as gospel truth. Like a prospector, the would-be historian has to scrape away successive layers of nonsense to get at the pay dirt.

The western saloon is a controversial subject. Every statement made about it has been contradicted by another:

"The saloon was a vile robber's roost where the dregs of humanity reveled in swinish drunkenness."

"The saloon was a bulwark against drunkenness, the poor man's only club, the place where mine owner and beggar rubbed shoulders as equals."

"The saloons were all the same and looked the same. If you had seen one, you had seen a thousand."

"The saloons were of fantastic variety, of different architecture as well as clientele."

"The saloons were dingy holes in the wall, made up of unpeeled boards, overflowing spittoons, and sawdust covering unspeakable things."

"The saloon was an oasis of glamour in the wilderness, a place of shining brass, flowered carpets, and glittering chandeliers."

"The bardog was a loutish, tight-fisted, monosyllabic brute with a shotgun under the counter, who loved to use his bung starter on his meeker customers."

"The bartender was a philosophic gentleman overflowing with the milk of human kindness, a peacemaker if for no other reason than to protect his backbar mirror and crockery."

"The western barkeep served nothing other than the straight undiluted road to ruin."

"The proprietor was an accomplished mixologist who could be depended upon to serve up a hundred and fifty different concoctions satisfying even the most exotic tastes."

"The saloon was a pure-bred native American institution, Anglo-Saxon to the core, blessedly free from foreign influence."

"The saloon was a bibulous melting pot reflecting the drinking habits of Irishmen, Bohunks, Frenchmen, Germans, and Slavs."

"The western pouring spot was a den of vice in which degraded sexual debaucheries were the order of the day."

"Western saloon customers were excessively prudish, latent homosexuals, afraid of women, who treated even the soiled doves of the prairie like ladies."

"Western saloons were slaughterhouses spattered with the blood of their customers who always died with their boots on—most of the time right at the bar."

"The western thirst parlor was a place where endless talk was unrelieved by any kind of excitement and where nothing ever happened. Customers died in their bunks—sometimes with their boots on if they kept them on in bed."

All the above statements are true and all are false, depending on the time, the place, and the attitude of those who made them.

There was not one West, there were several—the Indian's, the mountain man's, the settler's, the miner's, the gambler's, the cowboy's, the railroader's, the woman's—all different though overlapping. There is not even a consensus as to what the "West" meant geographically. It was an ever-shifting, ever-changing, hard-to-define sort of thing. It was the Big Unknown beyond the Alleghenies, the Wilderness of Kaintuck, the far side of the Bloody Ohio, the Ocean of Grass beyond the Mississippi, the Indian Territory west of the Big Muddy, otherwise known as the Missouri, and finally the land beyond Zebulon Pike's "Shineing Mountains," the gigantic movie set of the horse operas. For the purpose of a study of western saloons it is mainly the West of the miners, ranchers, and homesteaders, the whole land mass between the Missouri and the Pacific. There are four fringe cities whose drinking spots are anything but typical western saloons, but who nevertheless were great influences in the shaping of the western saloon. The first, southernmost, and oldest was New Orleans, the jumping-off point for the settlement of Texas and exporter of slaves, gamblers, and shady ladies. The second was St. Louis, capital of the fur trade, starting point of the great overland trails, city of French voyageurs and keelboatmen. The third was sinful, alcoholic Chicago, the "Gem of the Prairie," shipper of barroom equipment and terminus for cattle shipments. The fourth was San Francisco, with its Barbary Coast, the forty-niner's gateway to the goldfields, a legend almost from the moment of its birth. None of them was a typical western town but all of them contributed to the saloon's development. Finally there was Alaska, geographically not fitting into what is commonly understood by the "West," but during the Klondike gold-fever period the host to many sa-loon keepers and their customers who had pulled up stakes in California and Colorado and gone north.

The western saloon existed because it filled a basic human need, which it is now hard to imagine. It was a place of comfort, a refuge, even a place of refinement where one could rub elbows with a fellow human being. It was a place where they spoke cow talk, where nesters could commiserate with each other about hails and dry spells. The saloon was a place to dispel the loneliness of a month on the range or two months in the back country with only the sheep for company. There were some people who spent most of their waking and a good part of their sleeping hours in saloons. The saloon was all things to all men. Besides being a drinking place, it was an eatery, a hotel, a bath and comfort station, a livery stable, gambling den, dance hall, bordello, barbershop, courtroom, church, social club, political center, dueling ground, post office, sports arena, undertaker's parlor, library, news exchange, theater, opera, city hall, employment agency, museum, trading post, grocery, ice cream parlor, even a forerunner of the movie house in which entranced cowhands cranked the handles of ornate kinetoscopes to watch the jerky movements of alluring cancan dancers. A saloon might fulfill none or several of the above functions at the same time.

It has been jokingly said that, with the exception of the Battle of the Little Bighorn, all western history was made inside the saloons, and there is a grain of truth in this. States were named, capitals founded, candidates announced, and elections held inside barrooms. The saloon was as red-white-and-blue American as apple pie, in the best tradition of the Founding Fathers. Ben Franklin painted his nose frequently; John Hancock was a rumrunner; Washington drank hot toddies in a hundred taprooms and ran up enormous liquor bills; Jefferson promoted home brewing of good native malt. Sam Houston, dressed in a fancy velvet coat trimmed with gold, invited passersby to come in and have a drink in his Texas capitol, a primitive log cabin that later was turned into a grog shop. Davy Crockett could outdrink ten keelboatmen. Daniel Webster was "as majestic in his consumption of liquor as in everything else." Lincoln was part owner of an Illinois general store licensed to sell liquor to "all except negroes, Indians and children." Of Ulysses S. Grant, Honest Abe said: "I wish I knew what brand of whiskey he drinks. I would send a barrel to all my other gener-

als." Major Reno was incoherent during the Custer fight. His nipping might have contributed to Sitting Bull's victory. The farther west, the greater the capacity of men to hold their liquor; at least, that is the claim. The saloon was the empire's cradle, the place where a boy became a man—

> At the bar, at the bar
> where I had my first cigar—

where his first visit constituted a sort of puberty rite. As an old-timer put it: "We was weaned on it. The saloons were mighty pop'lar places. We

"The ruin of an ancient saloon . . ." St. Elmo, Colorado.

thought nothing of riding thirty miles jest to have a drink."

For some of the early prospectors and pioneers whiskey came before food, women, even gold. In one mountain pass stands the ruin of an ancient saloon—the only building left of a once-prospering mining town, its few remaining rafters covered with spiderwebs and festooned with clusters of somnolent bats. Tacked to a disintegrating wall of rotten pine logs is a faded sign:

> Thirst
> Comes first.
> Drink till you burst!
> Everything else can wait!

A saloon was often the first substantial building in a new settlement, the last to crumble when it turned into a ghost town. A story is told about an early St. Louis whiskey peddler crossing the Plains in his creaking prairie schooner. One day the oxen lay down and died. The peddler put his barrels of busthead in a circle and painted SALOON on a board which he nailed to the nearest tree.

One day later a town had grown up around him and his goods. Sometimes the saloon *was* the town:

> Dogville, Dogville . . .
> A tavern and a still,
> That's all there is to Dogville.

The names of some early Colorado mining settlements suggest that they were built around saloons, or at least that their inhabitants were preoccupied with thoughts of alcoholic refreshments. There was a Boozeville, Bugtown, Jackpot, Drunkenman, Delirium Tremens, Poker Flats, Red Elephant, Red Eye, Red Nose, Tin Cup, Winesville, Whiskey Diggings, Whiskey Hole, Whiskey Park, and Whiskey Springs. The western saloon had a way of springing up like a mushroom. It did not, however, spring up from the prairie soil like Pallas Athena jumping fully armed from the head of Zeus. It did not give birth to itself. It was begotten by the old London alehouse upon the colonial New England tavern.

CHAPTER 2

IN THE NAME OF THE GREAT JEHOVAH AND THE CONTINENTAL CONGRESS

Landlord, to thy barroom skip,
Make a foaming mug of flip—
Make it from New England's
    staple,
Rum and sugar from the maple.
Hark! I hear the poker sizzle
and o'er the mug the liquor
    drizzle,
And against the earthen mug
Hear the wooden spoon's cheerful
    dub.
See the landlord taste the flip,
Fling the cud from his under lip.
Come, quickly bring the humming
    liquor,
Richer than ale of British vicar.

—Sung at Greenfield Tavern
    Rhode Island, 1730

The history of the western saloon began on America's East Coast the moment the first white man stepped ashore and rolled his keg of ardent spirits down the gangway to establish a still. In every group of bold newcomers there was always one who forthwith erected a structure, no matter how primitive, which served at least in part as a barroom where he dispensed some sort of alcoholic beverage. Among the first crude wattled huts of the Jamestown settlers was a part-time saloon. Captain John Thorpe, a James River Virginian, savant, and missionary, distilled "godly liquor," which he brought to the benighted heathen, persuading them to accept the true faith together with the exhilarating spirits. He was killed by the natives "who either got too much of his whiskey or his religion, or got the two confused," as one writer put it. In 1609 Henry Hudson sailed his *Half Moon* into New York Bay and lost no time plying fishing Indians with brandy. They in turn wasted not a single moment in renaming their island *Manahachtanienk* (Manhattan)—"The Island where all got crazy," or maybe, drunk. At least this is what some historians say, though there are other explanations. The *Mayflower* had in her cargo a generous supply of what Governor John Winthrop described as "hot waters." Some seventeenth-century passengers did not wait until reaching New England before setting up their stills, but "burned claret at sea," that is, distilled wine into brandy en route, which must have cheered many a seasick voyager on a cold and stormy night.

When Reverend Higginson sailed out to the Plantations in the good ship *Talbot* in 1629, he took with him a load of five tons of beer and twenty gallons of brandy to help adjust himself to the New World. Liquor was looked upon favorably by the clergy. It was termed "one of the good creatures of God to be received with thanksgiving." Churches even encouraged the building of taverns next door to be "within easy hail of minister and parishioners." Settlements did not receive their charter unless they had first built a tavern.

The first Indian drunk in New England was recorded in 1621. An old Indian saying went: "You white men invented the devil, you can keep him." The Pilgrims not only imported Beelzebub together with their brandy, but involved Old Nick in their alcoholic doings. During the Salem witchcraft trials persons accused of consorting with the devil were sometimes examined in a saloon.

"We went therefore into the alehouse, where an Indian man attended us, who it seems was one of the afflicted. To him we gave some Cyder, and [he] acquainted us that his wife, who also was a Slave, was imprisoned for Witchcraft." This was probably the first Indian bartender in America.

In New England it was the devils who made their "afflicted" victims drunk. In the words of Cotton Mather: "Both she at my house, and her sister at home . . . were by the Daemons made very drunk, though they had no strong drink (as we are fully sure) to make them so. . . . And, immediately the Ridiculous Behaviours of one Drunk were with a wonderful exactness represented in her Speaking, and Reeling, and Spewing." The devil also smuggled into one household a "galley pot of Alkermes," a liquor made from the kermes insect thought to be a berry. Examining bewitched and bewitchers in the alehouse anticipated vigilante trials later held inside western saloons.

The East Coast settlers set the pattern for their

The "good creature" arrives.

western descendants. Liquor consumption was enormous. In Philadelphia, the inhabitants of which were mighty tipplers in spite of its Quaker atmosphere, one Thomas Apty, at the Red Lion Tavern on Elbow Lane, in 1736, "laid a wager of Half a Crown that he could drink within the space of one hour and a half, a Gallon of Cyder Royall, which he had no sooner accomplished and said I have finished, but He fell down and then expired." It was no wonder that among favorite Pennsylvania concoctions was a drink called "Stewed Quaker." Nor was capacity for drink less in the southern colonies.

The London-directed Virginia Company accused Virginia settlers of being drunk at the time of an Indian attack and therefore being responsible for the great massacre of 1622. Governor Harvey reported that half of the planters' income from tobacco sales was spent on drink, tobacco being the main source of income in the southern colonies. When Virginia Governor Spotswood explored the Shenandoah and Blue Ridge mountains, his liquor supply, loaded on pack horses, nearly equaled all the other provisions combined, including the powder and lead. Every newly discovered hillock, valley, or stream called for a liquid celebration. In the words of George Fontaine, one of the expedition members:

We had a good dinner and after it we got the men together and loaded all their arms, and we drank the King's health in champagne, and fired a volley; the Princess' health in burgundy, and fired a volley; and all the rest of the Royal Family in claret, and a volley. We had several sorts of liquors, viz., Virginia red and white wine, Irish usquebaugh, brandy, shrub, two sorts of rum, champagne, canary, cherry, punch, water, cider, etc. I sent two of the rangers to look for my gun, which I dropped in the mountains; they found it, and brought it to me at night, and I gave them a pistole for their trouble.

Whether losing his gun had anything to do with the Irish usquebaugh George did not say. By 1700, when the colonies were less than a hundred years old and the number of white settlers still considerably below one million, some ten thousand people brewed, distilled, or fermented alcoholic beverages in a surprisingly large variety. Consumption has been estimated as averaging about ten gallons of hard liquor a year per capita, women and children included. By 1792, when licensing had been widely introduced, there were 2,579 licensed distillers. No count was made of the numbers who brewed unlawfully, but who brewed all the same. Consumption was down to a yearly 2 1/2 gallons per person, but here again the homemade product was not taken into account. Hardships, it was said, made for hard drinking, a softer life for a decline in imbibing. This theory was contradicted when, by 1810, the efforts of 14,200 distillers raised the yearly per capita quota to a robust five gallons. It was not to be wondered at that our forefathers often got "tolerably thin in the knees and thick in the tongue."

From crude beginnings the handsome stone or solidly timbered colonial tavern or ordinary evolved. Drinking inns rose on every village green and lined all roads at intervals of a half day's stagecoach ride. A good number of them are not only still standing, but continue to dispense cheer, good food, and liquid refreshments—treasured landmarks engulfed by modern traffic. The earliest descriptions of the settlement that was to become Boston mention by 1625 a place where drinks could be bought, though many consider the Cole House, inaugurated in 1634, the oldest tavern in the city. It was here that Chief Miantonomah and twenty of his braves were plied with ardent spirits in an effort to induce them to sign treaties giving their land away. Cole House was later renamed the John Hancock. Among its guests were Washington, Talleyrand, the future French king Louis Philippe, Madison, Jefferson, and, of course, the famous fellow citizen after whom the place was named. Another ancient pouring spot was set up in 1636 by one of the founders of Concord, Massachusetts, Captain Willard, to whom a grateful community granted the monopoly to "sell wine and strong water." The captain would probably have been dumbfounded to learn that one of his lineal descendants, Frances Willard, became a leader of the Prohibition Movement.

Following ancient English tradition all taverns had their names—and flowery ones too: The Star Chamber, Blue Chamber, Sun Chamber, Jerusalem Chamber, Blew Anchor, Raleigh Tavern, Bull's Head, Queens Head, Crown and Eagle, Pig and Whistle, Red Lion, Green Dragon, or the very American-sounding Catamount Tavern. A few of these names would later reoccur in the West. Some taverns were simply named after their owners: Cole House, Holsapple House, Fraunces' Tavern, or Buckman's famous grogshop, which is better known as Longfellow's Wayside Inn. Its taproom was called the "coop" on account of its cagelike construction and swinging gate.

One favorite New York dram shop was the White Horse Tavern near the Battery at the tip of Manhattan, founded and run by a Frenchman. It was always crammed during the legal drinking hours, which were from early morning until ten at night, but equally busy on Sundays, when guzzling was forbidden, providing schnapps and branntwein drinkers with their favorite essence during church-going hours. The memory of the White Horse lived on in a number of successive bars of the same name. One of them, by now venerable in its own right, still does a thriving business in Greenwich Village, a favorite hangout for writers, artists, and Bohemians. By 1648 nearly a quarter of all houses in New Amsterdam were drinking places. The city even had its own official city tavern, the Stadt-Herberg. Built in 1642, it was a sturdy stone edifice erected on orders of Director-General Kieft. It later became the "Stadt-Huys," or city hall, but still preserved a taproom somewhere in its bowels where the town fathers, puffing on their long clay pipes, could relax over

"Inns lined the road . . ."

a mug of Schiedam schnapps or Holland gin. Both the White Horse and the Stadt-Herberg were precursors of the western saloon—the one because of its cavalier disregard for the law, the other because it combined the functions of city hall and taproom.

In 1837, Nathaniel Hawthorne described Parker's Tavern on the court square in Concord. His narrative is interesting because it mentions certain aspects that later became characteristic of the western thirst parlor:

The door opens into Court Square, and is denoted, usually, by some choice specimens of dainties exhibited in the windows, or hanging beside the doorpost; as, for instance, a pair of canvas-backed ducks, distinguished by their delicately mottled feathers; an admirable cut of raw beefsteak; a ham, ready boiled and with curious figures traced in spices on its outward fat; a bunch of partridges, etc., etc. A screen stands directly before the door, so as to conceal the interior from an outside barbarian. . . .

At the counter stand, at almost all hours,—tipplers, either taking a solitary glass, or treating all around, veteran topers, flashy young men, visitors from the country, the various petty officers connected with the law, whom the vicinity of the

A Dutch coddling.

courthouse brings hither. Chiefly they drink plain liquors, gin, brandy, or whiskey, sometimes a Tom and Jerry, a gin cocktail, a brandy mash, and numerous other concoctions. All this toping goes forward with little or no apparent exhilaration of the spirits; nor does this seem the object sought, —it being rather, I imagine, to create a titillation of the coats of the stomach and a general sense of invigoration, without affecting the brain.

The inner room is hung round with pictures and engravings of various kinds,—a painting of a premium ox, a lithograph of a Turk and Turkish Lady . . . and various showily engraved tailors' advertisements . . . among them all, a small painting of a drunken toper sleeping on a bench beside the grog-shop,—a ragged, half-hatless, bloated, red-nosed, jolly, miserable-looking devil, very well done, and strangely suitable to the room in which it hangs. . . . From the center of the ceiling descended a branch with two gas-burners, which sufficiently illuminated every corner of the room. Nothing is so remarkable in these barrooms and drinking places, as the perfect order that prevails; if a man gets drunk, it is not otherwise perceptible than by his going to sleep, or his inability to walk.

Notable in this description is the screen concealing the door. Whether in New England or on the Lone Prairie, saloon patrons preferred to remain unobserved—especially by their wives. Notable also is the fact that even in the civilized East men preferred their drinks straight, though in both places the bartender was also often capable of mixing fancy drinks. Easterners then treated their fellows to a drink, as was the universal custom in the West. And it is interesting that the cocktail was already invented. Finally, the paintings of the prize bull and the Turkish Lady might be regarded as the forerunners of roundup photographs and harem scenes depicting the nude female form divine, often copied from Ingres, which later graced the walls of western saloons. Not parallel, however, was the eastern taproom's decorum and peacefulness. Such, then, were the public houses, mughouses, pothouses, ordinaries, and

The Fountain House on the Boston-Salem Road.

gin mills of the old colonists, who had not yet invented the word "saloon."

The bartender was called landlord, tapster, hostler, publican, ganymede, and tapper of strong waters. He was carefully picked by the town fathers, local justices, or board of selectmen as a "person of sober life and Conversation . . . fit to keep a house of entertainment." In the words of Timothy Dwight, president of Yale: "A great part of the New England innkeepers and their families treat a decent stranger, who behaves civilly to them, in such a manner as to show him plainly that they feel an interest in his happiness; and if he is sick or unhappy, will cheerfully contribute everything in their power to his relief."

An early Virginia newspaper carried a "help wanted" ad for "a single man, well recommended, who understands the business of bar." Obviously it was thought that marriage would interfere with his business, yet many colonial women were "tappers of ardent spirits." Widows were often given the job of tavern keeper, possibly to save their community the expense of looking after them. Probity and a reputation of chastity were essential for such a lady to obtain a license to "entertain travelers in the absence of relatives." In 1714, when Boston was a city of just under ten thousand inhabitants, there were thirty-four keepers of taverns and ordinaries, of whom twelve were women; four "victuallers and ale sellers," of whom one was a woman; forty-one retailers of strong waters, of whom seventeen were women; and a score of cider sellers.

Most innkeepers brought a stirrup cup on a tray to a horseman in a hurry who did not wish to dismount—an early example of "drive-in" refreshment. As in the early West the stagecoach

Stirrup cup—eastern style.

trade was important. The arrival of a coach was always a colorful event. Sometimes the coachman blew a horn to announce his arrival, or he made his whips snap like rifle shots while his passengers tumbled out and headed to the taproom. Dealing with the carriage trade was done in an efficient and curiously modern way. Men arriving on their own mounts, or with their families in their own coaches, were welcomed by the hostler, who led away the horses and wagons, giving them a "parking ticket" in return. While the travelers sat down to a meal, made jolly by ample quantities of punch or burned wine, the animals were fed and watered. Sometimes the coaches were cleaned too. Upon departure they turned in the tickets and redeemed their horses and vehicles. Some tavern keepers handed out smoked kippered herrings free with every drink, their saltiness increasing thirst and improving business, a custom handed down in the traditional free lunch of later saloons.

The eastern barkeepers of old also set precedents for eccentricity. James Akin, an engraver and druggist as well as tavern keeper in Newburyport, once got into an argument with his employer, a certain Edmund Blunt, during which the latter hurled a hot skillet at Akin. In revenge Akin engraved Blunt's likeness on porcelain chamber-

pots which sold like hotcakes. In New York "Black Sam" Fraunces, Washington's friend, hired a philosopher to lecture his topers on Hume, Locke, Pascal, and Descartes. A Virginia bardog known as Fighting Cock Charlie challenged his patrons to duels with swords whenever he felt himself insulted by them. He actually fought two or three bouts, luckily with nary a scratch to either himself or his opponents.

The tavern keeper, just as the western saloon keeper later, was a person of consequence, often captain of the militia, postmaster, alderman, or mayor. After the Revolution many an ex-colonel became a tavern landlord, while his former aide-de-camp tended bar for him. Frequently a landlord was given the honor of sealing a bottle of whiskey in the cornerstone of a new church or town hall.

The customers were "full of fun, foolery, and mean liquor." Everybody tippled—high or low, rich or poor, male or female, farmer or sailor. Puritans, Pilgrims, Presbyterians, and Quakers, permanently at loggerheads over points of doctrine, were at one when it came to imbibing the "good creature." They all shared the same drinking tastes and habits, though some, curiously enough, objected to the "sinful use of tobacco." Interpretation of what constituted a case of inebriation was liberal:

He is not drunk who from the floor
Can rise again and drink once more.
But he is drunk who prostrate lies
And cannot drink and cannot rise.

For many colonists the day began with an eye-opener of rum mixed with usquebaugh for "man, goodwife and boy." Beer soup was a fitting breakfast for the Dutch child. A hot toddy for a phlegm cutter braced a fellow to face a cold dawn. At 11 A.M. shops closed so that all and sundry could enjoy their 'leven o'clock bitters. Lodgers at wayside inns got their free drink in the morning. A hot flip was an excellent remedy for a boy's whooping cough, a bumper filled half with milk and half with whiskey, a royal restorative for a poorly nursing mother. Water, in the opinion of most, was bad for one's health, while hard cider had great medicinal properties. As one Maine Yankee put it:

By a sudden stroke, my leg is broke,
My heart is sore offended:
The doctor's come, let's have some rum,
And then we'll have it mended.

In this aspect too, the westerner followed in the footsteps of his eastern ancestors, being addicted until well into the modern age to patent medicines and cure-alls that contained a whopping percentage of alcohol. It was said that one could tell the patent medicine addict by his fiery proboscis.

Every kind of human activity was an occasion to indulge. The building of a Connecticut stone wall was estimated as "a gallon per yard." Haying meant that a farmer partook of two tumblers of applejack instead of his usual one. The arrival of a ship, the raising of a roof or barn, a casual visit between friends, births, weddings, and death, all called for an abundance of the exhilarating essence. Even a tight-fisted man would not preside over the betrothal of a son or daughter without putting out on the road barrels of hard cider for every passerby to help himself while generously ladling out toddies, punches, slings, and flips for his guests. The twice-yearly-held drilling of the militia, the so-called trained bands, always ended in a great alcoholic debauch in the tavern. "Training days," scoffed the great Cotton Mather, "become little more than drinking days." The ordination of a minister was always the cause of "Sacrificing mightily at the Shrine of Bacchus." There was even a special brew called "ordination beer." At an ordination ball in a Hartford tavern the jolly men of the cloth consumed the following:

To keeping Ministers

2 Mugs Tody	24 Dinners
5 Segars	11 Bottles Wine
1 Pint Wine	5 Mugs Flip
3 Bitters	5 Boles Punch
15 Boles Punch	3 Boles Tody

A note was appended to the bill to the effect that all had been paid for except the "Ministers' Rum."

Taverns were convivial places where everything under the sun was discussed and commented upon. According to an early observer: "Americans discussed politics and government, while Englishmen talked about themselves." A Dr. Alexander Hamilton heard two Irishmen, a French Jew, and a Scot argue over religion. It seems to have been a favorite topic, because in a Saybrook pothouse Hamilton observed the "lower classes" disputing "so pointedly justification, sanctification, adoption, regeneration, repentance, free grace, original sin and a thousand other such pretty chimerical knick-knacks as if they had done nothing but study divinity all their lives."

Mark the phrase "lower classes." The mingling of high and low in American taverns appalled the English gentleman. The equalizing process began early. The indentured servant and the imported

"Taverns were convivial places."

tenant farmer quickly fell under the spell of frontier mentality. Each needed nothing but an ax, a long rifle, and maybe a little pot still to become his own man. From the first the untamed frontier, the boundless, unfathomed, unknown western land beckoned, severing the umbilical cord between landlord and tenant. Who could tell the runaway indentured girl from the free farmer's daughter after she "had gone west" for twenty miles? "Yr Lordship be damnd. I have had enow. I am goink. Yr obdt sarvant Liz." Thus the earliest royal land grants withered, and the hopes of founding duke- and earl-doms in the New World collapsed. The West always exerted its powerful pull, even though it was still a very narrow West—the Adirondacks, the Blue Ridge Mountains, the Cumberland, Kentucky. For a hundred years the West stopped at the Alleghenies, the Great Chinese Wall of budding America. Some people continued talking of the "lower orders" and the respect they owed to their "betters." Class consciousness lingered into the post-Revolutionary era and persisted into the twentieth century. But it lingered less and less the farther west one went. When the Alleghenies barrier finally burst and taprooms became saloons, it vanished altogether.

What did the eighteenth-century easterner drink? Almost everything alcoholic:

We can make liquor to sweeten our lips
Of pumpkins, and parsnips, and walnut tree chips.

Strong waters were distilled by the first New Englanders from a variety of fruits—cherries, plums, pumpkins, currants, and elderberries. From a mixture of wild honey, yeast, and water the Pilgrims brewed metheglin, a dark amber cordial with a wallop that made the imbibers hear "the bees buzz." Six gallons of metheglin could buy two prime beaver pelts.

The De Peysters in the Hudson Valley toasted the arrival of a new little burgher "in heroic amounts of caudle," a drink of uncertain qualities, seemingly strong Dutch malt beer mixed with equal parts of a great variety of different kinds of schnapps and brandies. The New York gentry "got their wet sheet aboard" with the meridian, a concoction of brandy and beer. They also drank Manathans (beer, rum, and sugar), unless they preferred a Hotchpotch, which was a Manathan served hot.

Some New England taprooms were justly renowned for their sassafras, spruce, and birch beer sprinkled with pumpkin and apple parings, sweetened with molasses or maple syrup, and spiced with a dash of nutmeg. Benjamin Lynde, chief justice of Massachusetts, according to his own diary was excessively fond of good Madeira, brandy punch, syllabubs, and sangarees; surprisingly so, since Madeira and sangarees were more apt to grace the tables of Virginia gentry. Chief Justice John Marshall was "brought up on Federalism and Madeira." The very best Madeira was therefore known as "Old Supreme Court."

In both northern and southern colonies cordials were the favorite refreshment of ladies who drank themselves into a condition known as "How came you so?" They got tipsy on gooseberry, rhubarb, dandelion, or chokecherry wine. Black walnut schnapps was drunk by Dutchmen around Albany. "It was very bitter and burnt like Hell." "Stewed Quaker" was a mug of hard cider in which a hot baked apple had been immersed; "perry," a fiery drink made from pears; "peachy," a potent schnapps made from peaches.

The Virginian gentry got "haily-gaily," as they called it, on claret, sack, sherry, fayal, malmsy, French, and Rhine wines. A local peach brandy called Virginia Drams was also popular. In the 1820s it became fashionable for taverns to create their own specialties with fancy names, such as Moral Persuasion, Ne Plus Ultra, Deacon, Fiscal Agent, Pine Top, and Sweet Ruination. The democratic spirit of the Revolutionary and post-Revo-

"Haily-gaily."

lutionary era expressed itself in drinks named Son of Liberty, Vox Populi, Old Hickory, Polk and the Union Forever, Split Ticket, and American Eagle.

These are what some people drank. What all people drank was cider, applejack, rum, brandy, whiskey, hot toddies or flips, and, of course, beer and ale. The apple was not native to the New World but was an almost instant immigrant. The first American apple orchard was planted in 1629 in Massachusetts, with the express intention of making not apple pie but applejack—that is, hard cider. The name cider, pleasing to the Puritan ear, derived from the biblical "shekar" (drunken). In 1632, Governor's Island was given to John Winthrop on the condition that he would plant an apple orchard on it. By the 1670s apple orchards covered much of New England and New Jersey, and hard cider, apple whiskey, and applejohn were set out in large tubs with a number of ladles on a "come ye one or all" basis on every suitable or unsuitable occasion. "Sweet cider," the unfermented juice, was given to children. Sour, sweet, and bitter apples were used. As the apple juice fermented it became "hard," and the longer it fermented the harder and more potent it became. Late apples were supposed to make the best cider.

Applejack made a triumphal march into the earlier West—Kentucky, Tennessee, Ohio, and Illinois—but withered when it reached the prairie, which furnished no soil conducive to growing apples.

Rum was "that most American of comforting stimulants," "a true childe of ye New Worlde, borne in Barbados." The word "rum" was an abbreviation of the West Indian "rumbullion," or "rumscullion." According to some it derived its name from "aroma," or *saccharum,* the Latin word for sugar. A few scholars maintain that it is a gypsy word meaning "potent" or "powerful." They cite in their support the sailors' drink rumbowling; or rumbooze or rambooze, a favorite of early Oxford dons, made of eggs, wine, ale, and sugar; and also rumfustian, a colonial "consolator" fashioned from a quart of strong beer, a bottle of sherry, half a pint of gin, twelve egg yolks, orange peel, nutmeg, and sugar. Rumbarge was another fanciful concoction, served hot. None of these contained any rum, but they were potent and powerful. Rum from Jamaica, Surinam, and Barbados, "a hot, hellish and terrible liquor" commonly called Kill Devil (also known as Barbados brandy and referred to by New Englanders by its Indian name of accobee and by the Dutch as branntwein), was first imported in the 1640s and soon made the colonies into a "Sea of Rum."

New Englanders quickly began to make their own rum in order to avoid high import duties. Six rum distilleries were operating in New York in 1750. Newport, Rhode Island, had no fewer than thirty rum manufacturers, underselling New York and Boston rum makers by hawking their own brand at a modest four pence a quart. Rum was indispensable to the English army in the colonies. Soldiers as well as sailors got their daily gill of rum, dispensed on his majesty's ships with great ceremony from a brass-bound barrel at the foremast. A double or triple ration of rum inspired the redcoats to advance upon the grapeshot-spewing guns of Fort Vaudreuil (later Ticonderoga) and to conquer Montcalm on the Plains of Abraham. An officer writing to General Clinton in 1781 pointed out: "I need not mention to you, Sir, that the severe duty and portion of fatigue that falls to the lot of the troops in this quarter make rum of importance here." Rum was said to have won the French and Indian Wars but did not help the British subdue the colonies, possibly because the rebels drank more and better rum than the lobsterbacks.

Rum overtook cider and reigned supreme during the eighteenth century. In its heyday rum was a sovereign remedy for all of mankind's ills. Rum and licorice "cleared the rheum." Rum, milk, sugar, and egg yolks constituted an "encouragement for ladies big with child." It also soothed sore nipples. Gallstone pains were relieved by rum and liverwort. A tankard full of rum mixed with the juice of oysters and certain herbs restored "waning powers of the genitories." A chaplain sent on an expedition to bring the light to the "Bloody Savages" of Carolina was overcome by exhaustion on the way . . . "Mr. Little, one of the Carolina commissioners, to show his regard to the church, offered to treat him on the road with a fricassee of rum. They boiled half a dozen rashers of very fat bacon in a pint of rum, both which being dished up together served the company at once for meat and drink."

Patients were given laudanum and as much rum as they could swallow before an amputation. Rum mixed with herbal potions was also recommended in cases of hysteria or depression to soothe a troubled mind. In the words of Lord Byron: "There's nought, no doubt, so much the spirit calms as rum and true religion."

Rum furnishes a good example of how the craving for a particular strong drink could influence a people's economy, social history, and politics. In its day, from about 1700 to 1770, the famous triangular rum trade—sugar and molasses from the West Indies to New England, where it was turned into rum, which was shipped to Africa in return for slaves, who were sent to the West Indies to cultivate the cane fields—helped make New England wealthy, affected American tariff policy, and possibly prolonged the slave trade another fifty years.

In the end, like the redcoats before the minutemen, rum gave way before good American "red likker." Native rye and corn vanquished sugarcane. Prohibition gave the coup de grace to what was left of the American rum industry. The manufacture of the old rumbullion returned to its original home—Jamaica, Puerto Rico, Cuba, and St. Croix.

Brandy was a close rival to rum on the colonial table. "Brandy," possibly derived from the German "branntwein," was also known as burnt wine, spirit of wine, ardent spirit, and aqua vitae or water of life. It was distilled from grapes or other fruits. George Washington lost to the British at Brandywine, a hamlet aptly named since the inhabitants both made and drank great quantities of "spiritus ardens." Brandy was the ideal, easy-to-make home brew. Like rum, it occurred in numberless concoctions and was credited with healing powers, such as refreshing the memory and strengthening the capacity for reasoning if drunk in moderation.

Punch was the favorite before-dinner drink. Its name came from the Hindustani word *panch,* meaning "five," referring to the five ingredients originally used in making it: tea, arrack, sugar, lemons, and water. It arrived in America, via England, shortly after 1670. Milk punches were for the elderly and women, concocted of "whiskey made palatable with sugar, milk and spices." Punches of all sorts were drunk in enormous quantities at weddings. A tavern keeper of any standing had his own recipes for punch served only in his own taproom. The drink bore either his name, or that of his tavern; hence, Red Lion Punch, Fraunces' Punch, King George's Punch, or Royal Punch. In Philadelphia, Fish House Punch was "held in almost the same regard as the Liberty Bell." Relatives of the punch were sangarees, syllabubs, and shrubs. All these concoctions could be served hot, cold, or iced. Some of them were simple. The recipe for Virginia Sangaree read: "Pour a quarter of a pint of old Madeira into a large tumbler. Add three lumps of sugar and as much of hot water as will fill the glass. Sprinkle a good measure of nutmeg on it, and serve."

Other drinks took some doing, and making them was a serious business. In the words of one jolly landlord, Bully Dawson:

The man who sees, does, or thinks of anything else while he is making Punch may as well look for the North-west Passage on Mutton Hill. A man can never make good punch unless he is satisfied, nay positive, that no man breathing can make better. I can and do make good Punch, because I do nothing else, and this is my way of doing it. I retire to a solitary corner with my ingredients ready sorted; they are as follows, and I mix them in the order they are here written. Sugar, twelve tolerable lumps; hot water, one pint; lemons, two, the juice and peels; old Jamaica rum, two gills; brandy, one gill; arrack, a slight dash. I allow myself five minutes to make a bowl in the foregoing proportions, carefully stirring the mixture as I furnish the ingredients until it actually foams; and then Kangaroos! how beautiful it is!

Drinks as complicated as this were later served to shaggy-bearded, unwashed forty-niners in San Francisco.

A peculiarity of early easterners was their inordinate fondness for strong hot drinks—flips, tiffs, toddies, and hot buttered rum. Flip was the favorite convivial poetic drink that gave rise to nostalgic reminiscences. The word "flip" brings to mind images of jolly fellows lifting the tails of their frog coats to warm their backsides at a friendly tavern hearth while drinking hot, foaming flips from pewter cups engraved with such mottos as:

> Merry met and merry part
> I drink to you with all my heart.

The cheerful landlord presided over the cozy gathering from his cagelike bar, surrounded by barrels, bottles, tankards, jars of fragrant spices, and sugar loaves. In the chimney's hot ashes he kept at all times the iron poker, the loggerhead, or flip iron glowing a deep comforting cherry red, ready to be plunged with a loud, joyful hiss into the mug of flip, giving it the puckering bitterness and tangy, scorched taste so beloved by the Founding Fathers. What pleasure to behold the foaming collar rise in the tankard as the metal ball at the end of the loggerhead brought to a bubble the mixture of rum, beer, and sugar. When buttered in addition, the flip was almost a meal in itself. The landlord at a Canton, Massachusetts, inn was famous for adding four great spoonfuls of mixed cream, eggs, and sugar to his flip. When an egg was beaten into the flip so that the foam spilled over the cup's rim the flip was called a "bellow's top."

Sudbury Tavern furnished with each meal one "Mug best India Flip, Toddy in proportion." Toddies differed from flips in that they did not call for a hot poker but for a swizzle or toddy stick, which had a knob at one end to crush the lump sugar. One such drink was the mumbo, a mixture of rum, water, honey, and sugar. Another was the negus, named for a colonel of His Majesty's 25th Regiment of Foot stationed in America. It was made up of port, lemon juice, sugar, nutmeg, and boiling water. Nutmeg was a favorite spice for hot mulled wines:

> And that you may the drink quite perfect see,
> Atop the Musky Nut must grated be.

Thus the colonial warmed his inner man or, as

later writers said, "invented central heating."

Beer was drunk from the beginning. In Virginia a kind of ale was made from Indian maize as early as 1620. George Thorpe preferred it to English beer. The Dutch lost no time setting up breweries in Albany and New York. The British had hardly taken over the city when a brewery "using only the best English malt" was operating in Maiden Lane. Virginians in 1725 drank strong Bristol malt beer said to be rendered "exceedingly fine & smooth" by having been tossed on ocean waves for weeks during long crossings. "Good wholesome beere, by the barrel, gallon, or smaller quantity, at one shilling per gallon," was sold by one Conrad Hoburg in Baltimore in the 1790s.

Beer brewers commanded universal respect. At New Amsterdam Myhnheer Jacobus established a brewery and beer garden in 1644 while also holding various offices for the city. At the same time William Penn was brewing and selling beer in Bucks County, Pennsylvania. He also owned a tavern. Matthew Vassar sold barrels of his mother's home brew in upstate New York markets. From this modest beginning sprang the famous Vassar Ale, which was sold up and down the Hudson Valley and whose profits founded Vassar College.

Beer played its part in the colonies' political and economic struggle for independence. Franklin, Hancock, and later Jefferson urged native beer manufacture because it hurt British interests, it profited America, and because they hoped (in vain) that it might induce Americans to consume the relatively healthful and innocuous malt drink rather than the ruinous hard stuff. Samuel Adams also pushed the local product: "It is to be hoped, That the Gentlemen of the Town will endeavour to bring our own OCTOBER BEER into Fashion again, by that most prevailing Motive, EXAMPLE, so that we may no longer be beholden to Foreigners for Credible Liquor, which may be as successfully manufactured in this Country."

Among early drinkers, however, beer and ale always ran second to the "good creature," ardent spirits, thought to promote longevity to the extent that the first life insurancers charged the abstinent a 10 percent extra premium for being a danger to themselves. Prices were reasonable, so that everybody could afford to drink, and everybody did, probably more than western sheriffs and badmen. Once a year prices were announced publicly by the Philadelphia town crier. In 1731 it cost a person two shillings for a quart of wine, tuppence for a gill of rum, one shilling fourpence for a quart of rum punch made with doubly refined sugar, three pennies for a quart of beer, "best" beer fivepence, a quart of flip eight shillings, cider ditto three pennies.

Daniel Webster once declared that the tavern was the headquarters of the Revolution. Others called it the Cradle of Independence, or the Seedbed of Rebellion. Patriots facing the lobsterbacks' bayonets did not do so on a diet of milk and weak tea. Liquor prices did not seem reasonable to the Yankee-Doodle-Dandy. The high import duties on molasses, excepting that bought and shipped in Britain, threatened New England's economy and over the years increased the cost of the beloved flip, raising the hackles of each true Son of Liberty; especially so because English molasses was not only more expensive, but of inferior quality and never available in sufficient quantities to make enough rum to quench the colonial thirst. Men like John Hancock took to smuggling rum and molasses for the cause as well as for profit. First the Molasses Act, then the Stamp Act aggravated matters and led to violent demonstrations in many places. On the fourteenth of August 1769, the Sons of Liberty assembled en masse at Boston's Liberty Tree Tavern and Robinson's Tavern at Dorchester to protest the stamp tax. Fourteen bottoms-up toasts were drunk at Boston, followed by forty-five more at Dorchester,

The Green Dragon Inn in Boston, where patriots dressed as Indians embarked on the famous tea party. *Above:* Colonial tavern signs.

which meant that most of the leaders had no less than fifty-nine tumblers of hot waters within the space of one day. John Adams noted in his diary: "To the honor of the SONS I did not see one person intoxicated or near it." A weakened and enfeebled generation of today's drinking men and women can only stand in mute admiration at the prowess of the Founding Fathers. The last toast of this mighty day was: "Strong Halters, firm Blocks, and sharp Axes to all such as deserve them!"

Rebellion was plotted in a hundred taverns throughout the thirteen colonies. After the dissolution of the Virginia House of Burgesses by the London government, outraged patriots repaired to the Raleigh Tavern drinking a "Toast to the King, the Royal Family and a speedy and lasting reunion between Great Britain and her colonies." The bill was thirty-two shillings and sixpence, paid by one Geo. Washington, Esqr.: "His first expenditure for liberty."

In Philadelphia Franklin sat at tavern tables, relaxing between political talks over a glass of port or claret, entertaining his seditious compatriots with drinking songs of his own composition:

From this Piece of History plainly we find
That water's good neither for Body or Mind;
That Virtue and Safety in Wine-bibbing's found
While all that drink water deserve to be drown'd.
                    Derry-Down
So for Safety and Honesty put the Glass round.

It was from the Green Dragon Tavern in Boston that men disguised as Indians embarked on the Boston Tea Party. In the South, Patrick Henry tended bar at his father-in-law's taproom at Hanover Court House, exhorting his patrons to strike a blow for freedom. A stout Son of Liberty was the landlord of Keeler's Tavern, a few miles north of New York on the Boston Post Road. He had a cartridge manufacturing operation going in his basement, which led to a bombardment of his drinking place by vengeful Britishers, a cannon ball lodging in the main beam of his timbered taproom. In New York, Black Sam Fraunces' Tavern is still standing. Its landlord himself went off to fight for independence, and, after victory, a great celebration was held in the long room of his tavern, with Governor Clinton as the host and General Washington as the guest of honor. Thirteen toasts were drunk from large tumblers—one to each of the new states—leaving some of the celebrants a trifle unsteady on their feet, while making the Father of Our Country oversleep the next morning.

When stout Rhode Islanders became angry at the British Schooner *Gaspee*'s interference with a little patriotic rum-running, they plotted the ship's capture over bumpers of hot toddies in the Red Sabin Tavern. Paul Revere did not set out on his epic ride until he had fortified himself with a dram or two of goodly Medford rum. And in John Buckman's alehouse at Lexington, in the cold dawn of a raw April morning, the minutemen also had their rum and a lot of hot, hard cider before stepping out onto the village green to fire the shot heard round the world.

The news of Concord and Lexington reached Ethan Allen, Remember Baker, Seth Hall, and their Green Mountain Boys while sitting at Steven Fay's Catamount Tavern on Bennington Hill. They were drinking the specialty of the house— "Stonewalls," a mixture of hard cider and rum, guaranteed to fire hearts and brains. It was served to them in stone mugs by pretty Prudence Arden. According to a number of accounts, not necessarily gospel truth, the Green Mountain Boys were rip-roaringly drunk as they followed Ethan Allen in the taking of Fort Ticonderoga "in the name of the Great Lord God Jehovah and the Continental Congress!"

Nearly every tavern and public house in the colonies played its part in the Revolution as headquarters for patriots or officers of the Continental Army. In their taprooms the volunteers were sworn in and drank their last toasts before marching off to battle. At the tavern they had their wounds tended. To the tavern they returned to celebrate their victories. As enthusiasm for the good cause waxed, tavern names were changed from the Lion and Unicorn, the Crown, and the King's Arms, to the Goddess of Liberty, the American Eagle, or the Congress. The sign of the Hen and Chickens Tavern, in Lancaster, Pennsylvania, bore the legend: "May the Wings of Liberty cover the Chickens of Freedom, and pluck the Crown from the enemy's head." The Earl of Halifax ordinary at Portsmouth, New Hampshire, a hotbed of unrepentant Tories, was stormed by ax-wielding patriots. Landlord Stavers swore the oath of allegiance and renamed his establishment the William Pitt Tavern, after the reputed friend of American independence. Almost every town and hamlet had its George Washington Tavern.

There were also Benjamin Franklin and John Hancock inns. It was fitting to honor thus the heroes of the Revolution. Samuel Adams was a brewer like his father and proud of it. General Israel Putnam, too, was a brewer's son and himself kept a drinking place, the General Wolfe Tavern. Thomas Jefferson roomed in Philadelphia's Indian Queen Tavern while penning the Declaration of Independence. Francis Scott Key composed "The Star-Spangled Banner" in the taproom of Baltimore's Fountain Inn.

The old colonial tavern was the forerunner of the western saloon. Like the saloon it also was all things to all men. In the words of Edwin Lasseter Bynner, describing the taverns of Boston:

They were the centres of so much of its life and affairs, the resort at once of judge and jury, of the clergy and the laity, of the politician and the merchant; where the selectmen came to talk over the affairs of the town, and higher officials to discuss the higher interests of the province; where royal governors and distinguished strangers were entertained alike with the humblest wayfarer and the

"The Redcoats are coming!"
Spreading the word from tavern to tavern.

meanest citizen; where were held the carousings of roistering red-coat officers, and the midnight plottings of muttering stern-lipped patriots; where, in fine, the swaggering ensign of the royal army, the frowning Puritan, the obnoxious Quaker, the Huguenot refugee, and the savage Indian chief from the neighboring forest might perchance jostle each other in the common taproom.

The Revolution burst the dam of the Allegheny border line, established and enforced for so long by the British. Over it spilled the mass of humanity eager to fill the empty land beyond. Toward the sunset with them marched the "Jug of Empire." The western saloon was about to be born.

CHAPTER 3

WESTWARD THE TANGLEFOOT

Come all ye fine young fellows
who have got a mind to range
into some far-off countree
your fortunes for to change.
We'll lay us down upon the banks
of the blessed O-Hi-O,
through the wild woods we'll
    wander,
and we'll chase the buffalo.
Take your powder, boys, and keep
    your rifles handy,
take your whiskey, and your rum,
    and don't forget the brandy.
and don't forget the brandy.

—Song of Ohio Settlers, ca. 1815

Like a huge swarm of bees, an army of would-be Davy Crocketts marched west. In the north a trickle of French voyageurs and coureurs de bois were canoeing or walking west. In the center thin-lipped Yankees were pressing into western Pennsylvania and Ohio. But it was the Virginians traveling the Wilderness Road, settling Kentucky, Tennessee, and the land beyond, who imparted to the West much of its character and traditions. They were at the beginning a homogeneous lot of Scotch-Irish Campbellites, Presbyterians, and hard-shell Baptists, full of Protestantism and strong likker, a people dour John Knox would have loved. They were wonderfully described by Irvin S. Cobb as a breed of

self-reliant, high-tempered, high-headed, high-handed, high-talking folk who would be quick to take offense and quick with violent force to resent it; a big-boned, fair-skinned, individualistic breed, jealous of their rights, furious in their quarrels, deadly in their feuds, generous in their hospitalities . . . a breed of lovers of women, lovers of oratory and disputation, lovers of horses and card-playing, lovers of dogs and guns—and whiskey.

The western saloon's customers in a nutshell, though Cobb had the first Kentuckians in mind. The later westerner, whether Yankee, Irish, German, French, or Slav, eagerly and successfully adopted the attitudes of the early pathfinders, thereby helping to create the mystique of the West.

They traveled light in homespun, buckskin, and fleeces of sheep sewn together by their womenfolk, barefoot in summer, or moccasin-shod. They were for the most part a scrawny lot, their prominent Adam's apples bobbing up and down as they took a swig from the jug carried on their backs whenever they rested. Among their essentials was the long Kentucky rifle, made by German and Yankee gunsmiths in Pennsylvania, a bullet mold and powder horn (which in a pinch made a good drinking vessel), a tinder box with flint and steel, a sharp ax, and a keen knife. Some, but not all, had a horse or mule to ride on. Not the least of their basic equipment was a pot still. From it would emerge the whiskey and bourbon—the famed "red uprising"—which later became the staple western drink.

It was after the War of 1812 that whiskey came into its own on the frontier. In the words of one "Kaintuckian":

Every Boddy took it. It ondly cost Twenty Five Cents pr. Gallon. Evry Boddy was not Drunkhards. . . . A Man might Get Drunk on this Whiskey Evry Day in the years for a Life time & never have the Delirium Tremers nor Sick Stomach or nerverous Head Achake. . . . One Small drink would Stimulate the whole Sistom. . . . It Brot out kind feelings of the Heart. And in them days Evry Boddy invited Evry Boddy That Come to their house to partake of this hosesome Beverage.

In the mythology of Tennesseans three whiskeys and a "chaw of terbaccer" constituted a satisfactory breakfast while men sang:

> Mush-a-ring-a-ring-a-rah!
> Whack fol'd the dady Oh!
> Whack fol'd the dady Oh!
> Thar's whiskey in the jug!

On his deathbed an old pioneer made his last will leaving "to my oldest son, Ebenezer, my Great Distill and from my celler 12 brrls. of Doubled & Twisted Whiskey & the House, and to my y'ger son, Thomas, my least distill & 6 brrls. ditto, and from my lande 20 acres of Indian Corne and ten of Rye and both to share my booke from which it may be Learned how to make good Whiskey with God's Blessing." Pioneers drank because drinking was the only entertainment they had, and the fearful concoctions they swallowed were the only spice in an otherwise monotonous bill of fare. Life was hard and people needed cheering up. It was said of the pioneers that "cowards never started and the weak ones died on the way." Not for nothing did Kansas adopt for its motto: "To the stars by the hard ways."

Folks ate homemade gritted hominy and pounded their own corn in wooden mortars made of hollowed-out tree trunks left by Indians. They made their daily gruel palatable by sweetening it with syrup from the sugarbush. They called themselves lucky if they could rob a hive of wild bees of its honey, taking the stings in their stride. They got salt to preserve their venison and johnnycakes from buffalo licks, using a pinch of gunpowder to season their meals if they had nothing else. They had to hunt their meat. If they lacked skill or ran out of powder or lead, they did without. They relied entirely on their own resources, which were meager and which they had had to create themselves in the first place. Their women were veritable human factories, shucking corn, spinning and weaving wool, knitting stockings, making moccasins, caps, clothes, and shoes, manufacturing soap from lye and candles from tallow and beeswax. Every year, with monotonous regularity, they gave birth to a child. Unlike the men who, if they survived Indian attacks or accidents, sometimes lived to a great age, the women generally died young, worn out before their time. Men, women, and children fell victims to consumption, the bloody flux, swamp fever, and a host of other ailments vaguely described as the "aigers." Whiskey was supposed to be good for all these sicknesses and was taken religiously, but it was not always efficacious—not even against snakebite. The demand for new settlers to fill the vacuum left by those who perished was inexhaustible: "Send us your paupers, except lawyers, have each bring at least one woman. We want girls to whip their weight in wildcats, outscream the cormorant, give the young badger heartache and grace a wild home."

The early settlers of the middle frontier were backwoodsmen who fought the forest and pushed it back, a tough, exhausting work. But these frontiersmen have been idealized to such an extent that it is necessary to remind romanticists that they were as well greedy and heedless men on the move who rooted up the soil, fenced in the best places, killed off the Indians, trapped out the beaver, hunted out the game, fished out the lakes and streams, cut down the trees, and recklessly robbed the earth of her hidden treasures with never a thought for tomorrow. When asked to leave something for their descendants they were apt to say: "Why should I? They hain't never done nothin' for me." They were often bad and unscientific farmers, slashing, burning, and then going on, not necessarily because they didn't know better, but because there was always new land to be had a little farther west. So they did not bother to fertilize or to let some of their land lie fallow for a few years: "Why, son, by the time I was your age I had wore out three farms."

They felt no ties to land that had nourished them for a generation or less, suffering chronically from Kentucky Fever, Ohio Fever, Illinois Fever, California Yen, Dakota Boom, or Oregon Itch. At the news of a new territory to be opened, or of rich, black soil abundant a few hundred miles yon-

"They pulled up stakes, hitched up their wagons, and moved on."

der, or a gold strike a thousand miles farther, they pulled up stakes, hitched up their wagons, and moved on—unstable as gypsies:

Where is your House?" "House! I ain't got no house." "Well, where do you live?" "I live in the woods, sleep on the great Government purchase, eat raw bear and wild turkey, and drink out of the Mississippi! . . . It's getting too thick with the folks out here. You're the second man I've seen within the last month, and I hear there's a whole family come in about fifty miles down the river. I'm going to put out into the woods again."

They were hospitable, though, either by inclination or out of the knowledge that the stranger asking for a bite and bed today might be host a year farther west. Curiosity played its part. The stranger might carry some news from what had been one's home, or have an amusing story to tell. Hospitality was therefore lavish:

"You'll take the sowbelly, stranger, and the wolf skin. I'll rough it."

or:

"May we sleep on the floor?" "No, you and your wife take the bed, and the children can have the bear rug by the chimney." "Where, the deuce, will you sleep?" "I'll be outside, leaning up against the wall."

Later, in cow country, it was:

"Jest tie up your hoss in the old corral, and 'light stranger, light! 'Light and fill up!"

As time went on and the trickle of settlers into what eventually would become Ohio, Illinois, Minnesota, Wisconsin, Iowa, and Kansas swelled into a torrent, some commerciality made its appearance. Travelers could not always rely on the hospitality offered by ranchers and homesteaders who were often fifty or sixty miles distant from each other and in certain areas altogether missing. The earliest saloons therefore doubled as inns,

Stirrup Cup—western style. *A Strong Cup,* by W. M. Cary.

places to eat, and relay stations for stagecoaches offering "acomidation fer man and beast." But their main business was the selling of liquor. These "road ranches," as they were called from the 1850s on, were rough places, a far cry from the decorous Aulde Tavern.

The first western saloon truly deserving the name flourished in the mountain man's West a generation before the existence of roads and the coming of the Conestoga wagons. It was set up in 1822 by a trapper named Brown in a place appropriately called Brown's Hole, at a spot where the present states of Wyoming, Colorado, and Utah meet, in a lush, canyon-rimmed valley. It was the focus of one of the "Great Rendezvous," where once a year the beaver men, the wild and woolly free trappers, congregated, coming from near and far to barter their beaver plews for "foofaraw"— baubles, beads, and red trade cloth—for their Indian squaws; and for a year's supply of tobacco, hardtack, powder, lead, and likker for themselves. They came also to go on the wildest, most complete drunk ever, to meet old friends, to shed tears over "a hoss who had gone under," or to pick a fight, usually decided with knives. Likewise to gamble, dicker for an extra squaw to help the old one with the cooking, tanning, beading, quilting, sewing, and beef jerking; race one's horses and do some betting, drink Brown's Old Towse, and eat his "boudins"—lightly roasted buffalo intestines with all their fermenting contents, the trappers' favorite dish.

The hard stuff dispensed straight from the keg was Taos Lightning, guaranteed to maim and kill. Some trappers blew a whole year's catch on one glorious drunk. Brown's Hole was more than a mere saloon. It was the largest settlement in the mountain man's West, the yearly host to up to five thousand traders, trappers, Indians, coureurs de bois, lone missionaries, squaw men, and famous pathfinders such as Jedediah Smith, Bill Sublette, Jim Beckwourth, Captain Ben Bonneville, St. Vrain, Kit Carson, and Thomas Fitzpatrick—Jedediah Smith reading his Bible while the others caroused. Brown's Hole flourished for eighteen years until 1840, when, simultaneously, the beaver was trapped to near extinction and beaver hats went out of fashion. The mountain men disappeared with the beaver, and Brown's Hole was abruptly abandoned and quickly reclaimed by nature, so that in a short time no trace remained.

The mountain men were followed by the settlers and California-, Colorado-, or Montana-bound miners. They, too, needed a watering hole for man and animal. Often the early saloon was ambulatory—a covered wagon, some barrels of rotgut, a lesser number of boxes containing hardtack, a crude sign spelling WHISKEY, maybe a few boards placed over empty kegs to serve as counter or tables whenever the wagon train came to rest.

The paddle wheelers chugging along western rivers were also moving saloons. Every boat offered whiskey and gambling. Alcohol on board was a necessity, not a luxury. Being proprietor of a bar on a popular packet was a surer way to wealth than possessing a gold mine. Bartenders

knew how to mix cocktails and made brandy out of burnt peach pits, nitric acid, cod-liver oil, and raw Kentucky whiskey. These booze wagons and boat bars anticipated the later "Hells on Wheels" of the railroaders.

When the whiskey peddlers first settled down, their road ranches were nothing to crow about. Horace Greeley described such an establishment in Kansas:

It consisted of crotched stakes . . . which supported a ridge-pole, across which some old sailcloth was drawn . . . forming a cabin some six by eight feet, and perhaps from three to five and a half feet high—large enough to contain two whiskey barrels, two decanters, several glasses, three or four cans of pickled oysters and two or three

Coureur de Bois, by Frederic Remington.

Above: A whiskey peddler on the plains.
Below: Mountain Man, by Frederic Remington.

boxes of sardines but nothing of the bread kind whatever. The hotelkeeper probably understood his business better than we did, and had declined to dissipate his evidently modest capital by investing any part of it in articles not of prime necessity.

In the 1850s a Kansas traveler found in Great Bend a sod-house saloon and several little huts along one side of a road created by the passing of many wagons. Large numbers of these crude shacks bore signs SALOON, DANCE HALL, or BILLIARDS. Occasionally just a broken-down prairie schooner and tent served as saloon, in front of which was an open campfire surrounded by men in broad-brimmed hats with their pants tucked into high-topped boots.

Another visitor to Kansas complained of having to depend for sustenance and liquid refreshments upon "as scurvy a set of bipeds as ever demoralized any community." Drinks served were "wretched Kansas water at five cents a glass with whiskey added to conceal the smell." The road ranches were as "civilized as an African hut," the "food bad, water worse and cooking the worst." A guest, objecting to dirty linen was told: "Twenty-six gents have used this towel afore you, stranger, but you're the first to complain." *Bois de vache,* buffalo chips, often constituted the only fuel to warm the guest. Frequently a "bitch," a tin cup of bacon grease with a rag for a wick stuck into it, was the only source of illumination. Breakfast invariably consisted of beans and whiskey.

In saloons plain and simple, without any pretense of serving also as inn, wayfarers who had spent money on drink were allowed to sleep on the sawdust floor. In the so-called road ranches, the sexes were mixed up together willy-nilly in the same bed, sometimes also shared by chickens, cats, and dogs. Outhouses were distant and "unspeakable," vermin plentiful:

Town of Coyote, Montana.

The June bug has a gaudy wing,
The lightning bug has fame,
The bedbug has no wings at all,
But he gets there just the same.

On the other hand, the run-of-the-mill guest was not fastidious. Customers had a quiet "spit at the stove" "spit out the candles," and had to be reminded to take boots and spurs off in bed and not use the tablecloth—in the unlikely case that such existed—as towel or blanket. An early San Francisco saloon, the Apollo, was a decaying ship hulk cut down to the main deck, roofed over, with a porch, and reached by a gangplank. Early El Paso saloons were crude adobe buildings with earthen floors and no windows, serving only Mexican aguardiente or mescal.

One Arizona saloon was a mud-brick structure with a few stones embedded in the lower walls. The ground floor was used as a saloon, the upper story—a mere afterthought of rickety, flimsy boards—served as a U.S. Customs Office. The bardog, an Anglo, was both the saloon owner and customs inspector. Attached to the building was a corral consisting of a circular coyote fence of upright poles. Goats, horses, and sheep shared this enclosure, which also had a well, usually dry in summer. The thick-walled saloon originally had only one doorway, combining the functions of entrance, exit, and window. In case of Indian raids, the opening could be barred with heavy, four-inch-thick boards fortified with studded nails. In later years, when Apaches no longer were a consideration, the owner knocked a hole in the wall into which he cemented a piece of broken glass to obtain additional daylight. And so it stands to this day—a remnant of an earlier time.

Some prairie saloons masqueraded as groceries. The "storekeeper" and his family lived in the back of the store among saleratus, flour sacks, twists of chewing tobacco, barrels of vinegar, powder and lead, kegs of nails, and similar frontier

First store in Lakin, Kansas.

goods. The main sales item, however, was whiskey, often kept in the cellar in a tub, the customers drinking from a tin cup or helping themselves with a ladle to the raw stuff.

The early western saloons did not fit the stereotype image. They were often a dugout sunk into a hillside with water seeping down from the cave roof dripping steadily upon the customer's neck, or a tent with a stovepipe stuck through its slanting walls, or perhaps a crude lean-to open at the front. They were cheap to put up. To make a dug-out saloon cost one entrepreneur $1.65 in materials and labor. This was a bargain indeed, even taking into account that a farmhand or a drover of the period worked for eighteen dollars a month. To replace the dugout later with a substantial false-front building necessitated an investment of five hundred dollars "because nails out here are so expensive." The investment in some cases was repaid within a week. An elaborate, hand-carved, imported hardwood bar, however, transported in sections on mule back to the same place five years later, cost fifteen hundred dollars or three times as much as the saloon itself. This, of course, included carrying charges.

The early saloon was an improvised, jerry-built affair, made up of whatever materials the environment provided. The typical saloon as depicted in innumerable horse operas came into being only after a community had settled down, when money began to flow, when the transport of fixtures and glass panes could be arranged, or when the first train came chugging into town. The moment when mahogany bars, pianos, gilded mirrors, and white-shirted bartenders appeared depended on location and developments. In San Francisco they made their appearance in the wake of the 1849 gold rush—that is, in the early 1850s; in Denver, ten years later; in the Kansas cowtowns, shortly before 1870; in some out-of-the-way places, as late as the 1880s. But eventually the swinging doors, shiny mirrors, and brass cuspidors spread to every part of the West to take their place in American folklore.

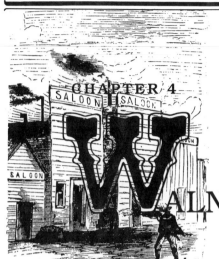

CHAPTER 4

WALNUT, GLASS, AND BRASS

At the Bucket of Blood
The drinks are good

At the Silver Dollar
For Jim Beam they holler.

And the Lone Star
Has the longest bar.

At the Bull's Head
You can lay a bet.

At the Exchange
The whisky tastes strange.

At the Teller House
I caught a louse.

At the Idle Hour
They serve Whisky Sour.

From the rise of the moon
Until noon
Look me up at the Saloon.

—Poem in a Jackson,
Wyoming, men's room

Right from the beginning the classic western saloon was a fraud. In a typical one-street western settlement of the 1870s every other building was a saloon, and every other building was also a "false front." The false fronts were pasted like sheets of cardboard to one-story log cabins or board shacks to give the impression of splendid two-story saloons. In character with the westerner's proclivity for bragging, for trying to appear a little more than life-size, the false fronts gave the western town the appearance of a stage set or a Potemkin village. And the false fronts are puzzling, because they deceived no one and the builders must have known it. In profile they were ridiculous. The fraudulent upper structure was often more than twice as tall as the real building beneath and behind it. It was as if the owners wanted to say: "We are exaggerating—don't take us seriously." Some of the bigger, better-known saloons did have second floors, but they were in the minority. Soon the words "false front" and "saloon" became almost synonymous.

Saloons were obviously important for the early mining or ranching community. A settlement's prosperity was calculated by the number of its saloons, which were its main business and served as an economic barometer. An 1879 census of businesses in the populous mining town of Leadville, Colorado, listed 4 banks, 4 churches, 10 dry goods stores, 31 restaurants, 19 beer halls—and 120 saloons and 118 gambling houses and private clubs selling liquor.

Minot, North Dakota, was barely five weeks old when it had twelve saloons and five "hotels" selling booze.

Deadwood, South Dakota, in its early days had more saloons than all other businesses combined. Moreover, the bigger saloons were the only buildings of substance, the miners and other citizens still huddling in dugouts and lean-tos.

In Georgetown, Colorado, the local newspaper complained that the town could support dozens of saloons and parlor houses, but not one single school.

In Ouray, Colorado, the first building was a saloon where "whiskey glasses were used faster than they could be washed." In no time the town had nine saloons but not a single preacher.

In Silverton, Colorado, notorious Blair Street, the "worst gaming street in Colorado history," boasted forty saloons and dance halls, twenty-seven gambling saloons, and eighteen houses of ill fame—and that was only one street among several. All these establishments were open twenty-four hours a day.

The mining town of Irwin was laid out in 1879 "to last forever," with fire hydrants and iron street signs. These were the only landmarks to survive when the ore gave out and the town gave up its ghost in 1885. Irwin's main street was a mile long, lined with twenty-three saloons and "nineteen other places of various nature in which liquor was sold."

Little Creede, "a swallow's nest pasted to a cliff," had five saloons, three dance halls, one variety theater, and a hundred places euphemistically called hotels for a population that never got above six thousand, giving rise to the saying:

> It's day all day in daytime
> And there is no night in Creede.

An average prairie town was described as having one preacher, one blacksmith, one druggist, one undertaker, one teacher, and seventeen bartenders. So much for statistics.

Saloons generally reflected the locality and customers they served. On the prairie, where wood in certain places was almost nonexistent, the first saloons were often sod houses. Where rocks were plentiful, saloons appeared in the form of stone edifices. In the Southwest they took the shape of one-story adobe structures. The majority were made of wood. In larger towns the early crude wooden buildings were replaced by brick saloons. Whenever silver, gold, or money was plentiful, saloons became ornate "palaces." The customers gave a place its particular flavor, determining mannerisms and behavior as well as the lingo spoken. Saloons in mining communities were different from those in cow country or the growing cities.

In the first boom days of the West, landscape and conditions varied widely. Some mining towns nestled in gulches, such as Deadwood Gulch or Last Chance Gulch, which spawned Helena. Others clung to steep mountain slopes like ivy to a wall. In the case of Butte, Montana, the mountain became the town—a huge, breast-shaped mound filled with an inexhaustible supply of copper. The town's male population hacked away at the rock inside, the houses sprawled on and around it—Swiss chalets, Slavic dachas, English Victorian cottages, German brick and timber structures—reflecting the multinational makeup of the population. Often the available timber around mining settlements was immediately and rapaciously cut down: "And there was no longer a lot of trees. The trees on all the hills around were chopped down fast to build the city and the mine shafts, and were used for firewood. . . . The hills of Leadville, where once great forests grew, were now as bald and barren as a baby's bottom."

So steep were some of these inhabited ravines that from their porches some families could look

Above: False-front saloon in Crested Butte, Colorado.
Below: Tom Anderson's Place, Silver City, New Mexico.

Gold Hill, Colorado.

straight into the chimneys of the houses below, while the people in the gulches often felt imprisoned, cut off from light. Some hoped for the day when their stake had paid off and they could escape. Others enjoyed their picturesque surroundings. What was squalid to one was quaint to another.

While the prospector and miner suffered from claustrophobia, the homesteader was often crushed by a landscape described as "a great lot of nothingness" or "an endless pancake." Some settlers, and the majority of cattlemen, loved the immense skies and the emptiness, waxing lyrical over the feeling of being liberated in space, extolling the endless, fragrant prairie where "all that stood between a man and the North Pole was a barbwire fence." It should be noted that those who loved the harsh but grandiose environment were mostly men, not always the women, stuck away all day long in their cabins and soddies doing

chores under appalling conditions. Many women kept diaries in which they enumerated the comforts they had left behind and the things they had to do without. Most of all they complained of isolation and the absence of another woman to be close with. Some men, too, reacted negatively:

> 10 miles to the nearest water,
> 20 miles to the nearest tree,
> 30 miles to the nearest house,
> Grasshoppers aplenty.
> Gone back East to the factory.

In the wide-open spaces temperatures were extreme and subject to abrupt changes. In the Dakotas, the stranger was told: "If you don't like the weather, jest wait a minute." Icy storms with hailstones the size of golf balls occurred during summer months. An Arizona legend has it that the devil, come to fetch some lost souls from a jughouse, recoiled in horror from the heat, fleeing back to the netherworld to cool off. Temperatures soared to 130° in the summer and dropped to 50° below in winter. The great blizzards of the 1880s temporarily wiped out the whole cattle industry, while droughts lasting over a number of years blotted out many nesters.

Dakota Land, Dakota Land,
As on thy fiery soil I stand,
I look across the wind-swept plains,
And wonder why it never rains.

During the great blizzards it became so cold that people did not dare touch anything made of metal, lest skin stick to it; exposed fingers became frostbitten within two minutes. All outside human activity came to a stop. In the words of James W. Gally: "On such a day the saloon, by which I mean the whiskey mill, is the headquarters—perhaps, more exactly, the stomach-quarters—of mountain society. Here is comfort—the truth is the truth! Here is warmth, jokes, all sorts of characters, and a thoroughly entrenched scorn of the howling, white-robed battling of the elements."

Parched for months, the settlers were often plagued by flash floods. Streets were unpaved. In one town a traveler reported "six inches of dust by measurement." The next day he noted in his diary that knee-deep mud prevented him from crossing the street. A standing joke was about a living human head sticking out of the mud in front of a

"Banking up" for winter in Dakota.

saloon asking for a drink. After it was brought and consumed, the head was asked whether it needed further assistance. "Thanks, no" was the reply, "I have my horse under me." It was on account of the mud that streets had wooden boardwalks along which people could creep. Mud inspired an early lady resident of Chicago to compose this poem in 1868:

Dearest Cousin

I should have written long before
But trouble entered at my door
And with it I am quite bowed o'er,
   The mud.

I strove to visit you last week
But went no farther than the street
Ere I was buried up complete
   The mud.

Indoors all things with blackness spread
E'en to our butter and our bread
And out doors nigh up to your head
   The mud.

Afflictions not from ground arise
If that is so, I have no eyes
You'll not see me until it dries,
   The mud.

Roads were unspeakable. A Californian traveling on horseback bogged down in saddle-deep mud and put up this notice:

This place is not crossible,
not even horsible.

Soon after, a man arriving at the same spot riding on a burro added to the sign:

This place is not passable,
not even jackassable.

As to the towns: "Yes, sir, this town looks as if the seed for a multitude of tenements had been scattered yesterday on a bed of guano and had sprouted up into cabins, stores, sheds, and warehouses, fresh from the sawmill since the last sun shone." Thus the St. Paul *Pioneer Press* when Minnesota was "the West."

A month's hammering built Sheridan, Wyoming. In 1859, the very best homes of treeless Denver were primitive log cabins with dirt floors, canvas or earth roofs, pole and rope beds, and chimneys made of sticks plastered over with mud. Windows and doors were covered with deer and elk hides—glass panes were yet to come. One year later, houses had wooden floors and shingled roofs. A few months later houses were routinely painted and some were made of brick. All had glass windows. By 1860 the city had a lending library, a debating society, one chess and two glee clubs. Peddlers had to be licensed in order to protect the numerous stores from unfair competition. By 1883 electric light and telephones were commonplace.

But a jumble of huts growing into a town did not mean immediate civilization. A Montana lady pioneer remembered:

There were practically no women, except the working girls up from Bannack, and far too few of them, even at their ruinous ten-dollar an hour rates.

Of whiskey there was an endless variety, all from the same green barrel, and selling by the shot from fifty cents to five dollars, depending on how new you were in town, or how far above discovery lay your claim.

Add to this 4,000 frontier toughs from every state in the Union and sixteen foreign lands, including China and the Solomon Islands; shake well with equal parts of gold dust, greed and gunpowder; put along a five-mile stretch of a small Montana stream and stand by with a lighted match; there was Virginia City up in Alder Gulch the early summer of 1863.

Sanitation did not exist. Sewers were lacking. Bad food and housing brought on epidemics of smallpox, typhoid, diphtheria, and dysentery. Fatalities from mining accidents were sickeningly high from "exploitation too rapid or too greedy to timber properly." The early cowpuncher, too, frequently fell a victim to accidents inherent in his profession. The saloon or barbershop had the only bathtub in town. Streets were enhanced—or disfigured, depending on one's outlook—by a profusion of advertising signs and posters, such as:

Above: The National Saloon, Breckenridge, Colorado.
Below: An early canvas saloon in Creede, Colorado.

Just arrived
A right smart of bacon!
A good many molasses!
A power of dried apples!
You bet!

Every saloon or store had its hitching rack with horses tied to it at all hours. The ground became a mire of liquid horse manure. Hogs rooted in the streets and chickens walked in and out of grocery stores, pecking and clucking. Men chewed and spat about them streams of dark-brown tobacco juice.

A fair sample of what we may expect in the way of variety and kinds of smell was given last Saturday, when it was a little warmer than any previous day this spring. . . . Oh! was the exclamation of those who had their olfactories saluted while plodding nose high in the different stratifications. . . . A tall man who was sitting on the sidewalk said that there were two hundred and forty distinct and odd smells prevailing there and then. All agree that some sanitary measures are needed, and heavy fines should be imposed on those who will throw slops, old meats and decaying vegetable matter at their doors or on the street.

The fact that women at this time wore long, cumbersome skirts which had a tendency to sweep up the accumulated filth did not improve the humor of the ladies.

It must be stressed that the southern sharecropper, the slum dweller from New York's Hell's Kitchen, the Irishman who had fled from the potato famine, the Rhineland Democrat who had escaped Prussian bayonets, and the Jew from out of the Russian Pale were all happy in the West, which offered them unhoped for, previously unimagined freedom and opportunity. The frontier was in almost every case better than what they had left behind.

For the whole male population the saloon was a refuge from dreariness and toil, a place of light and human companionship—the "apex of masculine society and the epitome of its culture." The western saloon was known by many names: bughouse, jughouse, whiskey mill, whoop-up, cantina, pulqueria, water hole, pouring spot, sala, hop joint, doggery, grogshop, bodega, gin mill, gin point, snake ranch, jugtown, watering trough. A "bit house" was a saloon where every drink cost a bit, or twenty-five cents. At "short bit houses" the drinks cost half that. A "barrelhouse" dispensed whiskey from open barrels so delicately balanced that a child could decant them. A "shebang" was a saloon of green lumber with some sawdust to stand on, but no chairs or tables. A "deadfall" was a drinking place of evil reputation. "Pretty waiter" saloons had girls in short skirts who induced lonely miners or cowboys to buy a drink for them. A "fandango house" was a dance-hall saloon. A "day-and-nite" saloon never closed. "Hells on wheels" were rolling saloons, transported on trains, following the railroad-building crews from place to place. A "company saloon" was a drinking establishment owned by a mining company, recycling the miners' wages back into its own pockets. It was sometimes called the place "where a rattlesnake wouldn't take his mother."

During Prohibition James Stevens wrote a nostalgic piece for H. L. Mencken's *American Mercury* magazine, trying to recapture the wicked allure a "saloon held for a young boy trying to act like a man." Stevens vividly remembered how his uncle took him inside his first saloon, the Old Judge, a decorous Idaho watering hole:

At last I was to see the inside of a "Saloon Hell." At last I was to take the first real step down what the revivalists called the bright and flowery road of sin! I was speechless with joy. . . .

As we stepped inside, my imagination was ablaze with all the Dantesque pictures of saloons that had been painted for me by Iowa revivalists. The day was heavily clouded and the light in the barroom was dim. Yet the great mirror shone gloriously, and at its base the glasses sparkled between the colored labels of stacked bottles. Never before had I seen such an array of glasses, or such vivid colors, or such a vast mirror, or such huge carved and polished pillars and beams, or such enormous vessels of brass as the spittoons. . . .

The banker and two other prosperous-looking citizens were talking quietly over mugs that steamed as if they held coffee. . . .

The Hell pictures had vanished, and I was feeling very small as I sat down. The heat from the big stove warmed me all over. The bar-room was strange and wonderful to look at, and even the smells were curious and pleasant to breathe. So for a good while I forgot to look for the shooting and stabbing to begin, and I forgot, too, the angel-faced little girl who was to come in and plead for her father to come home with her now.

Stevens' quest for wickedness, shooting, and stabbing was to remain unfulfilled, but the magic, warmth, and splendor lingered forever in his memory:

I simply couldn't imagine a handsomer or more comfortable place than the "Old Judge." The two rooms of the homestead shack looked mean and ugly by comparison, and so did the schoolhouse and the Adventist church, though they had been handsome enough for me before.

After the western saloon graduated from its crude, rudimentary beginnings, it became sleek, even baroque, wherever it was favorably situated. Splendid or dingy, the basics were always the same. In front of the saloon was the wooden boardwalk, sometimes in a perilous state of dis-

The Teller House in Central City, Colorado.

repair. In Abilene, Kansas, the thoughtful owner of the Alamo Saloon built a boardwalk from the back of his place to the nearest cat house, so that his customers would not have to get mired when in search of female companionship. The boardwalk was separated from the street by a rail, the hitching rack, to which were always tied a few patient nags with their cinches loosened. The wooden posts upholding the awning above the boardwalk had to be periodically replaced because they were constantly whittled away by the customers. Every puncher had a knife and loved to carve hearts or his initials or those of his girl friends into whatever came handy, and those posts were handiest for men who spent hours sitting on the boardwalk chewing the fat. Next to or behind the saloon was usually a livery barn. Sometimes a cowhand with too much of a load on would forget all about his horse, leaving it tied to the rail while staggering off for his ranch on foot. Some of his pals would check the brand of his pony and turn it loose. The smart and sober animal would go straight home, usually overtaking its rider on the way. Some customers had an arrangement with the stable next door to take care of their horses if they intended to go on a drunk of more than a day. The town's sheriff could read brands just as easily as a modern city cop can read license plates, and he would take care of the "parking" problem if he saw a horse tied to the rack overnight.

Entrance to the saloon was by way of the famous swinging doors. They could be plain or fancy, with panels of frosted cut glass in places that catered to a more civilized clientele. In busy pouring spots they were permanently wired open for easier access. Generally they were shuttered to obstruct the view. Customers were not always eager to be observed. As one man remembered his own boyhood:

I always wanted to see the picture of the "nakkid lady" over the bar and would sneak back and forth in front of them swingin' doors hoping to get a good look, but them doors were working too business-like, operating on steel springs. You could peek under them and see a lot of boots and spurs lined up by the bar, or you could stand on your tippie-toes and admire a bunch of big hats, but I never got a good look at that nude lady until I was old enough to walk in and buy a drink.

To prevent looking in, the windows had grilles, rodeo posters, or "Wanted for Horse Theft" bills stuck into the panes, maybe potted ferns in the better places. Wherever drinking hours were enforced, proprietors hung up double curtains so that patrons could go on enjoying their nightly measure after midnight unobserved by the law, or at any rate to make it easier for the law to overlook the violation. Windows in cowtowns were often shielded by heavy grates, because in bad weather the horses had a tendency to get up on the boardwalk, sometimes backing into the glass panes and breaking them.

The coming of the railroad exerted a powerful, improving influence upon saloon interiors. In El Paso:

The railroad got there in 1881, bar fixtures, lumber, and furnishings came in by the trainload. Brick saloons soon began to go up all over the place, floored with hardwood, equipped with mahogany bars, plate glass mirrors, roulette wheels, decorative blondes and square pianos. The bartenders, who had hitherto worked in gaudy flannel shirts and brown corduroy pants, assumed white aprons, and sometimes jackets.

A number of saloons were delivered on flatcars, section by section, to the farthest railroad terminals. In Forsyth, Montana, the last station of the North Pacific Railroad, each saloon was delivered with a carved bar, hardwood tables, a beer cooler, and a piano. Some saloons aspiring to grandeur did not wait for the first train to arrive. The Impe-

Above: The Pioneer Club in Leadville, Colorado. *Below:* The Rifle Saloon, Colorado.

rial in Silverton, Colorodo, had its huge intricate bar and diamond-dust mirrors transported by mules over what later became known as the Million Dollar Highway. In 1880, in Tombstone, Arizona, the interior of one of these newly opulent saloons, the Oriental, was lovingly described in the town's local paper, the *Epitaph:*

Last evening the portals were thrown open and the public permitted to gaze upon the most elegantly furnished saloon this side of the favored city of the Golden Gate. Twenty-eight burners, suspended in neat chandeliers, afforded an illumination of ample brilliancy, and the bright lights reflected from the many colored crystals on the bar sprinkled like a December iceling in the sunshine.

Denver's Brown Palace had a huge bar of veined marble topped with dark wood. It also had marble columns, five crystal mirrors, and ornate, pear-shaped light globes.

The typical western saloon was considerably longer than wide. On the business side stood its most important piece of furniture, the bar. It was in most cases placed on the left as you came in, though old photographs show plenty of barrooms with the counter on the right. It became almost second nature for a man automatically to turn left in order to belly up for his special poison. Tortoni's, in Denver, had bars on both sides, opposite each other. Bars were hand-sculpted in oak, mahogany, or walnut, the most prized of all. They were manufactured in Chicago or sometimes imported from England. Especially handsome were Eastlake Bars, but the Cadillac of them all, the ne plus ultra, was the Brunswick-Balke-Callander Bar, which gave a joint real class. In its days of glory, Brunswick of Chicago used the noblest of all woods for its bars—Circassian walnut. It was imported from Caucasian mountain valleys peopled by fierce Osset, Mingrelian, and Cherkess tribesmen who in the 1890s still roamed their

craggy "auls" in chain mail and pointed Turkish helmets. One walnut tree was reckoned to be worth ten olive trees. A quarrel over the ownership of two large ones, according to the writer Essad Bey, once became the cause of a blood feud lasting three generations. While the natives prized the trees for their prolific production of protein-rich walnuts, Brunswick admired them for the whorled grain of their wood. Gnarled, wind-buffeted trees growing just below timberline had the finest grains. Trunks were logged down to Tiflis and then began their long journey to America to wind up as bars in places like Telluride and Silverton, Colorado, or Virginia City, Nevada.

Owners prided themselves on the length of their counters. Fifty- and sixty-foot-long bars were by no means rare. Breen's, in San Francisco, has a straight bar of Brazilian mahogany measuring seventy-two feet, supposedly the longest bar in America today. Denver's Albany had an unbroken counter of 110 feet backed by a flawless mirror of the same length. That city's shortest bar was Walker's on Arapahoe Street, just long enough to accommodate six tightly packed gents. It was strictly an in-and-out saloon, whose customers finished their drinks quickly to make room for the next fellow. Its main attraction was the price of its fine, mellow bourbon—two bits per pony. The record was probably held by Erickson's Saloon in Portland, Oregon, which boasted of a bar measuring a stupefying 684 feet.

Characteristic of the old western bar were towels hanging from the edge of the counter at regular intervals so that customers could wipe the foam from their mustaches and beards.

Around a bar's base ran the brass rail, over which a man could hook his boot heels and be comfortable. Some say that it was invented "so that the shorthorn could stand on it and get his." Placed alongside the rail were the spittoons, cuspidors, or goboons—ideally one for every four gents. Some spittoons were built like vases reaching almost to the knee for "aiming convenience." They were necessary because most customers entered with a "chaw of 'baccer" lodged firmly in their cheeks, making them look as if they were suffering from chronic toothache. The story is told of a sourdough sitting in a saloon expertly spitting gobs of ambeer at flies crawling on the floor without availing himself of the proper facilities. A bar attendant discreetly placed a cuspidor in front of the gentleman, moving it from time to time, trying to make him use it, until the exasperated customer finally lost patience and threatened: "Iffen yer don't take the goldurn thing away I'm l'ble to spit in it." According to one old Montana cowhand, the big, vaselike spittoons came in mighty handy in a free-for-all. Men simply plunged their arms into the goboons, using them like boxing gloves—with telling effect. The saloon's hardwood floor was sanded or covered with sawdust for easier cleaning and to catch the drippings. Patrons often slept their jags off where the sawdust was thickest.

Behind the bar rose the backbar, mantel, or "altar." It was generally built around a huge mirror flanked by brightly labeled bottles. The implication was that the customers were connoisseurs of fine wines and liquors, as well as that the proprietor dealt in ladylike table wines beside his usual brand of liquid TNT guaranteed to blow the head off. Sometimes there were two smaller mirrors on each side of the big one. The 1880 Denver Palace prided itself on having a sixty-foot-long mirror. The mirror was not there just for aesthetic reasons. In the rougher places it enabled a man to see what was going on behind his back while gulping down his nightly ration. The backbar had shelves for pyramids of glasses and knickknacks, which formed the saloon's "museum." It was also a good place to display some favorite work of art such as an oil of "Undraped Pulchritude." If there was no

room, such a painting was prominently displayed on the opposite wall.

The light in most saloons was dim, as it is in most bars today, though some high-toned establishments illuminated the area above the bar so that "a fellow could see what was in his glass." At first, light was provided by candles, then by coal-oil or kerosene lamps hanging from the ceiling. Some of the bigger places had such lamps in clusters of four, suspended from wooden crosses or even wagon wheels. Coal-oil lamps were soon improved by the addition of large metal reflectors. After that, in the bigger cities, came globe-shaped gaslights and finally electric light, often only a naked, dangling bulb, sometimes mercifully shaded. Not a few saloons made the switch from candles to electricity without any intermediate stages. To sell kerosene lamps to cowtown saloons must have been a thriving business:

The "Klondyke" . . . was the village hot spot and had larger mirrors and bigger hanging kerosene lamps to amuse the cowhands when they got frisky enough to use their guns playfully. The man who owned the Klondyke bought his hanging lamps in large quantities and bought lamp chimneys by the barrel.

Some prosperous saloons, such as the appropriately named Crystal in Virginia City, Nevada, sported huge, resplendent cut-glass chandeliers for light.

With the coming of electricity, some prairie saloons acquired rotating metal fans resembling helicopter blades that whirred away suspended from the ceiling. The ceiling itself often consisted of squares of intricately hammered or pressed tin. A central fixture was always the pot-bellied iron stove. Cowboys loved to spit their wads onto the red-hot stove, the sizzling and hissing being music to their ears. Some owners had a desk just at the left of the entrance to do their figuring, and behind it a safe where they kept their clients' valu-

An old player piano at Tiffany's, Cerillos, New Mexico.

portant, because they gave a bar its personality.

Interior decoration depended largely on the location and clientele. Zoological specimens were always favorites, making some saloons look more like an old-fashioned natural history museum than a drinking place. A saloon frequented by stockmen and cowhands usually reflected this fact in its displays. The walls were hung with mounted longhorns, elaborately crafted saddles, huge Mexican spurs and sombreros, shooting and branding irons of all kinds, and every imaginable piece of gear connected with the cattle trade. Interspersed with these were faded photographs of horses, prize bulls, roundups, varmint hunts, rodeos, posses, and hangings. Local cattle brands were sometimes burned into the paneled walls. A miners' saloon was usually full of prospectors' tools, glittering ore samples, fossils, crystals, hunks of rose quartz, miners' lamps, and gold scales. In the early days the scales were no mere props, since drinking debts were settled in gold dust.

The saloon has been called the homesteader's and cowboy's art gallery. A barroom was rendered cheerful by oils and oleographs of a patriotic, sentimental, classic, sportive, religious, or carnal nature. The all-time favorite, hanging in almost every other bar, was Cassily Adam's "Custer's Last Stand," distributed by the thousands during the 1880s to advertise Budweiser beer. The company bought the rights to reproduce it for ten thousand dollars, a phenomenal sum in those days. The painting showed "Old Yellow Hair" in buckskin, his golden locks dangling to his shoulders, surrounded on all sides by savage fiends, laying about him with a huge saber. Historically the "Last Stand" was a dismal failure. No golden locks had been fluttering at the Little Bighorn, as Custer was getting bald, nor had anyone wielded a saber, because the general had ordered them to be left behind as obsolete encumbrances; but no customer has ever been known to object to the picture on grounds of historical inaccuracy. It was,

ables so that they would not be robbed when their "sights doubled on them."

Various saloons maintained letter boxes in which steady customers could receive their mail, others lured patrons with a rack of hard-to-get newspapers. Many places had a rear saloon or back room which served as a private club in which habitués played poker, held private conferences, or indulged in a game of billiards. One beloved barroom fixture was the "pianner," often the only one in town. In a few old saloons one can still see player pianos with their stack of up to a hundred punched paper rolls, each representing a different tune. Occasionally one could find a barber chair tucked away in a corner—sometimes with a live barber at hand. These, then, were the fixtures that made up the classic western saloon. The inessentials, namely the decor, in a way were equally im-

"Zoological specimens
were always favorites."
The Pioneer Club,
Leadville, Colorado.

however, the cause of innumerable fistfights, since tipplers disputed heatedly about what had happened at the Little Bighorn. Hot arguments made for thirst and careless drinking, thereby improving business.

Barroom nudes were equally popular, feasts for the eyes of every red-white-and-blue drinking man. The taste of the time ran to ladies shaped like bass fiddles. The ideal beauty was one whose waist could be encircled with two hands but who had trouble squeezing her posterior into a theater seat. In spite of the ample expanse of bare flesh these nudes were always classic, never obscene, very often the only original piece of art a cowboy ever saw. The most notable, a thinly veiled odalisque, hung in a Denver saloon. Two cleverly hidden rubber hoses led to the back of the picture. By

slyly pressing a little rubber bulb, the bardog could cause the painting's left breast to heave while, at the same time, making the navel palpitate. It was an unforgettable spectacle, giving many an unsuspecting miner the impression that he had drunk more than was good for him.

One ornate Teller House bar in Colorado's Central City had its walls covered with murals of undraped gods and goddesses—Leda and the swan, Aphrodite and the apple, Mars girt for battle. One goddess had only a single breast, another had two left feet walking in opposite directions. They were painted by an itinerant English artist, St. George Stanley, in exchange for room, board, and apparently unlimited liquid refreshments.

Most pictures of this genre showed a single, plump, and rosy lady artfully posed on an otto-

Above: The main bar in Central City's Teller
House. *Below:* "Saturday night art" and a
crystal chandelier in Leo's Place in Denver.

man, but there were plenty of "Susanna and the Elders," "Satyrs and Nymphs," "Le Bain Turque," "Aphrodite Emerging from the Bath," "Rape of Lucretia," "Mars and Venus," and "Innocence Betrayed." Here was history and mythology as well as art.

All these pictures were lumped together under the name Saturday night art. The divine female form was always discreetly veiled in the right places. Anything explicit would not have been tolerated by the somewhat prim cattlemen and miners. One of the most famous and often imitated pieces of artwork was not a nude at all. It was the "Face on the Barroom Floor," painted in 1936 by Herndon Davis in Central City's Teller House, a likeness of the sculptress Challis Walker. Versions of it can be seen on a hundred saloon floors.

Some famous western artists found their first sponsor in the person of a saloon keeper. Charles Russell was a forty-dollar-a-month cowhand when he traded his paintings for drinks at his friend Sid Willis' Mint saloon, at Great Falls, Montana. To other saloons he charged ten dollars per picture. One bartender promised him seventy-five dollars a month "and grub" for a whole year's output of paintings and sketches, establishing this saloon keeper as a patron of the arts. His offer, after all, amounted to more than double the wages Russell earned as a competent cowboy. One of Russell's oldest friends said later that the saloon owners were the first to recognize Charlie's genius and that there was no difference in quality between the pictures he sold for ten dollars in saloons and those he later sold for ten thousand dollars in New York.

Beside the pictures there were the signs. A poster frequently seen in bar windows read: "BIGGEST 5¢ BEER IN TOWN." One of the most opulent Colorado saloons displayed a sign: "Teller House, well supplied with things to cheer and inebriate." Popular signs inside a barroom were "In God we trust—all others pay CASH," or:

"Face on the Barroom Floor," Central City's Teller House.

My liquor is good, my measure is just,
But, gentlemen, I will not trust.

Or, in a high-class joint:

If you wish here to remain,
Do not swear or talk profane.

A sign in a Tombstone's Nugget saloon admonished:

Call frequently, drink moderately,
pay on delivery, take your departure quietly.

In early Georgetown, Colorado, an illiterate miner who had made a strike opened a saloon. He got into an argument with a revengeful artist, who painted his sign to read: "We sell the *WORST* whiskey, wine, and cigars!" This proved an irresistible attraction to the local prospectors, who obviously had a sense of humor, and the saloon did such a thriving business that the proprietor left the sign up even after finding out what it meant.

All these signs, paintings, knickknacks, polished walnut, and brass had one purpose only: to sell a short- or long-bit glass of whiskey. What impression it all made lay in the eye of the beholder. One thing was certain, one could not tell what kind of place it was by just looking at the outside. La Fonda, in Santa Fe, was a crumbling mud cantina, but once inside visitors were pleasantly surprised by its coziness, its comforts, its good dining and drinking. The Varieties in Dodge City, Kansas, was described by one visitor as: "Gleaming, swell, palatial, and luxurious, with clean, sparkling glasses, elaborate spittoons, effi-

cient and polite bartenders, pretty waitresses and smashingly beautiful female dancers."

The same Varieties was condemned by another as "sleezy, unadorned, stark, with rough tables, mismatched chairs, a splintering floor, unshaven trailhands with their hats on, dogs on bar and tables, and a few awkward, gawky, raw-boned, horse-faced women with clumsy, over-sized boots protruding from beneath their long, dirty calico skirts."

The first description was from a nostalgic cowboy, the second from a passing journalist. Neither of them mattered to the customers or the owner. The classic western saloon was a little empire ruled by a king: the gambrinus, mixologist, or booze boss, otherwise known as the bartender.

THE MIXOLOGIST

CHAPTER 5

The cheapest and easiest way to become an influential man and be looked up to by the community at large, was to stand behind a bar, wear a cluster-diamond pin, and sell whiskey.

—Mark Twain

Inside the classical saloon, the "sober side" of the bar was the bartender's, the "mixologist's" domain. It was the bardog's job to "keep yawning on the glasses" to give them a polish, to use chamois on the woodwork, and to shine the brass. He had his workbench under the counter, where he also usually kept a bung starter and a revolver or shotgun—just in case of trouble. Here he also kept boxes of crushed ice, but only in the later, "civilized" bars. Many saloons got along without it. In the famous Texas saloon, the Jersey Lily, the proprietor, Roy Bean, had a lump of glass. He would pop it into a tumbler and stir it around as if it were ice to impress his customers. The barkeeps ranged from barrelhouse and hog-ranch toughs to gentlemen in white shirts and red vests who sold neither to minors nor to those who in their opinion had already had too much.

In fact, there were as many types of bartenders and owners as there were saloons. It depended upon the time and the place. The tavern landlords of the early frontier, tending their taprooms in Ohio, Illinois, and Wisconsin from 1820 to 1850, were plain, homey characters, as homey as their inns and customers. They served men who had come to settle. Their taverns might be primitive, the food they served nothing more than a chunk of venison, but those who ate it while sampling the landlord's liquid goods were solid folk, peacefully inclined, in a great hurry to have laws and preachers and schools.

It was different in Kansas. The antebellum hatred between pro-slavery and free-soil immigrants was particularly evident in the saloons, where whiskey brought feelings to the boiling point. Most impartial travelers in Kansas during this period describe the barrooms as dens of violence, the bartenders as unshaven murderous brutes, just as likely to cut a free soiler's throat as to serve booze.

Farther west early bartenders also intimidated the eastern tenderfoot. Even at work, they usually wore slouch hats, red flannel shirts, and dark pants stuffed into high boots. They were armed, as a rule, with bowie knives as well as pistols. Their patrons were made up of the human flotsam come to search for gold and silver, first in California, then in Nevada, Colorado, and Montana, much later in Alaska—and also of those who preferred to take their gold from the diggers rather than the ground. It needed rough men to keep a bar in such surroundings.

There were exceptions. San Francisco, as early as 1851, had comparatively luxurious bars tended by well-groomed, white-jacketed mixologists, often highly paid easterners who could shake up a hundred different drinks. Yet side by side with these rather decorous places existed the low dives of the Barbary Coast, probably the worst in the whole country.

The cattle drives of the sixties and early seventies created the railheads for shipping beef, such as Dodge and Abilene, with their great number of saloons. These catered to cowboys and trail bosses, together with the gamblers and con men who gathered to fleece the cowpuncher with three months' wages in his pocket. The men who kept saloons in the early cowtowns were rowdy because they had to be, adopting the swagger and readiness to fight of their customers.

Wealth in minerals and cattle gave birth to the more ornate drinking parlor with its stereotype bartender. The classic saloon age arrived earlier or later depending on the locality. In some areas

The Barkeep, by O. C. Seltzer.

it lasted longer than in others. By 1900 it was generally over.

The typical classical bartender was an imposing figure indeed. A boniface rather than a booze boss, he was "always tidily dressed, appeared in a white shirt, his sleeves and wrist bands protected by calico cuffs; his cleanliness and his not wearing a hat, at once separated him from his customers." His outfit was predominantly "white-white shirt, white apron, white four-in-hand, spotless in the high class places."

In some fancy pouring spots the barkeeps wore

red or brocaded vests. The affluence and tone of a place were measured by the bartender's jewelry. A sparkling solitaire holding his white tie in place was smashing, even when tinctured with a little yellow. A diamond horseshoe pin likewise aroused admiration. Few customers were able to tell the difference between a real diamond and crystal or glass. Glittering rocks sparkling on the ring finger or on the bosom of a stiff boiled shirt were much appreciated. A Waterbury watch with a massive gold chain worn across an equally massive belly was an absolute must. A geranium and a sprig of fern wrapped in silver paper and stuck in the lapel were a nice extra touch. Ivory sleeve buttons were considered very elegant, more so than heavy golden ones. Elastic women's garters worn to hold up the sleeves were popular, especially when embroidered with fancy sayings: "I love my wife, but, oh you kid!" or, "The ladies, God bless them!"

Most proprietors and bartenders sported their characteristic well-waxed handlebar mustaches, in the case of one bartender six inches long on each side, and hair parted in the middle, festooned into spit curls, well oiled with "Lucky Tiger" or "Prince Albert's own hair pomade." Around 1900 not a few of the old professors under the spell of the German Kaiser's portraits ordered that monarch's hair wax, manufactured by a hoflieferant (that is, a "purveyor to the courts"). It was named "Es Ist Erreicht," meaning "it has been attained," and came with a *schnurrbartbinde*—a netlike strap that held the mustache in place during sleep. Attention was also paid to the back of the head, brilliantly reflected by the backbar mirror. The hair in back was pomaded to a glossy shine and artfully arranged in a sort of triangle, the point at the nape of the neck. Sometimes the hair was parted in the middle from the forehead down to the nape in what has been called "Moses parting the waves" style. It was no wonder that a man thus arrayed occupied the same social stratum as the lawyer, editor, banker, chief gambler, and chief desperado—namely, the highest. As Mark Twain said, "I am not sure but that the saloon keeper held a shade higher rank than any other member of society. His opinion had weight. It was his privilege to say how elections should be run. No great movement could succeed without the countenance and direction of the saloon keeper. . . . Youthful ambition hardly aspired so much to the honors of the law, or the army and navy as to the dignity of proprietorship in a saloon."

In its heyday the better-class drinking place's bartender was both a native philosopher and born anthropologist, to whom nothing human was alien, a rough-cut gentleman and far cry from the flannel-shirted brutes serving rotgut in the earliest mining camps. He solved the drinkers' problems of heart and mind, or at least pretended to. He had to be something of a psychiatrist, a patient listener to endless monologues, an impartial umpire of wagers and disputes over how much gold had been taken out of the glory hole or how many rounds it had taken John L. Sullivan to demolish a certain opponent. The smart saloon keepers never discussed religion or politics but stuck to sex and sports. They developed the fine art of seemingly listening with rapt attention without really doing so.

Will Thompson, who ran Denver's Brown Palace bar, was famous as a master storyteller who entertained his customers with racy gossip about the secret lives of the town's upper crust. Hinton Helper described the typical California bartender of the 1850s as

a red-nosed, jolly fellow of burgomaster proportions who treats his victim-patrons with the utmost courtesy and politeness. He is every man's man, and always has a smile and a smart saying prepared for the entertainment of the bystanders. His two clerks are equally urbane in their deportment and may be found at their posts from six o'clock

"The typical bartender was an imposing figure." *Above:* The bardog of the Tollgate Saloon, Black Hawk, Colorado. *Below:* In front of Andy Nelson's Saloon, Boulder, Colorado.

in the morning ready to flavor and tincture mixed drinks, to prepare hot punches, and to deal out low anecdote to vulgar idlers.

Besides dispensing drinks, the western mixologist's main task was as a peacemaker, never an egger-on. After all, diamond-dust mirrors imported from France cost money. So did the chimneys of his kerosene lamps. He had to be watchful. A third or fourth "cow-swaller of liquid fire" could transform a timid drummer into a raging lion ready to devour a timber jack. Bartenders of the 1880s and '90s were usually, but not openly, contemptuous of their heavy-drinking patrons. Competent bartenders were almost totally abstinent or drank only moderately—and never in their own saloons. One of the bardog's major problems was the westerner's custom, still adhered to in some out-of-the-way places, of buying the man behind the counter a drink to the customer's every three or four.

He might be forced to accept a beer, in which case he resorted to his "snit"—a private glass kept on the shelf beneath the bar. The snit was lilliputian in size and contained mostly foam. "A hundred snits wouldn't get a canary bird tipsy." In the case of whiskey, the bartender by some sleight-of-hand known to many of his calling could give the impression of drinking while pouring the red-eye back into a special bottle under the counter; or he filled his glass from his own special bottle, which contained tea the color of aged bourbon. Alternatively, he might accept a cigar at the customer's expense:

I never drink behind the bar,
but I will take a mild cigar.

He never smoked these but collected them in a special little box, the contents of which went back into the saloon's general supply after closing time. Of course, he rang up the wholesale price of these coronas to his own credit. In some places it was always the same cigar.

The genial barkeep of a first-class saloon was a well-remembered friend, who, when after years of labor, went to his just deserts, rated a bishop's or mayor's funeral.

While the majority of reminiscences of bartenders, genus 1880 to 1905, describe them as jolly fellows, there were also some detractors. A man who had sampled a multitude of saloons from New York to Denver wrote two articles, "What I Know about Saloons" for *The Independent,* a sort of radical periodical of the early 1900s. The anonymous commentator had this to say about bartenders:

In reviewing a rich and variegated personal experience of saloons, . . . the feature that stands out most prominently in my recollection . . . is the hard, listless, unfeeling type of man who keeps saloons. . . . The keeper of a swagger place is just the same type as the keeper of a humble little joint, only that he is harder. The bonhomie, the goodfellowship supposed by some to prevail among saloon habitués, is totally lacking in saloonkeepers. There is plenty of it of the artificial variety when a man has money, but a man may spend a hundred dollars in a saloon one night and have the saloonkeeper refuse to give him a drink the next morning when he is suffering for it, or give it to him in such a way as to spoil the drink. I never knew a saloonkeeper who was a really good fellow.

Other men, who had equally "rich and variegated experiences" with barkeepers, had nothing but praise for them, describing the dispensers of drink as usually quiet characters, keeping respectable places, with reputations for generosity.

From the beginning, they were often free-handed with their whiskey. When "Uncle Dick" Wooton arrived in his prairie schooner at Denver on Christmas morning, 1858, he put up a saloon tent with its stock of nine barrels of his famous "Old Towse." A tenth barrel of Taos Lightning he set out before the tent's entrance, inviting some two hundred onlookers to gather around him. He called to his wife to hand out all the tin cups, pots, and pans in their possession. With an ax he then staved in the top of the barrel and shouted that in celebration of Christmas and his own arrival the "drinks are on the house." It was the first big drunk in the young mining camp's history.

D. H. Edmonds in his reminiscences about life in early Montana wrote about Joe the Barkeep, an ex-cowpuncher who would always help a down-and-out cowboy, supplementing each loan with a quart of the hard stuff and a Colt .45 wrapped in a towel—"the traveling kit."

Some saloon keepers gave more liquor away for free than others sold in a lifetime. It was, of course, good and cheap advertising which made a place popular and created a crowd of faithful, steady customers. Other booze bosses were tight-fisted. Cripple Creek's Jim Prescott, bartender at the Palace, forced freeloaders to pay on the point of two guns, one in each hand, exacting gold watches and chains in lieu of cash from reluctant customers. Others pounded the bottle cork home with the heel of their hands, a gesture meaning "no more credit." Some very bad ones rolled their drunken customers, or even put knock-out drops in their booze to make plundering the old yeggs easier. Some miserly ones used glasses with deceptively thick bottoms, not giving the short-horn his fair measure.

An early western traveler recalled the following peculiar encounter:

At Nevada I am called upon, shortly after my arrival, by an athletic scarlet-faced man, who politely says his name is Blaze.

"I have a little bill against you, sir," he observes.

"A bill—what for?"

"For drinks."

"Drinks?"

"Yes sir—at my bar, I keep the well-known and highly respected coffee-house down street."

"But, my dear sir, there is a mistake—I never drank at your bar in my life."

I know it, sir. That isn't the point. The point is this. I pay out money for good liquors, and it is people's own fault if they don't drink them. There are the liquors—do as you please about drinking them, *but you must pay for them!* Isn't that fair?

Generally speaking, writers extolled the barkeepers' or proprietors' generosity in the 1890s, while decrying their avarice during the fifteen years preceding Prohibition. There is a reason for this. After the turn of the century the immense proliferation of saloons, as well as of distilleries and breweries, made keeping a bar into a dog-eat-dog business. In order to survive, saloon owners broke the law, kept open after legal hours or on Sundays, served to minors, and encouraged their patrons to drink to the limits of their purses and constitutions. Saloons and bartenders became sleazy, in the big cities even criminal (although all agreed that the western bartender as a man rated high above his counterpart in Chicago and New York). This finally led to Prohibition and the death of the old-style saloon.

Much time has been lost in arguments about how good the old western bartender was as a mixologist. One school of thought maintained that to serve the western cowhand or miner did not require much skill. In most western places the old professor just slammed a bottle and a glass down on the counter before the customer, who from then on did all the work himself. In the Mapleleaf at Maple Creek, Montana, "it was customary to belly up, nominate your 'pizen,' drink fast, and make room for the next comer. The barkeep didn't put the likker into glasses. If you asked for Scotch or what-have-you, he'd grab the bottle in his right hand, a glass in his left, cross hands, and plunk the two down before you. You took a small or a big drink as you wished—for ten cents, the tariff didn't vary."

Near forts, in places where soldiers went on payday in companies and troops for their evening measure, hops and malts ruled supreme. The rush was so great that bartenders did not bother to draw beer but dumped it into washtubs behind the counter, one bardog readying receptacles and dipping them into the foaming tubs, another passing them into eager outstretched hands.

In places where the customer was left alone with his bottle to do as he saw fit, a man with pride poured himself three fingers of bug juice. He never filled his glass up to the rim. If he did, someone, most often the bardog himself, would inquire solicitously whether he was taking a bath. It was said that for the bartender's question, "What's your pleasure?" there were few answers. It was always rye whiskey in the "near," and red likker in the "far" or "wild" West. Cowboy writers always asserted that the real honest-to-goodness bardog would have dropped dead had someone asked him for a Tom and Jerry or Sazerac or an old-fashioned. Such old-timers insisted that "in them days we threw it down without a thing to chase it but the pleasant memory." Likewise, they denounced the sissified custom of using ice in drinks, saying that as they never had enough ice to keep milk from turning sour and meat from going bad, they surely wouldn't waste the precious substance by throwing it in their likker, especially since it spoiled the kick. For all these reasons this group of specialists maintained that the bartenders never had anything more to do than polish the cherry-wood and keep the walkway behind the counter dry and slip proof.

On the other hand, there was a different school of those who remembered. Why, they asked, did the ole professor invariably greet his customers with a cheerful "What'll it be, gentlemen?" if the answer was always going to be "bourbon"? They asserted that many western barkeeps were accomplished mixers who could "shake up a good one," and they had plenty to back them up.

Legendary among publicans was Jeremiah Thomas, "the Michelangelo among bartenders," born in 1825 in New Haven, Connecticut, who became a true westerner dispensing drinks in St. Louis, San Francisco, and Virginia City, Nevada. He designed and had made a set of his own bar tools, done in sterling silver and worth five thousand nineteenth-century dollars! Customers called him "professor" and tried to confound him with the fanciest orders imaginable but, legend has it, never succeeded. Ample-bellied, walrus-mustachioed, with a lustrous jewel glittering on his stiff shirt bosom, dressed in an immaculate jacket of snowy white, he served up a bewildering variety of cobblers, slings, juleps, sours, sangarees, toddies, and cocktails. He himself invented a number of memorable drinks, such as the Blue Blazer, a boiling hot concoction, or the beloved Tom and Jerry, conceived on the spur of the moment when a gigantic miner asked for the sort of drink that "would shake him down to the gizzard." Thomas was not the only barkeep skilled at shaking them up. From the earliest days men in San Francisco, Denver, Virginia City, Leadville, El Paso, Gunnison, Sheridan, Miles City, Dodge, and Abilene asked for mixed drinks and got what they asked for. If the barkeeper felt himself on uncertain ground in the face of some exotic demand, he generally managed to come up with something to satisfy a customer who himself had often never tasted the concoction he had requested.

Sly bartenders disguised the poor quality of their cocktails with bitters and other flavorings and the "mixture was then kept in subjugation by liberal use of ice." In contradiction to the ex-cow-hands quoted before, the universal use of ice in western saloons astounded English travelers, one of whom wrote home that "iced drinks are consumed by classes in America far below the social level of those who never taste them in this country." The warm uncooled beer and stout served up in English and Irish pubs to this day would have

The "Michelangelo of bartenders," Jeremiah Thomas, at work.

been disdained by Montana miners in the 1880s. Some skillful bartenders prided themselves on being able to gauge any number of drinks by a certain acquired sixth sense, so that, when pouring from the shaker, they would fill just the number of glasses ordered. The author Robert E. Pinkerton described the rare skill of a Milwaukee saloon man:

This particular barkeep was one of those old-time experts who could slide glasses of beer along the bar and have each stop in front of the right customer. It was uncanny. The end of his bar was open, without a rail, and it was our favorite stunt to take a stranger there and have him stand at the end. The barkeep would shoot a full glass down swiftly. You'd think it was going right on thru the wall—and the stranger was always sure of it. He'd duck and run, but the glass would stop four to six inches from the end, and nary a drop spilled. I've seen others do it but I never saw that fellow miss.

In the opinion of most westerners "barkeeps were on-doubted the hardest worked folks in camp, an' yet none of 'em ever goes on the war-path for shorter hours or longer pay. Barkeeps that a-way is a light-hearted band an' cheerful onder their burdens." One of these burdens was to act as a human fire alarm. Western saloons never closed, and whenever a fire broke out the saloon owner would dash into the street, running up and down hollering and emptying his six-shooter at the moon. The commotion would have the volunteer firemen pouring into the street in their long johns to put out the fire. Having done so, all and sundry naturally assembled in the saloon to mull over the event while imbibing a tumbler of gut-warming red-eye.

Bartending in the West was not without its dangers, though most of the old professors retired with a nest egg and died peacefully in bed. Still, some places were rough. In 1852, at Yreka near Klamath Camp, everybody went around armed. The first building was a saloon. The bar had to be sandbagged and bullet-proofed in order for the proprietor to survive. The bartender had to keep his revolvers "cocked and capped at all times."

In 1889 things were not much better in Helena. A greenhorn went into what he described as a brightly lit saloon with chandeliers, carpets, and gold-framed paintings. One customer had taken on too great a load and was invited to leave. Enraged, he drew his six-gun, fired at the bartender, and missed. The bartender got the gun away from the man, fired, and did not miss, disabling the drunk with a shot in the shoulder. The greenhorn stood dazed, wondering where all the saloon's numerous clientele had gone, since nobody but the bartender and his victim were in sight. The patrons eventually emerged from under tables and from other hiding places. One local citizen patted the tenderfoot on the shoulder: "You must be from the East, otherwise you would have ducked like everybody else." Bartenders, however, were more often the victims than the victors in shoot-outs. The notorious killer Slade killed a number of saloon keepers. In one case he refused to drink the house whiskey, saying: "None of that! Pass out the high-priced article!" The poor barkeeper had to turn his back to get the quality brandy from the shelf; and when he faced around again he was looking into the muzzle of Slade's pistol. "And the next instant he was one of the deadest men that ever lived." Slade also murdered a saloon keeper called Jules, after whom the town of Julesburg is named, using him for target practice, killing his victim inch by inch. In Idaho, the ill-famed Plummer Gang murdered a jocose, well-liked Lewiston saloon proprietor named Hildebrandt, seemingly for fun. Ben Thompson, a notable saloon brawler and exterminator of men, boasted that among his many victims were four saloon owners, three barkeepers, and two uninvolved tipplers who happened to get in the way.

Among western bartenders were many whose names later became famous in frontier history. At Denver, Count Henry Murat hoisted the Stars and Stripes over his saloon, the Criterion, a high-class place with a gambling casino, thereby becoming "the first man to let Old Glory flutter over the new city." The flag, so the story goes, was made of the countess' blue cape and red flannel underwear.

Legal tender in Bodie.

Count Henry claimed to be the nephew of Joachim Murat, marshal of France, leader of Napoleon's cavalry, grandduke of Berg, and king of Naples. The count fled to Denver from the "upper Mississippi to the great bereavement of his creditors," and became Denver's first barber, while his wife, the Countess Catherine, took in washing. The count asked for, and sometimes got, five dollars for a shave and haircut, while the countess charged two and a half bucks for a load of laundry. The rates were exorbitant; but, as the count did not fail to point out, it was worth something extra to be shaved by the nephew of a real king.

Wyatt Earp was, according to one of his biographers, a saloon keeper, as well as lawman, gunfighter, gambler, con man, bigamist, and church deacon. Almost as famous as Earp was Bat Masterson, who ran saloons in between policing the streets of Kansas cowtowns. His brother George was in charge of Dodge City's foremost dance hall and gambling saloon, Varieties, where he served French brandies and Corona cigars. "Doc" Holliday, professional gambler, dentist, and notorious killer, once kept a saloon in Las Vegas, New Mexico.

The highly respected lawman Bill Tilghman first owned the Dodge City Crystal Palace saloon, and later the Oasis, which he sold to his brother in 1884. According to a notice in the Dodge City *Democrat*:

William Tilghman, Esq., proprietor of the "Oasis" has sold out to his brother Frank, who will refit and fix up and make everything smooth and harmonious to the visitor. Methodist cocktails and hard-shell Baptist lemonades a specialty.

If one can believe those who sampled them, Methodist cocktails and hard-shell Baptist lemonades were mighty powerful stuff.

Two San Francisco waterfront bartenders and owners, Jim Flood and Bill O'Brien, born in New York of Irish parents, financed two fellow Irish prospectors, John Mackay and James Fair. Out of this four-man venture grew the fabulous Comstock gold mines, the four partners taking out nearly two hundred million dollars, which enabled Flood and O'Brien to give up bartending.

Among the profession's oddballs were the gentlemen who shook them up on Mississippi and Missouri steamboats. A floating barkeeper with a good stock of rye whiskey and corn likker, who, in addition, knew how to fashion a satisfying mint julep, could easily clear two thousand dollars on a single trip. Paddle-wheeler bars were not managed or even owned by the ships' proprietors, but were leased to outsiders. Some men held the concession for several floating saloons. The business was highly profitable until the railroads put the steamboats out of business.

Bartenders came from every walk of life and from every corner of the globe. Among early California booze bosses were Kanakas, Mexicans, Indians, Irish, English, blacks, Frenchmen, Swedes, at least one Chinese, and judging from description, one Alaskan Eskimo. During the 1849 gold rush days, Coloma had a German Jewish barkeeper. He had "a few tin cups and a whole army of long and short-necked, gaily labeled bottles, from which he dealt out horrible compounds for fifty cents a drink." With his scales for weighing gold dust—the only currency available to pay for drinks or anything else—he would inquire: "Vat ye takes?" or holler: "Shtand back, poys, and let the shentlemens to the bar." In the 1880s the Irish took over to such extent that it was remarked that nine out of ten bartenders were Catholics. Thirst parlors sprang up everywhere with names like Emerald Isle, the Harp, Shamrock, or the Home Rule Bar. In the West, these places catered to the "paddies who worked on the railway."

The youngest bartender on record was thirteen-year-old Fred Lambert, who slung beer and whiskey in his father's Cimarron, Colorado, saloon. His French-born father, Henri, said of him, "In case of trouble, he has a quietening influence." Possibly the oldest was a Nebraskan called Pierre—part French and part Scot, with a dash of Oglala mixed in, who still shook up a good one at the biblical age of a hundred and one.

While it is generally true that barkeeping was an occupation exclusively reserved for the lords of creation, some two dozen western ladies defied male prejudice and successfully presided over the sober side of the bar. For some of them their sex was an asset. A female bartender was always a novelty one took a stranger to gape at. At Alkali Flat a man asking a local citizen for a place run on the ancient lines was told in the words of Frederic Remington: "Sure there is, Cap, right over to the old woman's. They don't have no hell round the old woman's. That's the old woman's over thar whar yu see the flowers in front and the two green trees—jes' nex' the Green Cloth Saloon."

In Pierre, South Dakota, a very much admired widow ran a "Clean Barrel House" dressed in bloomers, and did a thriving business. Another midwestern lady boniface was Milwaukee's Mother Heiser, who managed a Teutonic saloon known as The Reichstag with German no-nonsense thoroughness and propriety.

In Wichita, Kansas, "Rowdy Kate" owned a saloon together with her husband, "Rowdy Joe" Lower. They earned their nicknames by their rowdy ways of subduing rowdy patrons. Kate was said to be able to drink more rotgut and be faster on the draw than most of her male customers. During her somewhat hectic and exuberant career she reportedly shot and sent up the flume five citizens, among them two ex-husbands. She was described as petite, extremely attractive, well groomed and perfumed, a "swell dresser after the latest fashion." She ran the whole outfit—bar,

dance hall, and gambling tables—during Rowdy Joe's frequent absences. As a saloon keeper Rowdy Kate had a reputation for "acting straight" and being well able to take care of herself in "wild, woolly and wicked Wichita."

During the 1890s John L. Sullivan, stewed to the gills, walked into Frisco's Midway Plaisanceon vaudeville saloon, smashed his mighty fist on the bar while roaring: "I can lick any man in the world!" None of the male drinkers rose to the challenge but barmaid Bessie Hall walked around the counter and with one blow knocked the great John L. down. Sullivan looked up at her from his sitting position, smiled, and exclaimed: "Great gods, what a woman!" They became friends, and the champion reputedly helped finance Bessie's new business, a cat house on O'Farrell Street.

In a class by themselves were parlor-house bars behind which the prairie nymphs decanted the water of life. An old photo of the bar in Laura Evans' Denver Bagnio shows a regular saloon bar of carved hardwood with space for six gentlemen callers, two thoughtfully placed spittoons, an array of bottles of various sizes and shapes, foaming mugs of beer, an iron stove, a naked light bulb, framed pictures, a large cash register, and a sign admonishing: "Do not swear." The only features to indicate that this was not the interior of an ordinary saloon are chintz curtains and two pretty smiling "ladies" behind the bar busily mixing drinks.

In the words of a miner's wife, Anne Ellis, "There were good and bad saloon-keepers and good and bad saloons. As I remember now, O. T. ran a high-class place in Bonanza, having no drunken men around, getting his bouncer busy as soon as a fight was started; his fixtures were the best—the goldenest, heaviest frames on his pictures, his carpets the reddest and thickest, the glassware the shiniest, his mirrors the largest. He

The Bung-Starter, by John Held, Jr.

At last we got very confidential—and then what did he do but begin to deliver beery lectures on Bach and Handel, Beethoven and Wagner! One night he laid off and took me to a concert! The band played the grand piece called the Eroica. After the concert the head bartender cried into his beer as he told me how he had always wanted to play the flute in an orchestra. . . . He went to moaning and swearing in German; and I listened to him and felt sick as I began to realize that, actually, bartending was just a common job. . . . Certainly a man wasn't wicked who cried because he couldn't play the flute. . . .

The last hope was gone.

So I gave up at last and took the saloon for what it actually was: a handsome, comfortable, fine-smelling place, where a man could drink liquors . . . and where the best in him would be brought forth and paraded for the inspiration and instruction of his fellowmen.

By the beginning of this century, the bartender was no longer the all-important man he had been earlier, the equal of judge and mayor. He was, however, still a man of some consequence, regarded as a solid citizen and a regular fellow one could trust. It was held in the saloon men's favor that there were no known cases in which they used the information gained from a befuddled customer to blackmail him, and yet the old professor was the repository of more secrets than a priest in his confessional. The bartenders always knew whether the judge or governor had a woman tucked away somewhere on the wrong side of the railroad tracks, even knew her name. They knew a lot of things but never told. They usually were ready with an alibi for an erring husband and were most reluctant ever to testify against one of their regular customers. In the event of one of the more and more infrequent shoot-outs, they usually stayed at their bars like captains on the bridge of a sinking ship.

Those who criticized the bar owner most were anti-saloonists and missionaries who never knew

made his money honestly, never rolling the men when they were too drunk to protect themselves." Newspaper articles and books abound in memories of universally popular saloon men. Who but a good and warm-hearted fellow could have penned the following poem to his lady love:

> Take pity, Miss Fanny,
>   The belle of Pioneer
> And grant some indulgence
>   To a vendor of beer
> Whose heart-rending anguish
>   Will bring on decline
> Oh, God of creation
>   I wish you was mine.

In *Saloon Days,* James Stevens recounted the end of his futile quest for barroom wickedness in Los Angeles' Harbor Bar:

My last hope was to become a bartender. That trade still glittered and smoked for me with the flames of Hell. So I made myself as agreeable to the head bartender of the Harbor as I knew how.

him. They had some idea of what the booze boss in an eastern slum, at the worst period, was like and took him as a symbol for all bar owners. This was unjust. The western saloon keeper during the better days was as tough as he had to be, as charitable as he could afford, and often as sentimental as a sob-story heroine. Taken as a whole the old bardog was quite a man.

Boniface and his patrons, Old Town, Albuquerque.

CHAPTER 5
PAINTING ONE'S NOSE

When I'm dead and in my grave
No more whiskey will I crave
But on my tombstone shall be
 wrote,
They's many a jolt went down his
 throat.

—John Copeland

The men who bellied up to the bar and acquired calluses on their elbows by prolonged and heavy leaning on the counter did not patronize the saloon simply for its alcoholic refreshments. Many old habitués pointed out repeatedly that if a fellow wanted to hear the owl hoot, it would have been more effective and a lot cheaper to buy himself a gallon of barrelhouse whiskey and retire to his dugout or bunkhouse to work himself up for his case of jimjams. Men, however, did not drink alone, and they did not drink at home. Westerners were a gregarious lot. They needed each other's company, even if only to pick a fight. They all went to their favorite booze parlors to h'ist a few jolts of conversation fluid, of tongue oil, of tonsil varnish, to gather up a talkin' load. The fact is that the old whiskey mill was the only club the West had. Even when a cowhand went on a high, lonesome drunk, he did so inside a saloon, within a crowd.

The cowboy artist Charles Russell, himself no enemy to the red essence, who in his own estimation spent half his waking hours in Montana saloons, made these observations: "Whiskey has been blamed for lots it didn't do. It's a bravemaker. All men know it. If you want to know a man, get him drunk and he'll tip his hand. If I like a man when I'm sober, I kin hardly keep from kissing him when I'm drunk. This goes both ways. If I don't like a man when I'm sober, I don't want him in the same town when I'm drunk."

Saloon customers were a varied lot, as were the bars themselves and the men who tended them. The customers, too, went through a series of metamorphoses, from prospector, desperado, and gambler, to cowhand, stockman, coal miner and railroader, clubman and mining baron, as well as drummer and honest workman "with lunch pail and mourning bands under his fingernails," until he finally turned tourist. The early patrons were described as a tough bunch, but those who wrote about them were often prejudiced travelers who judged men by the standards of class-conscious Europe and studied westerners as specimens of untamed wildlife. Between 1840 and 1860 frontiersmen were said to constitute "a striking gradation to the savage," and to revel in drinking, dancing, and whoring. A minister commenting on Tennesseans, Kentuckians, and Missourians noted that they "live in concubinage, swapping wives like cattle, and living in a state of nature, more irregularly and unchastely than the Indians." The early central West was depicted as a gathering place for "one-eyed savages, semibarbarians" and a "kind of humanized ourang outang." A Denver variety and thirst parlor of the 1860s and its customers were thus described:

Imagine if you can a long, low room, dimly lighted but by no means illuminated, with bare walls and floors and ceilings; chairs and tables ranged along the walls and in the center . . . crowded with bummers of both sexes smoking, playing poker and talking all at once and at the top of their voices; the women no longer young, no longer fair; the men as various in appearance as the leaves of the forest; ragged miners from the mountains rejoicing in their brawny strength; dapper clerks from Larimer Street in shiny hats and faultless linen; gamblers of high and low degree, young boys taking their first lesson in lewdness; long limbed ranchermen and cattle boys, hearty and generous to a fault; a noisy but inefficient orchestra hard at work in one corner adding to the general confusion; waiters calling; chairs shuffling; drunken men shouting, women's voices joining in; coming and going feet and the rattle and clink of glasses and all the noises of the noisy street blending together in one deep deafening din; and you can have some faint idea of a Denver concert saloon.

In front of the Empire Saloon, San Francisco.

On the other hand, there was a certain romantic air about the gamy, long-haired, buckskin-clad frontier character who, from the very first, fascinated the foreign visitor, especially the lady visitor. One English woman, Iza Duffus Hardy, was thrilled to meet her first specimen of "the perfect presentment of the western man as we had read of him, but as we had never hoped to see him in the flesh." This particular example turned out to be "tall, dark, pale, hollow-eyed, and hollow-cheeked —an expression grave even to gloom—truculent-looking top-boots, a red shirt, a conspicuous lack of linen, a fiercely brigandish hat tilted over his dark brows—and withal the sweetest, saddest smile and the softest voice. . . ." Travelers often commented on the gentleness and respect with which westerners treated women, but this endearing trait cannot be absolutely taken for granted. Western men slapped women around occasionally. Bat Masterson once did so publicly in a Kansas cowtown saloon.

While in certain areas saloon customers were a fairly homogeneous, Anglo-Saxon lot, in others they represented an incredible mixture of races and nationalities. San Franciscans during the gold rush era were described as "mostly men, young or of middle age, very few women, fewer children, with here and there a bewildered matron or maiden of good repute. Here were British subjects, Frenchmen, Germans, and Dutch, Italians, Spaniards, Norwegians, Swedes, and Swiss, Jews, Turks, Chinese, Kanakas, New Zealanders, Malays, and Negroes, Parthians, Medes, and Elamites, Cretes and Arabians, and the dwellers in Mesopotamia and Cappadocia, in Boston and New Orleans, Chicago and Peoria, Hoboken and Hackensack."

The writer, oddly enough, failed to mention the original Indian inhabitants and the Mexicans who had so recently ruled California, as well as the Chilean women who made up the core of the city's prostitutes.

In some places, Denver, Colorado, among them, men tended to patronize saloons whose booze bosses "spoke their own language." Blacks with money to spend found acceptance at the faro and keno tables of gambling saloons, but they felt considerably more at ease in Bill Jones's all-black watering spot on Upper Arapahoe Street. In December 1881 an item in the *Rocky Mountain News* dealt with a riot inside a saloon on Delaney Street patronized almost exclusively by Italians. The *News* reported that "the Italians had really been the aggrieved parties and . . . the assault had been made upon them in this saloon by a crowd of thieves, blacklegs, and shoulderhitters, who hang around the place." The Irish congregated in at least four saloons of their own. Even the Chinese had two or three drinking places in their Sons of Heaven section. A similar process had taken place in St. Louis as early as the 1840s. The French had their own typical absinthe and wine houses in the Vide Poche (empty pocket) quarter, and according to George Ruxton, "The Dutch and Germans have their beer gardens, where they imbibe huge quantities of malt and honey dew tobacco; and the Irish their shebeen shops, where Monongahela (rye whisky) is quaffed in lieu of the 'rale crather.'"

Though western saloons were overwhelmingly egalitarian for whites, as a rule drinking democracy did not extend to other races. Indians were excluded by law. An occasional black man might be grudgingly accepted, or at least ignored, if he happened to be a noted gambler or badman. He was also left alone if he entered the saloon as a member of a particular gang, a certain crew of railroaders, or a group of cowboy bunk mates, but his position at the brass rail was always precarious. The attitudes of white saloon patrons toward blacks were more tolerant in the early, fluid days than in the 1880s and 1890s, when things had settled down.

The most offended against were the Chinese.

Barely suffered as long as they did coolie work, they risked their lives if they ventured into a white man's drinking place. In October 1880, two Chinese walked into a saloon on Denver's Wazee Street and began shooting a game of pool. They were immediately attacked by four so-called shoulder hitters. Thus started a major race riot. As the news about the two "uppity Orientals" spread, three thousand drunken whites stormed the Chinese quarter, setting fire to joss houses and looting stores. The riot was finally stopped by a courageous saloon keeper, Jim Moon, owner of the Arcade, who stood in the doorway of a Chinese laundry, six-gun in hand, offering to shoot anyone trying to enter. He was supported by a single citizen, an eccentric English nobleman, Lord Lyulph Ogilvie, who brandished an ivory-handled revolver, laying about him with a cane, bellowing: "Back, back, you bloody bastards, mind your betters!"

One seldom-mentioned but generally excluded minority was, of course, women. The saloon customer did not want them around unless they were pretty waiter girls or ladies of the night. The old tale, however, that respectable women never, *never* entered the western saloon has to be taken with more than a grain of salt. In larger cities women sooner or later, generally sooner, asserted their right to a public nip of the forbidden fruit and were sometimes provided with a discreet la-

A tavern for "hot waters" in Santa Fe.

dies' side entrance. Visitors to San Francisco in the pioneer era pretended to be shocked by women openly drinking at bars, gambling among men, and strolling tipsily in the streets. The same was true in early Denver, but emancipation of the drinking woman was a lengthy process. In the smaller towns of the cow country an unspoken taboo against women in saloons lasted until World War I and beyond. In retaliation the ladies managed to dry up large regions of the West. Thus the war of the sexes unfolded on the alcoholic battlefield.

The westerner was a drinking man. Every boy looked forward to that moment when his voice changed and he could strut up to the bar, slam his two bits down, and say, in as deep a voice as he could manage, "Gimme a Joe Gideon." The urge to rest one's feet on a brass rail was well-nigh universal. For a young'un not to have that desire was a sign of something wrong, of effeminacy. Men, once they had gotten drunk together, felt a special affinity for each other, a sort of brotherhood which might last their lifetime.

In Missouri, foreign travelers observed a "too free use of spirituous liquor." Kentuckians were discovered to be addicted to red likker. Tennesseans indulged "too great a fondness for whiskey." Ohioans drank too much Monongahela rye. In St. Louis and New Orleans everyone was in a perpetual state of inebriation, the upper classes on champagne and cocktails, the lower on barrelhouse rotgut. Coloradans had an unquenchable thirst for Old Towse. Dakotans became alcoholics due to the subzero winters and the need to warm their innards constantly with the most potent and fiery liquids in order to last until spring. The men of Cheyenne, Wyoming, had a greater capacity for the hard stuff than any other known humans, not excluding the Cockney regulars of Soho's and Liverpool's gin mills. According to Charles Rus-

sell, in *Trails Plowed Under,* the greatest thirst of all was an Iowan's because most of that state had been voted dry at an early time: "When Bill steps off the train there he has an Iowa thirst, an' . . . in them days an Iowan could drink more in one swaller than the average westerner can in three hours, so Bill's called on frequent by the barkeep to slow up, as they can only make just so much liquor every twenty-four hours."

Everybody drank. If a man wanted to get sociable there was nothing to prevent him except a lack of green frogskins—money—and even that was not always a hindrance. Owen P. White, a pre-Prohibition aficionado of good bourbon, described the saloon customers of his native El Paso:

Cow-men, sheep-men, doctors, lawyers, merchants, miners, bankers and gamblers all tilted the bottle for one another and entered merrily into a booze-histing contest, the results of which had a large bearing on the business of the community. The banker, for example, encountering all of his customers well lit, and hence honest, could make up his mind, better than at any other time, what to do about their notes. The prospective father, having the entire medical fraternity of the town paraded before him, all under a full head of steam, could judge the ability of each medico by his carrying capacity, and so decide which one to hire for the impending function. The litigant likewise, with the whole bar lined up at the bar, and mellow to the point of oratory, could select a lawyer to his liking. Even the average citizen, in the market perhaps for a thing as large as a trainload of cattle or as small as a white law cravat, was influenced by the way the cow-man or the haberdasher stood up under his liquor, and bestowed patronage accordingly.

As to the typical cowboy, one old-timer always said: "I never got into a fight when I was drinking, only when I was sober and knew what I was doing. Because I was always so happy when I was drinking. I loved everybody and everybody seemed to love me." According to him and others of his kind, one had to understand the life the westerner led

Texas cowboys enjoy themselves.

to understand his drinking habits. Cowboys and sheepherders did not get to drink often. They were cooped up in their line camps, bunk houses, and sheep wagons for weeks on end, either shivering in wet clothes or burned to a crisp by a pitiless sun, eating monotous grub, going without anything that means life to a man though incessantly dreaming and talking about it—

> The cowboy's life is a dreary, dreary life
> He's driven through the heat and cold;
> While the rich man's asleeping on his velvet
>   couch,
> Dreaming of his silver and gold.

On the rare occasions when they came to town— and precious little of a town it usually was—they made a night of it at the only place available, the saloon. And so they drank. Charles Kusz, the caustic owner-editor of the Manzano, New Mexico, newssheet, liked to fill his pages with items like this:

An Eastern Drug paper goes into ecstasy over "A Sponge weighing 11 lbs." Pshaw! Come West, young man, come West and see the sights. While in Santa Fe, one day last week, we saw more than 50 "sponges" at the leading hotels and boarding houses, any one of them weighing from 150 to 200 lbs; and we were told that it wasn't a very good day for sponges, either.

The development era in the West was hectic, flamboyant, violent, spectacular. So were many saloons and their customers. In mining towns the scene changed drastically as soon as the gold and silver gave out and big business took over. The rambunctious, adventurous, individualistic, solitary prospector was replaced by the grimy, hard-working coal and copper miner, an exploited proletarian who spent most of his waking hours underground and excited no romantic interest in the foreign traveler. After the settling of the West, which happened with stupefying speed, and the covering of an immense area with a network of

San Francisco drinking saloon.

railroad tracks, the great trail drives came to an end, and the cowboy, too, became a working stiff whose main tool happened to be a horse. The whoop-up Kansas cowtowns were tamed. The cattle barons, many of them English aristocrats and "remittance" men, disappeared together with the free range. The few who lingered were wiped out by the great blizzards of the 1880s. Wiped out with them were the fancy saloon clubs of the cow kingdoms, with their Victorian decor, Prince Albert syllabubs, and artillery punches.

Thus the transient, drifting population of adventurers and parasites quit the scene. What was left were working men with picks, shovels, or lariats, and they no longer went to the saloon as the poor man's club, because now there were churches, glee clubs, sports teams, libraries, and lecture halls. The western workman went to the saloon to get drunk. When the prairie proletarian went out on Saturday night he drank to get plastered. He drank to get the happy feeling that made up for the hardships, monotony, and often physical danger of his working life. Yet even at that stage the western saloons and their customers retained their special flavor, customs, and drinking rituals. The prairie saloon remained different from the New York, Pittsburgh, or Detroit grogshop, the working cowboy and miner different from the mill hand.

As the old western saloon degenerated, drinking places began to split up along professional class lines. The early thirst parlors had tended to be egalitarian. According to the English writer Marryat:

There is no limit to the introductions one is subjected to in a Californian crowd. If the "monte" dealer rises from his chair, you will probably be introduced to him, and I had the honor of shaking hands with a murderer quite fresh from his work, who had been acquitted a day or two previously by bribing the judge, jury, and the witnesses against him. I should have declined the honor had I learnt his profession with his name, but custom insists on your shaking hands on being introduced to a fellow-mortal; and to refuse to do so is tacitly to deny one of the great principles of the model republic, which holds that "one man is as good as another"; and as I heard a democratic Irishman observe, "a d———d sight better!"

The democratic spirit in which poor and rich, high and low drank together on an equal footing survived for a long time in the West and does so generally still, but in some towns stratification set in. Lee Casey, a writer for the *Rocky Mountain News,* described the Denver saloons and their customers at the turn of the century:

Along 17th St., in that hallowed era, the statement of the old song was apt—"You never went far till you came to a bar," and usually a very good one. . . . The Brown, then as now, got the society trade along with that of some politicians, mainly Republicans. Cattlemen and Democrats mainly frequented the Albany, whose bar was the longest in town and was the place where Colonel Cody could be sure to get any word left when he happened to be in town. Metal mining rather clung to the Windsor, although they didn't mind drinking at the Albany or Brown. Bob Stockton's Bar in the Equitable Building was headquarters for more dis- tinguished members of the bar. Tortoni's, 1541 Arapahoe Street, attracted the "Sacred 36" and upper crust journalists.

Some journalists, it should be noted, made a regular round of the bars because news was either made there or talked about and saloon gossip fur-

"In later bars there was a chillier, more formal atmosphere." The Navarre, in Denver, famous for its private rooms for entertaining women.

nished material for many newspaper items. Western reporters were given an allowance of "whiskey money" besides their wages. Members of the Denver press also patronized Volk and Uhlin's or Garrity's. Some went to Gahan's opposite the old courthouse to pick up news on crimes and scandals. Policemen, attorneys, and some politicians also liquored there. The Navarre, according to Casey, drew the sporting crowd. It was a place where a man could take a girl up to his room. If he didn't have a girl, meeting one could be arranged. Surgeons patronized the Denver Club, general practitioners the Metropolitan. The old saloons, whose decline or demise Casey bewailed, were already thoroughly stratified.

In the later high-grade bars, there was a chillier and more formal atmosphere. Since they were expensive as well as attractive they could not depend on the local trade alone and catered to the rich transient customer, especially the hotel bars. Unlike the small-town saloon they were filled with strangers, unknown to the bartenders and to each other. There was seldom a disturbance or unseemly noise, yet in many ways they were tougher than the small-time places. They had wine rooms filled with willing and available women and private rooms upstairs where these women could be taken. According to one who knew such places, they had a "quiet, unobtrusive, concentrated toughness" quite lacking in the average cowhand's thirst parlor. A few spectacular murders of passion were committed by respectable and wealthy men in ornate, even exclusive high-class saloons. A steady customer of such places, from Denver to New York, was the aforementioned Colonel Cody, better known as Buffalo Bill, whose invariable answer when asked if he would accept a drink was: "Sir, you speak the language of my tribe!"

In the old days, a cowhand rode thirty miles to the saloon on payday to throw around his compe-tence—thirty dollars, or a dollar a day for a month's wages—on Old Crow and cards. Some came early for their morning bracer, in accordance with that glorious western institution known as First Drink Time. The customer might be a dehorn, or a hard, fighting drinker, but most often he was a young cowhand chiefly concerned with raising a mustache. For the timid townsman the saloon often had a barbershop set up in one corner so that a pious fellow who publicly decried drinking, but who nevertheless had a thirst, could come through the barbershop for a couple of jolts and then leave the same way with nobody any wiser. Gentlemen of the cloth subscribed to this method. Once at the bar the customer was like a fish in a school of other fishes—they all talked alike and drank alike enveloped in the warm, sour, smoky, reassuring world of the old whiskey mill. All kept their hats on. Some were known to wear them even in bed. The typical westerner was baby-white and tender-skinned above the brow, sunburned and leathery below. Custom also demanded that an armed man toss down his shot with his right, his gun hand.

The vast majority drank only the straight stuff —rye or bourbon. All else was considered giving oneself airs. Men who went in for fancy or mixed drinks were said to have an "educated thirst." Their tastes were respected as long as they were known as regular fellows who had proven themselves at work on horseback or with a pick below ground. A foreigner, however, who asked for a cocktail might find himself the object of derision. Sometimes such an unlucky dude was forced to swallow a fifth of white lightning at gunpoint— "for his own good." An easterner in a Colorado jug joint who said: "I guess I'll take a cocktail," was forcefully instructed: "You don't guess, you drink, and you gets it straight and in a tin cup!" Foreigners used to nursing their drinks were horrified at the speed with which westerners tossed off their nightly ration. It seemed that they were "more interested in results than pleasure." One English writer described a prospector who once asked him for a drink, saying that he needed one badly but had no money. "I gave him a tumbler full of good old whiskey which he drank off at one draught as an ordinary man would ale. As he put down the empty glass he exclaimed, 'D———n, it, Paul! That was three parts water. You're a sly fox!' "

A man who did not treat found himself nudged by his neighbor with a "Say, stranger, ain't ye goin' to invite me to drink with yer?" To refuse a drink, even of the vilest rotgut barrelhouse whiskey, was a deadly insult not infrequently fatal to the offender. It invited the challenge: "Stranger, will you drink or fight?" A dude in Tucson who did refuse was kept in enforced hospitality by a gang of cowhands who, at gunpoint, dragged him from bar to bar until he had learned some manners.

The British writer Marryat recalled experiences in San Francisco during the gold rush days:

Perpendicular drinking at the Pioneer Club, Leadville, Colorado.

Everybody in the place is generous and lavish of money; and perhaps one reason for so many drinks being consumed is in the fact that there is ever some liberal soul who is not content until he has ranged some twenty of his acquaintances at the bar; and when each one is supplied with a "drink," he says, "My respects gentlemen!" and the twenty heads being simultaneously thrown back, down go "straight brandies," "Queen-Charlottes," "Stone-fences," "Champagne-cocktails," and "sulky sangarees," while the liberal entertainer discharges the score, and each one hurries off to his business.

And an anonymous writer remembered a big Leadville miner with a red shirt and a red beard

who had had just enough when he came in to make him dignified. He stepped up to the bar, raised his hand, and "Give 'em all a drink," he said with the dignity of a duke; "Give 'em all a drink." It was a time when all the miners were coming in with money in their clothes, and many were giving similar orders. So the whole house was treated. When it was all over Red Shirt said solemnly to the barkeep: "Well, it's on you; I haven't got a cent." The next minute he hit the floor.

A poor opinion was held of the man who did not from time to time invite the crowd, including perfect strangers, to "step up and liquor at my expense." In some out-of-the-way places, it was—and is—the custom for the booze boss to say, at fixed intervals which vary from place to place: "Gents, this one is on the house." Being treated meant, of course, that one had to buy back, which made for continuous boozing, pleasing alike the patrons and the old professor.

The treating habit aroused the particular ire of the temperance people, and attempts were made to suppress the custom. The city of Tacoma enacted an ordinance which forbade treating with fines leveled against the saloon keeper who tolerated it on his premises. An appellant argued that treating was an act of hospitality which had always been exercised by a free people. A Washington state court ruled that bars and alcohol consumption were regulated by the police who had the power to say what a citizen could do or not do inside a public house. But treating was an ingrained American habit, whatever the police might say about it. It might lead to drunkenness, but it was against human nature not to treat. Governor Winthrop of the Massachusetts Bay Colony legislated against it in 1639, Cotton Mather preached against it in 1687, it was made unlawful a hundred times, but it still went on at a son's graduation, or whenever the price of hogs rose, or when a wife got over a spell of bad cough, at a wake, or just to toast the grand old flag. It was the custom for the house to treat a miner coming from the shift to his first drink. In Virginia City a gent in good repute could get a free first jolt at a dozen different bars.

Another custom prevailing at the bar was to address a man by his "front name" and not to inquire into his second, or where he came from. Too much curiosity was impolite, besides being unhealthy. The West cared little for a man's, or a woman's, past and solemnly accepted any name voluntarily offered. Many persons were known only by their nickname. In 1969 the writer met an old man who had been known simply as Toad ever since, at the age of six, he had fallen into a well. He himself had forgotten his proper name. You did not loudly pronounce a man's second name even if you knew it. Many a quiet, flint-eyed stranger coyoted around in saloons trying, for reasons of his own, to catch a surname. Therefore, from mining king to the down-and-out prospector and from cattle baron to saddle bum it was always Pete, George, and Willy; or Lizzy, Sue, and Nellie. Since there were always several Joes or Charlies, first names were prefixed according to physical peculiarities—Handsome Bob, Limpy Willie, Splay-Foot Pete, Big-Nose Kate, One-Eyed Jack, and so forth. If a stranger came drifting through the country "just to see the sights" that was his business. If he had a reason to be secretive about his comings and goings, his silence was respected. One also never asked a rancher the size of his herd; that would have been like asking to see a man's income tax return today. Bret Hart once described the following dialogue:

Approaching the owner of the horse and cart, we asked:
"Whither bound?"
"Don't know," he replied sententiously.
"Where are you from?"
"Over yonder," he replied, pointing his finger toward the direction of Washoe County.
"Prospecting?" we asked.
"Spect so," he replied. Then glancing up at the sign in front of the *Reveille* office, he remarked:
"I'd just like to see the shape of one of you newspaper fellers that could pump *my* true-inwardness dry."
We gave him up.

As the cowpuncher put it: "Minding one's own business is the best life insurance."

The men with their feet on the brass railing respected a fellow's privacy, but they hated deception. Should a gent call for a drink and turn out to be unable to pay for it, he might be in for a beating, or worse. But if he owned up that he was broke and had a five-dollar thirst, few men would refuse to treat him. They were compassionate in the face of human suffering and generous to a fault. Cardplayers and boozers would take up a collection for a circuit-riding preacher ranting against gambling and drinking. Untalented and elderly actresses and warblers, on their way out and no treat for eye or ear, were showered with silver dollars or gold nuggets to help them retire. Everybody chipped in toward the cost of a funeral for a dead hooker.

There were other western customs to intrigue or shock the foreigner. Female English tourists were fascinated watching the frontiersman light up a lucifer by lifting up his leg and striking his match deftly on his Levis stretched tightly across his backside. "Why does the Westerner spit?" mused Rudyard Kipling. "It can't amuse him, and it doesn't interest his neighbour." Another traveler remarked: "True, they are good shots, and can generally make sure to three square inches of the spot they aim at, still, when you are surrounded with shooters, you feel nervous." Nervousness was also engendered by making the tenderfoot from the East fair play for all kinds of practical jokes and horseplay. Usually one tried to frighten him, and the greenhorn's behavior during this kind of hazing often determined his future standing in camp and saloon.

The drunken westerner was like the drunken easterner in running his mouth off, except in subject matter. The one talked about his fancy new saddle and the way his horse sunfished, or about how the assay of his ore had come out; the other might talk about stocks and bonds, or comment on who had gotten a new position. James Stevens found this out to his sorrow:

The team-hands were talking loudly about all the big reclamation and railroad jobs they had ever worked on, and I began to wonder about that, for out at camp they talked about their great drunks and their performances with wicked women. This was my first big disappointment in my career in saloons: the talk was always so infernally educational. Cowboys, it appeared, would tell bawdy stories and sing ribald songs only when they were in camp. In the saloons they talked about horses and beef, and told how to handle them and bragged about how good they were at it. It was the same with team-hands, railroaders and loggers. I was learning the truth of the old Western saying that men did their best work in the saloons and their best drinking and women-chasing when they were out on the job.

While endless talk was the rule in some nesters', stockmen's, and railroaders' saloons, taciturnnity was practiced in certain southwestern cow-poke bars. In Calabazas, near the Mexican frontier, customers were described as having said little more than "I don't care if I do," "Make your game," or "Gimme a Jim Beam." In San Antonio one enthusiast said nothing during a long night on the town but: "The man who invented bourbon sure was a genius!"—repeated over and over again.

A few little vignettes stand out in reminiscences about the customers of old. There is the tale about the man who galloped from town to town and bar to bar shouting: "The Injuns have burned down Trinidad and killed everybody—man, woman, and child." While recounting the gory events, which were entirely the figment of this western Paul Revere's imagination, he was naturally plied with free drinks, going on one of the greatest binges in Colorado history. Or the story about a befuddled drummer, nearly gone but not quite, trying to pick up the change which the barkeep had put down for him on a wet, foamy counter. After half an hour's attempt to pick up the two bits with trembling fingers, he blushed embarrassedly, resolutely pressed his finger down on the coin, and pushed it slowly toward the professor, saying resignedly: "Gimme a cigar . . ."

The West had a sympathetic understanding for the man who had made a night of it. A fellow unsteady on his legs after having taken three or four shots of Forty Rod beyond his capacity fell into an uncovered hole in a sidewalk, got hurt, and sued. A lower court held that the accident had been his own fault, the result of his drunkenness, but in 1855, the California Territorial Supreme Court reversed the decision, ruling: "If the defendants were at fault in leaving an uncovered hole in the sidewalk of a public street the intoxication of the plaintiff cannot excuse such gross negligence. A drunken man is as much entitled to a safe street as a sober one, and much more in need of it." The judges, obviously, knew the score.

Westerners who chose to spend a good part of their lives in saloons also practiced a wide variety of life's activities there. Doctors sometimes plied their trade inside the old thirst parlor, and occasionally customers turned to what they considered a place of comfort among friends, or perhaps a stage on which to play out a part of their lives, to doctor themselves. Tom Marshall once asked the keeper of Denver's Albany saloon for a pair of pliers to yank out an aching tooth, performing the operation upon himself right at the bar among a fascinated crowd of onlookers, using seven straight shots of bourbon for anesthetic. A miner whose leg had been crushed by an accident had himself carried straight to the nearest saloon, put his leg on the counter, himself applied the tourniquet, and then had his leg sawed off by the booze boss, loudly encouraged by friends and well-wishers. It is not known what particular brand of liquor this patient used to deaden the pain except that the amount consumed exceeded that swallowed by Marshall by a considerable margin.

Molly Demurska, a notorious lady from Butte, Montana, had herself married to Jack Jolly, the town marshal, inside the Clipper Shades Saloon, making her vow to love and obey right at the "altar"—namely, the backbar, after which a toast was drunk while bride and groom departed on their honeymoon on a fire engine. In Leadville, Colorado, a miner's wife had such a jolly good time socializing in a saloon that she seemingly was unaware that she was about to give birth. She was delivered of a healthy baby boy behind the counter with the assistance of the bartender, who held up the lustily crying infant for all to admire, whereupon one miner promptly baptized it with a shot glass of the very best.

Holidays were of course celebrated in saloons. Anne Ellis, a miner's wife, recalled: "Part of this winter I was the only woman in camp. At Christmastime, there was only another woman and myself, but lots of men, and they began early to fill up on Tom and Jerry. By night every man in town was either crying or singing drunk. The street was full of men; even those who had never been the worse for wear before were down and out today. They staggered and stumbled, fought and fell. One of the soberest, most reliable men in town fell by the town pump and was unable to get up."

After the elegant professional gamblers had disappeared, the transient drummers became the most glamorous customers to frequent the saloons. They were clad in flashy, citified suits, wore snappish bowler hats and spats on their shiny patent leather shoes. Their mode of dressing and general appearance proclaimed their profession. The traveling salesman became the prototype for the villain of the melodrama and the earliest one-reel moving pictures. This is odd, because the drummer was welcome. He had desired goods in his satchel, was a wandering newscaster, the bearer of tales, scandals, bloody deeds of horror, and the likely trends of the beef market. It was great to watch their spiels, especially those of the cigar salesmen, the aristocrats of the drummers. They conducted a lot of their business inside the saloons, where they told jokes to an entranced male audience. Their stories were usually "spicy," not fit for a lady's ear.

There was one type of man not included in the general saloon bonhomie. The soldier from the nearby fort was not welcome. There were three reasons for this animosity. Rightly or wrongly, the cowpuncher suspected the soldier of infecting the local parlorhouse girls with the clap or worse. The cowboy suffering from venereal disease generally did not blame the girl but the soldier who had given it to her. The military were also resented because they policed the early West, and neither cowboy nor miner had any love for that sort of thing. Finally, the independent-minded westerner despised any man who had to obey and stand at attention.

A better reception was given to the politicizing customer. The saloon was a place

Where politicians most do congregate,
To let their tongues tang arguments of state.

In 1849, in a California mining town, voters were called upon to ratify or reject the state constitution. Polls were set up in the town's largest tent—a saloon. "The voting inspectors," wrote one observer, "stood behind the counter, in close proximity to the glasses and bottles, the calls for which were quite as frequent as the votes." In the 1870s the state governor of Kansas entered a saloon with a dented stovepipe hat, frazzled pants worn over mud-caked boots, a bottle of Jim Beam protuding from one pocket, an old navy Colt from the other, greeting the customers with a jovial: "Step up to the bar, gents, and liquor at my expense!" It was a politician's standard opening gambit, setting the proper mood for an impromptu election rally. An offer of free drinks was always a good investment in future votes, and where else could the western office seeker always find a crowd to talk to but in the nearest thirst parlor?

In Chicago and elsewhere wardheelers assembled bums inside saloons, bought their votes with whiskey, and then formed them into columns and marched them off to the polls. Kansas City and state were given their name in a saloon, after an Indian tribe, the "Kanzas," during a long, acrimonious, and alcoholic debate. A plot to shift Minnesota's capital from Minneapolis to St. Paul was hatched in one saloon and foiled in another. For a number of years the Colorado State Senate assembled for its official deliberations in the bar of the Windsor Hotel. In San Francisco's Blue Wing Saloon, according to Hinton Helper, "We find the governor of the State seated at a table surrounded by judges of the supreme and superior courts, sipping sherry cobblers, smoking segars and reveling in all the delights of an anticipated debauch."

Politics was mixed with patriotism and maudlin sentimentality. The average customers believed in the American flag, motherhood, the Declaration of Independence, the sanctity of marriage, Irish home rule, the dignity of labor, the inviolability of women, and the right of a free citizen to be treated to a drink and to buy back. They believed in the equality of all men, provided they were white. To these noble sentiments subscribed alike the humble, peaceful nester and the ferocious road agent.

Politicians, in the general opinion, were just one cut above the far-gone derelicts who were at the bottom of saloon society. These, in the words of George Ade, were hangers-on "who showed up early, to sweep out and empty the fly-traps and crack the ice and set the stage for another performance. They received no money but got the compensation they wanted—about two raps of the hard stuff and the remnants of free lunch. They stayed around to do menial chores and sponge enough pick-ups to keep them alive and semi-conscious for another day." Most old-style saloons kept one or two of these characters, who in a few cases slept in the backyard.

In the beginning there were more customers than a saloon could handle. In some places one row of thirsty fellows was waiting for those lined up at the bar to get done and let them take a turn. But between 1895 and 1915 the saloons proliferated and had to fight fiercely to attract and hold a crowd of regulars. The reason for the mushrooming was twofold. Men thought that they could make more money for less work by keeping a saloon. Later they found out that too many others had the same idea. Even more significant was the astronomical increase in distilleries and breweries. In order to find an outlet for their product they had to create saloons in the same way oil companies franchise filling stations. This meant a certain loss of freedom on the part of the saloon keeper, who was often financially dependent on the distiller and obliged to take and dispose of a certain amount of booze every month.

After 1900, arithmetic began to work against the grogshop owner. If there were two thousand inhabitants in a one-horse town of, say, six saloons, which was about average in cow country, then slightly more than half of them were women. Two hundred more were boys below drinking age. Of the remaining eight hundred males—and we are talking now of the late, sedate period—four hundred did not drink, or rather piously drank at home where they could not be seen. That left about sixty-five potential imbibers for each saloon. Of these one-third were in-and-out men, who came in for their early morning eye-opener or their nightcap. The poor saloon keeper was no longer permitted to sell the homemade brand, and whiskey was more expensive than in the good old roistering days. Saloons cost more to build or rent. The owner had to employ every device he could think of to induce his small group of regulars to keep boozing. This hustling did not endear the owner to the wives and families of the regulars who came home every day in the wee hours with noses painted red. The upshot generally was that the community voted itself dry, which in turn made the booze boss an opponent of women's suffrage. In the end the women and the crusaders won out, and the old-style saloon died. It was a great institution while it lasted, and the customers were a colorful, exuberant breed of individualists who have become extinct. In *Trails Plowed Under*, Charles Russell captured a scene in a latter-day bar, and one senses a feeling of gentle demise:

Me and a friend drops into a booze parlor. . . . The man that runs this place is a friend of ours. I ain't mentioning no names but his front name's Dick. He's an old-time cowpuncher. He's bought a lot of booze in his day but right now he's selling it.

When me and my friend name our drink we notice there's about ten men in this joint. There actions tell us they've been using some of Dick's goods, but there ain't no loud talk. They are

"Saloons became the workingmen's clubs." Last drink before New Mexico voted itself dry.

. . . talking low like they're at a funeral. I get curious and ask Dick if these gents are pallbearers that's spreading sorrow on his joint.

"No," says Dick, looking wise. "This ain't no cow-town no more. It's one of the coming farmer-cities of this country, and the sellers of all this rich land don't want nothing that'll scare away farmers, and I'm here to please the folks. Most of these tillers of the soil come from prohibition states where men do their drinking alone in the cellar. . . . The old-timer that you knew was generally on the square. When he got drunk he wanted everybody to know it and they did. . . . Folks today . . . like some old bachelors I know, they've swept the dirt under the bed, and what you don't see don't look bad."

The gent that sold me that brand of booze told me there ain't a cross word in a barrel of it, and he told the truth. All these gents you see in here are pleasant without the noise. This bunch, if they stay to the finish, will whisper themselves to sleep. This booze would be safe for a burglar. I call it "whisperin' booze."

So much for the customers, from the frock-coated judge who could not face the litigants without having something stronger for breakfast than coffee, to the gambler who could keep a game going for three days and nights in a row with the help of an occasional shot of Joe Gideon, to the beer drinker who dropped in all day, to the peg-legged veteran of Chancellorsville who came in for a nip whenever the weather changed and made the old stump hurt—and out on the prairie the weather changed every five minutes. They went to cool off, or to get warm, propping their boots up on the pot-bellied stove, spitting their wads of "chaw" and admiring the fellow who "could drown a fly at ten paces." They came to get into a discussion or into a good fight, to complain or boast of the little woman, to laugh and to weep, to get that certain sad-happy feeling, and most of all, to get recognition as men and as individuals. Only the saloon could give them all of those things.

CHAPTER 7

THE STUFF THEY DRANK

The Horse and Mule live thirty
    years,
Yet know nothing of wines and
    beers.

Most Goats and Sheep at twenty
    die,
And have never tasted Scotch or
    Rye.

A Cow drinks water by the ton,
So at eighteen is mostly done.

The Dog in milk and water soaks,
And then in twelve short years he
    croaks.

Your Modest sober, bone-dry Hen,
Lays eggs for Nogs, then dies at
    Ten.

All Animals are strictly dry,
They sinless live and swiftly die.

But sinful, ginful, beer soaked man,
Survives three score years and ten.

While some of us, though mighty
    few,
Stay sozzled till we're ninety-two.

          —Anonymous

In Chicago it was: "Name your family disturbance." At Omaha: "Nominate your pizen." In Cheyenne: "Will you drive a nail in your coffin?" At Salt Lake: "Well, shall we irrigate?" In Virginia City: "Shall we lay the dust?" But what did the westerner drink?

He drank Red Dynamite guaranteed to blow his head off. He drank Brave-Maker, which made a hummingbird spit in a rattlesnake's eyes. He drank Joy Juice. A single nip would tempt one to steal his own clothes, two would make him bite off his own ears, while three instilled in him the desire to save his drowning mother-in-law. He drank Bumblebee Whiskey—the drink with a sting—which made one's ears buzz. He drank Brigham Young Whiskey—one jolt and you're a polygamist seeing double, or Dust-Cutter for those dry enough to spit cotton. Red Disturbance raised a blood blister on a rawhide boot. Block and Tackle made a man walk a block and tackle anything. Forty Rods brought a fellow down at exactly that distance. Taos Lightning struck a man on the spot. A fiery liquid called Skull-bender, served only at McHugh's in Custer City, got a gent floored and frenzied. Apache Tears made the roughest customer weep. It was brewed in Tombstone. Tongue Oil induced a man to talk his head off. Corpse Reviver made the dead rise. Snakehead Whiskey had a rattler's head nailed to the inside of the barrel "for flavor." Jig Juice or Jig Water was the freighters' favorite. Lamp Oil kept a man well lit. White Mule was the logger's corn whiskey. It had a mighty kick.

Tiger Spit made the keelboatmen row. Who Shot John felled a man instantly. Tangle Leg was made of tobacco, molasses, red peppers, and raw alcohol. It tied the imbiber's feet up in knots. A liquid called Miner's Friend was advertised to "outblast any other explosive." Tarantula Juice and Scorpion Bible were powerful poisons. Blue Ruin, also illogically known as Torchlight Whiskey, was a concoction whose main element was cheap gin. It was dispensed at Leadville. Nockum Stiff was a fearful type of rotgut brought West by Civil War veterans. Red Dog Whiskey, powerfully malignant, hailed from Tucson. Wedding Whiskey was, and still is, a favorite with the Swedes of North Dakota. It is made of 120 proof Everclear Grain Alcohol, burned sugar, and crushed peaches. Aphrodisiac herbs were added to "make the bridegroom go." Panther Piss, a brew of thirty-two different ingredients, now forgotten, inspired the poem:

> Panther Piss, Panther Piss
> Spit it out and hear it hiss.
> It's pure bliss.
> Little miss.
> Taste my kiss of Panther Piss.
> Panther Piss I love you.

White Mare's Milk was described as the "fightingest liquor ever to come out of a bottle." Roockus Juice made a mule grow horns. Base Burner was "hot as a she-mink." Creepin' Whiskey "creeps up behind you and knocks you down."

Further there were Widow-Maker, Wolf Whiskey, Pine-Top, Stump-Puller, Gut Warmer, Phlegm Cutter, Neck Oil, Popskull, Red Eye, Scamper Juice, Sheepherder's Delight, Nose Paint, Tonsil Varnish, Tornado Juice, Stagger Soup, Kickapoo Jubilee Juice, Gas Remover, Fool Water, Moral 'Suasion, Diddle Liquor, Coffin Varnish, McKinley's Delight, and Snakebite Medicine. Which of these a man drank depended on "where you're headed from and what church you went to."

On these concoctions a man got drunked up or pickled, blossom-nosed and struck with bottle fever. He painted his nose and rusted his boiler. He suffered an attack of the prevailing epidemic and got the jimjams. He looked down the neck of a bottle until he was affected with the trembles. He went booze-blind. He gathered a talking load. He went on a high and lonesome. He loaded up on patriotism and firewater. He drank pulque and became a borracho or a walking whiskey vat. He roostered until somebody stole his rudder. He belted the grape and imbibed his forty drops. He was drunk as a boiled owl. He was so drunk he opened his shirt collar to piss. He slept his jag off in the livery stable and woke up feeling as if a cat had kittened in his mouth, or as if he had breakfasted with a coyote. Then he "aired his paunch" —that is, vomited.

Early western drinks were raw, often homemade, the kind that "never paid no taxes." One such concoction, possibly the most famous of early western drinks, was Taos Lightning, also known as Taos Dynamite or, among mountain men, as Old Towse or Touse. It was made at San Fernandez de Taos in New Mexico and drunk by trappers and Indians alike. It was the first alcoholic refreshment of the pioneer Denverites, brought to them over 350 miles of mountain passes in an ox wagon driven by "Uncle Dick" Wooton. It was a variety of aguardiente, or burning water, made most often from corn or wheat. According to Lewis Garrard, a traveler on the Santa Fe Trail in the 1840s, it was the "Mountain Dew of New Mexico . . . imbibed before attaining a very drinkable age, by both foreigners and residents with great avidity." It "was as good as any, except it lacked color and age"; better, in the opinion of some, than aguardiente but inferior to Kentucky bourbon. One visitor to Taos was given

Making Old Towse in
Taos, 1895.

for his dinner a large tumbler of Taos Lightning
in which a baked apple was immersed.

Old Towse had come into its own in the 1820s
when a trapper named Peg-Leg Smith—a hardy
character who had cut off his own leg when it was
smashed by an Indian's musketball—opened a still
and distillery cabin for its manufacture. He produced an extrapotent strong water which made
those who swallowed it "knock around like a blind
dog in a butcher's shop." Taos Lightning eventually conquered much of the West, moving steadily
"upstream," beyond Denver, Georgetown, and
Leadville.

When the Yaller Flower of the Forest, Davy
Crockett, passed through Little Rock on his way to
meet destiny at the Alamo, he polished off a horn
of what he called "Green Whiskey" at a single
swallow. He later owned up that it was so hot that
he didn't need to have his food cooked for two

months—"The grub was cooked afore it got settled in my innards."

The strength of the stuff with which the rafts-
men of the Mississippi and the Big Muddy warmed
their guts may be gauged by the following ancient
anecdote:

"Hey! Don't let that stuff drop like that on your
boots!" I heard one raftsman say to another that
was passing him a bottle. "I spilt some on my new
shore shoes last week and it ate the uppers clean
off down to the soles."

"Was them shoes tanned with oqueejum?"
asked the other.

"No, sir. That there leather was tanned with
the best hemlock bark, and the shoes cost me $3."

"Now, say, my friend"—gently remonstrative
—"don't you know better than to buy leather
tanned with hemlock? What you want is leather
tanned with oqueejum and then whiskey can't eat
it. You see, whiskey and hemlock, they get together on social terms, same's you and me, and

then the whiskey does its deadly work and swallers the leather. But whiskey and oqueejum's enemies, and when they meet whiskey gets licked every time. That's why I keep my stomach lined with it."

Held in almost as much respect as Old Towse was Mormon Whiskey, or Valley Tan—

Valley Tan, Valley Tan
Maketh glad the heart of man.

It was an invention of industrious Mormons, and though the Latter-Day Saints in the beginning suffered no saloons in their midst, they were not altogether averse to imbibing their very own liquid balm—"Mighty as the hand of an avenging god."

And as for Mormon Whiskey, Wh-e-u-w! It was sod-corn barefooted. The Valley-Tan these Mormons make ain't nowhere. I mind Old Mike Gardner drunk a pint of it, and went home and stole one of his own plows and hid it in the woods, and didn't know where it was when he was sober, and had to git drunk agin to find it.

The humorist Bill Ney met up with Valley Tan in the early 1900s:

In Salt Lake City a man once said to me: "William, which would you rather do, take a dose of Gentile damnation down here on the corner, or go over across the street and pizen yourself with some real old Mormon Valley tan, made last week from ground feed and prussic acid?" I told him that I had just been to dinner, and the doctor had forbidden my drinking any more, and that I had promised several people on their death beds never to touch liquor, and besides, I had just taken a large drink, so he would have to excuse me.

Brigham Young is said to have been no stranger to the local product which warmed alike the heart of saint and gentile.

Pass Brandy or Pass Whiskey was an equally murderous fluid which was made in El Paso, Texas, and drunk on both sides of the border. Charles Russell mentions a Montana drink called Shelby Lemonade. "It's a mixture of alkali water, alcohol, tobacco juice an' a dash of strychnine—the last to keep the heart going."

Virile and robust, many of these liquid refreshments were well above 100 proof. The westerner liked his bug juice strong. It generally resembled the "corn licker" described by Irwin S. Cobb: "It smells like gangrene starting in a mildewed silo, it tastes like the wrath to come, and when you absorb a deep swig of it you have all the sensations of having swallowed a lighted kerosene lamp. A sudden, violent jolt of it has been known to stop the victim's watch, snap his suspenders, and crack his glass eye right across."

Suspicious cowhands shook their bottles to watch the "bead," the bubbles forming on the surface, from which an expert could tell the strength of the brew, but weak stuff could be given a fake bead with soap. Customers asked for "sink-taller whiskey," for it was believed that tallow floated in a weak drink but sank in the high-proof article. They did not like their liquor "baptized," that is watered, but tossed it off straight. A hapless Englishman who was so rash as to order a pint of Prickly Ash Bitters with some water in Tombstone's Crystal Palace was forced at gunpoint to take his whiskey neat, or "we'll blow a hole in the top of your head and pour it in!" The westerner drank cowboy cocktails—that is, straight rye or bourbon. Real Scotch was not known until the end of the century. A man's usual order to the bartender was: "Give me a tumbler and a bottle of your best drinking liquor."

What was called rye or bourbon often bore no resemblance to the genuine article. What was available was barrelhouse whiskey. The "barrelhouse" was born in New Orleans' French Quarter. It was a doggery frequented by men grimly intent on getting beastly drunk. "No lower guzzle-shop was ever operated in the United States." It was

A Missouri tavern in the 1830s.

usually a dank, tunnellike cave with a row of racked barrels on one side and bins with large-sized earthenware crockery on the other. For a nickel a patron was allowed to fill a mug from any of the barrels, which were labeled differently but all contained the same kind of vile rotgut. A customer who lingered instead of promptly refilling his mug was thrown out instantly.

This sort of concoction was not improved by a long journey west in a pitching, tossing wagon. Even better-grade "pure" whiskey was usually doctored as soon as it arrived at its destination. As the Tombstone *Epitaph* lamented: "Bad men and bad whisky are said to be plentiful . . . and measures are being taken to stop the mingling of the two. In a climate where the mercury sports around 110 the whisky should be only of the best quality."

But it wasn't. Low dives sold as whiskey colored camphine, fusel oil, and oil of turpentine whose legitimate use was as a varnish solvent. In southern California mining camps, bottles of cheap tequila were given labels with the names of choice bourbon. Cincinnati Whiskey, also consumed widely in the West, was suspicious to begin with: "A man out in Kansas said he could drink a quart of Cincinnati Whiskey, and he did it. The silver mounting on his coffin cost $13.75."

The notorious and murderous keelboatman Mike Fink, according to a farcical anecdote:

drank so much whiskey that he destroyed the coating of his stomach, and the doctor told him that before he could get well, he would need a new coat for it. Mike thought the thing over, and said, when he had a new coat for his stomach, he would have one that would stand the whiskey; and he made up his mind that a buffalo robe with the hair on it was just the thing, and so he sat down, and swallowed it. He could drink any amount of whiskey after that, and never so much as wink.

Some early Denver saloon keepers diluted their whiskey to make one barrel into three by means of additives that gave it an artificial kick. This "inventive whiskey" was definitely poisonous, brought on the DTs, and "left a fellow so shaky he couldn't pour a drink into a barrel with the head out." In New Orleans cheap wine became "Irish whiskey" when a pint of creosote was poured into it. A pound of burned sugar in grape juice, an ounce of sulphuric acid "to make it convincing," and a plug of "chawing baccer" to give it a bead, also made a powerful if not altogether satisfactory mixture. One thirsty traveler through Colorado, asking for whiskey, was told to wait awhile to give the "baptized" home brew which had frozen in its bottle time to thaw out.

In Creede, Colorado, Robert Ford, "the dirty little coward who shot down Mr. Howard"—that is, Jesse James' murderer—operated Ford's Exchange Saloon. In his cellar he made "overnight whiskey," "as deficient in proof as it was in the aromatic characteristics of genuine bourbon."

There were some who did not use any whiskey at all in their concoctions, no real, clear alcohol. They dosed creek water with any, several, or all of these: tartaric, citric, and sulphuric acids, fusel oil, ammonia, black bone meal, gun powder, molasses, oak bark, oatmeal, cayenne pepper, tobacco, snake root, nitre, juniper berries, creosote, and turpentine. A horrid something called "grains of paradise," infernally hot, acrid, and bitter, was sometimes added for an extra illusion of strength. Still, men drank everything aspiring to the name of whiskey or bourbon. Rye was supposedly the favorite in the East; bourbon the preferred drink of the South and West—the beloved red likker, the prestige drink. But rye was also tremendously popular in the wide-open spaces, and whiskey went down in American folklore as the stuff legends are made of.

If the ocean was whiskey and I was a duck
I'd dive to the bottom and get one sweet suck.

But the ocean ain't whiskey and I ain't a duck,
So we'll round up the cattle and then we'll get
   drunk.

Sweet milk when I'm hungry, rye whiskey when
   I'm dry,
If a tree don't fall on me, I'll live till I die.

I'll buy my own whiskey, I'll make my own stew;
If I get drunk, madam, it's nothing to you.

Whiskey was the thing that kept a man going, looking for a lost dogie in a blizzard. A western store, if it didn't have anything else, could at least be counted upon to have a barrel of gut warmer.

Whiskey, the king of liquors, was first known by its Gaelic name *uisge beatha*—the water of life. This, in time, was contracted into usquebaugh, which became uisge, whiskie, and eventually, whiskey. As the Scottish writer Aeneas MacDonald put it so poetically: "Whisky is a reincarnation; it is made by a sublimation of coarse and heavy barley malt; the spirit leaves that earthly body, disap-

pears, and by a lovely metempsychosis, returns to the world in the form of a liquid exquisite and impersonal. And thence whisky acquires that lightness and power which is so dangerous to the unwary, so delightful to those who use it with reverence and propriety."

Whether it is to the Irish or the Scots that we owe this exalting liquid is still hotly debated. As in America, it played its part in the songs and epic stories of Scotland as well as the Emerald Isle. Scotch and Irish warriors were alike mighty in battle and in the consumption of the water of life. The Irish hero Red O'Neil, who made the English tremble before him, always kept a great store of usquebaugh in his cellar. He drank it in such stupefying quantities that his men had to bury him in cool, moist earth up to his chin to counteract the heat generated in his body by the fiery liquor. Of whiskey, the Scot Aeneas MacDonald wrote:

"Whiskey was the stuff legends are made of. . . ."

It sloweth age, it strengtheneth youth; it helpeth digestion; it cutteth phlegm; it abandoneth melancholy; it relisheth the heart; it lighteneth the mind and quickeneth the spirit; it keepeth and preserveth the teeth from chattering and the throat from rattling.

The Scotch-Irish are generally credited with being the creators of whiskey in America. It was Scotch-Irish pioneers who, after the Seven Years' War, swarmed into western Pennsylvania to plant their rye, corn, barley, and potatoes. St. John Crèvecoeur, an early traveler along the Allegheny frontier, bemoaned the settlers' fate: "They have not, nor could have, any place where they might market their produce." Cattle could not easily be driven two hundred miles through dense mountain forests. It took too much time, and the bad roads ruined too many horses, to get the grain harvest to the eastern cities—and grain and cattle were all the frontier had to offer in the way of produce. Whiskey was the answer to the pioneer's prayer. A horse could carry at the most four bushels of grain—about 250 pounds. But grain could be made into whiskey at the ratio of two gallons per bushel. The old nag could manage to carry two eight-gallon kegs of the good creature—and at a most wonderful profit. What it carried was Monongahela rye, in most cases distilled solely from rye, sometimes from grain and potatoes. Monongahela was noble stuff. Men waxed lyrical when describing its mellowness and its satisfying effects upon the human system. It became the settlers' cash crop, their liquid gold. It took the place of coined money, which was rare on the frontier. Workmen and judges alike, preachers, teachers, artisans, mechanics, and carters were paid in whiskey. Whiskey bought a horse or a rifle, sugar and tea, a looking glass for the farmer's wife and shoes for his children. Whiskey kept up its value, year after year. Best of all, it was easy to transport. Heat or cold could not spoil it.

By 1790, the smoke from more than five thousand still houses curled heavenward in the Monongahela Valley. Just before the Revolution a whiskey-sipping Pennsylvania frontier character named John Harrod led forty hardy men into the wilderness of "Kaintuck," where they set up copper stills and, in time, produced that soul-inspiring drink called bourbon. Later the Scotch-Irish pushed farther west and produced yellow Tennessee Sipping Whiskey. And so whiskey traveled together with the pathfinders and trappers to conquer the West.

Life, as the Russian anarchist Bakunin remarked, would be quite livable if it were not for governments. On March 3, 1791, an excise tax upon distilled spirits, the brainchild of Alexander Hamilton, became law. Its purpose was to pay the national debt grown huge as the result of the War of Revolution. The effect on the frontier Virginians and Kentuckians was the same as that produced by the Stamp Act, which had brought on the American Revolution in the first place. In sparsely settled Kentucky, where every red-blooded man kept his planished copper still going to turn out the double-twisted, rectified stuff, the people rose in wrath. Everywhere revenue collectors were physically attacked, their tax forms and receipts stolen, their horses' ears cropped, their wagon wheels smashed. At Lexington, the chief tax collector was hanged in effigy, the dummy cut down and burned on a bonfire with the approval of a great crowd of onlookers quaffing red-eye. In the four western counties of Pennsylvania, where rye was the staff of life and chief source of income, the settlers' fury led to the uprising known as the Great Whiskey Rebellion, which was suppressed only with the help of the regular army. Ever since a citizen has had to pay exorbitant taxes whenever he feels like buying a bottle, and may no longer legally make his own hard stuff with which to regale himself and his friends. However, the wild, woolly, and lawless "real" West was for a long time yet outside the United States and continued to enjoy various forms of powerful home brew—untaxed and unlicensed.

Because it originated at what was then the wild, untamed frontier, whiskey was hailed as a western drink. This "western whiskey," as it was called, came in three main varieties—rye, bourbon, and corn whiskey. Corn whiskey was made from corn, with just enough barley malt to aid fermentation.

It was a "man's drink, fit for frolickin' and fightin'," hailed by thirsty Tennesseans:

> Here's to old Corn Likker,
> It whitens the teeth,
> Perfumes the breath,
> And makes birthing a pleasure.

It was, however, looked down upon as bourbon's poor country cousin by serious drinking men, who contemptuously referred to it as "yak-yak bourbon" or field whiskey. Irvin S. Cobb called it the "unlawful offshoot from the bourbon tribe . . . an illegitimate orphan of the royal line, born out of

wedlock in the moon, left as a foundling on the doorstep of some convenient bootlegger and abounding in fusel oil."

Jonathan Daniels wrote:

At its best, aged in home-sized kegs . . . corn liquor was a potable drink full of the mule's heels. Gentlemen exchanged private systems for reducing the shock to the palate, which extended all the way from the introduction of dried fruits into the liquor to advanced chemical procedures. Sometimes they succeeded. But at their worst, corn liquor and monkey rum were concoctions taken stoically, with retching and running eyes. There was certainly a democracy in drinking then. Rich and poor drank with the same gasping.

As some said, corn likker was a drink to make a fellow belch fire. It found its way in huge quantities to Louisville, Cincinnati, St. Louis, and points

Above: The apotheosis of corn. *Below:* Trying to collect a tax on whiskey in the Great Whiskey Rebellion of 1794.

west. It supplied fur traders, trappers, keelboat-men, and Indians in and around the forts and stockades along the Missouri River with something to cheer their innards. It was mostly transported by boat and the rocking motion of gently lapping waters was said to mellow it some. Corn likker would do for a man whose thirst still needed some education. But bourbon, ah, here was the good, red creature, "going down slick," the "stepping stone to eminence," "that famous soul-inspirin' liquah; the joy of every American father, the pride of every American mother, and for which American children cry."

In *Red Likker* Irvin S. Cobb sang a hymn of praise to the red essence:

Let me tell you, suh, there's only one likker that's properly qualified to caress a gentleman's palate in the way a gentleman's palate deserves to be caressed; and that's red likker—the true and uncontaminated fruitage of the perfect corn, and that, suh, is Bourbon. . . .

We make our mash by hand in small tubs—by hand, mind you—and of the finest corn these Kentucky lands can produce—and we ferment it right there in those small tubs, and the beer we get by that treatment is first singled in copper over open wood-fires—always over open wood-fires here—and the singlings are doubled also in copper over more open wood-fires; and from the spent mash, the waste you understand, which remains after the elimination of the alcohol by the boiling, we get a residue of slop, or as we say, sour mash, which provides the exciting properties for the next batch, so that the very soul of the grain goes on perpetuating itself, and reincarnating itself, world without end.

Take it straight, or in a toddy or julep, but never otherwise under any circumstances. For Bourbon stands on its own merits—the king, suh, and the queen and the whole royal family of likkers.

Bourbon is said to have been accidentally invented by the Reverend Elijah Craig in 1789. The reverend scoured the inside of his empty barrels with glowing ashes to clean and ready them for the next batch of wet goods. He then forgot about some of the barrels left standing in a dark corner for three or four years. When opened, they contained the aged, mellowed, full-bodied spirit, turned its characteristic reddish color by the charred oak. As early whiskeys were named after their places of origin, bourbon got its appellation in 1846 from the Kentucky county where it was first made.

Favorite brands were Old Pepper—"born with the Republic," Old Crow, Old Anderson's Little Brown Jug, Old Tub, Clark's, Hermitage, and of course Old Gideon. In Denver, the Grand Central Hotel Bar bottled bourbon under its own label. Jackson's Sour Mash had many admirers and was sold by Bob Ford in Creede, Colorado. Chicago loved Lake Whiskey, "fine as silk," which was recovered from eighty barrels of prime bourbon rolled into Lake Michigan to preserve it from the Great Fire of 1871. Some midwestern and western bars displayed signs "Gentlemen imbibing foreign and alien spirits other than good American bourbon and whiskey are required to pay cash." A Texan ran an ad in his local paper: "Strayed—one holstein heifer. I will give to the one who returns her a bottle of 10 year old monogram bourbon." Reputedly he found himself confronted the next morning by twenty-five hopeful neighbors leading Holstein heifers by the rope.

In spite of the "nothing but straight whiskey" mystique, a lot of other stuff was available and was drunk. This was especially true in early San Francisco—"Hail to the San Franciscan, whose cool climate both fosters a desire for liquor, and enables him to carry it!" In the 1850s Hinton Helper once enumerated the bill of fare of one California groggery. The list began with—"Bowie knives and Pistols," and ended with "Tobacco and Segars." In between were 110 different drinks, including Scotch Ale, English Porter, Portuguese Port, Tog,

Smasher, Ginger Pop, Hairs, Horns, Champagne, Apple Dam, Ching Ching, Burgundy, Spanish Sack, French Claret, Jamaica Rum, Holland Gin, Veto, Stonewall, Rooster Tail, Vox Populi, Tug and Try.

Virginia City, Nevada, saloons offered local, St. Louis, Milwaukee, and Clumbacher beer; French, German, and California wines; porter, stout, and ale imported from England; and about twenty different brands of bourbon and rye whiskey. As early as 1860 Denver saloons served champagne and Catawba wines besides Old Towse.

During the 1870s the favorite San Francisco drink was Pisco Punch, made on a base of Peruvian Pisco brandy. Its exact composition was a secret which died together with its inventor, Duncan Nichol, after Jeremy Thomas the most famous of California bartenders. It was thus described by one lucky enough to have tasted it:

It is perfectly colourless, quite fragrant, very seductive, terribly strong, and has a flavor somewhat resembling that of Scotch whiskey, but much more delicate, with a marked fruity taste. It comes in earthen jars, broad at the top and tapering down to a point, holding about five gallons each. We had some hot, with a bit of lemon and a dash of nut-

The Sour Mash Express.

meg in it. . . . The first glass satisfied me that San Francisco was, and is, a nice place to visit. . . . The second glass was sufficient, and I felt that I could face small-pox, all the fevers known to the faculty, and the Asiatic cholera, combined, if need be.

Pisco brandy was also used in mixing Button Punch, a drink Rudyard Kipling extolled as the "highest and noblest product of the age . . . I have a theory it is compounded of cherubs' wings, the glory of a tropical dawn, the red clouds of sunset, and fragments of lost epics by dead masters."

Cocktails and mixed drinks found their way into the roughest six-gun country. Roy Bean, "the law west of the Pecos," was not ashamed to make eggnogs for special customers. Soapy Smith drank "giggle soup"—snow-cooled Pommery Champagne—at the burial of a friend in Creede, Colorado; and red-headed General Phil Sheridan downed Brandy Smashers with his friend General "War Is Hell" Sherman in a Dakota saloon. A concoction called Cactus Wine was a mixture of tequila and peyote tea. It is said to have been a favorite with U.S. troopers under General "Black Jack" Pershing during their fruitless chase of Pancho Villa. Another invention of the military was calvary punch, drunk by officers at Fort Lincoln and Fort Laramie. It consisted of very strong tea mixed with rum and blackberry julep. Medora Busthead was Missouri water mixed with pure corn likker and a generous dose of red pepper to "give it firepower." A drink called Velvet was popular in the plush hotel bars of Denver and Colorado Springs. It was a giant-sized glass filled half with porter and half with champagne.

Old standbys were Mule Skinner—whiskey mixed with blackberry liquor—and Grizzly Bear's Milk—raw whiskey mixed with milk and sugar—for the cowboy with stomach trouble. Old-timers, long in the tooth, had hot toddies on wintry mornings—hot whiskey with sugar water or "cough syrup" made of rye and rock candy.

Cocktails were gulped down in the West at a surprisingly early date. A visitor to Santa Fe shortly after that city became part of the United States observed a bartender called Long Eben mix a gin cocktail. The first cocktail, reputedly, was made by a New Orleans druggist-mixologist, Monsieur A. Peychaud. This was the famous "Sazerac," named after its main ingredient—cognac manufactured by Messrs. Sazerac-de-Forge, of Limoges, France. Later the establishment in which this drink was available was named Sazerac House. Sazerac was compounded of a mixture of cognac, sugar, and aromatic bitters, the composition of which was Peychaud's secret. Eventually American rye and whiskey were substituted for French cognac. Significant for the reputation of western drinking establishments is the fact that in the opinion of cocktail lovers Bob Stockton's old bar in Denver was the only place outside New Orleans where the educated drinker could obtain a true and absolutely perfect Sazerac cocktail.

Southern-style juleps were introduced to the West by migrating Kentuckians and Tennesseans. The first julep was always a revelation, the second pure heaven, the third a serious mistake. Some New Orleans absinthe also found its way into Denver and Virginia City. The green, cool French aperitif has long since been outlawed because it contains wormwood, considered to be a harmful drug.

A very popular western drink was the Shawn O'Farrel, which eventually became a universal favorite under the name of "boilermaker and his helper." It came out of Butte, Montana, where it was the custom of the copper miner emerging from underground to rush and have several Shawn O'Farrels before anything else.

> Her heart was in Texas,
> But her Butte was in Montana.
> God, how she loved them boiler makers!

The drink inspired the Montana poet Bill Burke:

Oh, yes, they boast of lordly liquors
Brought from corners of the earth,
Creme-de-menthe and Parisian absinthe
And high toned beverages of worth.

But I'd stake my bottom dollar,
Also my honor and repute,
On the humble Shawn O'Farrel
Sold at quitting time at Butte.

After this terrific build-up it may be surprising to discover that a boilermaker was simply a straight shot of whiskey chased with the "helper" —a glass of cold beer. Equally elemental was the "pair of overalls" served at the Diamond Belle Bar in Durango, Colorado—two shot glasses of straight rye.

Beer made its appearance early in the West and was consumed in great quantities. "Willy the Brewer" McGlover began brewing beer in California in 1837, under Mexican rule. Beer was readily available to the forty-niners. The first regular brewery, William Bull's, was operative in San Francisco by 1850, the second year of the gold rush. From the very first, lager beer made by Luke and Thacheimer was popular in hot and dry Phoenix. An immigrant from Alsace-Lorraine brought the first keg of beer to Colorado miners and started a brewery in Denver as early as 1859. Soon the city had over a dozen. In Portland, Oregon, an ale brewery was opened in 1860. The Civil War gave a mighty impetus to beer drinking, a "lager-beer wagon" accompanying the numerous German Union troops everywhere during summer campaigning.

By 1880, brewing was mostly in competent German hands, and Germans were also among its biggest consumers. In Milwaukee, beer brewing was the chief industry; in St. Louis and Cincinnati it was the second largest business. Three billion gallons of beer were produced by the major licensed breweries in the 1880s. In spite of the great volume of business they did in the West

every mining camp or larger cowtown had its own brewery soon after it was founded. In Tombstone, Arizona, the Golden Eagle Brewery was built in 1879, when the town had barely three hundred inhabitants. Kegs were bulky, and beer was so cheap that it did not pay to ship it to the outlying areas—hence, the proliferation of local breweries.

Beer was sold in most saloons. Besides the places for hard stuff, there were also beer gardens, which sold nothing but beer. In Leadville, Colorado, these became very popular. The kegs were handled by "schooner skippers," who served "high-collared beer in scuttles." A person coming in with a large can to take beer home was said to be "rushing the grower." Shine Philips, writing of his hometown, Big Spring in West Texas, a typical cattle town, described a local beer garden:

George Brown's place sold beer only. It was across the street. Draft beer was in order—"big 'uns" for ten cents, "little 'uns" for a nickel—but it was beer, just beer, no hard stuff at that place. In front was the sloping board walk and on the edge of the walk was a bunch of empty kegs that the loafers used for chairs.

The bar was twenty feet long, with an enormous ice box behind it, where the kegs of beer were covered with ice. The nickel boys kept the place busy, as it was very democratic. It's a lot easier being democratic with nickel drinks than with fifteen cent 'uns.

There are many similar descriptions in western literature, hinting that the beer-only places were often as popular with cowboys as with farmers and miners. There was "lager bier," beer stored, table beer, small beer, bock beer (which was strong lager), and dark and light ale—from 3 percent "near beer" to 10 percent "triple XXX." While whiskey and bourbon drunk by westerners improved steadily, beer declined in quality between the years 1900 and 1915 due to price wars between competing English and American firms. An anonymous writer of the period complained:

It is a burning shame that if the Government permits its manufacture it does not compel a pure product. There is no doubt that the hops in America go into beer. But there is so much beer and so few hops that the latter are used only in special brands such as one finds in clubs—brands that cost ten cents for a small bottle at wholesale. In the common saloons a "scuttle," which holds as much as three of these bottles, can be had for five cents, which shows the kind of stuff the working-men are pouring into their unhappy stomachs.

Beer had been popular in Jamestown and New Amsterdam. It traveled west with the miner and sodbuster. It was the favorite refreshment of the European immigrants who swept westward during the second half of the nineteenth century. Beer was what the working stiff drank when he had a thirst. Beer consumption skyrocketed until, in the end, westerners swallowed considerably more beer than whiskey.

Wine came to the Southwest as early as 1630 when Franciscan friars planted the first vineyard in New Mexico near the present town of Socorro. In a report made to his superiors in Mexico City, the eighteenth-century traveling monk Fray Francisco Dominguez wrote in 1776 that the seven hundred residents of Albuquerque had "little orchards with vinestocks. . . . Not all those who have grapes make wine, but some do." At Isleta the wandering monk encountered Indian villagers growing and drinking wine—civilization indeed!

Wine was also brought to California by Franciscan monks during the eighteenth century. Moving northward from Mexico the brothers established a chain of missions along the coast, planting their vines as they went. In 1820, a Mexican woman, Maria Marcelina Felix, planted a vine near

Above: The Parkhurst Brewery and Saloon, Deadwood.
Below: "Indian Whiskey was in a class by itself."

97

Santa Barbara that attained a diameter of one foot at its base and eventually yielded twelve thousand pounds of grapes at every harvest. Clusters of its grapes weighed as much as seven pounds. Doña Maria finally died beneath the arbor formed by the branches of her extraordinary plant at the age of 107. Up to the middle of the nineteenth century, California wine, either red or white, was made from the "missios," the grapes the Franciscan brothers had planted. They are still used to make fine sherry. By 1865 other European and American varieties were grown, and ten thousand acres of vineyards were under cultivation, from which two million gallons of wine were produced for local consumption—sweet, tawny Angelica and muscatel, excellent port and hock, champagne, claret, bitters, and brandies. Soil and climate favored the California winegrower. An early traveler came across a cluster of Tokay grapes weighing seventeen pounds.

Wine grapes were also grown by the Anglo-Saxons of the early western frontier. The Ohio River became known as the Rhine of America. On its shores one vintner farmer, Nicholas Longworth, earned for himself the title of "father of American wine." His grape was the native Catawba, which inspired Longfellow to write:

> There grows no vine
> By the haunted Rhine,
> By Danube or Guadalquivir
> Nor an island or cape,
> That bears such a grape
> As grows by the Beautiful River.

Catawba was said by President Jefferson to be indistinguishable from the best French Chambertin. It was drunk by San Franciscans in 1850, and by Denverites ten years later. An early Missouri winegrower, who had learned his trade from St. Louis Frenchmen, predicted that American wines would soon be exported to all parts of a delighted globe, "unless we drink them all up ourselves."

The "whiskey and six-gun" literature has obscured the fact that a lot of wine was drunk in the West, occasionally even preceding the harder stuff.

In a class by itself was trade whiskey—that is, in a very low class. This was the horrifying and usually illicit firewater with which unscrupulous traders paid for the Indians' beaver and other pelts. One recipe was:

One barrel of Missouri water.
Two gallons of raw alcohol.
Two ounces of strychnine to make them crazy.
Three twists of 'baccer to make them sick,
   cause Injuns won't believe it's good
   unless it makes them sick.
Five bars of soap to give it a bead.
1/2 pound of red pepper to give it a kick.
Boil with sage brush until brown.
Strain through barrel.
Wall, that's yer Injun whiskey.

It was called firewater, because a little of it was always thrown into the fire to make a flame "so that the bucks knew it warn't jest plain Old Big Muddy water."

A drink learned from the Indians was tiswin—Apache cactus beer—while Mexican mestizos introduced southwestern Anglos to mescal, which became a favorite drink in the frontier towns. It was made from distilled agave cactus juice, the kind of stuff "that couldn't be corked," could only be kept in a glass, and had to be sweetened with salt before swallowing. If drunk immoderately, it made the imbiber see snakes and alligators. Modern mescal is much tamed—a rust-colored, highly palatable brandy. In 1880, at Tucson's Cosmopolitan Bar, customers were regaled with a drink made up of whiskey and mescal mixed in equal parts. The stuff was served "with the snakes strained out first." Pulque, the "grateful liquor," another drink made from agave, crossed the Rio Grande to become popular among Anglos and

Hispanics alike. Many southwestern saloons were simply referred to as pulquerias.

> Know ye what pulque is?
> Liquor divine!
> Angels in heaven
> Prefer it to wine.

Finally, there were the remedies and cure-alls. In the streets of cowtowns during the 1880s and 1890s could be seen little old ladies, fanatical abstainers, and vociferous denouncers of demon rum, who nevertheless tottered unsteadily on wobbly legs and did not seem to have all their marbles. They were the victims of Hostetter's Bitters or a number of other balsams, liver regulators, and restoratives guaranteeing exuberant health and long life.

Hostetter's Bitters was advertised as a "liver-regulator" and cure for chilblains, dyspepsia, evil humor, loose bowels, torpidness, and the ague, but was mostly double-distilled whiskey of the lowest grade with a slight flavor of honey. Hostetter's Bitters packed such a wallop that it was sold by the drink and became a favorite with clergymen who did not care to be seen inside a saloon but felt no guilt about visiting the pharmacist. Even more provocative was "Dr. B. J. Kendall's blackberry balsam, a remedy for diarrhea, dysentery, cholera morbus, biliousness and costive liver. Alcohol, 61 percent. Each fluid ounce contains 5 grains of opium. Adults, three tablespoons full, children 8 to 10 years old, one tablespoon, 4 years old, 1/2 teaspoonful, 2 years, 10 drops. Younger children in proportion."

Dr. Simmon's Liver Regulator was known as "the cowboy's friend," due to its high alcohol content. Sioux Indians at Pine Ridge and Rosebud got inordinately fond of Dr. Sweet's Infallible Liniment. It promised to raise hair on a bald head, if rubbed on, and to strengthen the roots if taken internally. Its efficacy was proven by the fact that no Indian suffered from baldness. The Infallible Liniment infallibly brought on tremendous drunks. Limerick's Great Southern Liniment was warranted to cure:

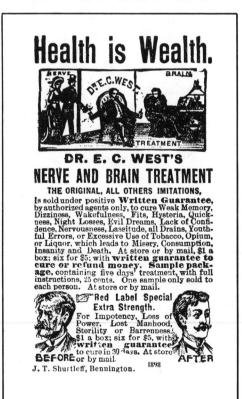

Health is Wealth.

DR. E. C. WEST'S
NERVE AND BRAIN TREATMENT
THE ORIGINAL, ALL OTHERS IMITATIONS,

Is sold under positive **Written Guarantee**, by authorized agents only, to cure Weak Memory, Dizziness, Wakefulness, Fits, Hysteria, Quickness, Night Losses, Evil Dreams, Lack of Confidence, Nervousness, Lassitude, all Drains, Youthful Errors, or Excessive Use of Tobacco, Opium, or Liquor, which leads to Misery, Consumption, Insanity and Death. At store or by mail, $1 a box; six for $5; with **written guarantee to cure or refund money. Sample package**, containing five days' treatment, with full instructions, 25 cents. One sample only sold to each person. At store or by mail.

☞ **Red Label Special Extra Strength.**
For Impotency, Loss of Power, Lost Manhood, Sterility or Barrenness, $1 a box; six for $5, with **written guarantee** to cure in 30 days. At store or by mail.
BEFORE — **AFTER**
J. T. Shurtleff, Bennington. 1898

Rheumatism	Burns	Eruptions
Neuralgia	Bruises	Broken Breasts
Erysipelas	Scalds	Boils
Scald-Head	Sprains	Fever Sores
Tetter	Wounds	Inflammation
Ring-Worm	Cuts	Swellings
Salt Rheum	Cancers	Felons
Sore Nipples	Corns	Sore Eyes
Chapped Hands	Gout	Headache, & etc.

It was also claimed to be a speedy cure for many diseases of horses. Whether horses got as drunk from it as men cannot now be ascertained.

Many patent medicines were made of cheap whiskeys and some additives. One was advertised as: DUFFY'S PURE MALT WHISKEY—Absolutely Pure and Unadulterated. Entirely free from FUSIL OIL. Other cure-alls with more than 60 percent alcohol were Ague Busters, the Colonel's Prickly Ash Bitters, Dr. King's New Discovery for Consumption, Indian Sachem's Electric Health Restorer, Indian Snake Oil Whiskey, Morley's Ague Tonic, the Great Sooliman's Oriental Malt Balsam, Plantation Chill Cure, Ballard's Horehound Syrup, Dr. Miles' Heart Cure, Mother's Friend, Mrs. Winslow's Soothing Syrup (and how it did soothe!), and innumerable others. Happiness, one ad said, was a pack of "star tobacco, three bottles of Garret's snuff, and a king-size bottle of Chickasaw Chill Cure." Or more poetically expressed:

> Little spells of fever
> Little chills so bland
> Make the mighty graveyard
> And the angel band.
> A little Cheatham's Chill Tonic
> Taken now and then
> Makes the handsome women
> And the healthy men.

Patent medicines were sold by drummers pretending to be doctors putting on a "medicine show" with the help of blackface minstrels, "Ethiopian" banjo players, and shills on crutches who were miraculously cured by a draught of "Doctor Von Vonder's Golden Wonder Elixir." These traveling doctors plied their trade at country fairs at a universal price of one dollar per bottle for their product, spiels and entertainment free.

Whiskey was thought to cure almost anything:

For croup: Put turpentine and rye whiskey into saucer and light. Hold baby's mouth over it, also black silk cord around neck.

Whooping cough: Mare's milk and whiskey.

Colic: Catnip tea and whiskey.

Dysentery: Burned whiskey.

Colds and pneumonia: Whiskey, more whiskey, honey, ground-up lamb's tongue.

Teething pains: Rub whiskey on baby's gums.

Toothache: Carry a pig's tooth in pants pocket, and a bottle of rye.

Asthma: Whiskey in mullein tea.

Sore eyes: A dab of whiskey on eyelid. Also wipe it with tip of black cat's tail.

Headache: Camphor mixed with rye rubbed into scalp.

Snakebite: "Cut a freshly killed chicken in half. Eat one half and press the other against the fang punctures to draw out the poison. Drink plenty of whiskey. Apply whiskey externally to affected part."

Folk cures involving a generous dosage of "the critter" were abundant throughout the South and West. They varied from region to region and depended largely on local superstition. Medical properties were even attributed to certain brands of beer. A faded poster which could still be seen in the 1960s, tacked to a wall in Georgetown's Red Ram Saloon, advertised "Selak's celebrated ale, takes right hold of the vitals and elevates the soul. It opens the faculties, clears the canals of the heart, and strikes down to the very bottom of contentedness." It could be had for a nickel a glass.

This brings up the subject of prices. A bushel of corn made three gallons of whiskey. Proprietors bought jug whiskey at twenty-five cents a gallon. In mining towns, during the height of a boom, they resold it to their customers at two bits, or twenty-five cents, a shot. This was taking unfair advantage of the situation, sheer inflation.

In the cowtowns whiskey was dispensed at two glasses for a quarter. A man slammed it down on the counter and received a drink and a brass check for change that could be used as payment for a second drink. It was calculated that the average customer drank a gallon of the hard stuff per week, which cost him all of a couple of dollars. Still a dollar was a dollar then—and it gave the owner a 400 percent mark up.

The pour-it-yourself stuff, drunk always in the perpendicular, was ten cents a glass—a "short bit." Fifteen cents was a long bit and gave a man a snort and a chaser. All this sounds very cheap and makes the West appear a drinker's paradise, but some men lived on three dollars a week then. Investing one-third of your income in drink was no small matter. There are plenty of stories describing cowboys blowing a month's, or even a season's, hard-earned pay on one glorious, rip-roaring night in the old thirst parlor. More often than not these stories were true.

In early Denver, California champagne sold for fifty cents a quart but imported giggle soup cost a dollar. In 1859 Taos Lightning was imported to Denver by mule train or oxcart and was sold in widely recognized turquoise green bottles. Old Towse had such a terrific reputation that it sold for a dollar a drink, while at the same time barrelhouse whiskey sold for three dollars a gallon. Colorado prospectors had palates that could distinguish the good stuff from the bad. Once the railroad reached Denver, Old Towse became superfluous and prices on all kinds of hard drinks dropped sharply. The highly admired "little brown jug of Anderson's pure rye" or bourbon sold for $2.50 a gallon. Champagnes, such as Mumm or Cliquot sold at $1.75 a pint, or $3.50 a quart in Denver and Colorado Springs. In the lower depths four glasses of "Green" beer sold for a dime. Before World War I department stores sold gin at 75 or 80 cents a bottle. For thirty years, from 1890 to 1920, prices were almost standard from coast to coast, rising very slowly from 10 to 12 1/2 to 15 cents for the staple shot of red-eye. Every ten years, whenever the price went up by two cents, there was a loud wailing and gnashing of teeth. The remarkable fact is that prices remained almost unchanged for so long that a man could do his drinking for very much the same amount of money as his father before him, that a grandson's dollar bought as much as had his granddad's silver cartwheel.

Knowing *what* the westerner drank, the question remains *how much* did he drink? The answer is a lot. A miner or cowhand was "not the kind of man that's satisfied with washing his mouth out." In vino veritas. If there is truth in wine, there is also truth in folklore—

A freighter on the trail to Deadwood met a second freighter going in the opposite direction. Outbound freighter: "What yuh loaded with?" Inbound freighter: "Twenty barrels of whiskey an' a sack of flour." Outbound freighter: "What in tarnation are you goin' to do with all that flour?"

Or:

"Mister, what would your father have said if he had known that you drank two quarts of whiskey a day?"
"He would have called me a sissy!"

Or, from *Wolfville Days:*

"My grandfather," says the Colonel, "is a gent of ironbound habits. He has his rooles an' he never trangresses 'em. The first five days of the week, he limits himself to fifteen drinks per diem; Saturday he rides eight miles down to the village, casts aside restraints, an' goes the distance; Sunday he devotes to meditations."

Or, a remark supposedly made by a customer in Virginia City's Sazerac House:

This, sir, is my sixty-fourth drink today. I must put on the brakes, or the first thing I know I shall degenerate into excess. Moderation, sir, moderation, the grand secret of health, has been the rule of my life.

Or a Texan's admonition to an abstainer:

We like to drink, suh, and we like people who like to drink!

While the westerner bragged of being able to hold more than the effeminate easterner, statistics seemed to prove that on the sober side of the Missouri men did not drink appreciably less than their prairie counterparts.

By any standard the westerner did all right. As the Englishman Marryat wrote in the 1850s:

From the time the habitual drinker in San Francisco takes his morning gin-cocktail to stimulate an appetite for breakfast, he supplies himself at intervals throughout the day with an indefinite number of racy little spirituous compounds, that have the effect of keeping him always more or less primed. And where saloons line the streets, and you cannot meet a friend, or make a new acquaintance, or strike a bargain, without an invitation to drink, which amounts to a command; and when the days are hot, and you see men issuing from the saloons licking their lips after their iced mint juleps; and where Brown, who has a party with him, meets you as he enters the saloon, and says, "Join us!" and where it is fashion to accept such invitations, and rude to refuse them, what can a thirsty man do?

Montana and Dakota hotel bills throughout the 1880s and '90s show a consumption of thirty whiskeys a day by single customers, "thirty slugs per diem." In the Dakotas it was estimated that the average cowhand and miner drank five tumblers of the hard stuff per day. Miners and soldiers are said to have consumed "oceans of beer." The Irish, by statistics, led all the rest in per capita consumption of liquor. Whether statistics at that time, or at any time, are reliable is open to question.

In Virginia City, Nevada, Mark Twain, the humorist and lecturer Artemus Ward, and two other cronies went on a binge. By the time Artemus Ward proposed a standing toast, nobody in the party could stand. At one place their bill came to $237, this at a time when a good dinner cost three dollars and the better places sold drinks for two bits. As to the westerner's capacity to hold it, a table at San Francisco's Embarcadero Restaurant

was always strictly "reserved for drunks." In 1852 the police court columns of Frisco's *Daily Alta California* ran everyday items such as these:

John Briggs, found comfortably drunk on Long Wharf. Discharged on promise to reform.

E. Jones was found by Officer Noeth on the corner of Long Wharf and Montgomery Street in a state of drunkenness and quite disorderly. He resisted the officer manfully, tearing his breeches and committing other small depradations. Fined $20 or ten days.

George Dits was found insensibly drunk in front of the Custom House. He was taken up in a hardcart and emptied in the police station. Fined $5.

Hyppolite Boveau, a Frenchman, fired a pistol in the street and did not know any better. Discharged.

Maybe the drunks were men who didn't have what it took, or maybe there were other reasons. Anne Ellis remarked: "It has always been an opinion of mine that if men were fed better they would drink less, as part of the craving they have for booze is hunger. Many times I have seen men coming off shift stop at the saloon for a drink, and I knew they had done a hard day's work on a half-cooked breakfast, and a lunch at noon which was not satisfying." There is, however, little evidence that a better-fed miner drank less or had greater drinking stamina.

The truth is, westerners liked whiskey, especially when it was red. They drank it "whenever the ground was wet" or, if soldiers, the day they got paid. They would rope the bar and drag it for five miles out into the prairie when they got high and pay for damages later. They drank beer on hot summer days, and there were weaklings among them who on rare occasions had drunk an eggnog —a tumbler of "baby titty." Those with some pride, and they were a prideful lot of men, took their whiskey neat "until it took them."

CHAPTER 8

"A COMIDATION FER MAN AND HOSS"

Beds, Board, and Booze.
All nations welcome except Carry.
Coffee, not like mother made but
   like she drank.

—Sign at Wisconsin tavern-saloon

No more than 5
To sleep in one bed.
No razor grinders or tinkers.
No dogs allowed upstairs.
No drunks in the kitchen.

—Sign in early South Dakota
   hotel-saloon

"Hotel de Drunk" was the nickname given to a number of early western saloons who also let stray customers, with no place to sleep, bed down on the sawdust. During the first half of the nineteenth century many whiskey mills doubled as inns, housing and feeding man and beast. At a later date specialization set in, the saloon, the hotel, and the livery stable (Hotel de Hoss) dividing between them the tasks formerly performed by a single road ranch. This was a matter of absolute necessity. Even in the earlier-settled Midwest roads were almost nonexistent before the 1850s, or even later. There were few stagecoach lines, and most traveling had to be done on horseback. Long stretches of corduroy roads in Illinois, Minnesota, and Wisconsin had to be negotiated on foot.

In 1895, an old man remembering the days of his youth commented that journeying from Fond du Lac to Galena or Prairie du Chien then was akin to traveling to China at the end of the century. Men were known to make their last will and testament before undertaking such a perilous journey. One could travel for days without meeting another human being. Often roads, or rather trails, faded without a trace, and the wanderer had to find his way navigating by the stars. On cloudy, rainy nights a wet cheek turned to the wind might give a hint of what direction to take. In 1836, a lone traveler on his way from Milwaukee to Prairieville was set upon by a pack of wolves. He frightened them off by shouting and waving his heavy cloak at them, abandoning it at last to their fury while running three miles to a lonely roadhouse, where he collapsed into the arms of the tavern keeper, who revived him with a heartening bowl of punch.

On these roads a horseman was not necessarily better off than a pedestrian. A Wisconsin man traveling on horseback had the lower parts of his boots—brand-new ones, be it noted—eaten by wolves, but managed to save his toes. And two friends, a Mr. Lewis and a Mr. Waterbury, set out on a trip of a hundred miles, Lewis walking and Waterbury riding. On his way back Lewis met Waterbury on a jaded horse which seemed to be dying. Lewis said that he "rested himself with running when he got tired of walking, and by walking when he got tired of running." In a few instances horses, drawing a coach or wagon, broke down, and the passengers had to yoke up, dragging the vehicle to its destination. When it rained hard, men emptied their boots of water before entering a saloon. As for the perils of the early frontier road, a man remembered losing a keg of whiskey from a wagon, discovering his loss and turning around to look for his keg. He found a huge Irishman, five miles back, sitting on the barrel.

"Hullo, sir! Have you seen a keg of whiskey?" asked the owner.

"Yes, sir, it is right here," answered the Irishman cheerfully.

"I lost it from my load and would like to have it again!"

"Well, sir," said the Irishman, "you will have to be a bigger man than I am to get it!"

In the barren West, road ranches gave shelter not only from fierce weather and beasts but sometimes also served as forts against Indian attack. Few and far between, settlers offered what hospitality they could, but the saloon, serving as an inn, was for long years the only place to offer "acomidation fer man and hoss."

Accommodations were not always the best. Upon arrival some of the more fastidious customers washed up by walking to the nearest stream with a lump of homemade lye soap in the North, or yucca suds in the Southwest. Bathtubs were unknown in most places. Only those "teched in the haid" bathed during the winter. The later, more opulent road ranches sometimes had a tin basin over a wooden sink. Under the sink was a malodorous bucket, watched by a barkeep or inkeeper who did not want it to overflow. A roller towel and a comb with teeth missing, hanging from a string, were sheer luxury. The wide outdoors served for purposes of sanitation. Better places had privies in back. These were sometimes two, three, or four holers for sociability. A western editor once asked his saloon-keeper host for some beef.

"I don't have any beef."

"Then bring us some potatoes."

"Don't have no potatoes."

"How about some wood for the stove?"

"Don't have no wood."

"Then bring me some cobs."

"Ifen I had the cobs, I wouldn't need your paper."

Saloons and taverns were expandable like accordions—always room for one more. A place was never full up even if "there were three in a bed with two more in the middle." In a California saloon, a man was charged three dollars for a quilt on the floor serving as a mattress. A woman's petticoat, instead of a blanket, was thrown in for free. In 1865, when Carson City, Nevada, was in the throes of gold and election fever, a traveler noted tongue-in-cheek:

For a bed in a house, barn, blacksmith shop or hay-yard (none to be had . . .) $10.—For sleeping on a billiard table, $5.—Ditto under table, $3.—Sleeping behind bar, $7.—For a horse blanket in an old sugar hogshead per night, $10.—For crockery crate with straw, $7.50. Without straw, $5.75. For cellar door, $4.00.

In Leadville, Colorado, during the mining boom, a whiskey mill owner built behind his saloon a "mammoth sleeping palace," a huge shed with double-decker bunks for eighty people. The typical saloon keeper in ranch country gave shelter for free, while the road ranches charged minimal fees.

An early frontiersman stopping at the Rowan Tavern in Wisconsin related:

I arrived in 1837, at about 11:00 o'clock P.M., on horseback. The hostler, a Frenchman, was yet up, making fires to keep those comfortable who were sleeping on the floor. After taking care of my horse, I went into the house. There was a good fire and the floor was covered with men sleeping. I asked the French hostler for something to eat; so he went into the kitchen and brought me a whole duck and two potatoes. He said that was all he could find cooked. After eating I felt like lying down. He pointed to a place between two men. I took my blanket and crowded myself into it. The next morning the teamsters got up to feed their teams and, in taking out their corn, they scattered some inside and outside the house. James Duane Doty was lying next the door in his robes. I was

Above: Sheep corral lodgings—and cheap at the price.
Below: A post for a bed.

next to him in my blanket. A lean long old sow found the corn that the teamsters had scattered outside. This encouraged her to follow up the corn scattered inside. Finding some among Doty's robes she put her nose under him and rolled him over, when he exclaimed: "Landlord! Landlord! You must postpone my breakfast for some time as I have not yet got rested."

If it wasn't hogs, it was something else. Indians perhaps.

Travelling on court business in Arizona Territory during the Sixties and Seventies had its hazards. Court was in session and not a room or a bed was to be had, our adobe cantina . . . had a upper story, something wondrously rare, but it was so low I had to stoop to find a corner to spread my coat. There was no way to separate the sexes, all had to bed down together, Judge "N." and a senora too dusky and young to be his wife. We were kept awake by Mexicans and miners downstairs drinking pulque, singing and quarrelling loudly. The noise had hardly abated, with only multifarious snoring reverberating, when the cry: "Apaches! Apaches!" resounded. All was confusion, fierce yells, the neighing of horses, barking of innumerable dogs, women's wailing! The lamp could not be found. Men and women tumbling down the ladder so as not to be caught in the windowless upper story, falling over each other. At last, Pedro, the owner, found and lit a candle. What a sight was revealed. Women clinging to the wrong men. Ladies in disarrayed nightclothing exposing a great deal of the form divine. Men with no nightclothes, some of them as nature made them. The contents of the slopjar and the upset olla of mescal making a puddle on the floor. And the whole commotion not started by Victorio's Apaches at all, but by a runaway horse!

Though this was the Victorian Age, during which legs were referred to as "limbs" and ladies' pantaloons as "unmentionables," prevailing conditions were accepted more or less cheerfully, including the fact that ladies had to share the same sleeping accommodations with strange men.

American guests took things in their stride. Europeans did not. The frontier attracted German princes, English sports, and Russian grand dukes looking for the noble savage or buffalo. Frenchmen searched in vain for the lost dauphin who was rumored to have escaped to America. Having come full of romantic ideas, they were often unwilling to accept stark reality. A French aristocrat complained about the lack of bedsheets, and one was miraculously produced. It had, however, a suspiciously colored spot. Queried, the tavern keeper identified it as pigeon dung. The Frenchman said his own senses told him "it proceeded from a different biped," and declared that up to that moment he had considered Russia the most barbarous country in the world, but that now he had changed his mind. America was much more barbarous. The great Talleyrand had come to a similar conclusion.

In the rare cases where the traveler found a bed, it was often swarming with unwanted bedfellows. According to one anguished Englishmen: "Forth rushed from tester pillow and post a horde of those 'blasted wonners' whose name I abhor to write."

Steven C. Massett, who arrived in California during the gold rush, reminisced:

Arriving at Sacramento City tired out and miserable, I . . . sought the comforts of a "bath" and a "lay down." The bath was accomplished by a "ducking" at even-tide in the river. As I think it might interest the present generation in general, and the keepers of inns in particular, I propose to give a sketch of the interior of my sleeping apartment. The heat was insufferable, mosquitoes were buzzing about, and with them their slow though sure attendents, fleas, and bed-bugs came in myriads to greet and congratulate me upon my arrival. Scratching and itching, itching and scratching, kept me awake all night; and then the stifled smell—the noise inside and out—the swearing and snoring of the occupants, the barking of dogs,

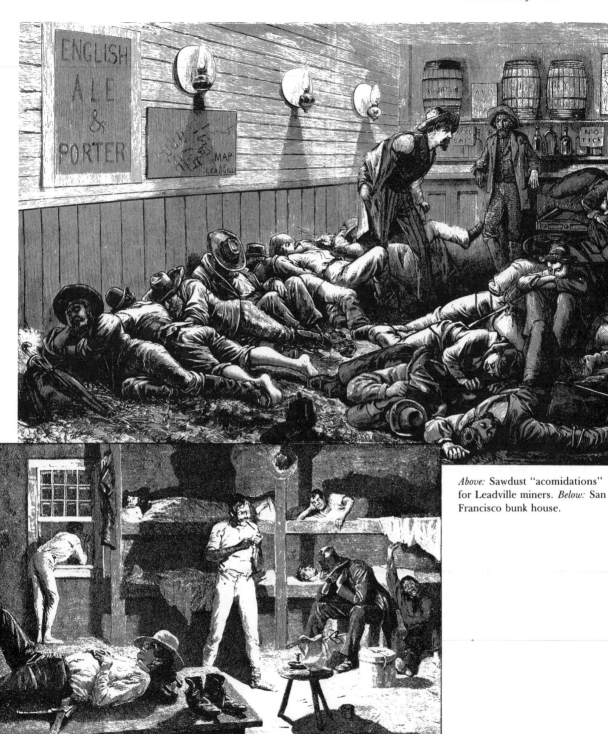

Above: Sawdust "acomidations" for Leadville miners. *Below:* San Francisco bunk house.

the leaving of numberless trains of mules and donkeys outside, the cries of children, rendered the whole scene a perfect pandemonium—and to crown the whole just as I had managed from sheer exhaustion to "drop off" into a doze, I felt a heavy bump come up against the slender board which screened me from the street—When to my astonishment the head of a big ox presented itself, and with its cold and moist snout commenced rubbing against my knee!

In Colorado, a fastidious miner who had shed his boots to sleep off a drunk on the sawdust before the bar found a live rattler in one of them when he put it on in the morning. In Arizona and New Mexico, shoes, beds, and pillows were at times invaded by centipedes, tarantulas, and scorpions. Befuddled men easing themselves in outhouses had their testicles bitten by black widow spiders lurking beneath the seat, attacking whatever touched their spun threads. The consequences were sometimes fatal. This gave rise to the superstition that black widows had it in for men and were easy on women. But western travelers were a hardy breed:

I have slept on beds active with snakes, lizards, scorpions, centipedes, bugs, and fleas—beds in which men stricken with plagues had died horrible deaths—beds that might reasonably be suspected of small-pox, measles, and cholera. Standing, sitting, lying down, doubled up, and hanging over; twisted, punched, jammed and elbowed by drunken men; snored at, sat upon and smothered by the nightmare; burnt by fires, rained upon, snowed upon, and bitten by frost—in all these positions and subjected to all these discomforts, I have slept with comparative satisfaction. There are pleasanter ways of sleeping to be sure, but there are times when any way is a blessing.

Among the hotel-saloons the bizarre was commonplace. One southwestern establishment, called the Palace, was run by a Chinese in a blue shirt with a queue and a tiny black skullcap. It was a large tent of cotton duck, partitioned by a canvas curtain into a saloon half and a hotel half. The "hotel" was further subdivided by muslin tacked from floor to ceiling into four cubicles—three "guest rooms" and the owner's private quarters, each furnished with a moss-filled sack, an army blanket of the type known as "henskin" on account of its thinness, a whale oil lamp, and a thunder mug. The saloon doubled as dining room, having an oblong table covered with black oilcloth. The bar consisted of a rough board laid across two empty whiskey kegs; behind it were two tilted barrels from which either white or red likker was drawn. The bar was kept by an Irishman, since customers would not have a Chinese handle their drinks. He was, however, acceptable as cook. Breakfast invariably consisted of a bowl of beans served with a large glass of mescal.

The Reese River Saloon in Nevada posted the following rules:

"Pocketing" at meals strictly forbidden. Gentlemen are expected to wash out of doors and find their own water. Lodgers must furnish their own straw. Beds on bar-room floor reserved for regular customers. Persons sleeping in the bar are requested not to take off their boots. Lodgers inside arise at 5 A.M., in the barn at 6 o'clock. Each man sweeps up his own bed. No quartz taken at bar. No fighting allowed at the table. Anyone violating the above rules will be shot.

The last rule was merely a threat, for emphasis.

One thing has to be said to the credit of the ancient road ranches, their keepers, and their guests. Though men and women were willy-nilly thrown together by circumstance, without privacy, washing up at the same stream, using the same outhouse, frequently forced to share the same bed though total strangers to each other, unprovoked sexual advances were rare. If they occurred at all, they were promptly and savagely punished by any man who happened to be near. Crude, often illiterate, even murderous, the frontier male was a respecter of women. As a matter of fact frontier conditions left him no choice but to behave. Or, in the words of one lady who had to share "acomidations" with them:

Yes! These ruffian miners and bullwhackers—many of whom had been for years absent from the softening amenities of female society, and the sweet, restraining influences of pure womanhood, these men hewn out of the rocks of the wilderness were, towards me, everyone in his own way—A GENTLEMAN!

Civilization spread westward from the Atlantic. Frontier conditions found in western Pennsylvania and Kentucky in the 1790s were encountered in Ohio and Tennessee in the 1820s, Iowa and Wisconsin in the 1840s, in Colorado in the 1860s, and in remote far western areas until the 1890s. Hospitality as well as whiskey were first offered in settlers' log cabins, then in road ranches and saloons and, only with the coming of railroads and wealth derived from gold and silver strikes, regular hotels. While initially the saloon doubled as "hotel," the later, sometimes opulent hotels doubled as saloons. Some of the greatest and most luxurious were often much more famous for their bars, mixologists, and brands of liquor than they were for their accommodations and food. The appearance of the hotel made the old-style tavern-saloon and road ranch superfluous.

The early saloon–road ranch was, of course, also a restaurant, at least a place where some grub, no matter how unpalatable, was always available. At the beginning, this was simply a matter of keeping the customers from starving. Later, when the money started coming in roughly in the years from 1860 to 1885, the patrons wanted something to eat while they drank, gambled, or ogled the hurdy girls. The food improved, and in gold and silver camps it became fancy beyond imagination. From the mid-eighties to Prohibition was the era of the famous "free lunch," of sardines and pretzels. For generations the saloon was a place where one could find something to eat.

With sources of supplies far away and roads and transportation insecure or nonexistent, providing food might have been a problem. Canned food was just becoming available, refrigerators uninvented, ice seldom available, cooking arrangements rudimentary. Mills were long in arriving, and the first crops of corn had to be ground by hand. Game, however, was abundant. Wild pigeons were netted by the thousands or knocked down from trees with poles. In the early Midwest fish were so plentiful that they could be taken from streams with bare hands. In 1850 there were still an estimated fifty million buffalo roaming the plains. In the sixties, railroad trains sometimes halted for days to let pass huge herds filling the prairie from horizon to horizon. Practically anything that swarmed, flew, crept, or ran was considered "good eatin'." The early tavern and road-ranch keepers were usually good hunters. If they were not they usually knew somebody who was. The emphasis was on meat, because often it was the only food available. The frontier relied on nature's bounty and this was reflected in the menu.

In the 1840s, when Chicago was still a raw frontier village, customers on the Tremont House Tavern porch shot ducks hunting for frogs in the mud which filled the road before them. For dinner they had, not illogically, roast duck and frogs' legs. In the 1850s, when the town had just been connected to the East by a single railroad track, one Chicago tavern offered this holiday bill of fare:

———— ◆◆ ————

Venison, Hunter Style   Game Broth
FISH
Boiled Trout
Baked Black Bass with Claret Sauce

BOILED

Leg of Mountain Sheep. Ham of Bear. Venison Tongue. Buffalo Tongue.

ROAST

Loin of Buffalo. Wild Goose. Quail. Mountain Sheep. Red Head Duck. Jack Rabbit. Blacktail Deer. Coon. Canvasback Duck. Prairie Chicken. English Hare. Bluewing Teal. Partridge. Widgeon. Saddle of Venison. Pheasant. Mallard Duck. Wild Turkey. Spotted Grouse. Black Bear. Opossom. Leg of Elk. Wood Duck. Sandhill Crane. Ruffled Grouse. Cinnamon Bear

BROILED

Bluewing Teal. Jacksnipe. Blackbirds. Redbirds. Partridge. Pheasant. Quail. Butterball Ducks. English Snipe. Ricebirds. Redwing. Starling. Marsh birds. Plover. Gray Squirrel. Buffalo Steak. Rabbits. Venison Steak.

ENTREES

Antelope Steak with Mushroom Sauce. Rabbit, braised with Cream Sauce. Fillet of Grouse with Truffles. Venison Cutlet with Jelly. Ragout of Bear, Hunter Style. Sauce Oyster Pie

ORNAMENTAL DISHES

Pyramid of Game en Bellevue. Boned Duck au Naturel. Pyramid of Wild Goose Liver in Jelly. The Coon at Night. Boned Quail in Plumage. Redwing Starling on Tree. Partridge in nest. Prairie Chicken en Sauce.

In 1865, a Chicago restaurateur was still able to offer wild boar's steak, boned wild turkey, patties of quail, aged bear's paws in burgundy sauce, ragout de coon, and squirrel pie.

While frontiersmen heartily approved of this fare, foreigners often complained that, in the absence of ice, the meat generally was in an advanced stage of decomposition, its taste disguised with hot sauces and pepper. Customers suffered from dyspepsia, colic, loose bowels, and the bloody flux. Englishmen and Frenchmen bemoaned the lack of fresh food. Coffee, to the foreigners' disgust, was often a brew made of brown bread, acorns, dandelion roots, barley, and snuff.

Poetry sometimes helped to whet the appetite. Saloons and taverns frequently advertised in verse. In 1842, the proprietor of the Public House at Elkhorn, Illinois, penned this:

> Accomodations of all kinds and good cheer,
> With Choicest liquors and strong beer;
> Lemonade, soda, wine, and Tom and Jerry,
> Which gentlemen can have to make them merry.
> My table is furnished with the substantials of life,
> Cooked and prepared by my daughters and wife.
> Myself will attend you and give you the food,
> With dessert and pastry, which shall all be good.

Customers also often versified, but were less lyrical. Thus one Utah miner describing the fare at his boardinghouse:

> The coffee has the dropsy, the tea has the grippe.
> The butter was consumptive, the flapjacks they had fits;
> The beef was strong and jubilant, it walked upon the floor.
> The spuds lost all their dignity and rolled right out the door.
>
> The pudding had the jimjams; the pies was in disguise;
> The beans came to the table with five hundred thousand flies.
> The hash was simply murdered, just as hard as 'dobe mud.
> We howl, we wail, our muscles fail on Baxter's awful grub!

From 1860 on, food in out-of-the-way places became somewhat standardized. For breakfast a tin cup and plate were filled with coffee, "sow-belly," bread, and syrup. In some years stewed tomatoes were plentiful. Lunch, and dinner again, consisted of bread and steak, the steaks being generally overcooked and hard as stone, "so that you had something to chew on for a while." Lamb fries

Taverns provided food.

and Rocky Mountain oysters (sheep and steer testicles) slightly shirred in a pan, or roasted in the ashes of a campfire until they "popped," were considered a delicacy. Rattlesnake meat was fancied by some and said to taste like the white meat of chicken.

Dried, pale red beans known as Arizona strawberries were the only vegetable besides corn and squash in certain areas of the Southwest. An old proverb went: "Beans is pizen lessen you're forking a bucking bronc which'll knock the accumulation of air outa you." The theory was that only the violent motion of a bucking and sun-fishing mustang could stir a man's innards to digest the tough western fare. Some people said that western saloon food was confined to the "Basic Four B's"— sourdough biscuits, beans, beef, and bacon ("overland trout" in cowboyese). Wild onions were sometimes served as a side dish "against scurvy." The chief complaint of travelers was the scarcity of vegetables. They were dumbfounded by seeing ranches pasturing fifty thousand head of cattle with not a single milch cow among them. Easterners could not get over the fact that, being in cow country, they could not get milk unless it was canned.

Coffee was the universal drink. Grounds were left in the pot to be boiled and reboiled again and again. It was jokingly said that coffee, also called "whistleberries," was not sufficiently strong unless you could float a silver dollar on it. It had to be:

> Black as the devil,
> Strong as death,
> Sweet as love, and
> Hot as hell!

To make grounds settle and clear the brew, coffee always had a few pieces of eggshell floating in it, a way of serving "black medicine" that still survives in a few places.

The saloon also sold chaw 'baccer, and especially "seegars," cheroots, or stogies. In Virginia City, Nevada, saloonists offered a wide choice of regalias, principes, and colorados. They advertised choice brands of "fine-cuts," "yellow-leaf," "honey-dew," "solace," and "eureka." At Salt Lake City, cigars were five dollars apiece for a time, because smoking them was against the law and sinful according to Mormon beliefs. Men paid the price, because forbidden pleasures never come cheap.

Westerners ate to fill the belly, not for pleasure. Food was food. One California traveler cheerfully commented:

We are now ready to replenish the inner man. The bar is convenient for those who wish to imbibe. Breakfast is announced. We seat ourselves at the table. Before us is a reasonable quantity of beans, pork, and flapjacks served up in tin plates. Pea tea, which the landlord calls coffee with a bold emphasis, is handed to us. We help ourselves to such other things as may be within reach. Neither spices, sauces, nor seasonings are necessary to accommodate them to the palate. Our appetites need not nursing. The richest condiments are the poorest provisions.

And again J. Ross Browne:

In respect to the matter of eating I am even less particular. Frogs, horse-leaches, snails, and grasshoppers are luxurious to what I have eaten. It has pleased Providence to favor me with appetites and tastes appropriate to a great variety of circumstances and many conditions of life.

As for the cooks in western saloons, the "grub-slingers" and "belly-cheaters," Charlie Russell described one of them, a personal friend:

Bill's chef was one of the most rapid cooks known in the West. He hangs up a bet of a hundred dollars that with the use of a can-opener, he can feed more cowpunchers and sheepherders than any other cook west of the Mississippi. There are never no complaints about the meat, either, for this cook's as good with a gun as he is with a can-opener. In fact, no one's ever claimed he ain't a good cook after taking one look at him.

Table manners were atrocious by European

"Table manners were atrocious."

standards. Food was wolfed down with a speed that astounded the foreigner. Philip Robinson, an Anglo-Indian writer, commented:

Dab, dab, peck, peck, grunt, growl, snort! The spoon strikes every now and then and a quick sucking-up noise announces the disappearance of a mouthful of huckleberries on the top of a bit of bacon, or a spoonful of custard-pie on the heels of a radish. It is perfectly prodigious. It defies description.

At saloons that were also stagecoach stations, with only a limited time available for a stopover, it was every man for himself. A run was made for the table set out smorgasbord fashion, guests elbowing and trampling each other, devouring everything in sight in record time. An easterner related that the much-repeated performance "resembled a feast of wild cats."

Things were no different on the northwest coast:

They breakfast in the middle of the night, dine when they aught to be breakfasting and take supper when they should be dining; and the "feed" is most distasteful—all noise, dirt, grease, mess, slop, confusion, and disorder; chunks of meat of all kinds and no flavor, placed in plates, and "sot" on the table; and before you had time to look at your meat, a piece of very flat pie, with a doughy crust, and dried fruit inside is placed under your nose, on the same plate with your meat. Men pick their teeth with forks and jackknives, gobble down gallons of water, and "slide." This is the style in Oregon.

In one place a man found his bed sheet being yanked from under him to be used as a tablecloth:

Thus it contrived the double debt to pay,
A sheet by night—a tablecloth by day.

Food was coarse, men rough, and manners deplorable but, again, women who had sat with frontier characters at the table said that amid confusion, blasphemy, and obscenity, no discourteousness was ever directed at *them.* Men, fighting like wolves among themselves over food, saw to it that the ladies were fed. Room was cheerfully made at the stove for the "weaker sex."

Sudden wealth from gold and silver brought sudden change. It came earliest in California. Bayard Taylor reported that in 1850 "it was no unusual thing to see a company of these men, who had never before thought of luxury beyond a good beefsteak and a glass of whiskey, drinking their champagne at ten dollars a bottle, and eating their tongue and sardines, or warming in the smoky campfire their tin cannisters of turtle soup and lobster salad."

San Francisco's famous oyster cocktail was born when a miner out of the hills strayed into Moraghan's Oyster Palace and Saloon and ordered a whiskey cocktail and a plate of raw California oysters. On a sudden impulse he dropped some of the oysters in his glass and let them soak. He then downed his drink and spread tomato catsup, Worcestershire sauce, and pepper over the oysters. He ate one and smacked his lips. The bartender tried one. He, too, smacked his lips. Moraghan, the owner, was attracted and tried an

oyster. He, too, experienced a happy glow. Thus drinking-gourmandizing history was made. Similarly, chop suey was invented in San Francisco by a Chinese cook who had run out of his regular food and served his miners a dish of "odds and ends" *(shop sui).* It quickly became popular among prospectors and sailors, but it was shunned by the Chinese.

Teddy Blue, a Montana cowboy during the 1880s, when the cattle trade flourished, wrote;

Talking about food, do you know what was the first thing a cowpuncher ordered to eat when he got to town? Oysters and celery. And eggs. Those things were what he didn't get and what he was crazy for.

It was not only oysters that, with the coming of the railroads, suddenly became available in Sheridan, Wyoming, in Miles City, Montana, or Virginia City, Nevada. Gambling and concert saloons as well as hotel bars offered their well-heeled customers fancy fare printed on equally fancy menus, often in broken French. When Eugene Field was a Denver newspaperman he wrote a poem about a joint named Casey's, which later became the Gold Hill Inn:

And Casey's tabble dote began in French,—as
    all begin,—
And Casey's ended with the same, which is to
    say, with "vin";
But in between wuz every kind of reptile, bird
    'n beast,
The same like you can git in high-toned
    restrants down East;
'Nd windin' up wuz cake or pie, with coffee
    demy tass,
. . . Or, sometimes, floatin' Ireland in a soothin
    kind of sass'
That left a sort of pleasant ticklin' in a feller's
    throat
'Nd made him hanker after more of Casey's
    tabble dote.

In Wyatt Earp's and Doc Holliday's Tombstone, the Occidental Saloon served a Sunday dinner to tickle "Doc's" fastidious palate:

———◆———

SOUPS
Chicken Giblet and Consumme, with Egg

FISH
Colombia River Salmon, au Beurre Noir

RELIEVES
Filet a Boeuf, a la Financier
Leg of Lamb, Sauce, Oysters

COLD MEATS
Loin of Beef   Loin of Ham   Loin of Pork   Westphalia Ham   Corned Beef   Imported Lunches

BOILED MEATS
Leg of Mutton, Ribs of Beef,
Corned Beef and Cabbage, Russian River
Bacon

ENTREES
Pinions a Poulett, aux Champignons
Cream Fricassee of Chicken, Asparagus Points
Lapine Domestique, a la Maitre d'Hote
Casserole d'Ritz aux Oeufs, a la Chinoise
Ducks of Mutton, braze, with Chipoluta Ragout
California Fresh Peach, a la Conde

ROASTS
Loin of Beef   Loin of Mutton   Leg of Pork
Apple Sauce   Suckling Pig, with Jelly   Chicken
Stuffed Veal.

PASTRY
Peach, Apple, Plum, and Custard Pies   English
Plum Pudding, Hard Sauce, Lemon Flavor

And we will have it or perish.
This dinner will be served for 50 cents.

———◆———

In Telluride, Colorado, the Sheridan Bar served steaks "Two inches thick, a foot wide, and 'mebbe two feet long, garnished in greens."

The railroad was the magic carpet that brought the oysters to Oklahoma and peaches to Arizona. Before the Civil War, the westerner had faced the same problems the Allegheny pioneer had struggled with fifty years before him. He had no way to get his product to market. Nor could the products of the big eastern cities reach him, except in a slow, uncertain trickle along forbidding and dangerous trails. The railroad changed this. The combination of railroad and refrigeration placed the oysters on a Leadville miner's table. Railroads got the cattle to Chicago and eliminated long, tortous trail drives. W. A. White, an Emporia, Kansas, editor, wrote: "The Santa Fe is the best thing that ever happened to Emporia, the best thing that ever happened to Kansas, and the best thing that happened to the country."

Railroads brought instant prosperity. They covered the West in an incredibly short time. Thanks to the railroad the population of some western states doubled and redoubled within ten years. It brought lumber, plows, window glass, and pianos to the prairie. It brought the first tourists to the Colorado Rockies, instantly dubbed "America's Switzerland." This in turn caused hot springs spas to come into being, complete with luxury hotels in the latest Victorian style.

Alongside the railroad station, sometimes part of it, the Harvey House made its appearance—the first one in 1876, at Topeka. Soon there was one at every larger railroad stop. Harvey employed pretty, polite, white-aproned, and very competent waitresses, who lived on the premises, their virtue carefully guarded by chaperones—a sort of early western den mothers. Guests ate from clean plates on spotless linen. The food was excellent because Harvey imported European chefs. It was also hot and cheap. Harvey revolutionized western eating habits. Wealthy cattlemen and mine owners wanted to live in the grand manner. Soon every sizable town had one or two good restaurants catering to their palates. Those close to a larger town, who had the taste for it and could afford it, ate well indeed. People in some of the smaller western cities probably ate better in the years between 1880 and 1910 than they do now. The majority of westerners, though, remained wedded to steaks the size and consistency of a slab of slate,

"In a surprisingly short time, railroads covered the West."

shunned fresh vegetables and salads, and continued to prefer evaporated to fresh milk.

Service and manners improved also. An English lady, Mrs. Carbutts, encountered in Wyoming:

A discreet waiter, who belongs to the masons, Oddfellows, Knights of Pythias . . . has been employed to carry milk punches and hot toddies to ladies' rooms in the evening. . . . The office clerk has been carefully chosen to please everybody, and can lead in prayer, play draw poker, match worsteds in the village store, shake for drinks at any hour, day or night, play billiards, is a good waltzer, can make a fourth at euchre, amuse the children, repeat the Beecher Trial from memory, is a good judge of horses, as a railway and steamboat reference is far superior to Appleton's, or anybody else's guide, will flirt with any young lady, and not mind being cut dead when 'pa comes down.

Food, accommodations, and service in Virginia City during the halcyon silver days were described as "sinfully Babylonian and sybaritic," with liveried waiters sliding noiselessly from bar to table on inch-thick carpets, serving bonded bourbon in goblets of rock crystal. The Golden Age of western eating came to an end with free silver and the fading away of blue-blooded English dukes and cattle and silver kings. The sumptuous places disappeared. The age of sowbelly and pigeon pie had been replaced by the age of filet à la Josephine aux truffes, which in turn was replaced by the age of the free (and undistinguished) lunch—which was finally followed by the age of the hamburger. For half a century the wide-open spaces became a culinary wasteland, except for a few oases in some larger cities. Dispensing food became a marginal business in all but a small minority of saloons.

There is a considerable argument about the free lunch's geographic origins. Some say it was inaugurated in New Orleans' Exchange Bar, where customers, after having paid for at least two cocktails, were entitled to help themselves from a table laden with bowls of Bayou Gumbo, smoked oysters, and barbecued pork. Some say that miners instigated the custom of serving free grub among booze bosses on San Francisco's Barbary

115

Coast. Wherever it originated, the free saloon lunch became a hallowed tradition from coast to coast. A Texan, remembering his drinking days around 1910, related:

A dollar was something then. If you made a hundred dollars a month, you had a good job. You could get whiskey at five dollars a gallon. You could get a hotel room for a dollar, and your meals would be a dollar and a half or sometimes only a dollar.

I've eaten many a meal at a free-lunch counter. You could get a glass of beer for a nickel and get a sandwich and some pretzels and go and sit down and eat 'em. If you got a stein for ten cents, you could have two sandwiches.

Loafers were always trying to mooch free lunches. I've seen more than one customer thrown out when he tried to sneak into the lunch counter without buying. Or they'd stand outside and say, "Buy me a glass of beer, Mister, so I can have a sandwich. Jesus! I haven't had anything to eat for a week."

After Prohibition had killed the saloons, old-timers waxed lyrical describing the free lunches of the grand old places, or rather the gourmet buffet dinners of tiny, savory meatballs, French Gruyère cheese, hickory-cured ham, and other dainties. There had, indeed, been a few high-class drinking places where the swells in silk hats and spats relaxed in wicker chairs with their aged-in-wood bonded stuff beneath potted palms and crystal chandeliers, contemplating the more than life-size voluptuous nudes on the wall, while discussing the stock market.

The narrow, twenty-foot-long tables in these establishments had indeed been covered with spotless white linen and plates of delicacies to please the most discerning tastes. The swells did not even have to get up to help themselves, but merely motioned to the circulating white-jacketed black waiters, who, more often than not, received a silver dollar for their efforts. Out of the thousands of saloons in the United States there were,

maybe, two dozen that had served that kind of free lunch.

Others served cold cuts, "cut so thin one could see through them like glass," limp and sweating slices of yellow cheese, beans grown cold in their pot, and, sometimes, stalks of celery wilting in a glass of water. Above all, the free lunch featured salted food—pretzels, rye bread, smoked herring, salted peanuts, peppery sausages, sauerkraut, kippers, rollmops (in German beergardens), potato chips, dill pickles, and sardellen—especially sardellen. From New York to Frisco the sardelle, or sardel, was the queen of the free lunch. In the words of George Ade:

The aristocratic sardine, immersed in oil and coming in small cans, was too expensive to be set out in large platters. Furthermore olive oil counteracts the influence of alcohol. But the sardellen, saturated with brine and probably sold by the hogshead, became one of the staple stand-bys of every saloon catering to a reliable beer trade. They were saltier than the Seven Seas and were served whole. No one had tampered with the heads, tails or interior arrangements. They were in great favor because a patron after he had taken a couple of them, draped across a slab of rye bread, had to rush to the bar and drink a lot of beer to get the taste out of his mouth. The sardellen were more than fish. They were silent partners.

The theory behind all this, and it was a good theory, was that a couple of shot glasses, or steins, produced appetite and that the salty goodies, in turn, produced a mighty thirst. The chain-reaction process of drinking and nibbling, nibbling and drinking could go on for hours during which the customers spent a lot on booze.

Free lunches varied, of course; in places where the barkeep was German, there might be slices of blutwurst, zervelatwurst, and landjaegers to tempt the patrons. Italian saloon owners might serve calzone and pepperoni, though seldom west of the Mississippi. Two places in Chicago gave away

"I guess there's not more than a dozen or so fellows alive who recall the free lunch. . . ."

thick, creamy pies to old customers. In the Southwest the faithful helped themselves from a bowl of chili con carne, or nibbled on nachos—small, salty squares of crisp tortillas covered with frijoles and melted cheese. The sardelle did not flourish in the desert country because it was not needed to stimulate thirst. Local boys licked up their quantum of salt from the back of their hand with lusty swallows of tequila or mescal. Even Mexican beer was traditionally drunk with a pinch of salt, and the glorious sun did its share to produce the desired effect.

Some bars had their daily free lunch specialties —franks on Monday, roast beef on Saturday, baked fish on Friday, and so on. Some saloons were more generous than others. Many advertised, "A fried oyster, a clam, or a hard-boiled egg with every drink." Charlie Brown, a Miles City, Montana, bar owner, kept a pot of "mulligan stew" bubbling on his stove twenty-four hours a day for the benefit of his customers. Charlie was a rough but gallant soul who on occasion chastised men with his bung starter who supposedly had insulted wives of customers.

The word "lunch" should not be taken literally. It blended imperceptibly into free breakfast and free dinner. A certain kind of dried herring— called black-eyed susan or blind robin—was known as the "booze-hound's breakfast." The same salted goods waited patiently on their fly-specked plates morning, noon, and night.

The free lunch posed problems for many bartenders. The institution rested on the honor system. Supposedly no creature walking on two legs would be so low as to approach the free lunch table without having first consumed, and paid for, at least two drinks. But there were human skunks —sad to say, great numbers of them—who were not honorable. In small western cowtowns, where people knew each other, the problem was inconsequential. Not so in the larger places like Kansas City, St. Louis, Denver, El Paso, or Amarillo. Hoboes, drifters, out-of-work cowhands, striking miners, even the wastrel sons of rich parents, considered it a sport, as well as a necessity, to get at the free lunch. In the words of George Ade:

Hunger will overcome modesty and weaken self-respect. The stony-broke who had seen better days would have died rather than go to a back door and beg for a hand-out, but he had no scruples against cleaning the lunch counter, trying to watch the rye bread, the Limburger cheese, the bar-keep and the door leading to the street, all at the same time.

In some saloons this was dangerous sport, akin to tiger hunting.

Bartenders were not selected for their weak physique but for muscles. Some of them came down on the offender with the force of an elephant stamping on a ladybug. The culprit was sometimes beaten, kicked, or belabored with the bung starter. Lo, the poor barkeep who worked alone behind the bar. Though he watched like a hawk, he had first to vault or get around the counter in order to catch the cadger. Muscular he generally was, but seldom nimble. The drifter had a good chance to escape through the batwing doors and disappear into the wide-open spaces.

In bars doing a good business and where, consequently, the free lunch counter was generously stocked with palatables, it was necessary to have a floor-walking bouncer to protect the tidbits from freeloaders. Sometimes the bouncer was coyly dubbed ''waiter'' and served drinks at tables, but everybody knew what his main job was. He generally placed himself strategically near the swinging doors so as to be able to cut off the retreat of any snake not doing the ''honorable thing.'' Undesirables were ejected without ceremony. Usually the bouncer grabbed them by the scruff and the seat of their pants, propelling them outside with great speed and dumping them in the mud or on the pavement. Bouncing became one of the martial arts. If the cadger resisted, stronger methods were used, sometimes resulting in fractures or, in a few cases, even death.

For the steady, paying customers the never-ending battle of wits between freeloader and saloon owner was a fine show to watch, often the subject for bets. Even without romanticizing, the free lunch was a noble institution, a glorious old-style coffee break, morning eye-opener, a relaxing bit of munching and boozing after a hard day, a fine way of occasionally showing one's independence from a wife's cooking and nagging. The Volstead Act killed the saloon and the free lunch with it. Many a man down and out during the Depression mourned it with nostalgia. A veteran of both the old-time saloon and World War I, living out the winter of his life in an old soldiers' home, said in 1976:

Whenever I was down and out, the free lunch saw me through the day many a time. When I had my pockets full it was still fun to nibble those smoked oysters and the crackers with the limburger on them. I guess there's not more than a dozen or so fellows alive now who can still recall the free lunch. Soon we'll be gone. Who'll remember it then?

After repeal, there was a comeback, but the free lunch was never the same again. The peanuts, breadsticks, and pretzels seen on contemporary counters can't hold a candle to the pot of mulligan, the peppery ''baloney,'' or the sardelle of old.

CHAPTER 9

THE SADDLE OF FAITH, THE BRIDLE OF SALVATION, AND THE SIX-GUN OF RIGHTEOUSNESS

Preacher McCabe put on a better
show than the wizard oil man
and the dance-hall girls.

—Reminiscences of a miner

When I hear a man preach I like
to see him act as if he were
fighting bees.

—Abraham Lincoln

Whenever a new territory was opened up, the first to arrive were
often the missionary and the whiskey seller. The first structure deserving to be called house invariably was a saloon. As a rule, a new
community had several saloons before the citizens got around to
building a church. Sometimes they didn't get around to the church
for years. The need for Jim Beam preceded a yearning for spiritual
refreshment. Since the saloon was the only place to accommodate a
crowd in some comfort, it was natural for the early thirst parlors to
double as churches, their bars serving as pulpits. A symbiotic relationship soon developed between the preacher and the saloon
keeper. Not a few preachers wound up as booze bosses, while some
bartenders turned parson.

The early West had a reputation of apathy, even hostility, toward
religion, especially among pious New Englanders who organized missionaries to bring the Good Word to the ungodly frontier. As the
saying went: "There is no Sunday west of Junction City, and no God
west of Salina." In 1836 one minister complained that the people of
Green Bay "seemed agreed in only one thing and that was to blas-
pheme God and indulge in all kinds of wickedness." Before the Civil
War less than half of all pioneer families belonged to an established
church. Clearly, the people living on the wrong side of the Mississippi
were mired in a swamp of irreligiosity and on the road to perdition.
Steeped in whiskey, they suffered from a thirst for spiritual drink.

Their souls, the people back east thought, needed saving as much as, if not more than, those of the heathen savages.

The eastern religious mind completely misunderstood the way in which the frontier shaped the thoughts of those who hacked and scratched a living out of it. They failed to see how the endlessness of space, the immense Ocean of Grass, influenced man's image of the godhead. The backwoods folk, trappers, and early miners were not churchgoers. On the other hand, they were not unbelievers. Among saloon keepers, someone said, there were hardly any atheists. The easterners misunderstood the westerners' casual, informal, intensely personal approach to the Lord of Hosts. They argued with God, speaking to Him almost as to an equal, "handwrasslin' Him," as one rancher put it. They talked back to Him if they thought He deserved it. One lay preacher supplicating God to end a bad dry spell shouted: "Lord, if you don't answer this prayer you have no business in cow country!" The early settler or prospector needed no learned divine to act as middleman between himself and God. He did not go to the preacher, the preacher had to come to him. He was apt to take issue with the parson: "Don't shake me so hard over hell, brother, or I won't be back!" What shocked the eastern ministers most was the frontier's lack of hypocrisy and

The first arrivals.

its tolerance. Americans have always prided themselves on their tolerance, on their creed of religious freedom. In reality, from the landing in Plymouth to the Civil War, they were as intolerant as could be. They harassed the Quakers, ran Roger Williams and his Baptists out of Massachusetts, persecuted the Mormons, and discriminated against the Irish on the ground that they were "popists." From 1890 to the era of Franklin Delano Roosevelt, Indians were forbidden by federal law to practice their native religions. The westerner's tolerance was therefore taken as an indifference to faith, a near cousin of outright atheism. The westerner did not mind a whore, drunkard, or gambling man praying by his side. They were all on a first-name basis—sinners alike.

The peddlers of the Word came to the West in a multiplicity of sects and doctrines. Besides the established churches—Methodist, Presbyterian, Episcopal, and Catholic—there also arrived Moravians, Dunkards, Shakers, Quakers, Mormons, and the Brethren of Christ. The West was derided as the "land of crazy religions where each man tried to preach the gospel in his own tongue and according to his own light."

First and most popular were the Methodists, who crossed the Missouri and preached in the Dakotas as early as 1854. The Methodist dogma of free will, free grace, and individual responsibility suited the western character. The Methodist preacher was most often a lay "exhorter" and circuit rider, frequently as uneducated as the listeners to whom he talked "in their own language." One of them, the Reverend Cartwright, remembered later:

We had little or no education; no books and no time to read or study them if we could have them. We had no colleges nor even a respectable school within a hundred miles of us. . . . We could not, many of us, conjugate a verb, or parse a sentence, and murdered the King's English almost every lick.

A Methodist preacher in these days, instead of hunting up a college, hunted up a hardy pony. He started with a text that never wore out or grew stale: "Behold the Lamb of God, who takes away the sins of the world!"

The pioneers took to that kind of preacher and to his emotional kind of sermon, which was always capital, down-to-earth entertainment.

> I'll tell you who the Lord loves best,
> It is the shouting Methodist!

The Methodists' chief rivals were the Baptists, who were on the far side of the Mississippi as early as 1800. They too licensed "local preachers," better known for the thunder and fervor of their sermons than for their book learning. They believed in immersion and close communion, allowing great leeway in expounding scripture to their individual churches. Baptist preachers often invited their listeners to follow them to the nearest creek to be washed in the Blood of the Lamb, shouting: "Water, water, follow your Lord into the water!"

The Baptists were the unwilling parents of the Campbellites, or Disciples of Christ. Founded by Thomas Campbell, a Scotchman who came to Pennsylvania in 1807, they preached simplicity in doctrine and organization, propagating a pure, primitive grass-roots Christianity among the Scotch-Irish. The founder himself traveled along the early frontier. Campbellites were all for poverty and self-denial but were said to have good heads for money—perhaps due to their Scottish background.

Presbyterians ran a poor third among the sects. Their gloomy, Calvinist doctrine of predestination was a hindrance among individualistic pioneers. So was their insistence on having only educated preachers and their interminable wrangling over fine points of dogma.

The Catholic missionaries were different from the others. As members of religious orders under discipline and obedience to superiors, they were

Reverend John Dyer, an early Methodist circuit rider, often preached in saloons.

more uniform and more tightly organized than their Protestant fellow divines. Before the Civil War they had a hard time finding enough parishioners. Since the early West was predominantly Anglo-Saxon Protestant, they concentrated upon bringing the light to the heathen tribes. Called "Black Robes" by the Indians, they arrived by boat, canoe, dogsled, or on horseback. Sometimes on foot or on snowshoes. As the post–Civil War flood of immigrants spilled over into the West, they caught up with the other denominations.

The mule-riding "Gospel Sharks," or "Sin-Busters," were a fierce breed of devil wrasslers with eyes like live coals—loud and strident preaching not only with their formidable vocal cords, but with their whole bodies. Shivering in ecstasy, they waved their arms, pounded their fists, stomped and kicked. The devil to them was an intimate acquaintance, an ever present personal enemy. In fighting the fiend, the circuit-riding parsons took their cue from their listeners. In the same fashion that miners and mountain men gouged out the eyes and bit off the ears of their adversaries, so no holds were barred in fighting the cloven-hoofed enemy.

The God of the American West, it was said, did his good work from the saddle. It was rumored that the typical circuit rider's buttocks had the hardness and consistency of sheet metal. They certainly were prodigious travelers. The Methodist bishop Asbury traveled 270,000 miles in administering to his western flock, mostly on horseback or by buggy. Father de Smet covered more than 180,000 miles converting Indian tribes. Some ministers, remembering their early years, said in all seriousness that they had spent half of their active life in the saddle.

Their efforts were ill repaid. One itinerant parson in Indiana received nine dollars and a pair of new pants for a year's work. As late as 1876, a Nebraska minister received as little as thirty dollars per annum. Some depended on being paid in kind, receiving hams, eggs, venison, corn, and whiskey instead of legal tender, collecting gifts to maintain the Lord's work. Some went from house to house, or rather soddy to soddy, when there was no church, knocking at any door, asking the settler's wife: "Sister, shall I pray with you?" For a meal they did chores, chopped wood, or watered the livestock. Some moonlighted as blacksmiths, miners, or even farmhands to make ends meet. Their overworked wives took in washing and sewing, slaved in backyard gardens, or taught school, although teaching paid even less than preaching.

The circuit riders were contentious and garrulous, never mealymouthed when taking a sinner to task or discussing scripture. In this, too, they resembled their flock. Preacher Riley, a Presbyte-rian New Englander who had spread the good tidings to many a western mining camp, remembered:

You talk of your church rows here in the east, why, they are no more like what we used to have out there than a hurdy-gurdy or monkey show is like a Barnum circus. Out yonder they were grand, with the grandeur of the Rockies and Sierras. We had none of your little quarrels you have hereabouts with small Christians in them saying mean things about each other in the dark. No, when a sister in Nevada buckled on the armor to do battle against the Midianites she was a Deborah, when a brother drew his sword he was a Gideon.

The westerner was as big in his faith or no-faith as he was in anything else.

Many preachers were indistinguishable from the gamblers—a long black coat, white shirt, and string tie were the trademark of both. One wandering preacher was described as long-legged, cadaverous, and melancholy, wearing a black linen duster and equally black wide-brimmed and low-crowned hat. He sported a scraggly beard of the variety known as Galway chokers and carried a large Bible under one arm, waving a horsewhip with the other. He rode a sad-faced mule so short-legged that the rider's boots barely skimmed the ground. He had a bowie knife stuck in one and an old rimfire revolver in the other, "which discouraged over-familiarity." The preacher's face resembled that of his mule "to such an extent one could have taken them for brothers." While most itinerant preachers wore solemn stovepipe hats and coats that came down below the knees, some dressed like miners or cowhands, wearing nothing that betrayed their calling, following the example of Christ, "who dressed like common folk when mingling with whores and tax-collectors."

The place where parishioners were most easily found was the old whiskey mill. Beer-soaked sawdust, fumes of the red essence, and the rattling of

Sunday in the Rocky
Mountains. *Below: Circuit
Rider,* by O. C. Seltzer.

dice never deterred the men of God. As a rule they were welcome. The bar often suspended operation for the duration of the sermon. Counter and bottles were draped with blankets or white tablecloths and bed linen when available. The pictures of languid nudes were covered up, the poker games stopped.

During the 1880s, a Wyoming traveler found a sign tacked to a saloon door reading:

Preaching in this room, next Saturday 7 to 8 P.M.
Dancing—Square, Polka, Waltz—8 to 11 P.M.
Poker—11 P.M. to daylight
No rough stuff!

In one Wyoming camp, an itinerant preacher entered a saloon asking the owner if he could hold a sermon in the place. The saloon keeper assented immediately. The drinking customers and gamblers roared their hearty approval and offered help. The bartender's arrangements were most satisfactory. Sheets were strung on a wire to "shut out the sight of the bar." Extra chairs and benches were borrowed from neighbors to seat all comers. A sturdy table was put in one corner. As the genial host explained to the parson: "I will place a whiskey case on it. The ladies will cover it with some nice cloth and it will make a fine place for you to lay your Bible on." There was one condition, however; the preaching had to be done on Saturday. On Sundays business was too good to be interfered with by religion. In some places liquor and religion mixed readily. The bar not only remained open, but served as pulpit. Men serenely drank and played poker while listening to the sermon, and the preacher himself unblushingly called for a shot of rye whenever his throat got dry.

Many sin-busters sermonized against the "cupbearers of devil rum," and it says much for the tolerance of saloon keepers and their patrons alike, as well as for their dedication to free speech, that they good-naturedly suffered the vilifications

Prayers sometimes interrupted poker games
—but never for long.

of Bible-thumpers denouncing the swinish sin of wine bibbing. It seems that some of them got a perverse kick out of being publicly assailed as sinners on the road to hell. Several saloon owners even thought that it was good for business. After a preacher had put the fear of God in him, a man needed a drink badly.

Preaching was muscular and flavorful, otherwise it made no impact. The most robust sermons were held by so-called Whiskey Baptists or Forty-Gallon Baptists, who were not abstemious. They were mostly "unlarned"; that is, illiterate and unequaled in doing violence to the English language:

Ef you're elected you'll be saved; ef you a'n't, you'll be damned. God'll take keer of his elect. It's a sin to run Sunday-schools, or temp'rince s'cieties, or to send missionaries. You let God's business alone. What is to be will be, and you can't hender it.

Whether they approved of or abhorred drinking, the tramp preachers spoke a language their listeners could relate to. Addressing a crowd of gamblers, one parson put it to them that:

the "Ace" reminds us that there's but one God.

The "Deuce" that God made Adam and Eve sinless.

The "Trey" of the Three Wise Men, Guided by the Star of Bethlehem.

The "Four" of the Four Evangelists . . .

"Knaves," who remind us of the false prophets of the Amalekites.

The "Queens" of the Queen of Shebah, Esther, Abraham's Sarah, and Pharaoh's daughter.

The "Kings" of King Saul, David, Solomon, and Herod.

One reverend exhorted players in a gambling saloon to repent, so that when death overtook them they could "call *keno!* and rake in the heavenly pot." Cowhands, listening to a Texas parson, must surely have enjoyed his sermon on God's pastures and the devil's range:

Hear what the great herd book says: "When the Son of Man (or the great herdsman of life) shall come in His glory and all the holy angels with Him, He shall sit upon the throne of His glory and before Him shall be gathered all nations, and He shall separate them from one another as a shepherd divideth his sheep from the goats." Now, when the herd is cut, the tailings are allowed to drift at will to be the prey of the cattle thief. But the cattle which have an owner will be cared for, taken into green pastures and fed through the cold, stormy weather. Hear the great stock-owner: "Then shall the King say to them on His right hand, Come ye blessed of my Father (or ye of my father's brand), inherit the kingdom." But hear what is to become of the tailings of that great roundup: "Then shall He say to them on his left, depart from Me, ye cursed, into everlasting fire prepared by the devil and his angels" (or the great thief of the human soul). . . . Boys, if you are in the old thief's pasture just take a run, and jump right through the fence out into the sunlight of God's own pasture green!

Some of the preachers were obsessed with sex:

When this man got to goin' good he held some meetings for men only. I went to one and I'll never forget it. It was held in the old opera house—a sanctuary of the devil which, the preacher said, was rendered holy for the time being because he was using it for God's purpose. The place was packed to the doors. There was a hymn or two, and then a sermon. At least, he called it a sermon. It was, in fact, merely a recital of page after page from Rabelais, the *Decameron* and the *Contes Drolatiques,* culled out by the parson and worked over to suit the taste of his customers. It suited me all right. I enjoyed it. Never anywhere, not even in the worst barrooms I have sinfully frequented, have I ever listened to as varied and as choice a collection of pornographic anecdotes. The preacher taught me things about women that I had never known of before—things extremely scandalous and surprising.

Frontier religion had its share of carnality. A man, asked who his father was, shrugged and answered: "Shucks, I'm jest a camp-meetin' baby." It was not just a matter of words. Saloon evangelists roared like lions when talking of Daniel in his den. They brayed like Balaam's ass, howled like wolves among the sheep, and wiggled lewdly when imitating the idolators dancing around the golden calf. One preacher impressed the brethren by crawling on all fours while impersonating the serpent that tempted Eve. Others frightened their congregation by convincing impersonations of Old Scratch himself.

The audience responded in kind—not the saloon regulars, but the few "decent wimmin" admitted into the barroom during gospel hour, and especially the nesters and their wives and offspring. They hollered, snorted, yelled, jumped, kicked, groveled on their knees, or had fits. Women fell down in a swoon or rolled up their eyes in ecstasy until only the whites showed. Worshipers made a noise "like a flashflood coming through a narrow dry gulch."

Fierce hellfire preaching did not fail to impress its hearers. According to the Las Vegas, New Mexico, *Optic,* two preachers accompanied by female missionaries entered Close and Patterson's saloon, where they harangued and baptized fifteen hurdy-gurdy girls and three gamblers with permission from the two proprietors. The girls approached the bar altar led by two nymphs of the prairie called Nervous Jessie and Lazy Liz. The gamblers were directed in their devotions by one French Pete. The twice-born sinners attracted a huge crowd and the saloon did a land-office business. Calamity Jane, a hard-drinking prostitute and bullwhacker, who spent a great deal of time inside saloons, once passed the hat for an itinerant preacher called Smith, who did his stuff standing on a whiskey crate outside Nuttall and Mann's Saloon in Deadwood. She exhorted the crowd: "You sinners, dig down in your pokes now; this old fellow looks as though he were broke and I want to collect about two hundred dollars for him!" She easily accomplished her purpose.

Bill Nuttall was also the owner of a combination concert, dance hall, and gambling saloon, the Melodeon. He allowed a minister named William Rumney to sermonize at his bar. Bottles, the keno goose, and roulette wheels were covered up during services. After Rumney had finished preaching, Nutshell Bill, a notorious faro dealer, exhorted the audience: "Now, boys, the old man has been showin' you how to save your souls; come this way and I'll show you how to win some money!"

Parson Tom Uzzel specialized in preaching in saloons—almost to the exclusion of all other places. He carried the word to dozens of Colorado mining camps, to Fairplay, Tincup, Independence, Gothic, Irwin, Silver Plume, and Georgetown. At Creede, Brother Tom asked Bat Masterson to be permitted to preach in his saloon. The frontier marshal banged on a whiskey keg with the butt of his six-shooter, ordering all and sundry to remove their hats and behave while Uzzel recited chapter and verse. Afterward the drinking men all joined heartily in hymn singing. Uzzel seldom collected less than five hundred dollars "for the building of a church" when preaching in saloons —at least as long as silver was king—in spite of the fact that Brother Tom preached mightily against drink and drunkenness. Nobody ever complained except the barkeep at Murphy's saloon in Denver, who pointedly remarked on the unfairness of parsons who were allowed to sermonize in bars but who did not permit saloon owners to tell their side of the story in church.

California saloons, during the gold rush, had many sermons preached in them. At Mountain Brow, Brother Magath held the first Protestant meeting inside the Headquarters, a gambling saloon. Magath approached the owner, Mr. Crowder, asking to have a word in private. Crowder thought he had a cadger on his hands and reached into his cashbox. The preacher was horrified. He wanted no money, merely permission to give a sermon. Crowder was incredulous: "Preach, h'yar? In this place?" He added that it was up to "the boys." He rapped on the counter with his bung starter, calling for everybody to calm down. When told that the strange gent in black considered the Headquarters wholesome enough to serve as his tabernacle, there were loud cheers and shouts of approval: "We'll all be hy'ar, d'ye think us a bunch of heathens like damn chinamen? Give the man a drink and put it on my bill!" After the sermon Magath somewhat shamefully admitted that he was tone deaf and needed help with the hymn singing. A prospector by the name of Wash White volunteered and led the chorus in a rich baritone:

> Am I a soldier of the cross,
> A follower of the Lamb?
> And shall I fear to own His cause
> Or blush to speak His name?

The first sermon in Bismarck, Dakota Territory, was likewise preached in a gambling saloon. One Sunday morning a man came into the place just as the gamblers sat down to begin their all-day poker games. Without explanation, the stranger climbed up on an unused faro table and started to pray. One gambler drew his gun, threatening to "stop the caterwauling with a bullet," but the man paid him no heed. Since he did not interfere with their cardplaying, the customers let him be. In a short while he won their attention and goodwill. When he finished, a collection was taken up and he was handed fifty dollars in poker chips. He was told he could either "cash them or play them." He politely declined to join in a hand, but cashed the chips.

The circuit-riding man of God did not always have an easy time. A one-armed minister preaching at Ford's Exchange saloon in Creede, Colorado, was told by a crowd of drunken miners to swallow a large glass of tarantula juice which they forced down his throat after he refused. The poor man was saved from further harm by, of all people, the con man Soapy Smith, who laid out the gang's leader with a blow of a pistol butt.

"The circuit-riding man of God did not always have an easy time."

In 1877, at Deadwood, South Dakota, the Reverend Dolliver was temporarily run out of town when he dared to preach against "King Faro, Prince Stud Poker, Bacchus, Gambrinus, and female depravity." In a Sheridan, Wyoming, saloon, a preacher was horrified when drunks parodied "Nearer my God to Thee" by raucously singing: "Nero, my dog has fleas." A minister who preached every Sunday in a Missoula, Montana, saloon had to be protected by the sheriff, who sat his horse outside the swinging doors, his pistol drawn, to enforce decorum.

Some of the preachers were tough hombres, who not only took it but also dished it out. In Butte, Montana, a man known as the Cowboy Evangelist enforced respect for religion at gunpoint. One gambler turned minister went further, giving a sermon on the prodigal son at the Show Mill, a Deadwood vaudeville saloon, shouting: "Get on yer knees, sinners, and yell!" The preacher lost patience with a drunken miner who kept haranguing him and, finally, drew from his pocket a "blood purifier" with which he silenced the heckler—forever. The event was preserved in a long epic by Bill De Vere, the "Tramp Poet of the West":

The preacher just straightened himself up, and
    said:
  "Then you think that I'm preachin' a lie."
And a forty-five cracked in a minute,
And the big gambler's turn came to die.

Then the preacher resumed, "Thar'll be
    preachin'
Next Sunday at just 10 o'clock.
We're goin' to run scripture teachin',
Right thro here, from soda to hoc.

My text is the Lord's first commandment,
And this is the rule I've laid down,
To run this game easy and quiet,
If I kill ev'ry sucker in town!"

It went to show that not all preachers had been

washed long enough in the Blood of the Lamb. Some were not preachers at all, but con men who found that passing the hat was the easiest way of making a living. One man in a stovepipe hat entered the Golden Rooms in Newton, Kansas, asking for permission to hold services. The outlook was not encouraging:

The games were going full blast . . . and the voices rose on the night air in discordant and babelic harshness. The fiddlers were squeaking their loudest, the melodeon was growling out its deepest bass. . . . A great crowd had gathered by the time the preacher came. He had to pass the bar.

"Say old chap, let's have a drink," greeted him on all sides. The preacher had a red nose. He disregarded the invitations, but his nose blushed deeper, and he sniffed spasmodically. Someone saw it and was crude enough to call out:

"Don't go back on your spiritual friends, old fellow."

Services began with a prayer. Somebody was playing faro in hard luck. The queen had beaten him three times. He lost again just as the prayer was drawing to a close. "Damn the luck!" broke from the gambler's lips just as Amen followed from the platform. The whole house roared. Someone let the dogs loose, and a dogfight, aided by the barking of the coons, was added to the scene. Nevertheless, the services went on, and hymns and a sermon followed.

The preacher took up a collection, had a drink, and left. A few days later it was learned that he was no preacher at all; merely a hard-up sharper in want of a week's board money.

In Black River Falls, an itinerant preacher named Snow brought God's word to taverns and saloons. Since he could not read or write, his wife had to announce the texts so that he could expound upon them. One day Snow vanished inexplicably until he was rediscovered in the Iowa state penitentiary, where he was doing time for horse stealing.

Some clergymen were incorrigible drunkards.

A traveler writing for *Harper's Monthly* described a Santa Fe padre, Father Ignatio:

At night, sounds of scandalous revelry and dancing emanated from the Father's room. . . . His Reverence professed himself unable to account for it, unless, indeed, it might have been a deception of the author of all evil, who was ever on the watch to take advantage, by interrupting the devotions of a Christian like himself.

In the California mining town of Olympia, an Irish priest was struck by gold fever. Obsessed by the idea that his churchyard rested on a rich vein, he dug up the bodies of his parishioners to get at the precious metal beneath. He shouted to his outraged flock: "Come on! Help me to mine out this place!" He had to be restrained with a leveled shotgun.

A most peculiar saloon preacher was "Butcher" John Chivington, a Methodist minister as well as colonel of the Colorado volunteer cavalry. In 1864 he wiped out a peaceful village of Cheyenne Indians, exhorting his soldiers to kill women and children with the shout, "Kill all, big and small, nits make lice!" Returning to Denver as a conquering hero, Chivington was invited to christen and bless Chase and Ford's new gambling saloon on Blake Street. As the Denver *Post* reported: "His Benediction was reverently received by the Ford's guests. All bowed their heads, and silence reigned as prayers went forth from our soldier-preacher."

It was the circuit-riding clergyman's job not only to preach to saloon patrons, but also to preside over their funerals. Given conditions on the frontier, this was one of their main jobs. Obsequies were jolly affairs, as great attractions as hangings. Beginning with great solemnity, the mourners relaxed into informality in proportion to the liquor consumed. Mourners raced their horses to Boot Hill and back to the saloon where bets were paid off. Bob Ford, the man who had shot Jesse James, was himself shot dead inside his own saloon at Creede. His wake, paid for by his gambling friends, was a tremendous affair. Mourners broke out the whiskey and champagne at the burial site and began dancing jigs on the fresh grave. As Creede's numerous "soiled doves" were present in force, the funeral degenerated into an orgy lasting for days which ended only "when the women and liquor gave out."

Almost equally rousing was a miner's funeral in Nevada. The parson's eulogy was so long that some of the mourners began idly to finger the dirt thrown up from the grave. Suddenly there were shouts and gesticulating. The minister interrupted his prayers to examine the dirt himself, with the surprising result that he hollered that it

Boot Hill, Dodge City, Kansas.

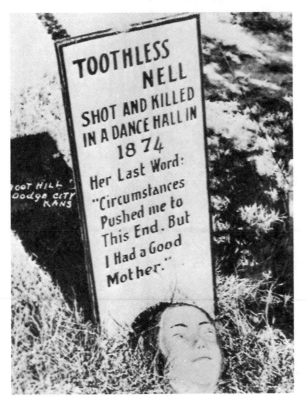

was the richest paydirt he'd ever seen. The corpse was unceremoniously lifted and dumped aside as the preacher led his flock in staking claims.

Early western funerals had flavor. Men died in saloons. Undertakers had their shops in the back, sometimes in a corner of the saloon. Wakes were held there too. Funerals were arranged and begun in the saloon. An 1884 announcement in the Laramie *Boomerang* read:

The friends of the late Whiskey Bill are respectfully invited to attend his funeral—he having gone up the flume on Friday—which will take place from Tompkin's Saloon on Sunday. The best ecclesiastical talent has been engaged and the services will be of a varied and interesting character.

One cannot help but detect a certain morbid humor in the accounts of western funerals. Death seems not to have been held in great respect, nor, for that matter, the eulogizing preacher. This is not surprising when one reads of a minister in Butte, Montana, being caught opening the coffin before burial to steal the corpse's new-bought clothes. Mortality in the early West was high. When the deceased had neither identification nor address on him, the tavern or saloon keeper was entitled to divide his belongings with the officiating minister.

Obituaries in the wild and woolly days had a charm of their own. One item in Ouray's *Solid Muldoon* read:

A tenderfoot over in the Animas Valley ascended the Golden Clothes Pole last week; the ascension being caused by getting outside the wrong brand of mushrooms.

A eulogizing Baptist minister was referred to by one western reporter as "an infinitismal pismire who worries me by perpetually crawling up my pants-leg."

Epitaphs were whimsical. A headstone on Dodge City's boot hill read:

Shoot-'em-up-Jake
Run for Sheriff 1872
Run from Sheriff 1876
Buried 1876

A Cripple Creek, Colorado, wooden grave marker proclaimed:

He called Bill Smith a liar.

Maybe the most famous of all was a headstone which for some years graced the cemetery in Ouray, Colorado:

Here lies Charlotte,
She was a harlot.
For fifteen years she preserved her virginity,
A damn good record for this vicinity.

In time obituaries as well as eulogies became less humorous and more decorous. The West became respectable and so did the preachers. They did their devil-wrassling in real churches and learned to speak the King's English and Latin, too; turned into shining examples; molded opinion; were a power in politics; influenced legislation; fulminated against smoking, gambling, and free love; and spearheaded the movement for temperance first and for Prohibition later—while a lot of old-timers longed for the return of the hard-riding, hard-assed sin-buster of yore who was not averse to lubricating his throat with a glass of good sippin' whiskey after a long sermon.

Fairplay, Colorado, 1975.

HIS HONOR (THE SALOON KEEPER) ON HIS BENCH (THE BAR), OR SALOON LAW

Gents, this Honorable Court is now in session, an' if any of you gander-eyed galoots wants a snort afore we start, let him step up to the bar and name his brand.

—Customary opening of Roy Bean's court

"Your fine is ten dollars and two bits." "Yes, Your Honor, but what's the two bits for?" "To buy your Honorable Judge a drink this fine morning."

—Early California saloon court proceedings

Just as a saloon bar occasionally served as pulpit, so it also functioned as a judge's bench, transforming the thirst parlor into a courtroom. In some cases the saloon keeper himself was the judge. Most of these barroom courts operated on "hope." There were no salaries or regular fees. Judges covered expenses through the fines they imposed. Men who upheld the majesty of the law west of the Big Muddy were untrammeled by a knowledge of law and Latin, which would only have gotten in the way of common sense. They kept an open mind when trying a case. If a law was needed, they promptly enacted it. If a law proved an obstruction, they ignored it. In the Southwest the community elected an alcalde, sometimes a saloon owner, who was bound by no specific law, because he was a law unto himself. He followed no precedent, decided cases as he saw fit, and allowed no appeal to higher authority. He might be illiterate, but if he had horse sense and dealt out justice after his fashion honestly, he earned the gratitude and respect of his community. In the gold and silver camps, miners' courts functioned in the same rough-and-ready manner, sometimes sitting in saloons or simply doing business in the shade of a convenient tree.

"There is more law in a Colt six-gun than in all the law books" was the motto in the early mining camps and cowtowns. A judge therefore had to be able to take care of himself. If he lacked that "certain presence which overawes and subdues," he did not last long.

One Texas pioneer judge known as Three-Legged Willy on account of his wooden peg leg, found himself confronted by a defendant who held a bowie knife to his throat saying: "Here's the law of Texas." The judge whipped out his navy Colt and roared: "Yes, and by the Great Jehovah, here's the constitution of Texas!"

A similar story is told of another Texan, Judge Williamson, who opened the first court at Shelbyville in 1837 in a tavern sitting behind a dry goods box.

In Silver Cliff, Colorado, Judge Slaughter dealt out justice with an even but somewhat heavy hand. Defied in court by a notorious badman named Bill Tripp, and his woman, Mollie May, "Judge Slaughter put the Indian sign on them by declaring 'I've seen and settled more hell than you could ever raise!' "

In spite of their supposed lawlessness, westerners were a litigating breed: the lawyer and the judge followed closely on the heels of whiskey seller and preacher. On the early midwestern border it was the saloon's precursor, the old-style tavern, which served as courthouse, also providing bed, board, and liquid refreshments for judges, attorneys, and litigants. In 1837, a tavern was built at Jefferson, Wisconsin, and in the barroom the first session of the circuit court was held by Judge David Irvin. Irvin was a bachelor, very able but, by modern standards, decidedly odd. One could say that time and place demanded of a judge that he be somewhat eccentric and adaptable to prevailing conditions. Irvin frequently adjourned court, ordering attorneys and jurymen to go fishing "to keep costs down and to ease the heavy demand on the Boniface's meager supply of victuals." Once, while Irvin was holding court in a Prairie du Lac barroom, a bear was sighted by a juror looking out the window and the judge led a general stampede to "bag bruin."

In 1840, Wayne Dyer, a tavern keeper at Portage, Wisconsin, was against his will appointed

Judge of the circuit court.

county clerk as "the only qualified person available." When he asked where to locate his office, since no courthouse had been built or was likely to be for some time, he was told to "carry it in your hat." Not surprisingly he established it in his popular tavern, where the hard-riding Judge Irvin arrived in due course to administer the law, make rulings, and set precedents in his own unique fashion, as he did in most of settled Wisconsin. Jurors loved to serve because according to territorial law, they were paid in hard cash, an article otherwise difficult to come by. They also were fed considerably better than at home, not to mention the double-twisted and distilled hot waters available in court.

Irvin's fellow judge, the Honorable Henry Jacques, also adapted himself to frontier conditions. When trying a horse thief by the name of Hull at the Hawk's Tavern at Delafield, he noticed that no lawyer was present to defend the accused. Jacques ordered the tavern keeper to stop tending bar, saying: "You will please act as counsel for this man, Mr. Hawks."

"Very well," answered the landlord, "but if I act, I shall clear him."

"With that I have nothing to do" was the judge's comment. Either the accused was a friend of Hawks, or the tavern owner had a good heart, knowing that horse thieves were occasionally hanged if found guilty.

The defendant was kept locked in the pantry, the constable sitting in the doorway to block all attempts at escape. When Hawks saw that the officer had imbibed freely and was fast asleep, he let the prisoner out, hiding him in an empty whiskey barrel. The judge, in the meantime, banged his gavel repeatedly, calling upon Hawks to defend his "client." The tavern keeper, "looking as meek as Moses," took up a volume of statutes and, holding it upside down, began reading from it in a decorous manner: "Whereas, it is further enacted, that when a prisoner gets forty rods the start of the officers of the court, he shall in such case be cleared, provided he runs fast. Therefore, in accordance with the law in such cases made and provided, I ask the court to discharge the jury."

This caused general merriment. Court was adjourned so that counsel for the defense could prepare a round of libations. The judge then ordered the constable to bring in the prisoner. The befuddled officer started a frantic search for the culprit in which the whole assemblage took a hand. Having searched long and in vain, intermittently refreshed by great draughts of the good critter, the exhausted dispensers of justice finally retired for the night, and Hawks let the horse thief loose with the warning never to show his face in the vicinity again. Instead of a fee, the grateful client gave the tavern keeper a heavy gold ring, which Hawks proudly wore to the end of his days. The judge for years lovingly recalled this trial, ending the tale always by saying: "It was a novel method of winning a case but one, nevertheless, which I could not conscientiously recommend to the legal fraternity."

Often the tavern keeper himself was the judge, as was true with Adam Smith, owner of a drinking place near Madison. Smith stood six feet four inches in his stocking feet and weighed 250 pounds. Litigants disputed his rulings at their own peril—the judge was willing to enforce them with his fists. He rivaled Judge Irvin in unorthodoxy, one time sentencing a defendant accused of assault and battery to walk twelve miles through a sea of mud to humbly beg his victim's pardon, then to return over the same unspeakable roads to receive a reprimand from the judge.

In his capacity of landlord, Smith once served drink after drink to a stranger, equally tall, stout, and confident. The man walked away after having refreshed himself, refusing to pay, pleading poverty as a reason. Smith pursued him in his capacity as judge and demolished him in an epic rough-and-tumble, which quickly established the authority of the court. The freeloader was brought back to the barroom and searched. A money belt containing three hundred dollars in gold being found on his person, the culprit was forced to settle his bill and to "defray the legal expenses of pursuit, capture, and return."

Improvisation was also the rule in Goldrush, California. In 1850 Stephen J. Field was alcalde at Marysville. Later he served on the supreme courts of both California and the United States. One day, Field happened to be out for a stroll when he came upon two men arguing vociferously. One of them, a respectable Marysville citizen, had been riding his newly bought mare when his bridle was seized by a pedestrian of equally good repute who said the horse belonged to him. The two men spotted the judge and appealed to him to settle the dispute. Then and there, Field swore them in as witnesses, listened to their testimony, decided for the pedestrian, asked for and received an ounce of gold for his fee, and adjourned court so that all three of them could get out of the sun into a nearby saloon for refreshment.

A judge of similar caliber was Major R. C. Barry, the "Texas Bantam Cock," who held court

Judge Brown holds court in Tuttletown, California.

in a saloon at the California mining camp of Sonora until a proper Ivolumne County courthouse was built. The major was elected justice of the peace "for his strength of character rather than for any attainments in the law." The judge kept records of some sort of most of his cases, written on odd scraps of paper. They are still a delight and wonderment. Take the case of the black mare mule:

No. 516. This is a suite for Mule Steeling in which Jesus Ramirez is indited fur steeling one black mare Mule, branded O with a 5 in it from sheriff Work. George swares the Mule is hisn and I believe so. On hearing the caze I found Jesus Ramirez of feloaniusly and against the law made and provided and the dignity of the people of Sonora steeling the aforesade mare Mule sentensed him to pay the Costs of Coort 10 dolars, and fine him a 100 dolars more as a terrour to all evil dooers. Jesus Ramirez not having any munney to pay with I rooled that George Work shuld pay the Costs of the Coort, as well as the fine, and in

defalt of payment that the said one mare Mule be sold by the Constable John Luney or other officer of the Coort, as also the payment of the fine aforesade. R. C. Barry, Justice Peace. John Luney, Constable.

The judge's action was typical of the gold rush era in that he didn't care who paid costs and fine as long as somebody coughed up the required ounces of gold dust. One can sympathize with the unlucky owner of the black mare mule, who got little satisfaction out of winning besides seeing justice done. He squawked, or rather his lawyer did, but to no avail as the following memo of the little judge attests:

H. P. Barber, the lawyer for George Work insolently told me there were no law fur me to rool so I told him that I did not care a damn for his book law, that I was the Law myself. He jawed back so I told him to shetup but he would not so I fined him 50 dolars and comited him to gaol fur 5 days fur contempt of Coort in bringing my roolings and disissions into disreputableness and as a warning to unrooly citizens not to contredict this Coort.

Barry was by no means unique in the California of the forties and the fifties. In 1850, at Downieville, one of the many California gold camps, a saloon keeper doubled as justice of the peace. He sentenced a man found guilty of stealing a pair of boots to return them to their rightful owner and, as a fine, to pay for three rounds of drinks for judge, jurors, and the crowd of onlookers. His Solomonic decision was greeted with wild enthusiasm, the judge, taking over the bar, dispensing its liquid assets. But when, after the third round, the time arrived for the culprit to pay his fine, he was nowhere to be found—and the judge-saloon keeper had to pay it.

In its own fashion, rule by law was established all over the West. At Mobeetie, Texas, in 1878, a number of solid citizens and drinking men assembled in the saloon and decided the time had come to nominate a judge. Their choice fell upon an

"In its own fashion, rule by law was established
all over the West."

upstanding early pioneer, Emanuel Dubles. They
sent an old buffalo hunter called Wilson Harrah to
acquaint Dubles with his nomination. Dubles
pointed out that he was a rancher, was building his
house, and had never studied law. Moreover there
was not a single law book to be found anywhere
within two hundred miles. All of Dubles's objec-
tions were brushed aside and he was unanimously
elected judge in the Panhandle, serving for ten
years with great distinction.

Perhaps one of the most inventive representa-
tives of civil authority was a Taos barkeeper, who
in his extra capacity of justice of the peace loved
to perform marriages with these poetic words:

Under this roof in stormy weather,
This buck and squaw now come together.
Let not but *Him* who rules the thunder,
Pull this buck and squaw asunder!

I now pronounce you man and wife
And may God have mercy on your souls!
Now, what's your pleasure?

The hard-drinking amateur judges who dispensed justice in saloons filled a vacuum. Unlettered, without any knowledge of the law, they
grew into their jobs as they taught themselves. Not
a few of them in time became able jurists. Others
were dismal failures or outright crooks. Some became laughingstocks in their communities.

The first trial held in Montana Territory, in
1862, at Hell Gate, ended in a near riot when the
defendant, a man named O'Keefe, shouted at the
judge: "Say, old Brooks, who in hell made you
judge? You are an old fraud. You are no judge;
you are a squaw man, you have two squaws now.
Your business is to populate the country with half
breeds. You old bastard!"

A newspaper in Manzano, New Mexico, reported the following goings-on in court:

Judge. "There is on this docket a case against you
for *arseny,* guilty or not guilty?"
Prisoner. "Guilty."
Judge. "The sentence of this court then is, that
you pay a fine of two hundred dollars, or marry the
girl."

In 1899, in Dawson, Yukon Territory, a drunk
stumbled into the Phoenix Saloon, reeling, making his way along the walls. He was James Church
McCook, in the States a justice of the peace, in
Alaska, the American consul. He offered to make
U.S. citizens of the Canadian, Indian, and Eskimo
patrons, and when nobody took him up on it, gave
away his gold watch and chain and begged the
hurdy-gurdy girls to search his pockets for money,
with which request they cheerfully complied.
Someone fastened an American flag to the seat of
his pants. McCook then bent over and invited all
and sundry to kick him. Pete, the bouncer, did so.
The incident eventually forced McCook to resign.
"Drunker than two judges" was a common western saying.

Little respect was shown to judges in Dodge
City, the Queen of the Cowtowns. As the local
paper reported on August 11, 1877:

"The marshal will preserve strict order," said the Judge. "Any person caught throwing turnips, cigar stumps, beets, or old quids of tobacco at this Court, will be immediately arraigned before this bar of Justice." Joe (the policeman) looked savagely at the mob in attendance, hitched his ivory handle a little to the left and adjusted his moustache. "Trot out the wicked and unfortunate, and let this cottilion commence," said his Honor . . . "You are here for horse stealing," says Walsh (the judge). "I can clean out the d----d court," says Martin (the defendant). Then the City Attorney was banged into a pigeon hole in the desk, the table upset, the windows kicked out and the railing broke down. When order was restored Joe's thumb was 'some chawed."

In a class by himself was the famous, or rather infamous, Judge Roy Bean, the "Law west of the Pecos." He was appointed justice of the peace for Pecos County, Texas, on August 2, 1882, qualifying for this office by posting a thousand-dollar bond. Bean held his trials inside his own saloon, the legendary Jersey Lilly, at Langtry, a whistlestop for trains crossing the Pecos River.

He was born one day near Toyah, where he
    learned to be a lawyer,
        And a teacher and a barber and
           the Mayor.
He was cook and old-shoe mender, sometimes
    preacher and bartender
        And it cost two bits to have him cut
           your hair.

The ballad had it wrong as far as learning to be a lawyer was concerned. The only written law he had any knowledge of came out of a single volume, the *Revised Statutes of Texas, 1879* edition. Over the years he learned to recite almost the whole of it by heart. Other law books, sent to him from time to time, he used to light his stove with, or tore them apart, stacking up the loose pages in his outhouse. Bean was unkempt in appearance, sported a scraggy beard, wore flat, wide-brimmed, and much-frayed straw hats or a sweat-soaked bandanna as headgear. He was otherwise clothed in a collarless, seldom clean shirt and a stained vest, which was always unbuttoned, except at the top, to leave room for Bean's ample belly. Across it dangled a huge golden watch chain.

He was a joke and a fraud but also, on occasion, a terror. He sentenced a number of supposed horse thieves and cattle rustlers to death, sometimes on the flimsiest evidence, and these sentences were carried out. "Give him a drink and tie him to the nearest limb! Well, what'll you have, feller?" And that was all. Newspaper clippings of Bean's trials make good and colorful reading, but there are in each case so many versions, embroidered and improved upon in the retelling, that it is difficult now to separate fact from fiction. Bean was sometimes merciful to ex-rebels and Irishmen, but hard on nonwhites. His judgments were colored by his racism. He acquitted one of the paddies working on the railroad for killing a Chinese coolie. As one newspaper reported:

At Langtry, Texas, Squire Roy Bean, who administers justice and keeps the leading saloon, had to sit in judgment on a railroad clerk who had killed Ah Ling, a laundry man for, as he claimed, insulting him. The man was arrested and brought before magistrate Bean, who listened to the evidence, which was given by the accused himself, and then proceeded to turn the pages of the revised statutes: 'This here book, which is a Texas law book,' he announced, 'says that hommyside is th' killin' of a human, male or female. They is many kinds of hommyside—murder, manslaughter, plain hommyside, negl'gent hommyside, justifi'ble hommyside an' praiseworthy hommyside. They is three kinds of humans—white men, niggers, and Mexicans. It stan's to reason thet if a Chinym'n was human, killin' of him would come under th' head of praiseworthy hommyside. The pris'ner is discharged on condition that he pays f'r havin' th' Chinee buried."

This is one of the earliest of a half-dozen versions describing the Ah Ling case, but the bare facts are not in question. Bean had as little liking for Mexicans as he had for Orientals. He once

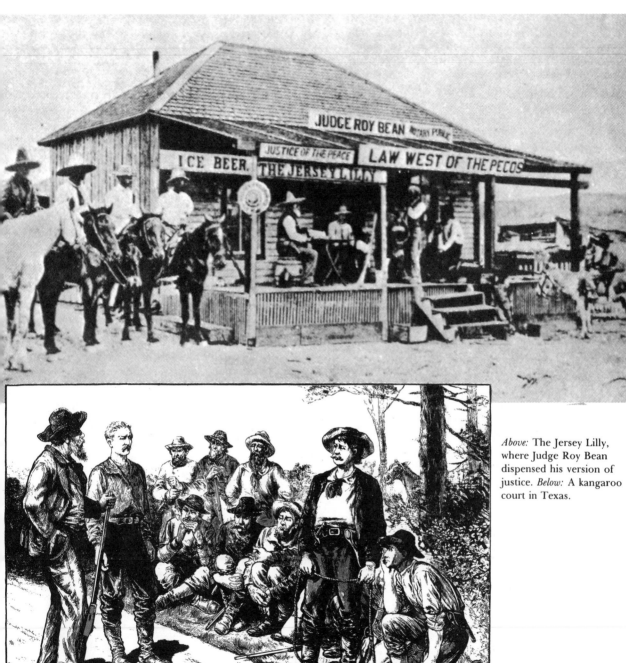

Above: The Jersey Lilly, where Judge Roy Bean dispensed his version of justice. *Below:* A kangaroo court in Texas.

tried a man named Carlos Robles for cattle theft:

"Carlos Robles, this court finds you charged with a grave offense against the peace and dignity of the sovereign State of Texas, to wit: cattle rustlin'. How do you plead?"

Unable to understand a word of English the defendant uttered a few sentences in Spanish.

"Court accepts yore plea of guilty. The jury will now deliberate, and if'n it brings in a verdict short of hangin' it'll be declared in contempt. Gentlemen, what's yore verdict?"

"Guilty as hell, your honor."

As far as can be ascertained, Robles was hanged from a nearby tree. According to custom, the jury ordered triple-x beer upon passing of the sentence, and rye whiskey after its execution.

"Hanging Judge Parker" in Oklahoma and Franklin Pierce Benedict in New Mexico are credited with the same kind of summary justice.

Bean used his position as justice of the peace ruthlessly to enrich and protect himself, as well as to further his saloon business. Defendants and accuser alike were mercilessly fleeced. Bean and Oscar, the saloon factotum, habitually rolled drunks. In his later years Bean developed the plundering of travelers into a fine art. He had shrewdly built the Jersey Lilly within thirty yards of where the trains stopped—for ten minutes—to take on water. The passengers always made a stampede to the bar. A bottle of cold beer cost them one dollar, an outrageous price for those times. Nobody, except a small handful of bold and vicious men, ever managed to get change for a five- or ten-dollar bill—Roy Bean was always "too busy" to get around to it before the whistle blew for the passengers to return to their compartments. Those who complained got short shrift.

Then a-down he threw ten dollars, which the
   same Roy quickly collars,
     Then the same Roy holds to nine
      and hands back one;

So the stranger gave a holler, as he saw
   the single dollar,
     And at that began the merriment
      and fun.

The dude he slammed the table just as hard
   as he was able,
     That the price of whiskey was too
      high, he swore.
Said Roy Bean, "For all that fussin' and
   your most outrageous cussin'
     You are fined the other dollar
      by the law.

Roy Bean was the law west of the Pecos for four hundred miles around, holding office in his saloon until 1903, when he died of pneumonia at the age of seventy-eight, the last of his kind. Bean became a folk hero in his own time, possibly on account of a certain sense of humor with which he carried out his depredations, but not necessarily. Frontier lore, reporters, and dime novels turned some of the most humorless killers into protectors of orphans and poor widows.

Jurors matched the saloon judges in thought and habits. The principle on which they operated was expressed by a "Cousin Jack" (a Cornish miner), serving on a Colorado jury: "I always come to a case wid this thought in me 'ead: if 'e idn't guilty, wot's 'e 'ere for?" A famous South Dakota story, perhaps true and perhaps not, concerned a cattle rustler tried by a jury of stockmen. Before the trial properly began, one of the jurors told the sheriff: "We'll make it fast. We know you'll want the barroom to lay out the body in." In Medora, North Dakota, the jury deliberated inside a saloon, charging their drinks to the county while taking their time deciding a case. In Tombstone, Arizona, an item in the local newspaper read:

One of the jurors selected Monday in the Hambleton case was taken violently ill with visions of

Trial scene in a Colorado mining town.

snakes and was in such a condition yesterday morning as to render his excuse only a matter of request.

In Miles City, Montana, one man among jurors waiting to be selected for a case inside a gambling saloon hit an out-of-town gambler over the head with a wooden beam during an argument, killing him instantly. The home boy's fellow jurors immediately hanged the dead stranger "as a 'dangerous' hombre" to save their friend from possible consequences.

The role of saloon as courtroom was short-lived, since courthouses were speedily built everywhere. They were cheap too, cheaper than saloons, and might have been built first, except that westerners needed their whiskey mills before the need for courthouses arose. The first Cook County courthouse in Texas, erected at Gainesville in 1850, cost only $29. It was sixteen feet square and eight feet high. The Ellis County courthouse, a glorified log cabin, cost all of $59. Grayson County courthouse, at Sherman, Texas,

was extravagant at $232. Up to 1847 court had been convened beneath a large pecan tree. Roy Bean's saloon-courthouse was already an anachronism during the 1890s, and its survival into the decadent, overcivilized 1900s something of a miracle. Possession of a courthouse was a matter of survival for many communities. Basically a county was supposed to contain at least 150 registered voters to get a court, though one county supposedly contained only "two Democrats, two Republicans and one sheepman." Communities, led by judges and lawyers, conducted regular wars to become county seats, burning rival courthouses down, stealing each other's court records, plying voters with whiskey, or offering them bribes.

The westerner's attitude toward the law was ambiguous. He wanted no judge and no law to interfere with his chosen life-style, whether it was a matter of making his own whiskey, or having two wives or three, or settling a personal vendetta with fist or gun. Many of the settlers were born rebels who had been in trouble with the law back east.

Some were survivors of the 1830 revolution in Poland or of the 1848 uprisings in Germany. The frontiersman had been able to observe his Indian neighbor, thereby getting a whiff of the kind of real freedom unknown to the white man, and was never the same afterward. Isolation and great distances forced westerners to improvise, innovate, and make do with makeshift justice. Vigilantes lynched men, and women too, for a variety of crimes, real and imagined, rather than let them go scot-free for lack of proper judge and jury. Most mining camps and early ranch towns had their "hanging tree." During the 1850s in California corporal punishment was meted out freely. Cheaters at cards, claim jumpers, and petty thieves on occasion had their noses slit or their ears cropped so that an honest fellow, meeting them by chance, could see what he was up against.

On the other hand, Anglo-Saxons were sticklers for the law; all of them attorneys at heart, born litigants and hangers around the courthouse, experts at judging a judge's gifts for elocution, secret yearners for law and order—as long as the law did not apply to them personally. Eventually those frontier dwellers who were not Anglo-Saxons adopted Anglo-Saxon standards in the process of acculturation. Unlettered miners, without benefit of Blackstone's precepts of law, quickly enacted their own regulations to fit their special needs. In 1850 in a California saloon, the following regulations were adopted by a crowd of prospectors:

1st Resolved:
That each individual be entitled to sixteen feet upon the River extending from bank to bank.
2nd Resolved:
That no claim shall be forfeited unless left for three consecutive days without tools, unless prevented by sickness or winter.
3rd Resolved:
That any Company designing to turn the River shall give at least one week's Public Notice in order to allow every person an opportunity of joining said Company. And said Company shall be entitled to all they improve.
4th Resolved:
That power to decide questions of conflicting claims or mining operations be vested in an Alcalde elected by simple majority.
5th Resolved:
That these resolutions may be altered or amended or added to in order to fit circumstances by a vote of the majority at Public meetings held for this purpose.

There were also the forty-niners' ten commandments, among them:

Thou shalt have no other claim than one.
Thou shalt not make unto thyself a false claim nor shall you jump one.
Thou shalt not go prospecting before your claim gives out.
Thou shalt not remember what thy friends do at home on the Sabbath Day, lest that remembrance compare unfavorably with what thou doest in your cabin.
Thou shalt not inquire into your neighbor's name in the states, or whatsoever he did there, lest he inquire into your past.
Thou shalt not steal a pick or shovel or pan from a fellow miner; nor borrow tools he cannot spare, nor return them broken, nor wash takings from his sluice's mouth.
Thou shalt not tell false tales about "good diggings in the mountains" to profit your mule and provision business.
Thou shalt not keep one or two squaws when a maiden pines for you in your old home.

Similar written and unwritten laws were conceived in saloons by cattlemen and cowhands, nesters and sodbusters to fill their particular requirements. The majesty of the law generally arrived together with the first group of "respectable" women and with the building of the first substantial church, making saloon judges and saloon courts superfluous.

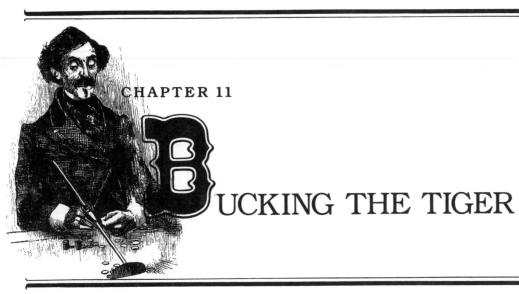

CHAPTER 11

BUCKING THE TIGER

I love not Colorado
Where the Faro table grows,
And down the Desperado
Where the rippling Bourbon
flows;

Sweet Poker haunted Kansas
In vain allures the eye;
The Keno game has charms
enough,
Yet its blandishments I fly.

—Song of a disgruntled gambler

There were saloons in which men drank and gambled on the side. There were others in which men gambled and drank on the side; these were gambling saloons, also known as gambling dens, gambling hells, slaughter houses, or skinning houses. Saloons, whiskey, and gambling went hand in hand. The difference between an ordinary thirstmill and a gambling saloon was merely a matter of emphasis. The urge to gamble is a universal human trait. After the basic needs of food, water, and shelter are met, the desire for sex, then for alcohol and gambling, seems to arise. It is one characteristic that differentiates *Homo sapiens* from other creatures. Animals will fight as fiercely as men for food, territory, or females, but no higher primate or dolphin ever wagered its property in order to con a fellow mammal out of his. Whether this proves the intellectual superiority of man over the other species remains debatable.

Gambling is as old as man himself. The land of Canaan was divided by lot. By lot Saul became king. Roman legionnaires threw dice for Christ's garments. Animal knucklebones used as game counters have been found in prehistoric caves. Sumerians, Babylonians, Egyptians, ancient Romans and Greeks all gambled. The Founding Fathers took time out from fighting the lobsterbacks to relax with a bumper of hot buttered rum over a game of whist. Gambling was the single vice the white man did not bring to the New World. Indians had hundreds of betting games—knucklebone, plum pit, stick, peb-

Bust! By W. M. Cary.

ble, moccasin, and hand games. Some of these were played with great solemnity as rituals with religious significance. The horse had hardly been introduced to America when Indians began to risk their possessions on the outcome of horse races. Mayan priests and nobles wagered wildly at ceremonial ball games. The players had most at stake, since the members of the losing team frequently had their heads cut off. Gambling was not a particularity of the American frontier alone.

A veritable gambling craze, which made gaming an obsession as well as almost the only entertainment available, was, however, a characteristic of the opening of the West. Life itself was a gamble. Settlers crossing the plains faced death from Indians, starvation, thirst, and cholera, as well as from each other. Everyday chores—prospecting, mining, cattle herding, hunting—were likely to injure or accidentally kill a person. Violent changes of fortune, for better or worse, were a part of the western experience. Men who had come to the gold fields pushing a handcart became rich overnight. Land, pelts, and precious metals could be picked up for nothing. The fever of speculation engendered by this seemingly limitless wealth reached all the way back to the eastern states. In

the mining camps prospectors wandered about with pockets full of gold dust and nothing to spend their easily won wealth on. As one old-timer said: "Faro and the bottle were the only relaxations for the motherlode." The prospector and gambler alike, as the saying went, "tried to knock Dame Fortune on her ass."

Westerners would wager on anything. A duel in Denver fought with pistols at ten paces drew a huge crowd of bettors who laid money on the man they thought was the better shot. California miners pitched twenty-dollar gold pieces at a hole in a large tree. Whoever managed to flip his coin into the hole took the pot. Men wagered at dogfights, pony races, and frog-jumping contests. In Olympia, California, prospectors picked lice from their shirt seams and threw them into a heated frying pan betting on which of the graybacks could scramble out fastest.

The mining king John McKay, of Comstock Lode fame, once bet five hundred dollars that he could produce a bug that could outjump the world's "farthest jumping grasshopper." He was set up by his opponent, who had McKay shown a tiny bottle of ammonia. When the hopper was given a sniff it immediately made a sensational jump. At the contest, McKay's opponent had the first jump and the distance was duly marked with chalk. McKay surreptitiously put the little bottle to his hopper's nose and the hapless critter made a feeble jump, fell on its back, and gave up the ghost. The bottle had been switched and contained chloroform. McKay had been beaten at his own game. One of the richest men in the country, McKay once told an associate that, since no amount he could conceivably win or lose at cards could excite him, life seemed hardly worth living.

Gambling in the West had no odium attached to it as it did back east. Judges, clergymen, army officers, and cattlemen gambled openly and unblushingly. In such an atmosphere the saloons, and especially the gambling saloons, thrived.

The development of the gambling den or skinning house closely paralleled that of the ordinary saloon. It started with the old colonial tavern. Gambling was as colorful and at times as violent in New York, Boston, or Charleston as it was in the West, but the frontier always fired the writer's imagination as the East never did, and the average New Yorker knew more about the wicked ways of the Barbary Coast than he knew about what was going on in the dives of Hell's Kitchen or the Bowery.

The early Midwest frontier also had a mining boom. Here prosaic lead, not gold, was king. Prosaic or not, there was money in lead and in the miners' pockets. In 1844 two professional gamblers traveled from Dubuque to Beetown, Wisconsin, put up at a tavern, and proposed to its owner to open a bank in his place for mutual profit. At the news someone thrust a gigantic bull's horn through a broken windowpane and set off a terrific blast, which shook the leaves on nearby trees and brought the miners at a run. They were well provided with Mexican dollars and French five-franc pieces, which soon covered the gaming table set up in the center of the barroom. The betting and drinking went on all night and continued during the day. When a miner got sleepy he crawled up into the attic, rested for half an hour or so, and then resumed gaming. There was good-natured fighting resulting in a few shiners. A wonderful time was had by all, and the general opinion was that civilization had finally arrived in Beetown.

At Carter and Giblett's tavern in nearby West Blue Mounts, poker was an obsession to such an extent that the settlement eventually was named Pokerville. While the lead-mining boom lasted, from 1845 to 1860, poker was the region's "leading industry and the melodious click-click of poker chips its only music." In the lumber camps, too, "gambling made short the night and poor the purse."

Alexander Pratt, an early traveler in the area, wrote about a night spent at Uncle Ab Nichols' famous tavern at Mineral Point:

Such a sight as presented itself to our view we never saw before or since. It seemed that the miners were in the habit of assembling there on Saturday nights to drink, gamble, and frolic until Monday morning. This was the only public house in the place. The barroom in which we were sitting contained a large bar, well supplied with all kinds of liquors. In one corner of the room was a faro bank discounting to a crowd around it; in another a roulette; and in another sat a party engaged in playing cards. One man sat back in a corner playing a fiddle, to whose music two others were dancing in the middle of the floor. Hundreds of dollars were lying upon the tables; and among the crowd were the principal men of the territory. Being pretty much worn out by our journey, we expressed a wish to retire. The landlord showed us to a dark room in which two men were also playing cards and a third lay drunk on the floor. . . . We sat down on the side of the bed, and began to figure in our mind upon the chances. We had several hundred dollars in our pocket. We imagined that in case they should get "short" they might call for our "pile."

After studying a while we threw down the outside blanket and quietly crawled into bed with all our clothes on except cap and boots. We had a good bowie knife in our belt and clasped a pistol in each hand, and in this way we lay until daylight; and a longer night we never wish to see. When we got up, our roommates were still playing cards.

Pratt ended his description by noting that he had seen enough of miners and gambling to last him for the rest of his life. This was Wisconsin, the supposedly tame middle frontier in the 1840s, but the description would also have fitted the typical western gambling saloon in Colorado or Nevada thirty years later.

In New Mexico, during the 1840s, according to one visitor: "Public gambling was both the leading industry and the leading sport in Santa Fe. . . . Liquor was cheap, women were bought and sold like horses, and almost everyone carried arms."

Gambling saloon in Santa Fe, 1854.

New Mexico gambling dens with their mixture of splendor and barbarism surprised the Yankee traders who had come down the eight-hundred-mile-long Santa Fe Trail. They were all low, one-story buildings with crumbling mud walls. They invariably had earthen floors, but there were also sparkling chandeliers, cut-glass decanters, and women—likewise barbaric and splendiferous. The gaming tables were piled high with gold and silver —Spanish reales, Mexican pesos, French francs bearing the image of Napoleon, Austrian Maria Theresa thalers, American eagles, and heavy octagonal California gold slugs. Among the bettors were Catholic prelates, American army officers, rich hacendados, shaggy-bearded mountain men, New England traders, French bourgeois from St. Louis, and cigar-smoking aristocratic señoras.

The typical western gambling saloon was born in California during gold rush days. As the saying went: "When a town can support three or four Faro games, a keno game, and can boast of a roulette wheel, it is a sure sign that said town is a good one."

The first gambling saloons were primitive. At Oroville the "town" consisted of a few tents. People slept in their wagons and oxcarts. Large prairie schooners served as hotels. The gamblers set up tables under brush shelters strung out along the road "to take in the cheerful but unwary miner."

At Virginia City the famous "Jones Canvas Hotel" was a tent eighteen by forty feet. The bar was an old sluice box, whiskey was kept in pitchers, dry goods crates served as gaming tables. "The yelling, cursing, clinking of glasses and clicking of roulette wheels was music to the gamblers' ears." In this place a man once stabbed a gambler to death and then peacefully went to sleep on the billiard table.

In 1859 the Denver House, better known as the Elephant Corral, was opened as one of the first Rocky Mountain gambling saloons. It was thirty feet wide and a hundred feet long, and most of the space was taken up by gambling tables, which were almost the sole furniture. The structure was built of cottonwood logs, with a slanting skeleton roof covered with canvas. Tamped earth served for a floor. Canvas nailed to rough, wooden frames partitioned off a few cubicles for accommodating guests. The front area was the barroom filled with rough card tables. The kitchen was outside. Guests furnished their own buffalo robes to sleep in. In a tunnellike corridor were kept water barrels, from which the patrons filled their wash basins. After using them they simply dumped the water onto the earthen floors. In case of gunplay, customers wishing to escape flying bullets jumped through the muslin-covered windows like so many grasshoppers. As with all gambling saloons, the Elephant Corral had an orchestra consisting of a fiddler, a cornet player, a fifer, and a pianist beating out the "Yellow Rose of Texas," "Lily Dale," and "Sweet Betsy from Pike" on an asthmatic upright. It also followed general custom by operating twenty-four hours a day, every day of the week, bartenders and gamblers working in shifts. The owner, Robert Teats, was not directly involved in the gambling, but leased out his faro, blackjack, and monte tables to professionals by the week or month for a good price. This had its advantages. If customers complained about marked cards or loaded dice, Teats looked piously heavenward saying: "Pray, sir, what has it got to do with me?"

The railroads furthered the spread of gambling saloons. As the iron trail was built across plains and mountains, "hells-on-wheels" moved from railhead to railhead. These railroad cars serving as saloons, gambling dens, or brothels were sometimes prefabricated and thus easily picked up again and moved along the tracks, section by section. If towns or settlements sprang up along the line, occasionally these outfits struck roots. While others kept rolling on with the hells-on-wheels, the stay-behinds generally put up an oversized pup tent, such as one called Keystone Hall, which advertised itself as an "instant gambling and pretty waitress saloon." When the tracks of the Union Pacific and the Central Pacific railroads finally met on May 10, 1869, linking the West Coast to the East Coast, the meeting place, Promontory, Utah, became a beehive of activity. Under the noses of pious Mormons, a row of false-front skinning houses, whiskey mills, and bagnios stretched along the tracks for nearly a mile. Three-card monte sharps set up tables in the open as the trains were serviced, separating the sucker from his silver before the cars rolled on again.

Cheyenne, Wyoming, owed its existence to the railroad, which arrived in 1867 and established a station and depot there. The town was aptly nicknamed "hell on wheels." A writer for *Leslie's Weekly* described gambling at Cheyenne in 1877, ten years after the town had become civilized: "Gambling in Cheyenne, far from being merely an amusement or recreation, rises to the dignity of a legitimate occupation—the pursuit of nine-tenths of the population, both permanent and transient. There are twenty gambling saloons in this diminutive town."

The opulent western gambling palace made its first appearance in San Francisco in 1850, not only because of the abundance of gold, but also because of its accessibility by sea at a time when inland territories were beyond the reach of civilization's amenities. Furnishings for the elegant gambling saloons were shipped from New York, Boston, and Philadelphia by three and four masters around the Horn, or unloaded at Colón or

Above: Instant town along the railroad track and games of chance in early Denver. *Below:* Keno in a Santa Fe saloon.

Portobelo, and transported across the isthmus to be picked up by another ship at Panama.

Among the skinning palaces were the El Dorado, the Mazourka, Dennison's Exchange, the Verandah, the Arcade, La Souciedad, the Empire, the Alhambra, the Fontine House, the St. Charles, the Aguila de Oro, La Varsouvienne, and many others. The first to open, and the best known, was the El Dorado, beckoning the miner "like a cool fountain beckons the thirsty wanderer in the desert." It was the forty-niner's dream castle. The original El Dorado had been a canvas tent, but within a year it had been transformed into a large square hall of rough-cut wood. Curtained booths were available for single gentlemen relaxing between faro and roulette in the arms of a nymph *du pavé*. The furniture was of baroque elegance. Ten large chandeliers hung from the ceiling. The backbar had large mirrors of fine cut glass. The walls were covered with "lascivious oil paintings of nudes in abandoned postures," according to one visitor. Another merely remarked "that these were the most relaxed nudes" he had ever seen.

At one end of the hall was a raised platform, draped with bunting, from which two alternating orchestras blared forth without interruption. All gambling saloons vied with each other in offering entertainment to lure customers. The El Dorado had a wheezy melodeon besides live performers. It also employed well-known soloists and dancers. An added attraction were short-skirted "pretty waiter girls." The bar was kept by the famous Jeremy Thomas, who was supposedly a greater attraction than the beautiful songstresses.

The main business, of course, was gambling, not drinking or wenching. The numerous gaming tables were heaped high with pokes of gold dust, nuggets, and coins. The El Dorado was so successful that it could afford a monthly rent of six thousand dollars. The whole trade was in metal—silver was slightly frowned upon, but paper was an abomination.

Gold dust was the standard medium of exchange. A pinch of dust, grasped between thumb and forefinger, was the price of a shot of whiskey; hence the question "How much can you raise in a pinch?" A man who "pinched well" could make himself some easy money. Every store, bar, and gaming table was furnished with a gold scale. The scale always rested on a small square of carpeting. By "carelessly" spilling a few tiny grains each time he weighed a quantity of gold dust and combing it out at the end of his shift, a bartender could "earn" himself twenty dollars a day on the sly.

A fellow was not supposed to have overlong fingernails when pinching or to dig too deep into a buckskin pouch or he'd find himself looking down the muzzle of a pistol.

The Verandah was a close competitor to the El Dorado. It gloried in floor-to-ceiling mirrors and red velvet curtains, and featured a one-man orchestra as its main attraction. The Aguila de Oro in 1849 advertised a "chorus of Ethiopians." The Alhambra featured a French lady violinist virtuoso who, on special occasions, performed Paganini compositions. Her daily wages consisted of two ounces of gold dust, worth thirty-two dollars. Well-pleased customers also threw nuggets and five-dollar gold coins at her feet. The Bella Union had a Mexican band, precursors of the mariachis, though its main star was a German violinist, Charley Schultze, who could make hardened prospectors weep. When he did his most famous number, "Flowers on My Sainted Mother's Grave," the Alhambra dissolved in tears.

Elegance spread quickly inland from the coast. At Rich Bar, another of the innumerable forty-niner gold camps, the Empire gambling-barroom was fitted out with "that eternal crimson calico," green baize tables, cut-glass mirrors, a flowered carpet, cigar vases, jars of brandied fruit, a backgammon board, and "a sickening pile of 'yellow-kivered' literature." Upholstered benches enabled tipsy gamblers to recover in comfort.

In the Rockies, "Pap" Wyman's saloon, at Leadville, Colorado, was a Mecca for miners from a hundred miles around. Pap's great saloon was a palace of pleasures—a saloon, a dance hall, a pretty waiter place, and a variety theater, but its main business was gambling. For the master of such a many-faceted emporium, Pap was an oddity. He had a conscience of sorts and strict morals to boot. Married men, especially fathers, were not allowed to gamble at his tables. Drunks who could not walk straight were not served at the bar. The girls were well mannered and well looked after by Pap. They might sit on a miner's lap stimulating him to order champagne, but the guest's hands were not allowed to fumble below the neck or above the knee. Vaudeville acts conformed to Victorian standards. Wyman kept a huge Bible chained to a pulpit next to the entrance, convenient for itinerant preachers.

Pap, who was said to have started as a preacher himself, was something of a showman. He believed in advertising. He wore brightly colored, flowered vests and carried his loose change in a purse made from a human scrotum. Every morning he invited Leadville's urchins to search his place, inside and out, for coins or gold kernels dropped by his patrons during the night. He generally scattered a few coins himself. He could afford it. His saloon, according to his own testimony, netted him $50,000 a year in spite of high wages he paid to his bardogs ($150 a month), gamblers ($10 a day; Pap did not lease his tables), actors ($75 a week), musicians ($35 per week), cooks (female, $25; male, $50; Pap seems to have been something of a sexist as an employer), and pretty waiter girls ($10 per week). The girls, of course, made their income from commissions on the drinks they sold. All these figures must be multiplied by five to approximate today's value.

By 1880 the gambling saloons in flourishing mining towns, such as Tombstone, Arizona, and Virginia City, Nevada, were all of the opulent kind with bartenders and chefs from New York and St. Louis, the mixologists boasting of being able to serve any drink known in the continental United States, the cooks taking pride in fashioning meals equal to any served in first-class places in the big eastern cities.

Before the railroads reached all over the West, immense cattle herds were driven overland from Texas and the Southwest to railheads in Kansas, beginning with Abilene in 1887. After homesteaders' fences had closed this trail, the railheads shifted to Dodge—the beautiful bibulous Babylon of the Plains—to Newton and Ellsworth, and finally to Ogallala, Nebraska. The roundups and trail drives took months. The cowboys were paid for the whole season in one lump sum. After weeks of hard, bone-crushing work, bad food, no liquor, and no entertainment, they were ready to blow their wad in one or two glorious weeks of carousing. The skinning houses were ready for them.

Kansas' most famous gambling saloon was the Alamo, on Abilene's Cedar Street, Wild Bill Hickok's headquarters when he was city marshal. The Alamo consisted of one very large room. Its street frontage was a full forty feet, and the saloon extended about 120 feet back. It had two entrances. The west, main entrance consisted of three magnificent double-glass doors which were never closed. The huge cavernous place was dominated by an ornate bar of polished, brass-trimmed mahogany with gleaming brass rails and knee-high cuspidors. Gambling tables covered the entire floor. Faro, monte, and poker were the popular games. The Bull's Head Saloon and the Applejack were also popular gambling places but couldn't hold a candle to the Alamo, possibly because of the latter's well-beaten and very short path to Abilene's foremost cat house.

In Dodge the Varieties was the best-known gambling palace. Here George Masterson, brother of Sheriff Bat, tended bar for a while, serving French brandies and bonded bourbon. In Newton it was Doc Thayer's Gold Rooms which took most of the gold. At Ellsworth, Joe Brennan's Saloon did its best to earn its nickname, "Gamblers' Roost." Famous or not so famous, all cowtown gambling saloons followed the same pattern. They were mostly rough, wooden false-front structures. The elegance, whatever there was of it, was inside; one has to take into account that the rapturous descriptions of their sybaritic luxuriousness came mostly from cowhands "who had seen nothing but cows' asses for weeks on end." They were essentially long and gloomy caves, getting darker the farther one penetrated. The bars were splendid, though, and the money real enough.

Cowboys, in the trail-driving days, were a raucous lot, more dangerous when drunk than the miners. Running a bank or a poker game in a cowtown took a special kind of man, and the professional gamblers were indeed a species unto themselves. Possibly their main characteristic was a penchant for easy living and an absolute aversion to work. George Devol, a gambler by trade for over forty years, remembered what made him become one:

I met my brother Paul, who was working at calking steamboats. He coaxed me to stay with him, saying he would teach me the trade. I consented, and soon was able to earn $4 per day. We . . . made a good deal of money; but every Monday morning I went to work broke. I became infatuated with the game of faro, and it kept me a slave. So I concluded either to quit work or quit gambling. I studied the matter over for a long time. At last one day while we were finishing a boat that we had calked . . . I gave my tools a push with my foot, and they all went into the river. My brother called out and asked me what I was doing. I looked up, a little

"Running a faro bank took a special kind of man."

sheepish, and said it was the last lick of work I would ever do. He was surprised . . . and asked me what I intended to do. I told him I intended to live off fools and suckers. I also said: "I will make money rain"; and I did come near doing as I said.

The gambler, from about 1850 to 1880, was among the aristocrats of western society. In the words of Bat Masterson, "Gambling was a respected profession, almost equal in rank to medicine and a lot higher than dentistry and undertaking." Many western gamblers had come from Mississippi steamboats, from New Orleans' Swamp section, from Natchez Plantations, from the Old Dominion, and from Chicago's Sand District. Not a few were ex-Johnny-rebs, some even former Confederate majors and colonels who, so they said, had gone west to avoid being interfered with by carpetbaggers. They all considered themselves gentlemen. What was acceptable behavior for a gentleman in mid-nineteenth-century America was somewhat different from what it is now. Consider the case of Dick Hargraves, son of a respectable and wealthy London squire. As a sixteen-year-old runaway he arrived in New Orleans in 1844. For a while he worked on riverboats tending bar. He won twenty-five thousand dollars in a poker game with a Louisiana cotton planter, took this as an omen, and became a faro dealer. He was trusted to run a straight game, saying that the odds favored the house in any case and made it unnecessary for a gent to *corriger la fortune*. Like all faro dealers, Hargraves was a womanizer and flashy dresser. He always wore a black suit, frilled snowy shirts, and brocaded vests. Surprised in a compromising situation with the wife of a New Orleans banker, he fought a duel with bowie knives that resulted in the death of the unfortunate cuckold. The lady's brother swore an oath that he would kill Hargraves on sight. They met in a Natchez gambling saloon, Hargraves dispatching his antagonist with his bare fists. That same night the woman, who had followed Hargraves,

slipped a knife under the pillow and, embracing the gambler, plunged it into his chest. She then stabbed herself and died. Hargraves survived to fight with distinction in the Civil War, winding up as a major in Abe Lincoln's army, living proof that a somewhat checkered past was then no barrier to social advancement. He eventually retired to Denver, boasting that as a gambler he had seen two million dollars cross his table. Again, true to form, he died of the gambler's disease—consumption.

They were all finicky dressers. Colorado Charlie Utter, a famous gambler and boon companion of Wild Bill Hickok,

always appeared in evening dress, with a silk hat, beneath which was coiled his long, yellow hair. When dealing bank or sitting in the "lookout" chair, he permitted his blond tresses to hang loose over his shoulders. A fortune in diamonds flamed in his shirt front, the broad expanse of which was studded with other precious stones. The buttons on his coat and cuffs were ten dollar gold pieces and on his vest five dollar gold pieces. And all these were set with diamonds.

Whenever Charlie was broke he was able to raise considerable sums with this outfit as collateral.

The westerner was given to exaggeration. Everything in his description grew bigger, vaster, and more grandiose. He himself was a walking exaggeration. This probably accounts a little for the image painted of the dandy-gambler. A more skeptical New Yorker, writing for *Scribner's Magazine* about his experiences in Leadville, remarked:

The traditional gambler, tall, slim, well-dressed, clerical-looking, with sharp features, thin, firmly set lips and iron nerve, is not here. I never saw him but once in all the west. The dealers are impassive enough, but that is habit and natural stolidity. They have nerve enough, but that is the courage of the rowdy.

But perhaps this is exaggeration in reverse. Possibly the easterner had a conception of elegance different from that of the frontiersman.

Snobbery existed within the fraternity. It was principally the faro dealers, and to a lesser extent the holders of lansquenet and Spanish monte banks, who made up the flashily dressed upper stratum of gambling society. Why this was so is hard to say. Dealing at faro took less skill than running many other games. "Any boy could do it." Possibly the faro dealer was esteemed because the odds favoring the bank were marginal. A player had an almost even chance—in a straight game. The faro dealers were, in any case, outnumbered by the multitude of jacklegs, bunko steerers, three-card monte artists, and tinhorn gamblers who formed the brotherhood's lowest stratum. These were neither well dressed nor gentlemanly, even by frontier standards. All agreed that the tinhorns were the scum of the earth. The deadly, fastidious, softhanded, and nimble-fingered gambler did exist, though, in fair numbers. The notorious, much romanticized Doc Holliday could serve as the prototype.

John Henry Holliday was born 1852, in Georgia, son of Major Henry B. Holliday, a lawyer, officer, and gentleman, who served in both the Mexican and the Civil wars. Holliday's mother was remembered as "a gentlewoman who played the piano beautifully." The future gambling man and gunfighter was therefore something of a southern blueblood. By the age of twelve he had acquired a reputation for straight shooting. It was said that with a pistol he could "shoot the eyes out of a rabbit when the rabbit would look at you before he started running." The young John Henry chose dentistry as his profession, a step down the social ladder, but not too far down. Being a dentist earned him his nickname "Doc." He went west for his health. This has to be understood in two ways. As a youngster Doc was stricken with tuberculosis, a common plight among southerners of his generation because of near starvation during the Civil War and its aftermath. This condition was later aggravated by his

gambling life, the days and nights in dark, smoke-filled rooms, the forty-eight-hour card games on a diet of black coffee, too much hard stuff, and cheroots. Consumption was an occupational disease and in most cases incurable. This gave the tubercular gambler an edge in a showdown. He knew he was going to die sooner or later, so what if it was sooner?

The second reason for Doc's departure for points west was that he had fired his pistol at some black youths who presumed to go swimming in the same river with him. By some accounts he killed one of them. And so Doc joined the legion of disgruntled "Southron gams." In 1872 he followed the iron horse to Dallas, Texas, then swarming with thousands of railroad construction men. Like most gamblers, who were the gypsies of

Doc Holliday.

the West, drifting from place to place, to a new mining camp or a cattle trail's terminus, swooping down wherever a herd of sheep was waiting to be fleeced, Doc left his traces all over the frontier—in Arizona, Colorado, Kansas, and South Dakota.

True to type, Doc was a fastidious dresser. Photographs show him with a stiff wing collar and a small, stylish bow tie. His suits were impeccable, black and conservative. He wore a vest even in hot weather. His sunken cheeks were partially covered by a luxuriant handlebar mustache. His hair, carefully pomaded, was slicked up into a jaunty curl.

He hung out his shingle in many places, promising to extract teeth painlessly and to refund the money to dissatisfied customers. But dentistry was only a sideline. His main, and in the end only, profession was gambling.

He was a killer. He had to be. In line with the requirements of his surroundings he carried revolvers, a small derringer, and an "Arkansas toothpick"—a thin sheath knife dangling from a string between his shoulderblades. Unlike the amateur gambler who could take his losses in stride, the pro had to win more often than he lost or he did not eat. Not all amateurs showed the required equanimity when losing heavily. They were apt to seize the dealer by the throat, sticking a pistol in his face while going for the pot. Their excuse was, of course, that the dealer had cheated. Probably he had. In order to live, he had to win. If he wanted to win, he had to give Dame Fortune a helping hand. Doc was no exception. He was proud of his skill in manipulating the cards. The code he lived by saw nothing wrong in this. The dexterous gent was admired. It was only the clumsy tinhorn who tried to deal from the bottom who was despised. Even if the pro cheated, he was sure that the greenhorn had not detected it, but merely *believed* himself cheated when his three aces were beaten by a full house. Having no proof, he was in the wrong. Once a dealer backed out in

a confrontation he was through. Hence the violence. Holliday supposedly killed thirty-eight men. The actual number might be less than half that, but it was substantial. Doc killed without compunction and often with little provocation. If the victim was a well-liked local character, Doc had to move on in a hurry. In many cases there was no prosecution. By the code of the time, a man accused of cheating, or being challenged to fight, had a perfect right to bring about the prompt demise of his assailant. Holliday by his own account practiced the fast draw as well as target shooting. At the O.K. Corral he used a shotgun. That dealers' hands were quick Doc proved in a fight with a man called Ed Bailey at Fort Griffin. The two had been playing poker. Being top dog locally, Bailey took certain liberties. He repeatedly looked at the discards, the so-called deadwood. This was decidedly bad manners. By getting a peek at an opponent's deadwood, a man found out what cards he did not hold, thereby gaining an advantage. A player whose discards had thus been peeked at had the right to take the pot without showing his hand. Doc admonished Bailey a few times "to play poker"—in professional parlance a warning to play by the rules. When this had no effect he quietly reached for the pot. Bailey went for his gun, Holliday for his knife. Before Bailey could get off a shot, Doc caught him below the ribs, practically disemboweling Bailey. It was one of two authenticated cases in which Doc's knife was faster than a six-shooter. It should be said in defense of Doc's character that he never killed a man until he had assured himself that he was "heeled"—that is, armed.

Doc, like many gamblers, prided himself on being a lady killer and openly set up house with his inamoratas without benefit of clergy. Big Nose Kate, a somewhat wilted flower of the prairie, had the longest stand. Doc died of consumption at Glenwood Springs, Colorado, in 1887, at the early age of thirty-five. The words on his headstone read:

DOC HOLLIDAY 1852–1887
HE DIED IN BED

Wyatt Earp, who had been his good friend and comrade at the O.K. Corral shoot-out, wrote later that

Doc was a dentist whom necessity had made a gambler; a gentleman whom disease had made a frontier vagabond; a philosopher whom life had made a caustic wit; a long, lean ash-blond fellow nearly dead with consumption, and at the same time the most skillful gambler and the nerviest, speediest, deadliest man with a six-gun I ever knew.

Wyatt Earp himself dealt faro in Dodge's Long Branch Saloon at night, while working as a peace officer during the day.

It was part of the legend about gamblers like Doc Holliday that they were generous, veritable guardian angels to widows and orphans, the Robin Hoods of the early West. Some were indeed generous. They had the money to be; besides it was good public relations and also raised one's ego. In the words of Alfred Henry Lewis:

Of course, a kyard sharp can make benevolences an' lavish dust on the needy on the side, but when it gets to a game for money, he can't afford no ruthfulness that a-way, tryin' not to hurt the sore people. He must play his system through, an' with no more conscience than cows, no matter who's run down in the stampede.

Still, they were generous after their own fashion. When a Methodist preacher arrived in the mining town of Creede, Colorado, and made known his intention to build a church, Browney Lee, a well-known gambler, invited the divine to the huge Watrous Gambling Saloon and introduced him to the crowd. After the sermon, which the man of God delivered standing on a pool table, about a hundred dollars was collected. "Hell!" cried Lee. "That won't build no church!" He took the money to the nearest faro table and there parlayed it into eight hundred dollars, which he handed with great flourish to the pleasantly surprised divine.

A faro dealer shot a friend and colleague during a sudden quarrel over cards. The killer immediately assumed the costs of a lavish funeral, bought the most expensive coffin available, hired a brass band of sturdy German miners to play Teutonic funeral marches, had himself let out of jail on bond as the chief mourner, and invited the entire male population of the camp to "step up to the bar and liquor at my expense," at the conclusion of this solemn ritual.

Gamblers were soft on women. Wives whose chicken-brained husbands had blown all the family's money on three-card monte sometimes made the tinhorn disgorge his winnings if they shed enough tears. Kids not quite dry behind the ears were shown mercy on occasion. A Victorian lady writing in the 1850s called gamblers the "knights of the green table," and described a young gamester she knew as toting little children around on his shoulders and distributing bright silver dollars among street urchins.

By no means all comments were favorable. A Canadian traveler, William Perkins, wrote about the dealers at Sonora, California:

They are the curse of this country; disreputable scoundrels who are ready for any act of atrocity. Nine tenths of the murders committed in California . . . have been committed by these ruffians; many of them once respectable members of the communities from whence they came, but brutalized by their habits and associations in this country. They form the most black guard and dangerous phase in the society of California.

The professionals could certainly be callous. The actor Eddie Foy, when playing in Tombstone,

Arizona, saw the gambler Lou Rickabaugh shoot an obstreperous drunk and order the body to be thrown out into the muddy street without interrupting his game. Johnny Ringo once killed a man who insisted on sticking to his beer after he had offered him champagne. In 1860 a faro dealer in the Southwest sold a Negro gambler who could not cover his bets into slavery. And the professionals certainly had pull. Dodge, the wicked city, was run by gamblers and saloon keepers who took turns being mayor. In 1878 they enacted a law against gambling. It didn't close down the games, but it did stop suckers from complaining about having been cheated. If they did they wound up in the calaboose for having broken the law. In some Kansas cowtowns the sheriffs and deputies were paid out of a fund raised by the gamblers—"when the dealer talked the sheriff listened."

Nobody ever took a census of the professionals who plied their trade in the West between 1850 and 1880, the gamblers' halcyon years. During the gold rush, San Francisco supported some three hundred gamblers. Among the Kansas cowtowns, Dodge kept a hundred and fifty professionals in beef and booze, Newton eighty, and little Ellsworth seventy-five. Chicago, at the end of the century, harbored twenty-thousand men who, in one form or other, maintained themselves by gambling. Of course, the same gamblers showed up in various places at different times.

The paladins of the green cloth played no mean part in western history. In their day they traveled the great circuit, from the Mexican border to the Canadian and from the Mississippi to the Pacific, unstable as fleas. They carried huge sums of money wherever they went, ready to bank games of any size. As the fancy took them, they also moonlighted as saloon keepers, bartenders, whiskey makers, prospectors, lawmen, smugglers, entertainers, or operators of hog ranches. Though some of them won hundreds of thousands of dollars from suckers during a lifetime career, most of them died broke. Last, but not least, they kept a generation of writers and newspapermen busy.

Was it because they so admired women that the professionals admitted members of the fair sex into their ranks? A surprisingly large number of lady gamblers managed to elbow their way into the macho world of the gambler, competing with men on an equal basis. One writer commented that the lady gamblers were in fact victims of a particular form of sexism, that they were used as come-ons by the men who were in control of the game. The women, he remarked, were possibly less skillful than men when running a bank, "but when a shill displayed herself to woman-hungry men, the lambs came more willingly to the slaughter and hardly noticed their losses at all." This theory is contradicted by the number of lady dealers who were extraordinarily adept at the game, with a courage that was in no way inferior to that shown by male dealers. Some of them had fame, eccentricity, and an ego equal to that of Doc Holliday, Wild Bill Hickok, or George Devol. Nor is it true that their sex always shielded them from physical assault. They might be given special consideration in a plush Frisco gambling palace, or a private club in Sheridan frequented exclusively by the cattle squirarchy, but in most places a gambling woman had to know how to take care of herself.

In gold rush California the majority of lansquenet tables were owned and run by French women. The first of these was Mademoiselle Simone Jules, described as "most beautiful, with ivory skin, lips of cherrywine, and enormous, coal-black eyes." Mlle Simone did such a land-office business for her house, the Bella Union, that soon all the first-class skinning houses in San Francisco leased their tables on commission to ladies, for the most part "recently at Paris." Mlle Simone was said to be as handy with "a deck of cards, a pistol, or a horsewhip as any man." As cool and collected as Simone was Mademoiselle Virginie, who saw two men, named Ford and Coffman, killed over a quarrel arising at her table. According to a contemporary, William Perkins:

I then paid a visit to the beautiful Mlle. Virginie, whom I found calmly continuing her game as if nothing had happened. She greeted me with a fascinating smile.
"Ah Monsieur, quel horreur!" turning up her brilliant eyes towards the roof and dealing slowly the cards at the same time.
I made her describe the circumstances to me, which she did with all the calmness she would have evinced had she been relating a scene from a novel. To me, her delicate white hands seemed smeared with blood and I left in disgust.

Newspapers lamented that the gambling hall was no place for women on either side of the table, but to no avail. At Santa Fe during the 1840s, Gertrude Barcelo was the reigning gambling queen. She suffered no equal—either male or female—and was said to be the most expert monte dealer of her generation. Originally a Taos prostitute known as La Tules, she managed to invest money earned in bed and at cards in a gambling saloon which soon became the social center in town. Immensely rich and stately, wearing diamonds and rubies on every finger, a massive cross of gold on her ample bosom, a servant used as a human footstool beneath her brocaded slippers, Gertrude's purple past was quickly forgiven and forgotten. Churchmen, army officers, and politicians felt themselves honored when invited to call. In time she became the town's foremost almsgiver and patroness of charities. Obese in middle age, she fell victim to fattening of the arteries. Her funeral was celebrated with befitting pomp as all the town's dignitaries solemnly followed her bier.

In a class by herself was Madame Vestal, the

La Tules.

"goddess of chance," who had started out in life as La Belle Siddons, a Confederate spy, "Jeff Davis' Mata Hari." As the most accomplished blackjack dealer west of the Missouri, she operated a tent-saloon skinning house on Denver's Blake Street, where the men thronging her bank pleaded: "Hit me again, ma'am!" When her lover, Archie McLaughlin, a gambler and noted road agent, was strung up by a mob of irate miners whom he had "relieved" of their earnings, Madame Vestal took it so hard that she swallowed poison, which, however, failed to kill her. She began hitting the bottle and faded from view, but not from memory.

It should be noted that gamblers, when coming to the end of the road, invariably blew their brains out with a derringer. Miners preferred clamping a stick of dynamite between their teeth and lighting the fuse, but lady gamblers either swallowed poison or jumped into the river in order to look pretty and undisfigured even in death.

The most famous "lady gams" were Madame Eleanor Dumont, also known as Madame Mus-

Madame Mustache—"She knew how to defend herself."

tache, and "Poker Alice" Ivers. French-born Mme Dumont started an elegant gambling saloon in 1850 at Nevada City. On opening night free champagne in unlimited quantities was served to all customers, and her place was a smashing success. Eleanor Dumont was at that time described as very pretty, dark-haired, and charmingly French. Every inch a lady, she allowed no profanity or ill behavior in her establishment.

She shifted her operations from camp to camp, following the gold and silver strikes, and when the Nevada mining boom collapsed, she drifted to Montana, New Mexico, and Colorado City, picking up several lovers along the way. She knew how to defend herself with horsewhip or pistol if the situation demanded it. The pickings grew slimmer as she grew older and lost her good looks. A luxurious sprouting of hair on her upper lip earned her the nickname of "Madame Mustache." She turned madam, running a parlor house in Eureka, Nevada, and ended up in Bodie, the wicked Hell-

dorado, losing whatever little money she had left in a faro game. Discouraged, she finished her career by making herself a cocktail—half champagne and half prussic acid.

English-born "Poker Alice" found herself alone in Denver after the Civil War, a penniless widow while still in her early twenties. In desperation she took a job dealing cards in a saloon and discovered her talents as a gambler. She soon was making twenty-five dollars a night at a time when a cowhand's wages were thirty dollars a month.

In the manner of male gamblers, she made the circuit of the mining camps, working up and down the line from Canada to Mexico. Sometimes she struck it rich, more often she was down to her last dollar. She began packing a pistol and took to smoking thick, strong cigars. When drunken cavalrymen tried to wreck her place she shot one of them dead. She outlived three husbands, and finally ran a bawdy house. Moralistic after her own manner, she would not allow her girls to work on

Sundays. She herself never touched playing cards on the Sabbath. In later life, with a stogie perpetually stuck in one corner of her mouth, she looked like Winston Churchill in a blouse with his hair done up in a bun. She finally cashed in her chips in 1930, at the ripe old age of seventy-eight.

The amateur gamblers on the far side of the table were very different from the professionals. One has to picture the West in the years from 1850 to 1875, when it was populated almost exclusively by bachelors with money in their pockets and nothing to spend it on at night except drinking, gambling, and whoring, of which pastimes gambling was the most expensive. Whiskey helped to lead the lambs to the slaughter. Frisco dealers ordered free drinks for big bettors to loosen lingering inhibitions: "Hey bartender, six brandy mashes and three cherry cobblers for these gentlemen, on the double! On my bill! Hurry up. Don't hold up the game!"

Each dealer had his own spiel to attract the greenies:

Come down! Come down! Come down on the red! On the black! Make your pile today, gents. Make it quick. Why work? The money's here! The money's yours! Walk up, gents, walk up, get it while it lasts! Step up, step up, step lively—

At Deadwood the spiel was:

Come on up, boys, and put your money down—everybody beats the old man—the girls all beat the old man—the boys all beat the old man—everybody beats the old man—forty years a gambler—the old fool—everybody beats the old man—put your money down, boys, and beat the old man.

But it was the old fool who always wound up with money.

The amateurs were a mixed and colorful crowd. In California, before the gold rush, they were almost exclusively Mexicans and mestizos with now and then a rare sailor among them. Gold made California cosmopolitan overnight. Gambling crowds consisted of Yankees, "greasers," Britons, Spaniards, Portuguese, Polynesians, "heathen Chinees," Chileans, "frogs," Indians, and blacks all talking in their native languages. Unlike the professionals, the forty-niners favored luxurious beards if they could raise them. Crowns were adorned by every kind of headgear known to man, from tall silk hats to wide-brimmed, flat "slouches," black felts, sailors' and stocking caps, berets, sombreros, and bandannas. In New Mexico, according to an old-timer, the gamblers were mostly cowboys and cattlemen at Las Vegas; at Socorro, miners and prospectors; at Albuquerque, men of all kinds with a leavening of hacendados; at Santa Fe, politicians, military gentlemen, and priests; in Taos, desperadoes—and always a few timid Chinese keeping in the background.

Gambling was the great equalizer. In a Sheridan gambling-saloon a British rancher was told: "You may be a son of a lord back in England, but that ain't what you are here!" Everybody's money was good, even that of ladies and children. In 1851, a reporter in California saw an eleven-year-old boy bucking the tiger:

"All down, gents?" inquired the dealer, as he rapped his knuckles on the table.

"Hold on!" exclaimed a shrill, puerile voice, as if coming from under the table. Everyone looked down; and there was a curly-headed boy, whose mouth was little above the level of the bank. He cautiously, coolly and methodically thrust forth a small hand, and laid down two dimes upon the ace. Everyone laughed—all but the dealer, who with the same placidity thrust back the dimes and dampened the little fellow's ardor by observing: "We don't take dimes at this bank."

But no, the little fellow had spunk; he was not so easily dashed. Picking up his dimes, his hand suddenly reappeared, this time holding a very weighty buckskin bag apparently filled with yellow dust. This he tossed upon the ace, exclaiming:

"There! I guess you'll take that six ounces on the ace!"

Everyone was astonished. All looked around to see if he had any relatives or friends in the crowd. He appeared to be entirely alone; but the game began—and, strange to say, the ace won!

For hours the boy bucked the bank until he had won two hundred ounces. Advised to stop while he was a small fortune ahead he coolly replied: "I'll break that bank or it'll break me!" The reporter went on:

This would decide the game. A stillness as of death was upon the crowd; our very hearts almost ceased to beat; even the banker wiped the cold drops from his brow . . . calmly, steadily, and without hurry the cards were drawn, one by one. . . . He had lost! The queen had thrown him; and his entire winnings were ruthlessly swept away by the sharp croupier beyond.

Dizzy and sick with the result, we turned our eyes upon the loser. . . . He looked about him with a stern, defying air, as if to chide us for our sympathy. As yet he had lost nothing; his large buckskin bag was still intact. Laying it upon the table, with the air of a Caesar, he put his all upon the throw, defying fate to do her worst! Our pity was suddenly changed to admiration. . . .

The cards were again shuffled and cut. The seven and the king were laid out; the boy chose the king. The cards were drawn; at last the seven appeared . . . and he saw his well-filled purse stowed away along with many others and, whistling "O Californy," turned his back upon the scene."

The reporter followed him and gave him a few dollars to feed himself. The boy accepted with a grin and confided to his benefactor that the buckskin pouch, which had been his original stake, was not filled with gold dust but with buckshot, and that the laugh was on the dealer.

The ideal of the amateur gambler was a man who went the limit in everything he did, who could lose a fortune at faro or poker and never bat an eye, a man who did not smile when he won, who spent freely and treated the crowd after a good spell at cards, a man who did not do his loving on the sly, but who picked the best-looking sporting girl and paid her lavishly. Such a man's check was good everywhere and for any amount, and if he ran out of money, his bets were accepted on his word.

Tales of fabulous sums won and lost were often exaggerated. The majority of gamblers bet only small sums and often as not played for drinks. A faro dealer needed a capital of from five hundred to ten thousand dollars or more, depending on the limit placed on bets. This limit, in Rocky Mountain camps, was usually twenty-five dollars a card, but there were banks in Denver, Leadville, and Central City that had no limit at all, where a man could, at least in theory, risk ten thousand dollars on the turn of a single card. In most mining towns the minimum bet was a two-bit white chip, sold in stacks of twenty at five dollars. Red chips were a dollar a piece, blue chips ten dollars. Yellow chips had an arbitrary value of from fifty to a hundred dollars each. Individual faro banks in Leadville netted an average of a thousand dollars per month, though some made a profit of ten times that much.

In 1888, Edward O. Wolcott, a candidate for the U.S. Senate, lost twenty-two thousand dollars in an all-night poker game at Ed West's Denver saloon. Criticized for this by his opponent, he answered in the *Rocky Mountain News* that his gambling was "nobody's business but my own, and besides, I had won the money at the races the day previous." Wolcott won the election—Colorado voters loved a plucky poker player. At Virginia City, Nevada, ranchman Joe Timberlake strode into a gambling saloon saying: "Give me a stack of thousand-dollar chips," and promptly lost forty-two thousand dollars at faro.

The biggest poker match ever played was between Isaac Jackson, a Texas cattleman, and John

Dougherty, a famous Arizona gambler, in Bowen's Saloon at Santa Fe. It is said that at one time the pot contained over one hundred thousand dollars in cash. The match ended in something of a draw, but with Dougherty ahead. He at least treated the crowd of three hundred onlookers.

One of the smaller pots was lost by "Fat Jack" Jones, in Butte, Montana, who staked and lost his set of false teeth.

Almost numberless were the games that lured the greenhorn—faro, also called tiger; draw and stud poker; roulette, also known as rouge-et-noir and chusa, Napoleon's favorite game; Spanish monte; twenty-one, also called blackjack or vingt-et-un; keno; lansquenet; seven-up; casino; chuck-a-luck; paddle-wheel; euchre; pedro; whist; backgammon; equality; the tobacco box game; old sledge; red dog; hieronymus; tarantula; wheel of fortune; craps; horsehead; Australian pooloo; highball; fantan; three-card monte; banco or bunco; and the nutshell and thimble games. Many of these games were regional. The miners' favorite was faro, the cowmen's poker. Games demanding either skill or intelligence were not popular. The miners and trail herders were in a hurry to win or lose without taxing their brains. A game's popularity depended on the time, place, and ethnic origin of the players. Whist and euchre were played by staid settlers of the early Midwest frontier. Roulette and lansquenet were favorites among the French in California, but did not catch on in the raw mining camps of the Rockies; roulette with its wheels and complicated layouts was more at home in a Sonora or San Francisco gambling palace than in a Colorado log cabin saloon. The variety of roulette called chusa was in favor among Mexicans and Yanquis at Tucson and Phoenix to the banker's cries: "Make yer little bets, gents; make yer little bets; all's set 'n the ball's a-rollin'." Horsehead was played in Kansas

cowtowns, hieronymus was the favorite in southwestern Colorado. Dice were almost unknown in Kansas railhead saloons, where both faro and poker thrived mightily. Lansquenet, forbidden in Paris because it led to too many bloody quarrels, was dealt mostly by French men and women.

Faro was the prestige game and the most popular, because it offered an exciting spectacle to the onlookers and gave a player an almost even chance. It was the "square" or "straight" game, since it was generally believed—erroneously—that it was proof against manipulation. Its name derived from pharaoh or pharo, the image of an Egyptian king on the back of the cards or, as some said, because in France, where the game originated in the eighteenth century, the king of hearts was also known as pharaoh. The box from which the cards were dealt traditionally had a tiger painted on its lid, hence "bucking the tiger" meant betting against the faro bank. After shuffling and cutting a full deck, the cards were put into the box. The top card was called "soda," the last "hoc." Both paid nothing. Cards were drawn from a slit in the side of the case in pairs face up. Each pair drawn was called a turn. Every card from ace to king was painted on the table on a wax cloth—the so-called layout. Players placed their chips or dollars on the card of their choice. If the card a man had bet on was drawn first, he lost. If it came up second, he won; and if neither he could bet again. The dealer raked in, and paid off each turn. There were twenty-five turns from soda to hoc, after which the game began anew.

Cards already drawn were exhibited by the dealer's casekeeper, who kept track of the game and gave the players, called punts or producers, a chance to figure out the odds as the game progressed. The producers generally played "straight up," betting on a single card to win or lose; if to lose, they "coppered their bet" by placing a Chinese copper token on their chips. Professionals

Above: Making the turn—the critical moment in a faro game.
Below: The Keno goose.

usually "coppered the heel" by playing several cards at once. In the larger gambling saloons the dealer also employed a "lookout" perched on a high stool, watching for trouble generally, and specifically for a player shifting his chips while the cards were drawn.

Spanish monte, faro's close rival, was a card game that came to California from Spain via Mexico and was played with extrathin cards—forty to a deck. The suits were clubs, swords, suns, and cups. Among the cards was a king, a knave, and—instead of the queen—a mounted knight. It resembled the modern game of "21," in that the players bet against the dealer, who first turned up two cards—the layout—and then another. The players bet on whether the third card, the "gate," matched either of the layout cards.

Keno was another popular game among miners, similar to modern bingo. Numbers were drawn from a bird-shaped cage called the keno goose. Players placed their bets on numbers shown on a layout. There was always the triumphant cry of "Keno!" when the right number came up. Mostly it was the dealer who wound up with the goose's golden egg. Keno is still played in Nevada.

Chuck-a-luck was widely played throughout the West. Of English origin, it was brought to America about 1800. Three dice were tumbled in a bottle-shaped wire contraption called the chuck cage. You could bet with an even chance that your number would show on one of the dice, or bet on combinations with odds as high as 180 to 1. The chuck cage was also called the tinhorn, hence the expression "tinhorn gambler"—a hint that chuck operators were not held in great esteem. They were, as a matter of fact, not allowed to mingle with the snobbish faro dealers.

Poker was the equal of faro. A story, supposedly true and often embroidered, tells of a Denver bank teller faced with three worn-out-looking citizens when he opened the bank one morning, one of them clutching an envelope to his breast.

"I want to negotiate a loan," declared the man with the envelope.

"Upon what collateral?" asked the teller.

The man explained that he had sat in an all-night poker game with the other two. There were almost five thousand dollars in the pot with everybody holding a good hand. He had run out of money and been given half an hour to raise five thousand dollars to "see" the others. He wanted to get the loan on his hand, which was in the envelope. The teller could have a peek, but of course not his fellow players, who had come along to watch that the cards in the envelope were not monkeyed with.

"What an idea, my dear sir," objected the bank clerk. "We don't lend money on cards."

"But you ain't goin' to see me raised out on a hand like this," moaned the gambler, letting the teller have a peek at his hand—four kings and an ace. "These gents think I'm bluffing, and here I could clean them out!"

"That's too bad," said the teller. The sad gambler was about to leave when the bank's president walked in and inquired about his lamentations. Being shown the cards, he immediately authorized a cash loan of five thousand dollars.

"Don't you have any sense?" he lectured his cringing employee. "Don't you even play poker?"

"No, sir."

"Ah, I thought so. If you did, you'd know what good collateral was. Remember now, four kings and an ace are always good in this bank for our entire assets, sir, our entire assets!"

Some games were nothing more than simple sleight-of-hand tricks and were not taken seriously by more sophisticated sports. Foremost among them was three-card monte, not to be confused with Spanish monte. The monte artist operated

Three-card monte—which gave the sucker no chance at all.

with three cards, one of them the ace of hearts—the eagle bird, baby, or winning card. He would show the sucker the ace, substitute the card behind it, and with lightning speed throw the cards face down on the table. The greenie had to guess which of them was the ace. This seemed to give the sucker one chance in three; in reality no chance at all. If the sucker got wise to the substitution, the dealer instead "accidentally" turned up a corner of the ace. Now the sucker was sure to outswindle the swindler. But no, the monte sharp had deftly flattened out the ace's corner and turned up that of another card, and the sucker lost again. The "thrower" always worked with a "capper," who won hugely and loudly, proclaiming that a little boy could pick out the baby card every time, thus luring the fish into the net. Monte throwers had their own spiel:

Here you are, gentlemen; this ace of hearts is the winning card. Follow it with your eyes as I shuffle. Here it is, and now here, now here, and now—where? You win if you point it out the first time; but if you miss, you lose. Here it is, you see; now watch it again. This ace of hearts, gentlemen, is the winning card. I take no bets from paupers, cripples, or orphan children.

The ace of hearts. It is my regular trade, gentlemen, to move my hands quicker than your eyes. I always have two chances to your one. The ace of hearts. If your sight is quick enough, you beat me and I pay; if not, I beat you and take your money. The ace of hearts—who will go me twenty?

It is surprising that such flimflam games attracted numberless tenderfeet, some of whom wagered thousands of dollars trying to pick out the "baby." George Devol conned a minister out of his church building fund of two thousand dollars, and his watch and chain to boot. He generously gave him his "ticker" and a hundred dollars back when he saw the victim on his knees, praying and weeping. Oddly enough, three-card is now played widely in New York. Every weekend one can see dozens of throwers busy at their tables in Central Park or on crowded corners with no lack of suckers.

Closely related to three-card monte were the old nutshell and thimble games. Here the tenderfoot had to pick one of three nutshells or thimbles under which a pea was hidden. Bunco was another con game, rigged in such a way that the sucker was bound to lose every time. It was essentially a numbers game played with a board, a sort of crooked bingo. Soapy Smith, the "King of the thimbleriggers and short-card artists," sold fifty-cent soap for five dollars. The come-on was that he pretended to wrap a fifty-dollar bill around one cake of soap:

Now, gentlemen, you will see that I have here a $50 bill which I wrap around this package of soap . . . so . . . and around which I place a piece of paper in this way, so the edge of the bill will stick out . . . so . . . and to further convince you that there is no fraud or deception to this, I will make a mark on the paper . . . so . . . and drop it in the box and mix it with the others so you can see the mark. . . . Now, who will give me $5 for the privilege of picking it out of the pile?

No sucker ever managed to pick that particular cake of soap.

The gambler's attitude toward his victim was epitomized by George Devol, who despised "kickers," that is, bad losers:

All men that bet should not be classed as gamblers, for some *THINGS* that style themselves *MEN* will bet (to win of course), and kick if they lose, which a gambler will never do, although he may sometimes be sucker enough to bet (to win) against a sure thing, like old monte or a brace game.

There were, however, more kickers than gamblers, and all over the West similarly worded post-

ers were seen prominently displayed in cowtowns and mining camps:

WARNING!

A word to the wise should be sufficient. All bunko steerers, confidence sharks, sure-thing men, thimble-riggers, and monte-throwers. You are not wanted here and will practice your tricks at your peril.

Prompt action will be taken!
Signed: The Committee of Honest Citizens

This never intimidated the sure-thing men for long, though a few of them were occasionally tarred and feathered, shot or even hung. It was part of the risk of their trade.

The thimbleriggers could be shrugged off; they were after all low-down, aig-suckin' no-account skunks, and if someone was dumb enough to be taken in by their spiels, he deserved to be cleaned out down to his socks. But poker players or faro dealers who ran crooked games were something else. They were supposed to be on the square, and of course were not. In the words of a Deadwood citizen: "That rara avis, the square gambler, and his associate, the law-abiding saloon keeper, were not much in evidence in any of the town." The games, said another old-timer, were "as crooked as a dog's hindlegs."

A regular industry existed in support of the dishonest gambler. The firm of E. M. Grandine, at 41 Liberty Street, New York City, marketed so-called advantage—that is, marked—playing cards. With these a professional could easily read every card by looking at its back. Advantage cards sold for one dollar a pack, or ten dollars a dozen. Doctor Cross & Co. manufactured marked decks in New Orleans from 1837 on. By 1850 half a dozen firms manufactured advantage cards, advertising their products openly in newspapers. Well-known back designs included calico, endless vine, stars, marble, perpetuum mobile, and mille fleurs. No experienced player would engage in a game where decks with complicated, busy back designs were used. Grandine also advertised loaded dice of the best ivory, at five dollars for a set of nine.

Loaded dice and marked cards in no way exhausted the inventive genius of such firms as Grandine. They produced a whole catalog of cheating devices, some simple, others veritable Rube Goldberg contraptions. Among these were "bags," which could be surreptitiously fastened to the underside of a table, and into and from which cards could be inserted or drawn at will. A friend in need was a sleeve or vest "hold-out." The simplest was a rubber device up the gambler's sleeve. A vest hold-out came with the direction: "The hand is held close to the body with the cards outspread while a string is pulled, and in that manner a card is shot into the hands under cover of the remaining cards." Thus the American language was enriched by expressions such as "pulling a string on someone," or "playing it close to the vest." "Bugs utterly defying detection" were devices for coming up with that extra ace. Some of the firms involved in this trade also retailed concealed weapons, such as derringers that fitted neatly into a palm or a vest pocket, belt guns, tobacco pipe guns, or sword canes, foreseeing that customers of their detection-defying contraptions might at some time or other have to fall back on them.

Some gambling saloons had holes bored in the ceiling concealed by painted designs or other ornaments. A gambler's accomplice, his eye glued to the hole, could see the hands of all players and signal to his friend below, generally by "pulling wires"—and so another Americanism came into being. Skilled gamblers needed no costly devices or assistants to cheat their opponents. They had mirrors hidden in pipe bowls which reflected each card as it was dealt. Some old pros had imitation diamond rings that did the same job, or placed a watch with a shiny lid in a strategic place. One riverboat gambler always managed to spill a few drops of dark brandy next to a candle and could actually read the cards reflected in them. Roulette wheels were almost always rigged. Even the supposedly foolproof faro game was crooked more often than not. In "skin faro," the dealer, whenever it was of advantage to him, could take two cards from the case instead of one by pressing a hidden lever. Two cards, "sanded" to stick together in such a way that players could not detect the deception, slipped out of the slit in the case's side. The casekeeper was, of course, in cahoots with the dealer and made sure the tally always came out right.

Many everyday colloquial expressions derive from gambling. Faro contributed "keeping cases" on somebody, "getting down to cases," "coppering a bet," and the western term "from soda to hoc," meaning "from beginning to end." "At the first rattle out of the box" meant "promptness." It was originally a dicer's term. To poker the American language owes such terms as "bluff," "kitty," "pot," "ante," "showdown," "call," "jackpot," "freeze-out," "see you," "raise," and so forth. When a man played the deuce, he was said to be "layin' down his character." "Sweatin' a game," meant "kibitzing." From seven-up came the expression "it's high, low, jack, and the game," meaning a task well accomplished, while a successful rodeo rider shouted "keno" when he had stayed the required ten seconds on a bucking bronco. To "cold-deck" a man meant taking unfair advantage of him or knocking him out. A four-flusher was at first a bluffer and later a show-off. "In a nutshell," of course, came from the old flimflam game.

Gambling also had its own superstitions. A one-eyed man was always suspect and bad luck to play with. The heart of a bat tied with a red, silken thread to the right arm guaranteed a man to win at cards. Aces and eights, the dead man's hand, were also unlucky. You never counted your poker chips, or allowed a fellow to look over your shoulder. A man who drew a pat hand of jacks full or red sevens was not expected to leave the game alive.

Everything comes to an end, and old-style western gambling was no exception. Cattle was shipped to Chicago, and the boisterous Kansas railheads became sleepy backwater towns overnight. The festive click of chip and wheel was no longer heard. The gold gave out, and mining camps turned into instant ghost towns. Far-famed Virginia City, as one sad ex-miner said, "is now like a big cheese, pretty well gutted with nothing left but the rind and the holes." The women also, that is, the so-called respectable women, reduced the roaring tiger to a declawed pussycat. The bachelors had implored the women to come out from the East because it was not good for a man to be alone. The women came and married the bachelors, and the first thing they did was to stop the gambling. The women seemed to frown on all the things that up to then had been considered fun. The haphazard posses and red-nosed, poker-playing judges were replaced by men of another breed. A man of a mind to hurrah a town found out quickly that it could no longer be treed. Respectability had suddenly arrived, and the flashy gambler was no longer respected, whether his diamond shirt studs were real or not. For a while more, there were still miners digging coal and copper, and cowboys reduced to the status of common laborers. The high-rollers were replaced by penny-ante players. The whole population changed. The land of bullwhackers and prospectors became the home of God-fearing farmers who went to bed with the chickens. The pistol-packing badman was rendered as helpless as a crocodile on Times Square. Finally, the women and preachers combined to outlaw public gambling altogether in most places just as, a few years later, they managed to outlaw public drinking.

Gambling at the Pioneer Club in Denver in the early 1900s.

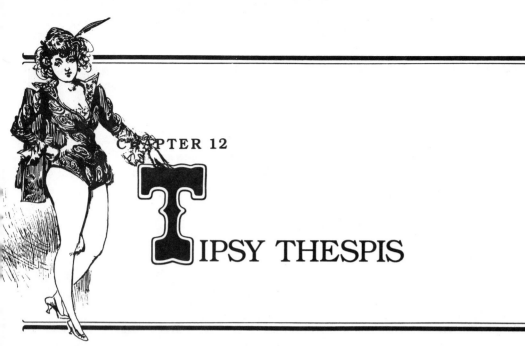

CHAPTER 12

TIPSY THESPIS

Full-Grown People
Are Invited to Visit the
Bella Union
If you Want to
"Make a Night of It."
The Show is Not of the
Kindergarten Class,
But Just Your Size,
If You are Inclined to be
Frisky and Sporty.
It is rather
Rapid, Spicy and Speedy—
At the Bella Union

—San Francisco advertisement

There is a cat in this town that
will fight any other man's cat,
either catch as catch can, or New
Orleans style, across a rope,
Particulars of Sporting Editor of
THE MINER.

—1884 Bodie
newspaper

For Western life ain't wild and
woolly now;
They are up on Wagner, Ibsen,
And adore the girls of Gibson
For Western life ain't wild and
woolly now!

—Cowboy song

The theater was the tavern. The show took place inside the saloon. Already in colonial New York during the early 1700s "a surprising MONSTER from the Woods of Canada" was exhibited at James Elliot's ordinary. According to an advertisement, the "Monster is larger than an Elephant, of a very uncommon Shape, having three heads, Eight Legs, three Fundaments, two Male Members, and one Female Pudenda on the rump . . . one very old Indian Sachem, remembered to have seen one when he was a Boy, and his father called it a GORMAGUNT." To see this amply endowed creature cost one shilling ninepence.

Executions were capital entertainment. On the 18th of September 1775, the whole town of Cambridge turned out to catch the hanging of a black slave and the burning of his woman, Phyllis. They had been found guilty of murdering the master. Onlookers watched from tavern windows quaffing punch and brandy. One diarist thought it a wonderful show: "Went home, went to bed and slept and woke up finely refreshed." Thus the style was set and, together with the jug, westward went Thespis.

Early western entertainment was as varied as the people who thronged to the variety saloons to take in a show of one kind or another. Amusements were robust, not designed for moralists or the squeamish. Bullbaiting, bearbaiting, dog- and cockfights were favorites among California miners, but couldn't hold a candle to a good multiple hanging. In dozens of California saloons men paid a dollar to see the severed head of Joaquin Murieta and the hand of his lieutenant, Three-Fingered Jack, neatly preserved in large pickle jars. Patrons of Nuttall and Mann's Number Ten Saloon in Deadwood paid the same to get a peek at the head of a Sioux Indian kept in a barrel of rye whiskey "until it soured."

European travelers shuddered to find themselves back in the Elizabethan or even Tudor age as far as American amusements were concerned and were horrified at what westerners considered good, clean fun. As the forty-niner said, "They's three things I'm goin' to have if I make a strike, boys, a fast horse, a fast woman, and a fighting dog."

Easterners turned up their noses at the forty-niners' barbaric pitting of dogs against badgers, conveniently forgetting that far into the Gay Nineties New York gentlemen lost large sums while they watched dogs tearing each other to pieces. As a matter of fact, a dogfight is probably in progress in Florida or Mississippi while these lines are being read. Ladies who were mortified to hear of bullbaiting became admirers of romantic matadors. Those who bemoaned obscene shows of half-nude wilted flowers in western whiskey mills often failed to mention that the saloon also featured Sarah Bernhardt, Edwin Booth, or a professor lecturing the miners on Plato's *Republic.* Entertainment could be raucous or innocent, learned or illiterate, cruel or gentle, depending on time and locality. It generally took place inside the old thirst parlor.

A fiddle or a fife was sometimes the only consolation of the lonesome frontiersman. Even Meriwether Lewis and William Clark leading their men across the "Shineing Mountains" to the western sea were cheered by the fiddling of Jean Cruzat, who played the violin "extreemly well." The traveling fiddler was an integral part of tavern life on the middle frontier.

He always brought whole-hearted vigor to his performance. Note his eyes sparkling like dewdrops on morning grass, nerves at high tension as his body swings in rhythm to the music. His feet tap the floor or rostrum and it is his nod that sets the company in motion in the ballroom lighted from end to end with tallow candles. It matters not whether he perches on a sauerkraut barrel or is seated on an elevated platform, he is the observed of all.

Dancing, quilting parties, barn raisings, and getting drunk were about all the frontiersman could hope for under the heading of entertainment. In the 1830s and '40s favorite dances were the Devil's Dream, Irish Washerwoman, Virginia Reel, Old Dan Tucker, Two Dollars a Week, and Pop Goes the Weasel. Besides such amusements there were only weddings to divert the early settler. Such occasions were rare, due to a distressing lack of brides. It did not take long for a man to make up his mind. In 1844 a respected citizen of Wawckesha was riding toward Milwaukee and encountered a lone young woman on the road. She asked him the way. He inquired if she was married. She said she wasn't and wanted to know how long it would take her to reach Mr. Newton's house. He said two hours if she didn't linger, asking how

Badgering the badger.

long it would take her to get married. She thought two hours would do it. He said it was a bargain and married her in the nearest tavern, the boniface doing service as justice of the peace. Getting wedded took some effort then. The tavern in which couples invariably were joined was often twenty or thirty miles distant, the preacher or magistrate had to travel a like distance from another direction. The man from whom the groom borrowed a horse or a buggy was likewise hours off. Wisconsin Judge Hall, wanting to marry his bride, Lydia, at Brigham Tavern, found that the preacher who was supposed to perform the ceremony was snowed in fifteen miles away. Hall being a justice, the couple married themselves, and a night of drinking, dancing, and mirth followed, the wedding party breaking up only after the sun had risen. Among the wedding presents were a milking stool and a fishing hook, things sure to come in handy for a judge's wife in those days.

By the mid 1840s entertainment became more varied. In a Fond-du-Lac tavern a Boston professor lectured on astronomy. At Prairieville a phrenologist felt the heads of the patrons in a popular drinking house. A mesmerist who displeased his audience was knocked out by being hit over the head with a live dog. Whigs had a political rally and a barbecued oxen feast, but while the Whigs relaxed their watchfulness over applejack, the Democrats stole the ox. Such was the entertainment on the tame middle frontier.

The California gold camps were something else again. Wrestling, prize fighting, bare knuckle contests, badger fights, bearbaiting, hunting coyotes on horseback, rifle-shooting and drinking contests were popular with the miners. On one occasion a bear broke loose and chased the manager twice around the saloon hall and then up a pillar supporting the roof with the audience loudly cheering bruin. Hinton Helper saw a "tremendous grizzly bear, caged, and drawn by four spirited horses." A large poster fixed to the cage announced to the sports:

FUN BREWING—GREAT ATTRACTION!
HARD FIGHTING TO BE DONE!
TWO BULLS AND ONE BEAR!

Programme—In two Acts.

Act I.

BULL AND BEAR—"HERCULES" AND "TROJAN,"

Will be conducted into the arena, and there chained together, where they will fight until one kills the other.

Act II.

The great bull, "BEHEMOTH," will be let loose in the arena, where he will be attacked by two of the most celebrated and expert picadors of Mexico, and finally dispatched after the true Spanish method.

Admittance $3—Tickets for sale at the door.

In Wisconsin during the 1840s, a tavern keeper advertised:

There will be RARE SPORT at which time a HE BEAR will be baited by relays of five dogs every thirty minutes, and that a SHE BEAR will be barbecued for dinner.

Bearbaiting was so popular among the forty-niners that over a hundred men made a good living scouring the mountains, trapping bears by various methods. To provide animals for these gruesome shows became almost a regular profession. The bears had to be grizzlies. If a manager tried to use a black or brown bear the "results were generally deplorable." The grizzly had to be chained because otherwise he might get it into his head to go after the spectators. This gave the bull an unfair advantage. Frequently bear and bull had not the slightest inclination for mayhem and wished only to be left alone, in which case the patrons complained and asked for their money back. It therefore became the custom to chain the two animals together in the justified hope that "proximity

Dogfight.

would breed contempt." Most of the time the bull emerged as the winner. The shows were liveliest when the chain broke.

Denny O'Brien's San Francisco saloon was *the* place for dogfights. He had a pit in his cellar where he staged fights between terriers and rats, or dogs and dogs. He employed a number of street boys who trapped the rats under the piers, selling them to O'Brien at from ten cents to two bits, depending on a rodent's size and ferocity. O'Brien advertised "the world's greatest rat killing match" for a purse of ten ounces of gold. One dog with a fighting weight of twenty-two pounds killed forty-eight large rats in under five minutes. A full thirty years after the beginning of the gold rush, such spectacles were still popular in California. In June 1880 a Bodie newspaper announced:

A wildcat and a bull terrier dog make the fur fly for one hundred dollars a side at Upper Dance House tomorrow night.

On January 21, 1884, an item in the same paper read:

Bodie has a chicken cock that will be backed against anything that stands erect on two legs and wears feathers and spurs.

Good entertainment also pitted man against man. The bartender at the Bullwhacker's Rest in Deming, New Mexico, arranged a boxing match in his barroom between a pig-tailed Chinese laundryman and a long-haired, breech-clouted Apache. The Indian won easily.

At Dodge City's Saratoga Saloon a free-for-all, no-holds-barred match took place between Nelson Whitman and Red Hanley, known as "the Red Bird from the South." The fight lasted for sixty-two rounds, ending when Nelson indicated that he had had enough—understandably. He had one eye out of its socket, both ears chewed off, a fractured cheekbone, a broken nose, and seven teeth knocked out.

Boxing was usually of the regular, less messy kind. Men challenged each other in the Tombstone *Epitaph:*

ACCEPTANCE

Having seen the challenge issued by C.C. Perry, of Tucson, to fight any man in the territory, I hereby challenge Mr. Perry to fight with naked hands, any time within two months, London prize ring rules, give or take 5 pounds from 145 pounds.

A CHALLENGE

Bob McDonald, of Bisbee, challenges Prof. Costello to a fistic encounter, as follows: Costello being a middle weight champion; I am a light weight. I will bet $500 that he can't knock me out of time in four three-minute rounds. Marquis of Queensbury rules. The fight to come off when or where Mr. Costello may choose.

Bob McD.

J.C. ("Con") Orem, "professor of pugilism," gave boxing lessons and staged fights inside the Champion Saloon in Omaha, Nebraska, one match lasting a record 193 rounds. Some preferred wrestling. The Bodie newspaper reported:

Saturday, March 15, 1884

This week some sport was had in Joe Rowse's back parlor between two well-known businessmen of Bodie. An Irishman thought, $20 worth, that he could throw a certain French gentleman twice out of three times, catch as catch can. And he thought right.

Sports were attuned to a man's way of life—drilling contests for the miners, log-birling and tree-cutting matches for timbermen, hay-bailing and mowing bouts or foot races for the sodbusters, as well as milking and quilting competitions for their women. The cowhands had their riding, lassoing, and bullwrangling contests, which eventually developed into rodeos. Among the more degraded pastimes of the crude frontier was a game called "hit the nigger," a favorite at all carnivals and fairs, often staged inside a saloon. A down-and-out black man was prevailed upon for a dollar, or the price of a meal and drink, to stick his head through the hole in a blanket or cardboard and drunken cowhands and miners were allowed to pitch eggs or tomatos at it at a dime a throw.

As the mining camps turned into cities, and as respectable women as well as eastern journalists ventured beyond the Missouri, a percentage of local citizens took pride in demonstrating that they were cultured folks, that they had a volume of Shakespeare or *Uncle Tom's Cabin* on the shelf, and generally aspired to the higher things in life. Another group delighted in shocking the easterner by slurping beans off bowie knives or clearing their nose by pressing a thumb to one nostril and violently propelling the contents of the other onto the floor—preferably at the dinner table—emphasizing that they were true westerners of the old breed, not given to hifalutin' ways, preferring a good, bloody dogfight to a poetry reading. But the more culture-minded citizens, trying to act like New York or Chicago swells, were gaining in influence. Among them social affairs were the rage. In 1882, at the mining camp of Decatur, Colorado, a ball was held. As the Montezuma *Mill Run* reporter described it:

All the elite of the Snake River country were present and helped to form an assemblage which for beauty and refinement has never been equaled in our lovely hamlet.

Everything was most recherche, chic and most utterly one, two, three; from the dulcet notes of the violin, superb banquet, and charmingly bewitching toilets of the ladies, to the smoothly waxed floor which glistened like our mountain peaks after a snowstorm.

In Goldrush, California, during the years when women were as rare as grizzly bears on Broadway, bearded miners waltzed sedately with each other, the "female" being indicated by a hankie tied around the left arm. Dame Shirley recalled a gala night at the Rich Bar Saloon with the ceiling so low that big men had to stoop:

There was some danger of being swept away in a flood of tobacco-juice, but luckily the floor was uneven, and it lay around in puddles, which with care one could avoid, merely running the minor risk of falling prostrate upon the wet boards in the midst of a galopade.

The gallop, the cross-eyed snap, the Irishman's trot, do-si-do, and schottische were among favorite miners' dances. At Salt Lake City Brigham Young gave a ball every month, gravely and impartially dancing with each of his numerous wives in turn, a habit that made these affairs rather lengthy.

The variety or concert saloon, a western institution from 1849 on, was born in New Orleans and San Francisco. Porn shows and topless-bottomless performances are by no means inventions of the 1960s and 1970s. A San Francisco paper reported:

Indecent exhibition.—Antonio Rico has got a music box and a magic lantern. His pictures represent members of the human family in the Texas costume. Whilst the exhibition is going on, he grinds Yankee Doodle out of the box and charges two rials a sight. He was discharged and the indecent pictures ordered to be destroyed.

One Mexican fandango saloon featured a group of dancing girls dressed in short red bolero

The cancan in a San Francisco variety saloon.

jackets, black garters, red slippers, and nothing else. The girls eventually donned pants, not because they were modest, but because they complained that on colder days "their derrières froze." At the Bella Union, the songs were risqué, and some of the skits frankly obscene. The saloon believed in vigorous advertising:

AT THE BELLA UNION
You will Find
PLAIN TALK AND BEAUTIFUL GIRLS!
REALLY GIRLY GIRLS!
No Back Numbers, but as Sweet and Charming
Creatures As Ever Escaped a Female
Seminary.
Lovely Tresses! Lovely Lips! Buxom Forms!
at the
BELLA UNION

And Such Fun!
If You Don't Want to Risk Both Optics,
SHUT ONE EYE!

As For the Program, it is Enough to Make
A Blind Man See—It Is An
EYE-OPENER!

We could Tell You More About It, but It
Wouldn't Do Here. Seeing is Be-
Lieving, and If you Want
Fiery Fun, and a
Tumultuous
Time,
Come to The
BELLA UNION THEATER.

California authorities were very broad-minded and did not believe in legislating the exact acreage of female anatomy an adult citizen was entitled to admire if he had a mind to; but in 1892 a law was passed that forbade serving liquor in theaters during performances. It was one of the few laws enforced in San Francisco. The variety saloons had for years proudly styled themselves theaters and had to pay the price for such pretensions. The law slowly but surely killed them.

Shows became a little more demure, but not much; with the onward march of civilization, coyly veiled nudes posed for "artistic living tableaus," such as Christian maidens being thrown to a stuffed lion. Early versions of the striptease featured girls in pink tricots, seemingly but not in reality naked. Throughout the West young and not so young ladies danced the cancan or its variation, the Clodoche, to the sound of wheezing melodeons, giving delighted miners and cowhands tantalizing glimpses of rustling froufrou, a froth of *dessous,* batiste bloomers, elaborate garters, and above them two fingers of white, real flesh.

Tombstone's Bird Cage variety saloon featured a belly-dancing odalisque whose striped Turkish silk pantaloons barely covered the pubic area and whose brocaded gypsy vest left her breasts bare. The Bird Cage was possibly the site of the West's first dancers in drag. As the Arizona *Star* reported in 1881:

Shortly after midnight the curtain rang up on the cancan in all its glory. As the cancan girls retired three men clad in tights with women's undergarments over them sprang to the stage and vied with each other in the obscenity of their actions. . . .

The audience did not appreciate this kind of show, whose time had not yet come. They lassoed the manager down from the stage and gave him a beating.

In Dawson, Alaska, the Oatley Sisters (Polly and Lottie), more modestly clad, possibly due to the climate, danced the buck and wing in the Regina Saloon, singing the whole night through, while their dog, "Tiny, a mite of a canine," joined in to the wonderment of all in "a soprano voice." The Wakely Sisters brought art and refinement to Central City, Colorado. For male support they would grab whatever prospector happened to pass by. These compliant amateurs "ad-libbed considerable profanity, suiting the taste of the miners." Horace Greeley once gave a lecture against the evils of drinking in the barroom of the Denver House, which was well received by the assembly of tipplers.

Such shows diverted the unregenerated old-timer. In Virginia City the "better element" attended a recital of Poe's "Raven." At Denver they watched an "Exhibition of the Great Stereoptician" and listened to a "Grand Vocal and Instrumental Concert under the baton of Mr. Alexander Sutherland." The programme consisted of:

Anvil Chorus (Mr. Meyers having kindly loaned six anvils, to render the chorus more effective) Full Chorus. Cornet Solo Mr. Olmstead. Overture, *The Lone Star,* or *The Opening of the Battle of Charleston* (the Overture to commence with a Salvo of Artillery, Col. Potter and Capt. Hawley having kindly loaned the use of cannon)... Full Chorus. Cornet Solo Mr. Sutherland.

The humorist Artemus Ward was immensely popular among the miners. When the owner of Maguire's wired him asking: "What will you take for a hundred nights?" the prompt answer was: "Brandy and soda."

Denver variety and concert saloons offered "the Wilson Brothers, World Famous Gymnasts" and "Miss Mayfield, an Unrivaled Contortionist, Pronounced by the Public as the WONDER OF THE AGE"; also "Professor James Clark, the armless wonder, the Political Orator of the Day." Magicians were frequent performers. In spite of all efforts such fare did not impress the eastern reporter who wrote about a Denver theatrical saloon:

At last the orchestra seems to play itself out of tunes, if it ever had any, and the shabby curtain rises up on the shabby stage, and the shabby artists ranged in shabby articles, ranged in a row of shabby chairs.

In a class by himself was Oscar Wilde, who lectured Leadville, Colorado, miners on the topic:

Oscar Wilde.

"The Practical Application of the Aesthetic Theory to Exterior and Interior House Decoration, with Observations on Dress and Personal Ornament."

He comes! The simpering Oscar comes.
The West awaits with wonder
As bullfrogs list to beating drums
Or hearken to the thunder.

The miners listened with great respect, since Wilde had proved that he could drink them all under the table. Wilde recalled one of his Leadville performances:

I went to the theatre to lecture, and I was informed that just before I went there, two men had been seized for committing a murder, and in the theatre had been brought on the stage at eight o'clock in the evening, and then and there tried and executed before a crowded audience. The people of Leadville are miners—men working in metals, so I lectured to them on the *Ethics of Art.* I read them passages from the autobiography of Benvenuto Cellini, and they seemed much delighted.

A local reporter commented:

Wilde stumbled on with a stride more becoming a giant backwoodsman than an aesthete, dressed in a suit of very elegant black velvet, which included a cut-away coat cut in circular form, knee breeches, low shoes, and black stockings. At his neck was a Byron collar with a flossy white neckhandkerchief, while from his snow-white shirt front glittered a single cluster of diamonds. His hair was very straight and very long, falling in a dark mass over his shoulders, and was parted directly at the equator. Without much introduction, he proceeded at once to business, pitching his voice at about middle C and inflecting only when tired nature asserted itself and compelled a rising inflection by a long-drawn breath. There was not a comma or a period in the whole hour, save when he came to a stop to take an unaesthetic drink.

Wilde also lectured in Denver but "stirred nobody except in the direction of the door." The great interest aroused by the "great aesthete" in western mining camps was possibly due to American clergymen who mentioned Wilde—unfavorably—in at least nine hundred sermons. Little boys asking their mamas why the parson came down so hard on Oscar were told "because he eats babies." If miners were disappointed in the topics on which he expounded, they didn't show it. He gave himself no airs, visited the mines coming down the shaft in a bucket, said that the miners were his best listeners in America, treated them to oceans of whiskey, and left them dizzy while he, having kept up with their drinking, left their thirst parlors cool, collected, and remarkably erect. For these

reasons Leadville denizens remembered him as a real gentleman.

The legitimate theater was there from the beginning, alongside the bearbaiting and freak shows. Almost with the first prospectors arrived the first actors, including many who had made a reputation for themselves on the eastern stage. Western audiences watched and applauded such stars as Junius Brutus Booth, Eddie Foy, John S. Langrishe, Ada Rehan, Lola Montez, Adah Menken, Julia Dean, the Great Modjeska, Minnie Fiske, Lotta Crabtree, Lily Langtry, and Sarah Bernhardt.

At first the saloon served as improvised theater. The Eagle, the first theater in California, opened in the fall of 1849 at Sacramento. In order to reach their seats in the "dress circle," theatergoers had to climb a ladder on the outside of the wooden building. The ladder's underside had canvas nailed to it to prevent gentlemen from looking up the ladies' skirts. On rainy nights water covered the floor but not to the extent that patrons "had to stand on their chairs." San Francisco's first theater, Washington Hall, occupied a saloon's second floor. It opened in January 1850. Opening night was slightly marred by the building sinking several inches into the ground under the weight of the spectators. The mining camp of Mok Hill created a theater complete with raised stage and candles for footlights in the back part of its biggest saloon. Amateurs did the acting, the female roles being filled by young, beardless miners. For a performance of *Richard III* some playful miners smuggled a jackass into the saloon, hiding it underneath the stage. When Richard sank to his knees exclaiming: "My kingdom for a horse!" someone kicked the animal vigorously so that it responded with an ear-splitting braying to the delight of the audience. In Olympia, another California mining town, young and pretty Julia Dean was such a smash hit that enthusiastic miners showered the stage with pouches of gold dust and hundreds of silver dollars.

John S. Langrishe, a talented actor who cut short a promising career in the East to play to Barbary Coast and Rocky Mountain audiences, became the "Prometheus of western theatre goers bringing the sacred fire of the love of art to the rude miner." In 1860 he appeared in Denver and organized a stock company that dominated Denver's theatrical scene for almost twenty years. He established a circuit and kept a half-dozen troupes of actors busy playing in every Colorado mining gulch and mountain settlement, in some cases importing stars of national fame. Langrishe was an all-around actor, playing tragic and comic roles with equal ease. Everywhere he charged patrons a uniform $1.50; it did not matter whether it was a box seat or standing room. For a while he performed at the notorious Deadwood Bella Union, a combination saloon, theater, and variety house which also maintained a few gambling tables and private, curtained boxes where customers could discreetly entertain waitresses and chorus girls. At the Bella Union troupers played Gilbert and Sullivan for 130 nights straight—during which period eight spectators were shot on the premises.

Thespis came to the cowhand, too. At Miles City, Montana, the first theatrical performance—*Uncle Tom's Cabin*—was given inside Charlie Brown's Saloon on an improvised stage made of planks supported by beer and whiskey barrels. As Elizah fled from the bloodhounds she stumbled, dislodged a board, and fell amid rolling kegs. When a theater opened in a Helena saloon, the sheriff and his deputies did not want to miss out and consequently had to take their only prisoner, a Flathead Indian, along. All went well until the actors started killing each other on stage and the frightened prisoner, who took the stabbings for real, nose-dived screaming through a window,

Exuberant cowboys sometimes lassooed the performers.

jumped on a horse, and was never seen again. At Dodge City, theaters were installed on the second floor of saloons and general stores. A cowboy caused a nonfatal shoot-out when he lassoed an actress from the stage into his lap. Many Kansas cowtown variety saloons called themselves "opera houses" rather than "theaters" because it gave a place tone. Having a theater was a sign of permanence, respectability, and sophistication. Even the so-called rougher element was proud of its "op'ry" and in some cases saw to it that objectionable material was omitted from a show. Shakespeare was the rage at first, though one Texas cowpuncher caused a commotion when, during a performance of *Macbeth,* he loudly and repeatedly protested that "the lady has her shimmy on!" On a less elevated plateau but nevertheless "quite elevating" were plays such as *The Union Spy,* which ran for a full month in Wichita and netted a thousand dollars on its last night, at a time when the city had a population of barely three thousand. Wichita also saw the first work of a native Kansan playwright performed. It was a monumental epic called *Homesteading in Oklahoma*—somewhat lengthy since the curtain rose at 8 P.M. and did not

The Palace Theatre, Denver. *Cameos:* Edwin Booth and Lotta Crabtree.

fall until 7 A.M., at which time audience and musicians were fast asleep. Other plays that met with success in Abilene, Dodge, Wichita, and Newton were *Under the Gaslight, East Lynne, Sea of Ice* (an English version of Goethe's *Faust*), an adaptation of Zola's *Nana,* and, of course, *Uncle Tom's Cabin.* Vaudeville skits were performed between acts of serious drama and even *Hamlet* was routinely followed by a humorous afterpiece, allowing the cowhand to depart in a happy mood.

The fare in all these "theaters" and "opera houses" was mixed. Even the most famous and luxurious of all, the Denver Grand Opera, built exclusively as such and not as a variety saloon, which allowed no drinking or unseemly deportment within the audience hall, offered during its first ten years, from 1881 to 1891, 345 weeks of plays, 54 of operas, and 24 of minstrel shows, acrobats, contortionists, magicians, and trained animal acts.

Mrs. Frank Leslie, the wife of the publisher of "Leslie's Weekly" described a Cheyenne, Wyoming, theatre saloon which she visited in 1877:

The auditorium departs from the conventional horseshoe pattern, and is shaped rather like a funnel. It is so narrow that we, leaning out of one box, could almost shake hands with our opposite neighbors. The trapezes through which the wonderful Mlle. Somebody is flying and frisking like a bird, are all swung from the stage to the back of the house, so that her silken tights and spangles whisk past within a hand's breadth of the admiring audience, who can exchange civilities, or even confidences with her in her aerial flight.

Below, the floor is dotted with round tables and darkened with a sea of hats; a dense fog of cigar smoke floats above them, and the clink of glasses rings a cheerful accompaniment to the orchestra, as the admiring patrons of the variety business quaff brandy and "slings," and cheer on the performers with liberal enthusiasm. The house, for all its barbaric red and yellow splashes of paint, and *bizarre* Venuses and Psyches posing on the walls, is wonderfully well-ordered and marvelously clean; the audience, wholly masculine, is unconventional (let us put it courteously), but not riotous. As for the performance, it is by no means bad. The hours of the entertainment are from 8 P.M. to 2 A.M. while the doors of the connecting gambling saloon are never closed.

In most saloon-theaters the lapses between acts were always "long enough to satisfy the thirstiest." And the connection between saloon, opera,

A Cheyenne concert saloon.

theater, gambling place, and disguised bagnio was widespread. "Besides a large Hall, and Stage and Bar Room the Cricket has an extensive room devoted to all the games of chance that were ever invented and back of the hall a sort of hypothetical Green Room—concentrated to purposes which we leave to our readers imagination."

Abilene had its Opera House Livery Stable, Dodge its Opera House Saloon. The Topic Theatre at Cripple Creek advertised itself as a "Temple of Thespis, Terpsichore and Bacchus." Eddie Foy and family performed with great success in the Alcazar Theatre, Café and Bar at Denver. By 1876 Denver had fifty-eight variety and concert saloons, but from the 1880s on, real, brick-built theaters began to replace them.

One of the first great stars to capture the West's imagination was the Spaniard Lola Montez, one-time mistress of Dumas Père, Franz Liszt, and King Ludwig of Bavaria, who created her Countess of Landsfeldt for devoted services in the royal bedchamber. According to Alexandre Dumas, the beautiful Lola had the evil eye, and her numerous lovers died like flies by suicide, accident, duels, or consumptive exhaustion. She certainly did Ludwig no good. He had to renounce the throne when his attachment to Lola and the sums spent on her became too much for the Bavarian taxpayers. In Europe Lola had been feted as a raven-haired beauty with eyes like burning coals, but impartial observers who saw her arrive in California thought that she was past her best days. She was preceded by her reputation and men flocked to see a real countess on the stage of the Bella Union. Lola had two specialties. One was a play, *Lola Montez in Bavaria,* a dramatized autobiography in which she starred as herself—the femme fatale, the seductress, the witch, the king's concubine, the wronged woman, the revolutionary. Her other act, and the one that made her famous—and maybe also ridiculous in California —was her celebrated spider dance. It represented, some said, a poor imitation of Fanny Essler's "Tarantula." Lola usually dashed onto the stage like an Arabian stallion stung by a bee, got entangled in invisible cobwebs, and was then attacked in various delicate places by an army of invisible spiders, but, as one spectator remarked:

One jumps to the conclusion that she is enough for them. It is Lola versus the spiders. . . . She apparently stamps daylight out of the last ten thousand . . . and glides from the stage, overwhelmed with applause, and smashed spiders . . . cobwebs and glory.

Another ballet-loving miner complained in a letter to his newspaper:

The Spider Dance was to represent a girl that commences dancing and finds a spider on her clothes and jumps about to shake it off. If that's it, Mr. Editor, then . . . I guess she must see the spider upon the ceiling, and that it's in trying to kick the cobwebs down that she gets the spider upon her clothes. She kicked up . . . and around in all directions, and first it was this leg and then it was the other and her petticoats were precious short, Mr. Editor, on purpose to give her a fair chance.

At which point the prudish, God-fearing miner covered his face with his slouch hat to see no evil, but enthusiastic yells and stompings made him uncover his eyes to

. . . see what was up. If the countess wasn't crazy, I don't know what on earth was the matter with her. She seemed to get so excited like, that she forgot that there was any men at all about there.

Whether they liked the performance or not, all spectators agreed that her movements were positively spiderly. Lola Montez eventually retired to Grass Valley, Nevada, to a picturesque little villa with her pets—various dogs, parrots, and one smallish bear.

Lola's close rival in fame was Dolores McCord, better known as Adah Isaacs Menken or simply the Menken, sometime mistress of Alexandre Dumas and Swinburne. Her stock in trade was performing Byron's *Mazeppa,* the high point being reached at the end of the play when the Menken was tied "naked" to the back of a wild horse, presumably to die a cruel death as the animal tore off with her through a dense forest. Actually the Menken was dressed in a skin-tight, flesh-colored leotard that covered all but her head, hands, and feet. The illusion of nakedness, however, caused one critic to write:

Her exhibitions are immodest and overdrawn caricatures, unfit for the public eye; degrading to the drama whose temples they defile; and a libel upon woman, whose sex is hereby depraved and whose chastity is corrupted.

Romantic rendition of the Menken as Mazeppa.

Such publicity in no way hurt the box office. Beginning her career at San Francisco in Maguire's Theatre Saloon, Adah was tied to a very real horse thousands of times for some twenty years before fascinated western audiences. A poster for a Virginia City, Nevada, variety saloon shows her languid form, apparently *sans* tricot, strapped to a wild, rearing stallion with rolling eyes. Adah had top billing over the famous writer Ross Browne, whose lecture following the Menken was printed in much smaller type. The poster also contains ads for Ayer's Tonic Pills and Brown's Bronchial Troches, together with a notice: "Have a good meal at the HOWLING WILDERNESS SALOON!"

Late in Adah's career the docile, aged beast which had carried her for so long stumbled on a ramp leading to the stage and fell upon her. The Menken never quite recovered from this injury. One thing remains a mystery. The original, historic Mazeppa was a fierce, bald-headed, bushy-bearded Cossack Hetman executed for treason by Peter the Great, reputedly by being bound to the back of a wild stag. By what sleight of hand the grim warrior was transmuted into an unclad voluptuous woman is still not clear.

The third star shedding light on the Plains was Sarah Bernhardt, the Great Sarah. She, too, experienced a mixed reception. Sarah Bernhardt's western debut took place in 1881 in Camille at Fottle's Opera House in St. Joseph, Missouri. As described by Ed How, the editor of the Atchison *Globe:*

At exactly 8:31 last night Sarah Bernhardt made her appearance walking down the centre as though she had but one joint in her body and no knees. Her dress was of white and costly stuff and cut so low in front that we expected every moment that she would step one of her legs through it.

If Sarah pasted her American write-ups in her scrapbook, it would be proof that her English was poor:

Sarah Bernhardt.

ugly, jaded, untalented, awkward, and tasteless, attracted and fascinated western males as no others in the nineteenth century. Possibly, as some said, it was because the pulpits rang with their denunciations, and the men of mountains and plains were determined to admire anyone the preachers frowned upon. It is more probable that open, honest, radiant sexuality was appreciated by men who themselves made no effort to hide theirs.

Opera—that is, grand opera—was rated higher than drama, even Shakespearean drama. It was the acme, the ne plus ultra of all entertainments. A new era was ushered in with the opening of the Tabor Opera House in Leadville, built by H. A. W. Tabor, the carbonate king, ex-grocer, owner of the Matchless Mine, and husband of the beautiful, ermine-clad Baby Doe, whose income from his Colorado mines alone was four million dollars a year. The Tabor Grand opened on November 20, 1879, a red-letter day in the West's cultural history. It was a solid, four-story building of red brick, rather ugly by modern standards but the ultimate in architecture by those prevailing at its birth in Colorado. Eight hundred seats were sold for the premiere, an ambitious double feature: *The Serious Family* and *Who's Who*. The Leadville *Chronicle* reported that in honor of the occasion "plug hats, heretofore a rarity, suddenly appeared on the heads of male bipeds," while the ladies adorned the scene "in full bloom; flashy dresses, white opera hats, and colors flying." The gala event was marred only by the corpses of a pair of horse thieves swinging from the rafters of the nearby unfinished courthouse, the result of a necktie party arranged by local vigilantes. One of the executioners later watched his first ballet at the theater and was asked how he liked it. He replied that it was all right as far as it went, but as to all those girls dancing constantly on their tippy-toes—"I jest can't see why they don't git taller gals." Another miner remarked that: "I like op'ry

We waited patiently for the embrace for which she is said to be the champion of two countries. It came in the third act, and . . . it was neither graceful nor natural, and only original in its awkwardness. The Bernhardt kiss is little better. . . . She has no new ideas on the subject, unless kissing on the ear is new.

The only thing Bernhardt does extraordinarily well is to put her arms around a man, and look into his eyes. If her face could be hidden at these moments, she would be sublime.

Whether the cruel comments journalists made about Lola Montez, Adah Menken, and Sarah Bernhardt are proof that the West was barbaric or merely honest is debatable. Certain is that these three remarkable women, who were described as well enuff, all but the singin'. The stage is hansum, all right, an' the fiddlin' fust rate, but so much singin' spiles it all.''

The Tabor Grand was lavishly furnished with flowered carpets and patent opera house chairs upholstered in wine red plush. The ceilings were adorned with frescoed allegorical paintings, and the curtain alone cost a thousand dollars. On its stage appeared Helena Modjeska in *As You Like It,* the New York Metropolitan Opera Company, John Philip Sousa and his band, the Chicago Symphony Orchestra, and Oscar Wilde in velvet knee pants; and yet with all that culture and refinement, the Tabor Grand Opera House could and would not hide its basic western character—its ground floor was occupied by Phil Golding's Saloon, the "neatest in Leadville," where tall-hatted theatergoers and opera fans could down a jolt or two of red-eye and play a hand of stud poker during the long intermissions.

The Tabor Grand.

CHAPTER 13

"WIMMIN", OR ONLY A BIRD IN A GILDED CAGE, OR WOMEN, GOOD AND BAD

Mattie Silks and Fanny Ford
Drank theirs from a gourd,
Poker Alice she smoked a cheroot;
Lily Langtry, they say,
Had been led astray
By the juice of the forbidden fruit.

—Old western song

The average man would rather
behold her nakedness than
Ulysses Grant in his full dress
uniform.

—Mark Twain's comment
on a high-class whore

She was only a convict's daughter,
but she knew all the bars.

—Western proverb

Westerners divided women into two categories—good ones and bad ones. For many years only the bad ones could be found in saloons. By the time the good ones were bending their elbows at the counter alongside men, most saloons had become—just bars. It was not that "respectable" frontierswomen never had a hankering to see the inside of one of those dens of iniquity and down a couple of burning sensations to find out what it was like. Men did not want females in their drinking places to spoil their "ethereally masculine aura." The role of women in the West was unique. At first men determined the role women should play. Later on women often determined the life men were to lead. Men were attracted by women while shunning them. They, at the same time, put women upon a pedestal and brutalized them. They worshiped and also looked down upon them. They dreamed of creatures in lace and silk when what they really wanted was a workhorse on two legs. They paid women an exaggerated respect, but slapped them around when that seemed to them the thing to do. Above all, the westerner in public (especially in print) and the westerner in private were altogether different species of the human race. Many a man, as the saying went, behaved like a parson at the north pole and like a hog at the equator. The overwhelming fact that determined the role of women in the West, and their relationship to men, was their almost total absence during the early years. Whores, of course, were there almost from the beginning:

> The miners came in forty-nine,
> The whores in fifty-one,
> They rolled upon the barroom floor,
> And made the native son.

But even those who were "neither widows, wives, nor maidens" never showed up in some places. It was said that in San Francisco during the gold rush days there were so few women that a female was as rare a sight as an elephant. The shout: "Look, a woman!" brought men running from saloons and places of business. Even the painted cats were treated with respect verging on reverence. A so-called respectable woman found herself surrounded by self-appointed guardians clearing the way for her, shielding her from the rowdier element, carrying her across the street so that she would not drown in mud. According to one historian only fifteen women in this category —"white and decent"—could be found in San Francisco in the spring of 1849. One is inclined to believe that the standards by which he judged women were a trifle too high. In the fall of 1849 a thin trickle of women arrived on the West Coast by the overland road. Almost none came by sea except those who wanted to turn their bodies into cash—great amounts of it—until 1850, when a few respectable ladies arrived by ship. Women seldom came with their husbands. In the rough conditions prevailing, men tried to establish a solid foothold first and create the rudiments of a household, however primitive, before having their wives join them. They were lucky if their spouses survived the perilous journey across the mountains or around the Horn.

Desperate bachelors wrote glowing letters describing California as a land of milk and honey to women of whom they knew only the name and address. If they received an answer, they promptly proposed and sent money for the trip. In other cases men advertised in eastern or midwestern newspapers for wives, "buying the goods un-

seen." These brides by mail were eventually known as "Monkey Ward women" or as "mail order wives." They were sometimes snapped up en route, never getting to the man they were originally intended for. So great was the demand for women, and so short the supply, that a Mrs. Eliza Farnham decided to bring out from the East, as a commercial venture, two hundred "cultured, educated, refined and respectable females." When she finally got to California, she was left with only three of these rarest of creatures. Even less-than-alluring spinsters were married almost as soon as they arrived, though one traveler, William Perkins, witnessing the arrival of an upper-class woman in Sonora, cautioned:

Eureka! We all exclaimed a day or two ago, on the arrival of the wife and family of our American doctor. But, good lord! And I confess my very pen is blushing while it writes the sentence; the comparison is anything but favorable to morality. What chance has virtue in the shape of tall gawky, sallow, ill-dressed down easterners, in rivalship with elegantly adorned, beautiful and graceful Vice! The strife is unequal. Virtue must put on some pleasing aspect to enable her to conquer the formidable enemy already entrenched so advantageously.

Many men discovered that strumpets made good wives. As for the homely ones, in the words of one miner: "She ain't nothin' for a drinkin' man to look at, but she sure can cook an' keep house. So I kept her."

In the beginning, women in the cow country were almost as scarce and consequently held in as much awe as in gold rush California. It was said that no other class of men behaved toward women with more reverence and chivalry, albeit a crude kind, than the western miner and cowhand. The prevailing legend, and it has prevailed for a hundred years, tries to convince us that a virtuous woman in a gold camp or among cowpunchers was

The Pioneer Mother, by O. C. Seltzer.

as safe as in church. In the words of an old stockman:

When I was a boy, a woman that had the reputation of being a good woman could go anywhere in the country, and nobody would touch her. A man that ever made a move at a woman got hung—and that was all there was to it. There was no foolishness. On the other hand, if a woman was promiscuous, why God help her if the boys took a notion to get heavy.

This is not altogether true. Wyatt Earp, made by eastern writers into the cow country's Sir Galahad, frequently slapped women around, and sometimes beat them savagely, "But these were *only* dance hall girls," as the Dodge City *Times* reported in 1877:

Miss Frankie Bell . . . heaped epithets upon the unoffending head of Mr. Earp to such an extent as to provoke a slap from the ex-officer. Miss Bell was fined twenty dollars the next morning; Mr. Earp was fined a dollar.

At Deadwood, Al Swearangen, owner of the notorious Gem variety saloon, physically abused actresses who refused to double as lady ushers and entertain customers in curtained-off boxes, causing one or two girls to commit suicide. Near Leadville, drunken drivers traveling in a stagecoach forced an exhausted songstress to sing to them for hours telling her: "Sing to us, we like it, and if you don't we'll dump you in the snow!"

There is a contradiction here, the contradiction between reverence and contempt for women, between protectiveness and brutality. Old-timers among cattlemen insist that respect for womanhood was the lodestone. Range etiquette, so they maintain, forbade a stranger to show interest in the woman of a household where he was a guest or merely had dropped in. The only permissible appreciation shown to the lady of the house—that is, a rancher's wife—was to eat heartily. But after, say, the 1880s, the human skunk who propositioned a good woman was no longer strung up or horsewhipped; he was merely ostracized and shunned by all "real men." What seems to have happened was that in the West as elsewhere, attitudes changed from time to time. At first, life was unsettled and unconventional. Women as well as men had a great deal of freedom. After the law of supply and demand became more favorable to men, exaggerated reverence toward women lessened perceptibly. Then came the era of respectability and the establishment of the "Bible belt." It was the women, the good, God-fearing women, who caused the outlawing of liquor, gambling saloons, and parlor houses throughout counties, states, and finally the nation. They paid dearly for their triumphs, since the madams, saloonists, dashing gamblers, and merry hell-raisers gave way to the rule of the kind of men who maintained that "a woman is news only three times in her life—hatched, matched, and dispatched."

The difference made between "virtuous" and "nonvirtuous" women lingered for a long time. During the rip-roaring second half of the nineteenth century, the only place a man met a woman —a willing woman—was the saloon. The "better element," meaning the respectable ladies and the men they had under their thumbs, tacitly supported the symbiosis between saloon, dance hall, and cathouse, as "protective institutions." In an essentially womanless environment the virile bachelor cowpuncher and prospector had no excuse to "bother" the "good" women. The "bad" ones were available in fair numbers. The presence of the "fancy women" shielded the married women and their daughters from unwanted attentions. After all, as one philosopher remarked, the average man, if he were not inhibited and hedged in by codes, laws, religion, and the threat of punishment, would kill his own father, ravish his mother, and violate every female in sight, and early westerners had considerably cut down on their inhibitions while the threat of punishment was often weak and distant. The decent women therefore showed great tolerance, one might say gratitude, to their errant sisters who acted as safety valves, and cheerfully accepted the former prostitute into their ranks once she was married and exhibited her marigolds, quilts, and preserves at the county fair.

This was true in gold rush California, as well as in Rocky Mountain camps and early cowtowns. As one early California traveler wrote:

In no part of the world, is the individual more free from restraint. Men, women, and children are permitted to do nearly as they please. High wages, migratory habits, and bachelor life, are not favorable to the maintenance of stiff social rules among men, and the tone of society among women must partake of that of men.

A woman who was shocked out of her Victorian sensibilities when she first came to California wrote in 1855: "The very air I breathe seems so free that I have not the least desire to return" (to the East).

The freshly arrived immigrant woman from "out east" found herself thrown willy-nilly into a whirlpool of alien morals outrageously different from her own—Chinese, Polynesian, Latin, Indian, French, sailors', mountain men's, and gamblers' morals. She had to sink or swim, and some swam wonderfully well. The Women's Movement arrived early, most commonly in the guise of a "bloomer girl," braless certainly and wearing that damnable, unmentionable, hellish nether garment instead of chaste pantaloons and layers of petticoats. "Bloomers" smoked, gambled, sipped strong waters, and were suspected of still darker deeds. Their reception was mixed.

Dame Shirley, who wrote wonderful letters about her travels in early California, half-admired and half-feared the "bloomers":

Apropos, how *can* women,—many of whom, I am told, are *really* interesting and intelligent—how *can* they spoil their pretty mouths and ruin their beautiful complexions, by demanding with Xantippean *fervor,* in the presence, often, of a vulgar, irreverent mob, what the gentle creatures, are pleased to call their "rights"?

Bluestockings were even worse; they were bloomers without bloomers, and unlike bloomers, who at least were truly if aberrantly American, they were French or under French influence.

Women's rights came to the Colorado mining camps in the shape of suffragettes and women reformers. Anne Ellis, who lived in Bonanza, a Colorado mining town, recalled a chat with a friend of hers, a local character called Slippery Joe, who told her:

Above: Bloomers draw trade in San Francisco.
Below: A miner's spree on the Barbary Coast.

"I was working in Lake City; in the spring of 1876. One day I saw all the boys gatherin' in front of a cabin. I figgered somebody had locked horns and sauntered over, an' by gol! It was a woman talking' politics, 'wimmin's rights,' she called it."

"Was she married?"

"She didn't look it. Her name was Susan B. Anthony. Another woman who was with her was called Elizabeth Cady Stanton. They was ridin' horseback from one camp to another."

Anne Ellis commented: "Women dream many dreams and see many visions while bending over the washtub."

Western women played a larger and more central role than their more sheltered eastern sisters. The frontierswoman could shoot straight if she had to, could ride a horse, drive an ox team, set a broken bone, make soap, grow her own food, make her children's clothing, slaughter a pig, and raise a family without many of the tools and gadgets normally used in a city household. The frontierswomen were therefore a lot more self-reliant, and consequently self-assertive, than women in the long-settled East, a lot more self-assertive than they ought to have been in the opinion of some. Women competed with men as bullwhackers, mail carriers, saloon and hotel keepers, bartenders, hunters, gamblers, prospectors, bandits, cattle rustlers, and owners of businesses.

The cowpunchers and miners were not a little intimidated, maybe even afraid of the brawny and resourceful decent women who presumed to lay down the moral law. They were more at ease with the fancy women and hurdy-gurdy girls who made their living by playing up to their machismo.

The owners of innumerable frontier newspapers, generally catering to the male mind, often had kind words for the ladies of the line, commenting on their good looks, fine clothes, and generosity, reporting at length how this or that wilted flower had given to the poor or nursed the sick during an epidemic. But they had little use for women in business or on a speaker's platform. One Colorado editor's comment on a lady reformer lecturing on raising and nursing children was: "An individual with a pair of bosoms that look like two gingersnaps pinned onto a cotton-wood shingle, must be an excellent authority on such subjects."

In the opinion of some, the long-limbed, true-shooting frontiersman was in some ways more self-reliant than is generally thought. Girl-shy, at least of the marrying kind, he has been described as curiously asexual—a latent homosexual. The hirsute forty-niners certainly managed to get along well without members of the opposite sex. An envious eastern reporter wrote about prospectors in wicked Bodie in the August 1865 issue of *Harper's Monthly:*

Miner's Ball, by A. Castaigne.

These jolly miners were the happiest set of bachelors imaginable; had neither chick nor child, that I know of, to trouble them; cooked their own food; did their own washing; mended their own clothes, made their own beds, and on Sundays cut their own hair, greased their own boots, and brushed their own coats; thus proving by the most direct positive evidence that woman is an unnecessary and expensive institution which ought to be abolished by law. I have always maintained, and do still contend, that the constant interference, and despotic sway, the exactions and caprices of the female sex ought no longer to be tolerated; and it is with a glow of pride and triumph that I introduce this striking example of the ability of man to live in a state of perfect exemption from all these trials and tribulations. True, I must admit that the honest miners of Bodie spent a great deal of time in reading yellow-covered novels and writing love-letters; but that was probably only a clever device to fortify themselves against the insidious approaches of the enemy.

Yellow-covered or "yaller-kivvered" obscene brochures are often mentioned as the favorite literature of the forty-niners—those among them who could read. They were nineteenth-century versions of *Playboy, Penthouse,* and *Hustler* firing the imagination of the celibates. The cowboy was, if possible, even more averse to the approaches of marriage-minded maidens. Folk songs can generally be trusted to express a people's true feelings, and cowboy songs are certainly a clue to the cattleman's mind:

> When you are single
> And living at your ease
> You can roam this world over
> And do as you please;
> You can roam this world over
> And go where you will
> And shyly kiss a pretty girl
> And be your own still.

> But when you are married
> And living with your wife,

> You've lost all the joys
> And comforts of life.
> Your wife she will scold you,
> Your children will cry,
> And that will make papa
> Look withered and dry.

> Come close to the bar, boys,
> We'll drink all around.
> We'll drink to the pure,
> If any be found;
> We'll drink to the single,
> For I wish them success;
> Likewise to the married,
> For I wish them no less.

Lee Sage, in "The Last Rustler," put it in prose: "I was horse-tied but skirt-free! Up to this time none of that disease called Love had ever crept into me. I figured you could reason with an old horse or else flog it out of him. You couldn't do neither with a woman. Women was mighty nice things but they was better free than captured."

There was sure more riding of mares than of lassies, and his good old pony seemed more important to the cowhand—in both fact and fiction —than a pesky female. On boot hills throughout the West can be found headstones or boards bearing the legend:

> JIM
> a reel hors
> oct 1, 82

or:

> HERE LIES
> "I'M HERE"
> The Very Best of Cow Ponies,
> A Gallant, Little Gentleman
> Died on this Spot, Sept. 3, 1890.

or:

> HERE LIES
> "WHAT NEXT"
> Born ----, ----, 1886, ----,
> Died July 16, 1892, near Ft. Washakie, Wyo.
> He had the Body of a Horse,
> The Spirit of a Knight, and
> The Devotion of the Man
> who Erected this Stone.

On the other hand, one can find stones inscribed simply:

WOMAN † 64

Gunmen were also mama's boys. Few old songs exist about a cowboy and his mistress, but innumerable ones about his silver-haired mama back home. Wild Bill Hickok shed tears if someone mentioned his mother. Billy the Kid, a heartless killer, once gazed at a ranch house and told a friend: "George, I wish I had a home like this. I'd send for my mother and be the happiest kid alive!" When the ferocious Cherokee Bill was about to shoot off his six-gun somebody admonished him: "Now, now, Bill, you know your dear old mother wouldn't want her boy to act like that!"—and Cherokee meekly holstered his artillery.

The westerner found the women he was most at ease with in the place he was most at ease in—the saloon. He also found them in the cat houses, but to visit those necessitated a trip to a town of some size. Two types of saloons specialized in providing the right kind of female companionship for the lonely cowhand and miner—the hurdy-gurdy house or "pretty waiter saloon," and the variety saloon disguised as a theater.

Hurdy-gurdy houses were essential fixtures of mining towns and cowtowns, but usually absent from the homesteader's community—for the simple reason that the nesters had wives. The hurdy-gurdy house existed to sell drinks. The girls existed to keep the wet goods moving. They were known as hurdy-gurdy girls, honky-tonk gals, beerjerkers, box rustlers, or pretty waiter girls. Some of them were prostitutes, but most of them just danced with men for a living. They were considered a cut above the fallen angels. In this respect they resembled geishas. They were there to entertain, to please men, and—most important—to make them buy drinks at outrageous prices.

"Pretty waiter girl" saloon.

They had their own places to live and sleep in. They might be snubbed by the so-called better element, and they were seldom virgins. They took lovers freely and defied convention by living openly with their paramours, but most of them were not whores and resented it if treated as such. They were proud that they picked or rejected their lovers as they pleased. They worked for saloon owners, not for madams or pimps—most of them, most of the time.

Like other saloons, the hurdy-gurdy house was a western institution with a long tradition behind it. It could be squalid or elegant, comparatively decorous or the nearest thing to a brothel—the line was often hard to draw. The word "hurdy-gurdy" comes from an old-time German musical instrument, a sort of hand organ on which tunes were ground out by street musicians at county fairs. In many of the first, most primitive dance-hall saloons a hurdy-gurdy man provided the only music and the name stuck. In the Old South "honky-tonk" was a word coined by black people for a place to hang around, a place of dubious reputation. Hence, honky-tonkers were people who made their living in questionable or at least unconventional fashion—gamblers, bartenders, con men, pimps, and errant sisters. New Orleans dance hall saloons were called honky-tonks, and the term spread to the West Coast. Also in New Orleans was born the "concert saloon," just another name for the same kind of establishment. "The pretty waiter girl" saloon was an original western creation. In 1869 the Mexican operator of one of the deadfalls lining San Francisco's Pacific Street fitted out his dancing girls with fancy jackets and ostrich-feather bonnets, while furnishing them absolutely nothing with which to cover themselves below the navel; he called his bottomless nymphs "pretty waiter girls." This name was innocently adopted by many saloon operators who would never have dreamed of imitating the creative señor. Likewise in Hispanic California originated the term "fandango saloon" for the same sort of place.

The San Francisco of the forty-niners is generally credited with having been the birthplace of the hurdy-gurdy house, but in New Orleans, and even New York, forerunners of the concert saloon were operating as early as the 1830s and 1840s. The first girlie saloons were little to look at from the outside; they might be a dugout or log cabin. Inside, one could usually buck the tiger at the faro table or sit in on a poker game if too tired to dance, but the bar was always the heart of the honky-tonk, which was first of all a saloon.

The hurdy house on the raw frontier was often a large tent supported by a framework of scantlings. The floor was tamped earth. This was the ballroom. Around the sides were rough benches for dancers and onlookers. Two or three oil lamps dimly illuminated the scene. The bar was sited where it was easiest for a man to get his liquid refreshment. A great variety of labeled bottles was a specialty of the hurdy house. The girl's partner was supposed to buy her a fancy drink—at an outrageous price—after each dance, not the one-bit

whiskey he himself was consuming. What the girl drank, for a dollar a shot, bore of course no relation to what was written on the label. The label might say champagne, but what the girls got was weak tea.

In a corner of the tent, placed at an angle, stood the battered upright piano, tinny and out of tune, often transported hundreds of miles on mule back to reach the end of its line. After the bar it was the saloon's most precious piece of equipment. On a stool before the "pianner" sat the "perfessor," almost but not quite the equal of the bartender. To receive a condescending nod from the piano player, or have him accept a drink at the customer's expense, was an honor treasured by the cowpuncher, miner, or farm yokel. As the place acquired "tone" a podium was added, upon which were placed chairs for a fiddler and banjo player, who took their lead from the professor. In front of the piano stood a row of chairs for the girls.

By eight o'clock the dance hall filled with clumsily booted miners, cowboys, or railroadmen, depending on the locality. The girls were waiting, sitting demurely on their chairs, the musicians at their stations, the faro dealers alert, the bar ready, the glasses washed. The proprietor was scanning the crowd for unwanted deadbeats or for men who seemed overattentive to one particular girl. The specter of marriage was an ever-present threat to the saloon keeper, who had a hard time replacing his girls. After having, in his own way, gotten rid of unwanted patrons, and after the boys had their hair of the dog and paid the ante for the first go-round, the fiddler called out: "Gents, take your partners for a dance!" and scraped away on his violin while the professor pounded out a Varsovienne or a waltz, a mazourka or a schottische. In some places the girls wore heavy, ungainly footwear as a protection against the customers' heavy-booted clumsiness or sheer exuberation. At the

Dances were exuberant in
the hurdy-gurdy saloons.

end of the allotted time—anywhere from five to fifteen minutes depending on house policy—the dance ended with a suddenness which left some dancers stumbling. The fiddler called out: "Gents, balance your partners up to the bar!" The girls immediately and deftly steered their partners to the counter, where the men obediently bought them drinks. While the boys downed their whiskey the girls took a nip of the colored sugar water. They had to remain sober, because a tipsy girl on the dance floor was a calamity. As they said in cow country: "A hurdy gal on a drunk raises more hell than a locoweed-fed bull." In some places a patron after buying a girl "five fancy drinks received one snake free and likewise a gratis hop-and-skip ticket." After the treats had been speedily consumed, the bardog rapped the counter with his bung starter as a sign for the girls to "weigh out" —that is, to sit down for a minute to "get their steam up," after which the dancing started all over again. A popular girl averaged about fifty dances, no mean feat of endurance considering the vigorous stomping and whirling of cowboys and miners intent on getting their money's worth. At a buck a dance this netted a girl twenty-five dollars, her half-share of the tickets initialed by her, plus her commissions on drinks she had induced her partners to buy, and that was no mean sum either, ample reward for the strain on her arches. It gave the girls independence, so that most of them did not have to entertain customers upstairs or behind the shed. Finally the fiddler called out: "One last dance, gentlemen," followed by, "Only this one more afore the gals go home," and that ended the long, long night.

In Alaskan gold rush camps, the hurdy houses had balconies. There the affluent prospector could sit and watch. It was the custom for a well-heeled miner to pick out a girl of his choice and shower her with gold dust, most of which was caught in her hairdo—usually an elaborate one during the "gay nineties." A shampoo usually yielded a girl from ten to twenty dollars. Miners also pitched pea-size gold nuggets into the hurdy girls' cleavages, enjoying the spectacle of seeing the young ladies trap the shining kernels between their ample bosoms.

The dance saloons of San Francisco's Barbary Coast had an evil reputation for rolling the befuddled sucker, for having waiter girls who were accomplished pickpockets and prostitutes for performers. The average pay of Frisco's pretty waiter girls was twenty dollars a day. They also received a commission on the booze they sold and half the earnings from the sale of their bodies. Some were classed as performers, artists, and chanteuses, but these were paid the same as the waitresses and were likewise expected to solicit drinks as well as the customers. San Francisco dance saloons usually had fifteen-minute intermissions between dances or acts on the stage.

In 1865, in Montana mining settlements, the hurdy-gurdy was a most popular place, and when Montana became cattle country, the cowboys put their own brand on the dance saloons. In a Billings watering hole a puncher and a waitress took first prize for dancing the "Bull Calf's Medley" on the grand piano at a gala Saturday night hoedown. The cowboy wore high boots which did the piano no good, and exuberant onlookers kept discharging their six-guns at the ceiling to the beat of waltzes and polkas.

Thomas J. Dimsdale, one of Montana's first authors, described a pretty waitress he saw in a hurdy-gurdy during the range war days:

Let us describe a first class dancer—"sure of a partner every time." There she stands at the head of the set. She is of middle height, of rather full and rounded form; her complexion is as pure as alabaster, a pair of dangerous looking hazel eyes, a slightly Roman nose, a small and prettily formed mouth. Her auburn hair is neatly banded and gathered in a tasteful, ornamented net, with a roll and gold tassels at the side. How sedate she looks during the first figure, never smiling till the termination of "promenade, eight," when she shows her little white hands in fixing her handsome brooch in its place, and settling her glistening earrings. See how nicely her scarlet dress, with its broad black band round the skirt, and its black edgings, set off her dainty figure. No wonder that a wild mountaineer would be willing to pay—not one dollar, but all that he has in his purse—for a dance and an approving smile from so beautiful a woman.

Beauty, of course, is not only a matter of personal taste, but also of time and place. Whatever allowances a writer might make for changing tastes, he is still confronted by a wealth of photographs that flatly contradict eye witnesses waxing lyrical over the beauty and elegance of western dance-hall girls as well as the opulence of hurdy houses' decor. While the onlooker's eye was distorted by lust, the camera's objective lens was impervious to sex appeal and dealt in reality. A whole row of tintypes and chromos of the interiors of hurdy houses in Montana, Kansas, and Nebraska cowtowns shows that the majority of dance-saloon girls consisted of raw-boned and gawky country girls. One out of twenty seems to have been pretty, some beauties in any age. Their unwieldy boots, fastened at the side with innumerable lentil-sized buttons, apparently gave them a lot of trouble. Usually they were dressed like farm girls going to church on Sunday. There is not an ostrich feather, any lace, silk, or velvet on one of them. Still, an old-timer who was asked if he thought that the girls had been good-looking said:

Ideals of beauty and fashion change. Hurdy girls in Cripple Creek saloon.

"The gals in the hurdy-gurdies were real purty. They weren't whores mostly, and with the money they made on drinks and all that gold dust on the side, they could take good care of themselves. The ones in the cribs were ugly. They got wore out fast, though not the chinee gals. They lasted longer. Pretty as dolls. They didn't come cheap but were worth it. The nester gals were in between, kind of homely with faces like horses, but white skin and rosy cheeks."

The hurdy-gurdies were mostly refugees from the mill or farm. Girls in the mills worked up to sixty hours a week for a dollar a day and contracted TB after a year. The sodbuster's daughters were no better off:

Pickin' up buffler bones to keep from starving,
Pickin' up buffler chips to keep from freezing,
Pickin' up courage to keep from leaving,
Way out West in No Man's Land.

A Texas girl remembered: "I never had no skirt until I was fourteen. Had worn nothin' but a long, gray shift made outen a flour sack after one of the city hombres in El Paso had eaten the flour out."

It was no wonder that girls were lured by posters and handbills such as:

LEADVILLE
WANTED: FIFTY WAITER GIRLS!
High Wages, Easy Work,
Pay in Gold promptly Every Week.
Must appear in short clothes or no
engagement!

or:

GOOD STEPPERS, make yourselves some money.
FUN GALORE! FINE CLOTHING!
Nothing untoward which could tend
to affect a lady's sensibilities allowed at
THE GOLDEN NUGGET SALOON.

Girls who could read and get their hands on a newspaper could pore over articles describing hurdy-gurdies "dressed as close to the Paris mode as did anybody in New York City." They could learn that "the fandango girl's wages of sin are not necessarily death, but often wealth, fame, and a respectable marriage."

It beat picking buffalo chips by a mile. And so they came, and hustled, and after the first night the short skirts bothered them no longer. Most were good girls, at least in the eyes of the average westerner. In the mining camp of Alma one of the hurdy girls became so popular that fans made her a present of a pair of solid silver heels for her slippers. After that the men just called her Silver Heels until her real name was forgotten. When a smallpox epidemic struck the region, the few "respectable" ladies departed in a hurry, but Silver Heels stayed behind to nurse the sick and comfort the dying. She caught the disease and survived, but her face was badly scarred. She disappeared soon afterward. As the miners had it, she did not want to be seen by them with her beauty gone. They named Mount Silver Heels in her honor.

Sometimes a whole cowboy outfit "adopted" a hurdy girl or fancy woman:

. . . Oh, Cowboy Annie was her name.
And the N-bar outfit was her game.
We'll work a year on the Musselshell
And blow it in, in spite of Hell.
And when the beef is four years old,
We'll fill her pillowslips with gold.

One Colorado cowboy recalled dance-hall keeper Kate O'Leary protecting him from her own overeager rustlers because she had a soft spot for youngsters who couldn't raise a beard yet. Such women were sentimental at heart, especially after hours when they could afford it. They didn't mind rough manners, but demanded a minimum of respect. One cowpuncher found a dance-hall girl he knew on a stairway, savagely beaten, the front of her dress covered with blood. She had repelled the brutal advances of a drunken client. "I don't mind the black eye," she said, "but he called me a whore."

Some of the girls had second thoughts about

the easy life with fun galore and good pay, especially those working in saloons that required them to be box rustlers—that is, to serve and entertain customers in private behind curtains. This was also true of those who had become old and worn out. They, as well as the disillusioned prostitute, often turned to alcohol and narcotics. They dosed their drinks with laudanum or they smoked opium, readily available in a town's Chinese quarter, and they sniffed cocaine:

Take a shot of cocaine,
And take a shot of gin.
You kin tell it'll kill yer troubles,
But you can't tell when.

Suicides were frequent. A several times repeated headline in a Leadville newspaper read:

DANCE GIRL TRIES TO ARSENIC HER WAY
FROM LEADVILLE.

The dead dance-hall girl was the subject of romantic outpourings:

Talk if you will of her
But speak no ill of her—
The sins of the living are not of the dead.

Remember her charity;
Forget all disparity;
Let her judges be they whom she sheltered
and fed.

A good part of the time there was a happy ending. Dodge's *Kansas Cowboy* of August 27, 1884, reported:

AN UNFORTUNATE MADE HAPPY
Her Lover Takes Her Away

While a reporter of this paper was making his round last Friday evening skirmishing for news he stumbled on to a sensation. A well-dressed gentleman stepped into the dance hall and to his surprise found his long lost sweetheart, whom he had given up two years ago as dead. Such a meeting of the two lovers was a sight. After wiping the tears away, the lover commenced propounding questions to her as how come she was living at such a place.

The lovely unfortunate with dazzling eyes gazed up at him and said, "Charlie, I don't know; it has always been a mystery."

She made all kinds of apologies and told him of her trials and tribulations for the past two years in such language as brought tears into his eyes. She pleaded to be taken away from "this den of devils" as she expressed it. He agreed to, if she would make up her mind to be his "future happiness." She consented, and the happy couple left on the late train for Pueblo, where they will be joined in the happy bonds of holy wedlock.

Not all honky-tonkers were fondly remembered. Some had crossed the fine line and were mainly whores who just happened to do a little dancing and drink rustling on the side. Among them was Lola, "a tigress, the very comet of her sex, a left-handed daughter of Lord Byron." There were Doc Holliday's Big-Nose Kate; and good-looking squirrel-tooth Alice, who kept a tame squirrel; and Tidbit, "pure as driven snow, but oh, how she drifted," who had the names of her lovers embroidered on her dresses, with those out of favor winding up "on that part of her anatomy on which she sat." Then there was the "Lost Chicken," who sang in a quavering tinny voice to forty-niners the only song she knew: "The boat lies high, the boat lies low; she lies high and dry on the Ohio." Her dancing was worse than her singing, but she was unsurpassed at picking pockets. The "Waddling Duck," too, did not shine on the dance floor, "but she was the one and only songstress of the age singing wonderfully in two keys at one and the same time, a feast for the discerning ear without parallel." Then there were Rocky-Faced Kate, Rockin' Chair Emma, Virgin Mary, Hop-Fiend Kitty, Diamond Molly, Ogallala Shorty, Jack-Rabbit Sue, Wingless Angel, Four Ace Dora, Kansas Cow, Razorback Jennie, and Society Annie. In Pierre, South Dakota, Nigger Jenny had a reputation for whoring when not dancing.

She told one drunken cowpuncher who complained of her kinky hair: "White man, what you expect for fifty cents—sealskin?!"

A young nester was waylaid in Omaha by a dance-hall woman:

A nice-looking girl asked me what time it was. I told her. Then we began to talk. She invited me to go home with her. When I said I had to catch a train, she wanted me to go a piece with her. When we went outside, she said let the train go to hell. Coming from such a pretty girl, this set me back. She told me she "could do the Landershuffle and if it ain't good mamma will sift for you." I began to catch on and turned back. She wanted me to give her a quarter for luck, which I did, and she said, "Good-bye, baby."

The dancing saloons were as different from each other as were the girls. Different also were opinions held of this hallowed western institution. The local boys sure liked them. Jesse Benton, an old cowhand, recalled:

I walked up to the dance hall and looked in. What a sight to anyone, the prettiest gals from all over the world, dressed like a million dollars, was all there. If you did not come in to dance, they would grab you and pull you in, whether you wanted to dance or not. All the girls acted glad to see you. Round after round of drinks, then all hands would dance.

An old saying went: "Many's the cowpuncher and miner who'd never wash his face or comb his hair, if it wasn't for thinkin' of the hurdy-gurdies and sportin' women he might meet in the saloon." Some commented favorably on the well-run, "morally unobjectionable" dance-hall saloon. One ancient fellow fondly remembered a sign in a hurdy house: A SKIRT IS A SKIRT AND MUST BE RESPECTED AS SUCH!

The Carbonate Concert Hall Saloon in wide-open wicked Creede advertised: Wine, women and song: These three are supposed to make life

palatial, and while nothing of an improper character is permitted, we can furnish all three any night. Some concert saloons formulated strict rules of comportment. The owner of the Alhambra in Sliverton, Colorado, posted the following printed set:

Rule 1. No lady will leave the house during evening working hours without permission.
Rule 2. No lady will accompany a gentleman to his lodgings.
Rule 3. No kicking at the orchestra, especially from the stage.
Rule 4. Every lady will be required to dance on the floor after the show.
Rule 5. No fighting or quarreling will be allowed.

As time went on those who had anything good to say about hurdy houses and the dancing girls were outnumbered by far by those who condemned both in the strongest terms. The critics were mostly eastern writers and local reporters catering to what they called the "civilizing element," but the worst epithets heaped on the hurdy-gurdies came from clergymen and women reformers.

A San Francisco newspaper described the Bull Run Concert Saloon as a notorious combination of dance hall, saloon, and parlor house in which customers were knocked out with Mickey Finns and then robbed. The San Francisco *Call* waxed positively lyrical in describing the Barbary Coast's squalid fandango houses, and then thoughtfully ended its long diatribe with: "We give the precise locality so our readers may *keep away*. Give it a *wide berth* as you value your life!" thereby transforming its sermon into advertisement.

A Chicago missionary did the *Call* one better:

The concert saloons are among the worst features of the social evil. They flourish in almost every quarter of the city, and are so many places where the devil's work is done. The better class of citi-

"The dancing saloons were as different from each other as were the girls." *Above:* A "squalid" fandango house. *Below:* A "morally unobjectionable" dance-hall saloon.

zens are helpless to abate the nuisance. The vipers in human form, who keep these soul-destroying places, are men so small in principle, that their paltroon souls would rattle in the eyeballs of the most infinitesimal animalculae that ever infested a stagnant mud-hole.

Thus the Chicago dancing saloon reflected in the eyes of a preacher. In the seventies the *Colorado Miner* similarly described the Leadville hurdy-gurdy houses as "breathing holes of hell, where customers imbibe torchlight whiskey and indulge in the quadrille and the whirling sinuosities of the waltz." The Leadville *Daily Chronicle* added: "Men are fools and women devils in disguise. That's the reason the dance halls clear from one to two hundred dollars per night."

The hurdy girl's life in a railhead town was not without danger.

The trail driver was afraid of nothing, "except a decent woman and being afoot." When he yip-yip-yipped into town "hell was in session." In Liquor Lane, as one early reporter wrote, he arrived to "loiter and dissipate, sharing the boughten dalliances of fallen women . . . and as soon send a bullet flying as cast a lasso over the horns of a wild steer." With spirits high, stomachs full of rotgut, tempers short, and guns being part of a man's normal apparel, it was no wonder that some got hurt and that this somebody frequently was the hurdy girl or the fallen angel whose sex supposedly should have rendered her bullet-proof:

Who shot Maggie in the freckle?
Who shot Maggie in the divide?
Who pierced her billowing bloomers?
And ran away to hide.

Slade, the notorious badman, terrorized dance-hall girls and actresses in Montana concert saloons, pointing his six-gun at them:

"Pull up your skirts, let's see your legs. . . . We paid our money. . . . Let's see your legs. . . . Hell, there's a couple of dozen girls here probably got better. Pull 'em up. . . . Take off that skirt."

Dora Hand, a supposedly ex-Beacon Hill blueblood, who loved to dance the fandango on tables, bar counters, and grand pianos, whose "Home, Sweet Home," sung in a rich alto, made hardened bardogs and muleskinners weep, whose smile, it is said, caused the deaths of ten men suffering from squaw fever, herself fell victim to an odd shooting affair. In 1878 Dora had two lovers—Doc Kelley, mayor of Dodge City and owner of the Alhambra saloon in which Dora worked as a dancing girl, and "Spike" Kenedy, a young Texan cowman. One dark night, after having drunk more than was good for him, a brooding Kenedy walked over to Doc Kelley's frame house and pumped sixteen .44-caliber bullets through the mayor's bedroom window. Unfortunately it was not Kelley who was sleeping in his bed, but Dora, and one of the slugs killed her instantaneously. Nothing happened to Kenedy. He had not shot the man he had intended to kill, he had killed his lady love to whom he wished no harm. The whole sad event was therefore dismissed as a deplorable accident. Dora was given an impressive funeral by her innumerable admirers. She is supposed to be the only woman buried in Dodge's famous boot hill, though she possibly shares this honor with another joy girl. Doc Holliday's Big-Nose Kate also fell victim to a shooting accident in Bisbee, Arizona's, notorious Brewery Gulch saloon.

Violent death was one of the hurdy girl's, pretty waitress', or nymph of the prairie's professional hazards, and more than a hundred cases have been documented, but a lot more westerners died for the love of a woman. In the words of a forty-niner: "I believe every woman was the cause o' fifty fights an' one or two deaths." To fool with another fellow's woman, legal spouse or otherwise, was also unhealthy. The West knew no friendly discussion about a triangular situation, as was the insipid custom in the East.

BOUND TO A HORSE'S BACK was the headline in Cheyenne's *Democratic Leader* of July 1884. It recounted the fate of a young Englishman who was found in a compromising situation with a rancher's wife. The injured husband, with the help of a few cowhands, firmly tied the modern Mazeppa to the back of a wild bronc, lashing the horse into a furious gallop. The amorous Briton was found seven days later and fifty miles away still alive. He eventually recovered.

Most adulterers were less lucky. In 1875 the Silver City, New Mexico, *Herald* reported:

We learn that on Friday, Jose Garcia, who lives at the Chino copper mines, caught his wife in flagrante delicto—we leave the reader to guess the crime—Jose, then and there, gave her the quietus with an axe. She's dead—deadest sort of dead, and it is said that Jose did not run away and intends to face the music.

Jose had little to worry about. A Utahan named Egan killed his wife's lover, though the woman had been the seducer. The defendant's lawyer thundered: "It is the God-given right of the nearest of kin of a female who is seduced to take the life of the seducer." The judge thought so too, saying that the killing "was in accordance with the established principles of justice in these mountains. . . . If Egan had failed to avenge the dastardly deed, it would have damned him in the eyes of everyone in his community."

The jury agreed and came in with a verdict of "not guilty" after deliberating all of ten minutes. Needless to say, judge, lawyer, and jurors would have taken a dim view of a woman shooting her man who had gone to meet a sportin' gal in a saloon. That was no dastardly deed but a mere peccadillo which judge and juror themselves indulged in occasionally.

Some saloons, whether straight thirst parlor, gambling den, or hurdy house, were places of assignation and hangouts for the frail sisters. On the other hand, some parlor houses advertising "choice cigars, bonded bourbon and the finest liquors and wines," with their elaborate bars and dance floors, seemed to some visitors to resemble a concert saloon more than a bagnio. A number of saloon keepers and bartenders were married to madams such as Jennie Rogers, whose husband was a barkeep in Denver's ornate and decorous Brown Palace. As a Montana woman wrote: "One of the chief evils of those early days was the saloon. . . . Women of easy virtue were always present in large numbers, habited in the most costly and attractive apparel, brazen-faced and bold." A woman who, as a young girl, had lived in both Montana and Colorado during the frontier years recalled:

[They] were easily recognizable by their painted cheeks and the flaunting of their gaudy clothes on the streets. They were always to be seen either walking up and down or clattering along on horseback or in hacks. . . . These women were so in evidence that I felt no curiosity about them. I knew that besides being so much upon the streets, they went to hurdy-gurdy houses and to saloons and that they were not 'good women,' why, I did not analyze.

The West had many names for them: giddy ladies, painted cats, fair but frail, scarlet ladies, come-on girls, fallen angels, "boarders" (in quotation marks), ladies of the evening, easy women, fast women, fancy women, fair belles, sportin' gals, owls (for nightwalkers), and, lowest in their profession, crib women. They were as much a part of some western saloons as the painted nudes on the backbar. They thronged Denver's Elephant Corral. When Bob Ford opened his Exchange Saloon at Creede, Colorado, in 1891, he brought with him his paramour, Dot, who operated part of the structure as an improvised bordello. Abilene's famous Alamo was connected in the back to a parlor house.

The Durango, Colorado, Strater Hotel and Saloon advertised:

BEST HOUSE IN TOWN!
Come all you boys who've been around,
Chambermaids you'll find at hand!
Best damn girlies in the land!
Press the annunciator and you get
All you want, and more, you bet!

The girlies lived on the fourth floor known as the monkey hall, officially off limits for the guests but, as one of them remarked: "It was bed bugs or monkey hall." Some saloons gave out one- and two-dollar brass checks, entitling the holder to the services of one of the place's female habitués.

Above: "Fallen angels" in a Denver bagnio.
Below: Dance Hall Girl, by O. C. Seltzer.

Some bore the legend: "Good for one screw." Another was inscribed:

$ 1.- lookee
$ 2.- feelee
$ 3.- dooee.

Still another, showing a bare-breasted lady on one side, bore the legend:

Silver Dollar Saloon
Eat, drink and go to bed,
or get out!

The term "red light district" originated in Dodge from a custom among uninhibited railroaders of leaving their red brakemen's lanterns hanging outside the door of their girl of the evening to discourage intruders. Robert Wright, one of the city's respectable citizens, complained:

Beautiful Bibulous Babylon of the Frontier. Her principal business is polygamy . . . her code of morals is the honor of thieves, and decency she knows not. Her virtue is prostitution and her beverage is whiskey. She is a merry town and the only visible support of a great many of her citizens is jocularity. The town is full of prostitutes and every other place is a brothel.

Puritanism reared its head wherever and whenever the number of good women caught up and surpassed that of the bad ones, when the fallen angels were no longer safety valves but competition. What had been thought good heman's fun was suddenly termed insufferable:

The Barbary Coast is the haunt of the low and the vile of every kind. . . . Licentiousness, debauchery, pollution, loathsome disease, insanity from dissipation, misery, poverty, wealth, profanity, blasphemy, and death, are there. And Hell, yawning to receive the putrid mass, is there also.

W. E. Stanley, a Wichita, Kansas, politician, lamented: "I am of the opinion that the time has come when these places of vice must be at least regulated if not entirely suppressed." In Tombstone, Arizona, whose citizens had long prided themselves on the rich flavor of their lingo, men suddenly became shocked by purple language:

A fallen angel was arrested last Wednesday on a charge of using profane and indecent language and had a hearing before Justice Hawke in the afternoon. The said angel vehemently denied the charge in terms so strong that His Honor turned pale and nearly fainted.

A minister visiting Denver in 1869 was outraged that the city's respectable ladies did not want to spoil their beauty by bearing children. He was more disturbed finding out that most Denver women knew the secret means to prevent conception and achieve their "unnatural resolutions." He wrote with horror that contraceptives "are advertised in every newspaper."

In Marysville, California, reformers had a parlor house dragged away by a team of four huge horses with the bewildered fallen angels still inside. Mining towns changed their names from Whiskey Bar, Last Chance Gulch, Delirium Tremens, Red Nose, Bedbug, and Hangtown, to names like Helena, Ione, or Placerville.

Instead of the lusty songs of the wild and woolly years, sentimental, sugary hymns became popular in the old variety saloon such as:

Take back the ring you gave me:
Take it back, Jack, I pray.
Wearing it would de-prave me,
More than I am today.
To make me your wife would wrong you,
Grief to your heart would bring—
So, please take it back, I beg of you, Jack.
Take back the engage-a-ment ring.

In 1878 state legislators from Sacramento studied immorality firsthand by making a tour of San Francisco's houses of ill repute and dancing saloons, "graciously accepting a glass of wine from the hands of lissome Cyprians and possibly sampling more than just that."

In Leadville a ministers' union was formed to watch over the mining camp's morals, to offer prayers and song for the surrounding sinners, and to hold temperance meetings. As the local paper reported:

Saturday night a party of four distinguished and extremely pious divines made the complete rounds of the camp. They visited the dance dangers, gambling shops, bunko-coolers, and May-Minnie unmentionables. It took these pious parsons almost all night to satisfy themselves . . .

Though the thundering preachers got most of their support from women, they were, by and large, rabid antifeminists looking upon woman as Eve, the eternal temptress, cause of man's fall from grace. As one of them said: "A dunghill covered with flowers." Not for them the old western dictum that every woman, no matter, was a lady and had to be respected as such.

Luckily, the typical Texan, Oklahoman, Californian, or Montanan did not share this viewpoint. But they gave in to the extent that they conformed outwardly. By the time the Noble Experiment became reality, the last of the old dance saloons had closed its doors. As early as the 1870s Denver passed a city ordinance fixing a "$100 fine for anyone who shall employ any women for the purpose of attracting customers, bar tending, dancing, etc. and if the place is licensed, the license is to be revoked." It was circumvented and periodically replaced, but it was a straw in the wind. Wild, woolly, and wicked Dodge unblushingly passed a law prohibiting dance halls or any similar place "where lewd women gather for the purpose of dancing," but not before the end of trail-driving days had made the hurdy-gurdy house economically unimportant. It was dead but not unmourned. One former Denver State Street hooker and rustler at the Pioneer Saloon wistfully stated in her old age: "These modern girls are a bunch of ninnies, and the modern man is worse—a sissy

of the first water. . . . In my day, you were either good or bad. These ninnies do everything that branded us as bad—and get away with it."

Of course, not all the women in saloons were pretty waiter girls, hurdy-gurdies, or brides of the multitude, though fiction would have it so. Good mothers and on the whole faithful wives did frequent the thirst parlors. As one old cowboy song had it:

My Lulu, she's a dandy,
She stands and drinks like a man,
She calls for gin and brandy,
And she doesn't give a damn,
And she doesn't give a damn.

Normal red-blooded American women drank. Colonial dames got their high colors from brandy mashes and cordials. Tennesse and Kaintuck pioneer ladies mixed a little honey and milk into their whiskey. Demure churchgoing spinsters in their attics got soused on Hostetter's Bitters. Many a First Lady of the land, from Dolley Madison to Mamie Eisenhower, was not averse to occasionally sampling the good creature.

In gold rush San Francisco there were many drinking places that had male and female patrons. One visitor saw a "loud" San Francisco belle, young, handsome, and beautifully dressed, march up to the open bar to have a nightcap with some of the finest gentlemen in town. Tessie Wall, admittedly not a lady but a madam, once emptied twenty-two bottles of French champagne without leaving her dinner table. San Franciscan ladies reputedly had a capacity equal to that of their male escorts.

Other towns also took pride in their drinking women. A Santa Fe newspaper of 1881 related how eight Anglo boys went to a *baile* and thought to have a great deal of fun with a hundred-year-old cigar-smoking Hispanic lady by each marching her in turn to the bar to treat her to a shot of fiery mescal and Old Towse, intending to repeat the performance until they had gotten her "blind drunk." When the *baile* broke up, the fellows found out that they had each spent over fifteen dollars and were no longer able to remain upright. While the fun-lovers were trundled home on a *carreta*, the "chipper dame, sober as ever, was standing up to the bar getting outside of another glass of *cerveza*."

Old cowhands still insist that no real lady ever darkened the swinging doors of their favorite watering spots. Shine Philips maintains:

Sometimes when I see these modern girls whipping into a bistro or whatever they call it, I get a picture of what would have happened if a Big Spring lady of the nineties had sailed into a saloon, wearing her good black skirt with the overdrape, her white shirtwaist with a collar up under her ears and high bones to make it stay there, her black sailor hat perched behind the smooth roll of her pompadour, no lip-paint nor rouge, and asked for a drink. Why a shooting would have been nothing compared to the consternation such a happening would have evoked. Strong men would have turned pale and everybody in the place would have known that he was drunk, including the bartender, who never touched a drop.

The facts are otherwise. The men tried to keep the women out, but the women eventually battered their way into the saloon or crept in by the side door. In some cases the solution was simple. In a Chicago saloon a headwaiter informed the great John L. Sullivan and his charming companion of the evening that "no ladies are allowed in this establishment," whereupon John L. threatened him with raised fists roaring: "When a lady's with me, she ain't no lady!" There were at all times ladies nosing their way to the bottom of a glass, "jug and thou" persons. A dowager who entertained the Grand Duke Alexis of Russia in Denver became so drunk that she collapsed and had to be carried off by concerned friends. A Deadwood

fallen angel was so distressed about alcoholism among the town's women, respectable and abandoned, that she advertised in the *Deadwood Pioneer:*

If there have been a lot of drunken women in Deadwood, then I for one am an exception, for I am not in the habit of getting in this condition, and no gentleman can say anything to the contrary, but that I always behave myself like a lady, even though a member of the demi-monde.

The onslaught females made on the batwing doors eventually led to the institution of "the wineroom in back" for lady topers and their male friends. They were comparatively tame but allowed females to get a toe inside the hallowed "for males only" drinking places. As Anne Ellis recalled:

Every saloon had its side entrance to the winerooms, where women went. There were also several places for both men and women. The Rendezvous is the only one I remember now. Here one

"Red-blooded American women drank."

could drink and gamble. Most of the women did lay bets on the roulette wheel, but I never did, as there was no money to lay. Once I did go in one of the back rooms with Billie and his wife, and have beer and club sandwiches, but considered it a very tame affair, as I didn't like beer, and you got only a rumble from the front, where things were really doing.

When even this got to be too much for the moralists and laws were passed forbidding a woman even to enter a whiskey parlor, imaginative saloonists invented the "ladies' entrance" by simply adding a second door. If a lady used that, rather than coming in through the batwings, her entrance into the den of iniquity was in some unfathomable way sanctified. Despite male resistance, Carry Nation, the Temperance League, and the Noble Experiment, the drinking woman, bent upon bending an elbow at the bar, prevailed over all. The men—poor, besotted men who had taken their women into barrooms to show them off—had done themselves in. As one of them ruefully said:

That the calamity was accomplished with the dazed and idiot connivance of men themselves but made it the more tragic. Like the British, the women were adroit colonizers. They still allowed the native males to inhabit the saloons and a pretense of liberty, but only in a paying and ornamental capacity. They became atmosphere, like the soap writing on the mirror and the framed bank note over the bar, while at the same time financing the entertainment of the conquerors. But they were allowed no voice in the conduct of the premises and revolt against female domination was ruthlessly suppressed.

Similar sentiments were expressed by a man from Olympia, an old California mining camp:

And the women haven't only took charge of the politics here, they've got the business too. They run the City Hotel, and the express office, and the water company, and practically all the stores.

Why, even the Stage Drivers' Retreat—Jack Douglass's fine old saloon—even that belongs to a woman. Us men, the few that's left of us, we're making our last stand at Fallon's Hotel. It's the only place now where a man can go and set in a broad old barroom chair and spit at the stove and express his feelings in just as strong language as he wants.

For a Texan the end came when they made Shirley Temple a rangerette. And old Shine ruefully commented:

Yes, times have really changed. The cowboys have learned bridge and up there in New York, I understand they have to have a special ruling in some hotels and places to keep women from taking over the bars entirely. They have to have special bars with a "MEN ONLY" sign or a man can't drink in peace.

Poor old Shine! He was wrong. The "men only" sign also lost its power. One hopes he was not around to read of that day in August 1970 when McSorley's Old Ale House had to open its doors to women, when old customers, urinating pensively in the single facility existent, were shocked to their very vitals by seeing a booted, braless female entering even there, making a beeline for the stall! The author, who'd rather talk to a companionable woman while sipping his brandy than to anyone else, has been in McSorley's since that fatal day. He liked seeing the women there, but has to admit that McSorley's famous aroma (under female ownership) is no longer the "rich compound of pine sawdust, tap drippings, pipe tobacco, coal smoke and onions." The smell, as Joe Mitchell said, was for mental disturbances "more beneficial than psychoanalysis." Teddy Blue, the old Montana cowhand, summed it all up: "Well, it was the way we were raised. If you mentioned a decent woman's name in a saloon or a sporting house in those days, you were liable to get your eye shot out. And now if you go in a saloon, there they all are."

CHAPTER 14

DEATH IN THE BARROOM, OR LIKKER AND LEAD

He shot a greaser every morning,
For to make his morning meal.
And let a white man sass him,
He was shore to feel his steel.

But one day he met a man
Who was a whole lot badder.
And now he's dead,
And we ain't none the sadder.

   —From "Billy the Kid,"
    old cowboy song

Whiskey en women en poker,
Monte en Faro en Stud,
Just a short wild race,
 who'd keep the pace
Would land in a river of blood.

Fightin' en drinkin' en gamblin',
Nigger en Mex en White;
'T was a riot of sin,
 iet the best man win;
'T was drink, when called, or
 fight.

 —Another old Billy the Kid song

"I always carried a gun because it was the only way I knew how to fight. 'If God Almighty'd wanted me to fight like a dog, he'd have given me long teeth and claws.' That was the feeling among the cowpunchers. They didn't know how to fight with their fists." So said Montana Teddy Blue in his old age.

The legend of the nonchalant gunfighter surrounded by his victims writhing on a barroom's sawdust floor has been repeated so often that in the end the white-haired ex-cowboys themselves believed it. It has been said that more men were killed inside saloons than in all the Indian wars on the Plains. Possibly that is true. Most of the killing was done within a period of some twenty-five years— say from 1860 to 1885, with a generous sprinkling of violent deaths in California whiskey mills during the preceding decade, and a modest afterglow that lasted into the early 1900s. Statistics are funny things. In a comparable period, an equal number of killings occurred in New York's Hell's Kitchen, Chicago's Tenderloin, and New Orleans' Storyville. More people were killed in New York's Civil War draft riots than in a wild and wicked Kansas helldorado in ten years.

The figure of the heroic killer has always loomed large in American history, which often is nothing more than folklore, for the simple reason that the western historian often has only a legend for his source material. In its formative years the frontier was certainly violent—as are the streets of our big cities today. Violence, it has been said, is typically American, but whether it is only American is questionable. From the beginning Americans carried guns because they had to hunt for their meat and because they insisted on moving into Indian lands against the resistance of the native owners. The average frontiersman did not particularly appreciate the frontier until it was gone and his rifle or six-shooter had become a mantelpiece decoration. The heroic gunfighter was an eastern invention; for the westerner he was a pain in the ass. Just as the present New Yorker dies of cancer or heart failure, and not of a knife wound or bullet, so the overwhelming majority of westerners died with their boots off.

Still there were sizable numbers of violent demises in the old western snake ranches. Men died in saloons first because they foolishly followed the prevailing fashion in going around "heeled"—that is, armed—while they really didn't know how to handle themselves with a gun; second, because the saloon was the place in which to get drunk—and drunken men fight; third, because the saloon was the place in which to play cards and meet bad women, and men quarreled over poker, women, and other things in that order. Poker mixed with alcohol accounted for more deaths than all other causes combined. A further reason for gunplay and knifings was the fact that the majority of shootists were Civil War veterans, and it was the most restless, adventurous, and embittered among them who moved west. Bull Run and Gettysburg were fought over and over again in western barrooms by former bluecoats and rebs full of firewater; the saloon, after all, was the most likely place for them to run into each other.

The frontier penchant for exaggeration and bragging also played its role. After a few jolts of whiskey, men began to believe their own bragging and found that they had to make it good. Not for nothing was red likker called the "bravemaker."

The fine art of boasting was born on Mississippi keelboats, in Louisiana swamps, and in Tennessee taverns, and it achieved its apotheosis among mountain men who carried it beyond the Rockies. Westerners would "wild up" whenever they had a good, preferably eastern, audience:

A'm raised in a swamp,
Fed in a hog trough,
Suckled by a she-bear,
The click of a six-shooter is music to my ear.

The further up the creek you go,
The worse they get,
An' I come from the head of it!
Wh-o-o-o-pee!

A cowboy might swagger into a whiskey mill challenging all and sundry to a fight, declaiming:

I got two rows of nipples and holes bored for
    more.
I pull up trees by the roots,
An' if a mountain gits in my way
I jest kick her to one side.
I'm a rarin', tarin' cyclone of chain-lightning
Loaded with destruction.
I'm the idol of all wimmen
And bad news to their men!

A fellow might ask: "Give me a baked horny-toad, two broiled gila monsters on toast with tarantula sauce, and a scorpion salad with a few poached centipedes on the side." A politician on the stump introduced himself as "The Tarantula from Calaveras, a Warhorse from the Hills, and a fighter from Hell!" A saloon keeper warned customers: "If any man says the Silver Dollar ain't a first-class drinkin' place, I'll put a bullet through him!" Miners encouraged a missionary wrestling the devil: "Gouge him, Billy, gouge him!" A cowboy asked a friend: "Didn't you tell me that "crookback Jack called me an ornery, low-down son of a bitch?" "Naw, I never said that." "Doggone! I've gone an' killed an innocent man!"

The bark was generally worse than the bite.

Home for the boys.

The real killer was a taciturn sourpuss, "short on conversation," who lacked the imagination for elaborate braggadocio.

Men delighted in boasting that their town was the very worst in the state, the territory, the whole West. California miners named their settlements Hell's Delight, Devil's Basin, Last Chance, Gouge Eye, Rattlesnake Bar, Graveyard Canyon, Dead Man's Bar, and Bloody Gulch. Sober-minded merchants, grocers, and newspaper owners gloried in making outsiders shudder whenever their particular burg was mentioned: "Deadwood, soaked in Blood, Whiskey, and Corruption." "Newton, Swiftest Joint in Kansas." "Abilene, Wild, Woolly and Wicked." "Ellsworth, that violent and Scarlet Spot." "El Paso, Toughest of the Tough in Texas." "Bloody, Beastly, Bodie." "Helena, a mighty Rough Hole." Dodge citizens loved to call their town: "The Beautiful, Bibulous Babylon of the Plains," which

Called that day lost whose low descending sun
Saw no man killed or other mischief done.

They impressed visitors with the "Immigrant's Prayer":

Oh, Lord, we pray Thee, protect us with Thy mighty hand. On our long journey Thy Divine Providence has kept us safe. We have survived cloudbursts, hailstorms, floods, strong gales, thirst, and parching heat—as well as raids of horse thieves and attacks by hostile Indians. But now, oh, Lord, we face our gravest danger, Dodge City.

The morbid enjoyment of one's hometown's evil reputation continued long after the wicked burgs had become sleepy and peaceful, long after the only stiffs in town were those who had died of cyrrhosis of the liver.

Violence and the worship of the romantic, superhuman killer were not uniquely American. Bandits and pistoleers had always loomed large in European folklore. They were subjects of songs, broadsides, biographies, plays and operas, even modern dramas. Famous English highwaymen kept gentle ladies for mistresses, had their deeds of derring-do avidly followed by an adoring public, and drew great crowds when they went bravely to their death on Tyborn Tree. Robbers like the Italian cutthroat Rinaldo Rinaldini, who waylaid travelers in the Abruzzi Mountains; the German Schinderhannes, terror of the Hunsrück; and the Hungarian Bettyars became folk heroes of legends and tall tales. Russians shed tears singing the sad song of the robber Stenka Razin; the Japanese have their outlaw Samurais, called Ronin.

Horrendous saloon fights likewise are not solely red, white, and blue American. The eye gouging, groin kneeing, ear chewing, and nose biting that went on in western saloons was popular entertainment in Europe. The immigrant did not learn about violence or down his first tumbler of hard stuff upon coming to the West. He came already well primed. There was, however, one big difference. The European did not come into his drinking place equipped with firearms. The mystique of the gun, the legend of the long rifle which had defeated the redcoats and blazed trails through the wilderness, did not exist in the Old World. The well-policed monarchies of Europe did not encourage good burghers to carry arms. Germans, Austrians, Slavs, Irishmen, and Scandinavians wanting to engage in a donnybrook had to use their fists instead of guns. Once in America, though, they caught on fast. Among the baddest of badmen were first- and second-generation immigrants.

The violence of the American frontier, the superhuman feats of bullwhip, bowie knife, rifle, and pistol are part of the nation's mythology. Inventive native imagination played a great role in its making. Frontier heroes sprang up as soon as there was a frontier. John Smith set the pattern, making himself into a sort of early-seventeenth-

Eye-gouging, groin-kneeing, and ear-chewing were popular.

century Buffalo Bill without help of a ghostwriter. In 1608 he published "a true relation," a short narrative of the Jamestown Colony and his experiences in Virginia. In 1624 he brought out another work, *General Historie of Virginia.* What had been an encounter with a single Indian in the first book became a fight unto death against swarms of savages in the second. Epic battles and miraculous escapes not mentioned in the "true relation" were expanded into grandiose exotic happenings. The London public loved it. Smith's rescue from having his head bashed in by Powhatan's lovely daughter Pocahontas became the great romantic story of the age, and Smith acquired a wide reputation as bold explorer, Indian fighter, and ardent lover, although his fame never reached Americans who were still busy hacking cabin plots out of the primeval forest. To appreciate the frontier hero one had to be at least somewhat civilized.

Daniel Boone was the first homespun, native-born hero appreciated by the home folks—that is, the city slickers of New York, Philadelphia, and Baltimore. John Filson's "Adventures of Colonel Daniel Boon" transformed the simple scout, land speculator, hunter, and farmer into the philosopher-trailblazer. One writer quotes Boone as saying:

"Why, thar's more real satersfactshun in Sarcumventin' an' scalpin' one o' them red heathen, than in all the amoosement you could scare up in a thick-peopled, peacable settlement in a lifetime."

Filson has him orating:

"No varieties of commerce and stately structures could afford so much pleasure to my mind, as the beauty of nature found here."

From what we know, Boone spoke neither stilted nor barbaric English but the normal jargon of time and place. Already at work in these quotes is the city dweller's yearning to "go back to nature," the admiration for Rousseau's natural man, for the elbowroom that made French aristocrats build themselves luxurious and expensive "shepherd's cottages" and log cabins. From the beginning the pioneer was shown as worshiper and protector of nature's beauty. In reality the typical frontiersman had gone beyond the mountains not because he loved the wilderness, but because he wanted more land or because he was a misfit who had no choice.

Early writers have Daniel Boone killing two Indians with one bullet, subduing a ferocious bear with his fists, swinging Tarzan-like from grapevines, and saving himself from pursuing hordes of Indian braves by sixty-foot jumps from towering cliffs. This set a precedent. All later frontier idols up to and including Buffalo Bill were credited with similar feats. The bare-handed fight with the grizzly, the bowie knife duel to death with the Indian chief, the death-defying leap, the miraculous shot, became standard "musts" in every biography of a western hero.

One could say that the frontier hero owed his existence to the educated easterner. Filson was a schoolteacher, Fenimore Cooper had gone to Yale for three years, Washington Irving had studied law and was a diplomat. It is only due to Ruxton, a British army officer, that such trappers as La Bonte, Killbuck, and St. Vrain are remembered now. Who would know of Bonneville if it were not for Irving? An article in *Harper's Magazine* made Wild Bill Hickok, the "King of the Pistoleers," a nationwide hero overnight. Buffalo Bill was, ninety percent of him, the creation of Nat Buntling. Deadwood Dick was entirely a penny-dreadful writer's brainchild, although he was resurrected in the flesh during the 1920s and '30s.

As every historian knows, legends are not made about men who never were. Daniel Boone blazed trails. He probably was right handy with his Kentucky rifle (made in Pennsylvania). Davy Crockett, who was his own best press agent, prob-

Above: Daniel Boone. *Below:* Buffalo Bill.

ably killed more than one bear, and he did die at the Alamo. Noble Kit Carson, "the prince of the pathfinders," who owed his reputation entirely to Frémont's narrative, was a scout and Indian fighter. As one writer had it:

Discharging his rifle and pistols at the first he came to, Carson raised himself in his stirrups, and swinging the former weapon over his head, with as much apparent ease as if a mere whisp, he brought it down upon the dusky horde around him with fatal effect. Not less than a dozen in the space of twice as many seconds bit the dust beneath its weight, while his horse, madly rearing and plunging, trod down some four or five more.

Diminutive Kit, weighing all of 150 pounds, swinging those heavy muzzle-loaders like "whisps"?—one wonders. But Kit lived. The Navajos still remember him for having devastated their cornfields, cut down their fruit trees, and killed their sheep to bring them to heel. Doc Holliday, Bat Masterson, and Wyatt Earp did exist; they tended bar, gambled in barrooms, and killed men in them. Wild Bill Hickok did not have a romantic love affair with Calamity Jane, but he did kill men, and was himself killed, inside a saloon. John Wesley Hardin did have notches on his gun, and each notch did represent a man shot down. All had their stories written, distorted, and changed to fit the taste of readers in big cities. The gunfighters did not write their stories. The men who did, for the most part, had never fired a shot in anger or seen a grizzly bear or witnessed a cattle stampede. They wrote the story as they saw it, from their point of view, and thereby changed it. The process is still going on, has in fact been given a new impulse by television. But the circus was there, from the very beginning, from the time Columbus

Hands of a famous barroom fighter, 1851.

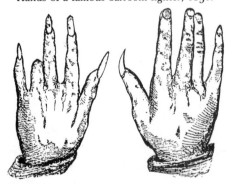

staged the first Indian Wild West Show for Queen Isabella. Wild Bill played himself on the stage. He was a bad actor. Sitting Bull, billed as Custer's slayer, appeared in Buffalo Bill's Wild West Show. Doc Holliday once played, appropriately, a gambler in a variety saloon. The gunfighter became the pretty singing cowboy of the Hollywood of the 1930s. The whole West was a stage on which a tremendous play was enacted. Unfortunately, a good many of the dead were real.

The typical gunfighter came in two varieties. The professional type was made up of men who were everything rolled into one, a sort of western dilettante—sometimes gamblers, lawmen, hired killers, saloon keepers, or bartenders. The second variety was made up of hard-working rural workmen, slaving from "can't see to can't see," known at first simply as drovers and later, cowboys. They were essentially amateurs, drawn into fights because they happened to be armed, armed because they had been soldiers fighting bloody battles and had never quite adjusted to civilian life; and because there were still Indians around; because of rustlers, road agents, and cheating gamblers; also because of the range wars for water, and against fences, during which their bosses handed them guns to fight for them. In movies and on television the cowboys almost never herd, brand, or feed cattle; they are always shooting up saloons or galloping madly in a cloud of dust and gunsmoke after some badmen. In real life they worked from dawn to dusk at a rather messy, bone-breaking, and, to be honest, unromantic job among the little dogies. On their rare days in town, cowboys did go to the saloons, fought, and sometimes killed. Mostly they were harmless. There were Mexican, Indian, black, and European-born cowboys. In the words of William Savage:

For the matter of a week, or perchance two—it depends on how fast his money melts—in these

Sometimes people went to saloons to get themselves killed. By Frederic Remington.

fashions will our gentleman of cows engage his hours and expand himself. He will make a deal of noise, drink a deal of whiskey, acquire a deal of what he terms "action"; but he harms nobody, and, in a town toughened to his racket and which needs and gets his money, disturbs nobody.

He might see himself differently, possibly tongue in cheek:

Oh, a man there lives on the Western plains,
With a ton of fight and an ounce of brains,
Who herds the cows as he robs the trains
And goes by the name of cowboy.

He laughs at death and scoffs at life;
He feels unwell unless in some strife.
He fights with a pistol, a rifle, or knife,
This reckless, rollicking cowboy.

He shoots out lights in a dancing hall;
He gets shot up in a drunken brawl.
Some coroner's jury then ends it all,
And that's the last of the cowboy.

To shoot a man one must have a shooting iron.

Most of the nonsense written about gunfighters is due to the fact that the writer never saw or handled the revolvers used by his heroes, and because he, like the hero, was in thrall to the mystique of the gun. It is indeed a peculiarly American phenomenon. Death in a barroom is incomprehensible without understanding it. The rifle, the six-shooter, stand for independence, for Concord and Lexington, for democracy, and especially for virility. The mountain man cuddled his Plains rifle, named it Betsie, Bess, Meg, or Mollie. The firearm was as necessary for the American pioneer as it was useless for the European farmer. Even today an American is thirty-five times as liable as a European to get killed with a handgun. It is still the custom in the West to give a boy his first .22 small caliber gun, " 'cause he's growing up, make a man of him." On the early Virginia, Kentucky, and Tennessee frontier, twelve-year-old boys were given a small-bore, lightweight rifle and shot pouch. At the same time they were assigned their porthole and firing position in the fort. Kids learned to shoot as soon as they could pull the trigger. During Tombstone's "palmy days," children, according to one observer, went to school with huge revolvers strapped to their waists.

It was not only that the pioneer needed a gun to hunt for his meat, without which he could not survive, and that crouching with his weapon behind door or window he could fight off a dozen Indians armed only with clubs, there was also the psychological factor. The early pioneer had been an indentured servant, a lord's tenant farmer, a deported criminal, a former slum dweller. Where he came from, to be armed had been the squire's prerogative. The game in the woods, the fowl in the air, the fish in the stream had belonged to the gentleman. If the poor poacher who snared a rabbit to put something in the family's cooking pot was caught, he got a savage and humiliating hiding from the gamekeeper and wound up in jail. If unlucky, he found himself with a rope around his neck. Sometimes the punishment for an incorrigible poacher was transportation to the New World. It was no wonder that stalking deer with his long rifle made him feel like a king, or at least like gentry, and that he passed some of this feeling on to his sons and grandsons. The gun, together with the ax and plow, made him the master of his environment. In the words of Emerson Hough:

The stars of a new heaven looked down on another king, a king in Linsey-Woolsey. France kicked him forth a peasant and, born again, he scorned the petty limitations of her seigniories, and stood on her rejected empire, the emperor of himself. England rotted him in her mines and ditches but . . . this same man under another sky, was offering hospitality, and not obeisance, to her belted earls.

The frontiersman went around armed, "feeling positively naked without his weapon."

An Englishman traveling through Arkansas asked a native if he ought to buy himself a revolver. " 'Well,' replied the citizen, 'you mout not want one for a month, and you mout not want one for three months; but ef ever you did want one, you kin bet you'd want it almighty sudden!' "

Another Briton, crossing the Plains by train, marveled at seeing his American fellow passengers armed to the teeth with every variety of shooting iron strapped to hip or cradled in lap at some discomfort. The natives kept a sharp watch for anything that moved on the prairie. As the train was passing a small herd of buffalo they banged away in a frenzy "from every available window, with rifles, carbines and revolvers. An American scene, certainly."

The early pioneer was a woodsman walking on foot through dense forests. His weapon was the long rifle, so accurate that with it he scorned to shoot a squirrel anywhere but in the head:

Witness this sweet ancient weapon of our fathers; the American rifle, maker of states, empire builder. . . . In outline severe, practicable, purposeful in every regard. It is devoid of ornamentation. The brass that binds the foot of the stock is here to protect the wood. The metal guard below the lock is to preserve from injury the light set-triggers. . . . This is no belonging of a weak or savage man. It is the weapon of the Anglo-Saxon; that is to say, the Anglo-Saxon in America, who invented it, because he had a need for it.

Mystique again. The prototype was invented by gunsmiths of the German Palatinate (Pfalz) in the early 1700s. Immigrants from that region made the first "Kentucky rifles" at Lancaster, Pennsylvania. The weapon was improved again and again until it became the dreaded "widow and orphan maker" feared by the lobsterbacks armed with the much inferior "Brown Bess" smooth-bore musket. Famous British regiments, which had defeated Napoleon's armies in Spain, recoiled before this weapon at New Orleans, half of their dead, it is said, shot between the eyes. Thus the mystique grew.

The mountain man beyond the Missouri needed a different weapon. Not necessarily "half-alligator and half-timberwolf," but "half-horseman and half-footslogger," the trapper had to have a gun that was short enough to be carried on horseback and was effective against big game, against the powerful buffalo or grizzly. The brothers Jacob and Samuel Hawken provided it with their legendary Hawken rifle made in St. Louis from 1822 to 1849. It was a heavy weapon weighing twelve pounds, a muzzle-loader with an octagonal barrel of .53 caliber firing a half-ounce round ball. It was the weapon of the mountain fur trade. It conquered the Rockies, an ideal weapon for its time and place. But it had its drawbacks. Good at long range, it was clumsy and heavy, not fit for hand-to-hand combat unless one hit one's opponent over the head with it. Also a muzzle-loader was no good for horseback fighting. The Indian's bow and arrows were faster and handier, and he usually was a better rider on a faster horse. A smaller weapon was needed.

The horse or dragoon pistol had already been used by Cromwell's Ironsides against King Charles's Cavaliers. It had nothing to recommend it but its shortness. A pistol became absolutely necessary for the mounted man facing Indians on horseback. It joined the westward march of empire in the form of the single-shot cap-and-ball gun. This was a good weapon for fighting a stately duel at ten paces, but not so satisfactory in a running fight with Comanche warriors. It was the revolver that vanquished the West—the Indians' West. At age twenty, in the year of our Lord 1835, Sam Colt patented the first multiple-shot revolver in England and a year later in the United States. His Patterson Colt was first used by Texas Rangers in 1844 against Comanches with such deadly effect that it broke the tribe's fighting power.

These early revolvers were designed not for cowboys and gunfighters, but for the United States Cavalry. Hence they were known as "dragoons" or "dragoon pistols."

They were all "cap-and-balls." It was necessary to load each chamber of the revolving cylinder separately with percussion cap, powder, and ball, and that took time. Most men therefore carried two guns. Later it became fashionable to have spare, exchangeable, loaded cylinders in one's pocket, sealed off with beeswax to keep the powder dry. A man thus equipped could fire off twenty-four rounds in almost as many seconds. The Dragoon Colt was the gunman's shooting iron's "granddaddy." Later models could be converted to cartridges (containing both powder and ball), making the separate actions of pouring and ramming superfluous. It was at about this stage that the old cap-and-ball became the gunfighter's weapon and found its way into saloons.

These old six-guns were all single-action revolvers, meaning that the hammer had to be cocked for every shot. Later double-action guns made this repeated cocking unnecessary. One just had to pull the trigger five times. Mark that number: FIVE. The six-gun had six chambers, but the wise man always loaded only five chambers—never the one beneath the hammer. A jarring motion could discharge it with the loss—in consequence—of the big toe of the greenhorn ignorant enough to have loaded all six.

Some experienced barroom-shootists, such as Bat Masterson, actually preferred the old-fashioned single-action gun, claiming that the trigger pull of the double-action model was too hard for accurate shooting. It sometimes took both hands to get a shot off. Not for nothing were these guns called thumb-busters. The cap-and-ball could be fired almost as fast as the double-action gun, especially after the trigger notch had been filed away so that the hammer dropped the moment it was

The classical shoot-out, Minden, Nebraska.

released. The single-action gun also lent itself to fanning, that is, to the rapid moving of the free hand, palm down, back and forth across the hammer resulting in staccato firing of all chambers. According to Masterson, an experienced man could draw and get his first shot off in half a second, all the shots in less than two seconds. The pistoleer often filed off the gunsight as well, because it occasionally got stuck in the holster at the most inopportune moment.

The West's most legendary weapon was, of course, the Colt .44 "Peacemaker." Also known as the Equalizer, the Frontier Colt, and the .44-.40, it was remarkable for its feel and balance. Remington and Smith and Wesson made equally fine handguns, but the Colt was the most popular, par-

tially because of Sam Colt's reputation: "Sam Colt, who found the pistol a single shooter and left it a six-shooter." And

God made some men big and some men small, But Sam Colt made them all equal.

Another reason the Peacemaker was so widely and readily accepted—more widely used than Colt's .45—was that its cartridge fit the equally popular Winchester .44 repeating rifle.

Colt and other manufacturers also produced .38, .36, and .32 caliber revolvers, but old-timers maintained that using anything less than a .44 was risky. According to them a man fatally wounded with a .38 or .36 might still take a good swing at you with his bowie knife, while a man hit with a .44

stayed down for good. In actuality, a man hit with either a .44 or a .38 was in serious trouble. Fatalities were high also because of the still primitive state of frontier medicine. A "paunched," that is a gut-shot, man was meat for the undertaker. The doctors, if any were available, did not even try to do anything for him. Nor did they try to probe for bullets lodged deep in the body—for instance, the lungs. They left it all to nature and gangrene.

The Peacemaker, as well as the old hogleg, weighing up to three pounds, had its day, and it was a long one. By the 1920s only a few Texas law officers still used it, and then mostly to pose in their old outfits for photographers. From the thirties on, for serious work western law officers used a .45 auto-loader, a .38 double-action Smith and Wesson or Colt, a Winchester .30-.30 carbine, and a Remington 12-gauge auto-loading shotgun full of buckshot and slugs, loaded alternately. In movies and on the TV screen sheriffs as well as badmen use six-shooters exclusively. The very word "gun" in the American mystique means a heavy six-shooter. In real life even the most celebrated nineteenth-century shooting iron was only a poor cousin to the rifle and shotgun, especially the latter. Whenever they could, sheriffs, marshals, Texas Rangers, as well as ranchers with rustler trouble, relied on shotguns. Even the baddest of badmen, all horns and rattles, with a six-gun on each hip, backed down when faced with a shotgun, also known as scatter-gun or Greener, which did terrible things at close range, virtually cutting men in half. They didn't need much aiming. Even a half-blind drunk, pointing one in the right direction, was sure to maim and kill. The Greener, made in London, England, was, in its day, the finest shotgun in the world, a favorite of the unromantic western fellow who meant business. As the saying went: "Buckshot meant buryin' every time."

The westerner was thus given a wide range of the finest guns the age could produce. How well did he do with them? Those wonderful heavy old handguns with their mighty kick didn't lend themselves to very accurate shooting the way a modern target pistol does. And it is a very different thing to shoot at a target for sport and at a fellow shooting back at you "with the lead flying both ways." There was also this dilemma facing the saloon fighter—should he go for speed or take time to aim? A fast man might beat the other fellow to the draw—but would he put the other fellow down? On the other hand, careful aiming might result in hitting the other fellow between the eyes, but only after he had first done considerable damage to the aimer. After studying the accounts of a great many saloon encounters, one comes to the conclusion that the average cowboy was no better a shot than the average sportsman of today and that even the most famous shootists often were less than accurate.

The great Wyatt Earp occasionally could be as careless with his artillery as a greenhorn. As the Wichita *Beacon* reported on January 12, 1876:

Last Sunday night while policeman Earp was sitting with two or three others in the back room of the Custom House saloon, his revolver slipped from its holster and in falling to the floor the hammer, which was resting on the cap, is supposed to have struck the chair, causing a discharge of one of the barrels. The ball passed through his coat, struck the north wall then glanced off and passed out through the ceiling. It was a narrow escape and the occurrence got up a lively stampede from the room.

In a gun battle in front of Abilene's Alamo Saloon with a gambler named Phil Coe, Wild Bill Hickok managed to slay his antagonist, but two of the bullets intended for Coe slammed into, and killed, his very good friend Mike Williams, who was rushing to his assistance.

If Wyatt Earp could almost shoot himself and

"More shooting was done in fun. . . ."

Wild Bill Hickok kill the wrong man, one could not expect the ordinary gunslinger to do better. Some cowpunchers "could not hit the side of a barn if they had the whole day to do it." Cowboys packed guns, but very rarely fired them in anger. If they had money in their pockets, they wasted costly ammunition by practicing on tin cans and bottles. Some oiled the insides of their holsters for that "snakelike, lightnin' draw." Some fancied themselves gunfighters to their ultimate regret.

Shooting, on the average, was bad because the shootists were drunk: "When a cowhand in town for a whing-ding had seen the bottom of a tumblerful of Nebraska Needle Gun a few times, his marksmanship was apt to be erratic." The six-gun heroes usually drank like fish. The consumptive Doc Holliday kept going with a daily quart of hard stuff. Even the pulpwriters glorifying Masterson and Earp admitted that drinking frequently affected their dignity as law officers and their aim as well. The great Wild Bill was occasionally found lying in the mud in front of a saloon, totally soused and oblivious to the world. Some called him Wild Bill Hiccup. Most of the badmen were alcoholics, punishing the bottle whenever they came to town.

Some shooting incidents make humorous reading. In Green River's Gold Nugget Saloon,

two desperadoes, having only one revolver between them, took turns firing solemnly at each other, doing no damage to themselves, but demolishing mirrors and glassware. A Tascosa, Colorado, newspaper dryly reported a man wagering that he could shoot off another fellow's bowler hat at a distance of a hundred feet . . . "The winner's body was planted yesterday in Boot Hill." During a tremendous shoot-out inside a Fort Griffin, Texas, saloon the antagonists swapping lead at close range missed each other, but shot two lawyers having a drink at the bar—one fatally—killed a young cowhand, and winged a deputy sheriff. In an Oregon saloon, Hank Vaughn, a noted gunman, and a cowhand named Jack clasped left hands, drew on signal from a third party, and emptied the chambers of their shooting irons at each other. Both survived. After reading numerous accounts such as these one wonders whether those involved were badmen or merely bad shots.

More shooting was done in fun than in earnest. Possibly the knowledge that some banging away was just friendly sport improved the aim. Teddy Blue recalled an incident inside a Montana saloon:

There was a fellow that used to be around Miles City, by the name of Tom Irvine, who was the best shot I ever saw. One night when they were all in the saloon, Louis King, that deputy I was telling you about, was standing there with a cigar in his mouth, and Tom pulled his six-gun out and shot the end off. Louis never budged. He just stuck his face out a little further and Tom clipped another half inch off the cigar so it was down to a little stub. Still Louis never moved, but only stood there with it held out between his lips as though he was daring Tom to come on and shoot again.

Tom said: "You go to hell," and shoved his gun back in the scabbard.

Such things happened, but not as often as the movies would have it.

George Ade thought that the worst ruckus he ever saw in rural prairie saloons were "fights between a couple of agricultural huskies trained on copper-distilled Kentucky sourmash." Shine Philips wrote about the shooting up of saloons and other "harmless high jinks" in his Texas hometown:

Some ranch outfits, when they came to town, would set up their own government for two or three days and the rest of us would kinder take out and make ourselves scarce in the interests of our health, but they would promptly pay for all the destruction—all the lights they shot out and all the mirrors they busted up in saloons. The better saloons carried spare mirrors for their backbars, because when the boys got around a certain amount of that electrifying pizen, they positively could not be deterred from shooting them up. Mirrors and lights just drew their gunfire like a magnet. Also some cowhand drunk always had an irresistible desire to ride his horse into the saloon and let him look around.

There are literally hundreds of anecdotes about cowboys riding their horses into saloons. According to one story, three young punchers at

Cowboys "hurrahing" a town.
By Frederic Remington.

Socorro, New Mexico, rode into a saloon making a considerable nuisance of themselves, one of the horses depositing a number of steaming samples into an elegantly dressed drummer's open sample case. The fastidious salesman, who was just having his nightcap at the bar, complained loudly to the mixologist, who was himself an ex-cowhand. This bartender looked hard and dolefully at the drummer and finally unburdened himself with a: "What the hell y'u doin' in here afoot anyhow?"

The pastime could be improved upon—for instance, by playing a game of billiards on horseback. On one occasion a California saloon keeper who tried to stop such goings on "because the billiard table cloth might get ruined" was shot dead by one of the annoyed players. In Dodge City a Texan was known for frequently riding his horse into the Alamo Saloon and asking for two drinks, one for himself and one for Old Paint; the horse was described as a habitual tippler. In Abilene a pesky cowpuncher with his hogleg drawn rode his horse into a barbershop and forced the barber to

stand on a high chair and give him a shave and haircut while he remained astride his mount. Such pranks were not always taken in good humor. At Fort Benton, Montana, a cowboy was riddled with fourteen .44 caliber slugs by a saloon keeper when he insisted upon riding his horse upstairs to his room.

Clean fun, or not so clean, there were fatalities. Upholders of the western mystique would have us believe that the saloon shootists conducted their bloody business in the manner of medieval knights jousting according to the rules of chivalry. As Gene Rhodes explained it:

To rise up from a man's table and war upon that man while the taste of his bread is still sweet in your mouth—such dealings would have been unspeakable infamy. . . . You must not smile and shoot. You must not shoot an unarmed man, and you must not shoot an unwarned man. Here is a nice distinction, but a clear one; you might not ambush your enemy; but, when you fled and your

Gunmen did not always observe the frontier code that their opponents should be "heeled."

enemy followed, you might then waylay and surprise without question to your honor, for they were presumed to be on their guard and sufficiently warned. The rattlesnake's code, to warn before he strikes, no better; a queer, lop-sided, topsy-turvy, jumbled and senseless code—but a code for all of that. And it's worthy of note that no better standard has ever been kept with such faith as this barbarous code of the fighting man.

Some knights of the prairie lived by that code, but there are abundant accounts of gunfighters bushwacking their enemies, blowing their heads off without warning, shooting them in the back, or killing them while they were helplessly sick in bed. One has to differentiate between the real bad badman and the pretended badman.

J. Cabell Brown described the type well:

The average western badman is not nearly so dangerous as is the California flea or the Hoboken bedbug.

The genus "KID" wore his hair long, and in curls upon his shoulders; had an insipient moustache, and sported a costume made of buckskin ornamented with fringe, tassels, and strings of the same material—the dirtier the better. His head was covered with a cowboy's hat of phenomenal width of brim, having many metal stars, half-moons, etc., around the crown. Upon his feet he wore either moccasins or very high-heeled, stub-toed boots, and an enormous pair of spurs, with little steel balls that jingled at each step. Buckled around his waist would be a cartridge belt holding two carefully sited revolvers, and a bone-handled bowie knife in his boot leg, completed his dress.

The "cayuse" was never far from his master, for when that gentleman wanted a horse he wanted him badly; either to escape from a worse man than himself, or to escape the consequences of having killed one.

These "kids" were almost as annoying as flies. There was a Nevada Kid, Wyoming Kid, Texas Kid, Pecos Kid, Colorado Kid, Pockmarked Kid, Billie, Willie, and Jimmy the Kid. The most deadly and obnoxious were seldom over twenty-five years old; some only seventeen, eighteen, or twenty. The generic name of all these juvenile delinquents throughout the territories was "kid." Today, many of them would have wound up in juvenile court with their names carefully withheld from the public and posterity. In fairness to the profession, these types should not be classified as cowboys. They herded cattle when there was absolutely no other way to make a dollar, get a cup of coffee and a bed to sleep in; but they were basically work-shy and spent more time in saloons rustling up trouble than on the range with the little dogies. As Brown put it: "It would be better to eat sand for a month than to truculently cross the orbit of this flaming meteor of a Kid."

Fortunately they did not live long. Jesse James died at thirty-five, King Fisher at thirty, the Nevada Kid at twenty-two, Doc Holliday at thirty-five, the Verdigris Kid at twenty-four, Curly Bill Brocius at thirty, the Dutch Kid at twenty-seven, Clay Allison at thirty-seven, the Ace-High Kid at twenty-eight, Johnnie Ringo at thirty-one, and Billy the Kid at a satisfying twenty-one.

The most famous Kid was, of course, William H. Bonney, better known as Billy the Kid. It is symptomatic of the great esteem in which Americans hold a killer that this vicious, unprepossessing, buck-toothed juvenile was made into a legendary Robin Hood figure, the subject of more hardcover books than Einstein and Picasso put together.

William H. Bonney, like many of the badmen, was not a born westerner. He entered this world in Brooklyn, in 1859. His greatest claim to fame rests upon the fact that he killed twenty-one men, one for each year of his life, and that he shot his first man when only twelve years old. Actually, he committed his first murder at eighteen, and even had he done this six years earlier it would not have been very remarkable. In 1885 a boy of ten named

Billy the Kid.

James Oscar Barker blew away a man with his shotgun inside an Idaho thirst parlor. And in 1872, at Gold Hill, Nevada, "John Williams called Willie Miller a liar, whereupon Willie shot John through the head with a revolver. Both were under twelve years of age."

Billy the Kid was, comparatively, a late bloomer. His first offense was stealing clothes from two Chinese laundrymen in Las Vegas, New Mexico—not a very auspicious start. At age nineteen he was hired by one of two rival factions of ranchers as a cowhand, but in reality as a hit-man, having already established his reputation as a horse thief and cattle rustler. He was described as a first-rate killer, but only a fourth-rate cowboy, looking like a teenager, an undersized fellow desperately trying to raise a little fuzz on his upper lip. After having, indeed, killed twenty-one men, "not counting Mexicans and Indians," within the space of three years, some of them unarmed or unaware, the Kid fell victim to Pat Garrett, who shot Billy down as he entered a darkened room of the Maxwell ranch in the wee hours of a July morning. Sheriff Pat Garrett became instantly famous and, naturally, wrote a romanticized *Authentic Life of Billy the Kid.* Pat himself was dry-gulched, shot in the back of his head, in 1908, long after the Southwest had, presumably, been made safe for little old ladies and retired peace officers.

Another typical frontier hero was Ben Thompson, typical because he was at various times a Johnny Reb, badman and marshal, professional gambler and saloon owner, womanizer and kind husband. He was soft-spoken and gentle, yet a brutal killer, a consumer of great quantities of whiskey, and a Texan. He started out as a Confederate soldier, and after the Civil War, became a mercenary in Emperor Maximilian's army. He won so much money gambling that he used his winnings from poker games to open a number of saloons, which did not prevent him from shooting up half a dozen similar establishments, sometimes in company with his bloodthirsty brother Billy. Inside Brennan's Saloon, at Ellsworth, Kansas, Billy gunned down his good pal Sheriff Whitney by mistake in a shoot-out.

Ben cried, "You've killed our friend, Billy!"

"I'd shot him if he was Jesus Christ himself" was the answer.

Ben killed a great many men on the merest provocation. He was that rarity among gunfighters, a good shot. He was seldom taken to account. Judges, jurors, and prosecutors were afraid to offend him. In Austin, Texas, he once went on a monumental spree, shooting up the local newspaper, a keno hall, the police headquarters, one variety saloon, three cat houses, and, for good measure, a poor Italian's hand organ.

After this exhibition, Thompson disappeared for two years, shooting people in various places all over the West. When he returned to Austin, the citizens thought that it was better to have him on the side of the law and elected Ben city marshal. After being a model officer for a while he got bored and moseyed down to San Antonio for a weekend of fun, killing a man named Harris, the owner of a hurdy-gurdy house. Thompson was acquitted, not unexpectedly, by fearful jurors, and returned to the same place for further amusement. This time, however, a reception party was waiting for him and his friend, King Fisher, also a gunman, whom Ben had taken along on his lark. What happened is obscured by clouds of black powder. As a San Antonio reporter lyrically described it:

There they lay, side by side, weltering in their own blood, with their hair and faces carmined with their own life fluid. The stairs leading up to this place of horror were as slippery as ice, the walls were stained, and the floor was tracked with bloody footprints, while dissolute women, with blanched faces, crowded around with exclamations, and amid broken sobs demanded to know, "Which is Ben?" "Show me Ben," "Is that Ben?", so that even in death the grim reputation of the man stood forth as strong as ever.

When Thompson still showed a flicker of life, the dance-saloon's policeman, Coy, blew out his brains with a six-shooter. In the excitement, Coy got the revolver stuck in his holster, shot himself in the leg, and died eleven days later.

A maverick among saloon fighters was Clay Allison, "the corpsemaker" and Don Quixote of the shootists, and possibly the inventor of streaking. Allison committed so many murders inside

barrooms that Colorado saloon keepers closed up whenever he came to town. He was a sandy-haired, brooding, not bad-looking man with a wild look in his "dancing" eyes. He has been described as a manic-depressive psychopath, forever wavering between elation and depression. A southern guerrilla in Nathan Bedford Forrest's outfit, he had been discharged for insanity. He had the southerner's exaggerated reverence for "sacred womanhood," and he respected clergymen, liking to sing hymns and improvising religious services in saloons. He was, however, hell on men who, for often obscure reasons, were "graveling" him.

He once fought a duel with a neighbor about the location of a fence. They battled it out with bowie knives, according to Allison's specifications, inside an open grave dug for the purpose of accommodating the loser. At the end of the gory affair of honor, Allison, dripping blood from crippling wounds and laughing insanely, had the satisfaction of shoveling the sod over his opponent's body.

In a more jocular moment Allison, at gunpoint, pulled three teeth out of a dentist's mouth without anesthesia—in revenge for pain caused to him. In a Texas town he galloped through Main Street stark naked except for sombrero, gun belt, boots, and spurs. Riding standing up in his stirrups, he shouted pleasantries to all the ladies present, waving the proof of his manhood at them. After having sent an estimated eighteen men up the flume, Allison was killed by falling from a wagon, to the great relief of all.

John Wesley Hardin, the son of a Methodist preacher, possibly holds the record for the number of men killed in and around saloons. He himself was killed shaking dice in El Paso's Acme saloon by Constable "Uncle John" Selman. They had been after the same girl. A year later Uncle John, in turn, got into a fight with a peace officer named Scarborough inside the Wigwam saloon.

Scarborough had called Selman John Wesley Hardin's murderer. A duel was arranged. When Selman's hand went for his holster, he was surprised to find that somebody had deftly lifted his gun, and Scarborough promptly shot him dead. Shortly thereafter, in a New Mexico barroom, one of the ever-present Kids, in this case Kid Curry, called Scarborough Selman's murderer and gunned him down. John Wesley Hardin had a nephew called Mannen Clements who, inside El Paso's Coney Island saloon, got into an argument over the multiple Hardin-Selman-Scarborough-Kid Curry feud and was promptly dispatched to the happy hunting grounds with a bad case of lead poisoning. In the meantime, in a Texas bucket shop, Kid Curry . . . Well, it was a perfect example of the chain reaction, or falling-dominoes syndrome, of western saloon fights.

Hardin had killed at least twenty-four men with his single-action Colt .45, and possibly as many as forty. On the other hand, it is quite possible that the famous Bat Masterson killed none. Typically, Bat was a jack of all trades—hunter, scout, gambler, Indian trader and fighter, faro dealer, saloon keeper, restaurant owner, politician, U.S. marshal, badman, railroad grader, mule driver, buffalo skinner, and sportswriter. He was not a reckless, trigger-finger-happy shootist, but rather, to his credit, a cautious diplomat who managed to persuade evildoers to surrender—often at the point of a double-barreled shotgun. He was a dapper, medium-sized man, who habitually wore a gray bowler hat and was as far removed in appearance from the stereotype frontier fighter as possible. His mustache was a small, bank-clerk type of thing, his eyes blue and gentle, his cheeks plump and rosy, his manners excessively polite.

His repute as a gunslinger was entirely due to the imagination of newspapermen. The first man he killed was a cavalry sergeant named King. The sergeant surprised Bat fondling his, King's, girl friend Molly in a Sweetwater, Texas, saloon. As the trooper unlimbered his artillery, Molly clung to Bat, shielding him with her body. As a consequence, she stopped the bullet intended for Masterson, who fired from behind her, killing King. Molly also died from the effects of her wound. According to the frontier code this was no kill at all, and did not entitle Bat to a notch on his gun handle.

Masterson became marshal of "hell-popping" Dodge. He drank, and sometimes subdued and arrested drunks. He gambled, and hauled gamblers into the calaboose. He was part-owner of the Long Branch Saloon, and later closed down saloons according to the law. He arrested lawbreakers, and as often sided with them against the law. He suppressed vice in various forms, but lived in sin with a fallen angel, Annie Ladue, age nineteen, and was known as the Fighting Pimp. He has been credited with killing two drunken drovers, Jack Wagner and Alf Walker, in a fight spilling over from the Long Branch into Hoover's saloon. A study of contemporary local newspapers makes it highly probable that it was not Bat, but his brother Ed, himself dying of a bullet through his abdomen, who accounted for the two drovers. Finally, Masterson supposedly killed Al Updegraff. However, four days after his supposed demise, Updegraff sent a note that he had been merely wounded and that he was doing nicely. It is possible that Updegraff died weeks later of blood poisoning. Which leaves only Sergeant King as Bat's verified victim, and he died, one might say, accidentally, by courtesy of Molly Brennan. Of such stuff are legends made.

This paucity of victims in no way discouraged the reporters. One stringer for a Kansas City, Missouri, newspaper wrote:

BAT'S BULLETS

. . . Your gentleman, who has dropped his man is

no uncommon individual, but when you see a man who has entered upon

HIS THIRD DOZEN

it is time to be civil, for he may begin to fear that material is about to run out, and may have an uncontrollable desire to hurry up and finish that third dozen. Such a gentleman . . . is the famous Mr. Bat Masterson, of Dodge City . . . (it is well to be respectful.)

Masterson became known as the Deadliest Gun in the West, Devil's Desperado, and the "greatest exterminator of evildoers who ever lived." A judge once asked him whether he really had killed thirty-eight men. He modestly replied: "No, unless Indians are counted. I don't let anybody shoot at me. If folks let me alone I never hurt them."

Probably due to his essential peacefulness, Masterson survived until 1921 as a sportswriter in New York City. The equally notorious Wyatt Earp, sometime saloon, brewery, and gambling-den owner, was also a rather cautious man, working by bluff whenever he could, thereby living to the ripe old age of eighty-one. That Masterson did some autobiographical writing, and Earp gave newspapers his story, did not hurt their public image.

The ultimate example of the man-killing lady-killer, the ne plus ultra of legendary gunfighters, was James Butler Hickok, better known as Wild Bill Hickok, King of the Pistoleers. Unlike other gunmen, Wild Bill came from an Illinois family of farming abolitionists and himself served as a Union scout. He went to Kansas at age twenty-two and did not kill his first man until he was twenty-eight. Known mainly as a peace officer and shootist, he actually spent most of his life gambling and drinking in saloons, which served him throughout as headquarters. As a peace officer he had one fatal weakness—he often shot the wrong man. As one Deadwood saloon keeper put it: "When it came to telling a bandit from an honest citizen,

Wild Bill Hickok.

Wild Bill couldn't tell shit from honey." Due to eastern writers and his own penchant for telling tall tales, Wild Bill's story became a fantastic mixture of fact and fiction. Every phase of his life is subject to conflicting accounts. People who knew him in the flesh could not even agree on his looks. A Kansas lady said that she had always thought John Wilkes and Edwin Booth the most beautiful men in the world—until she met Wild Bill. General Custer's wife, Libby, looked upon him as one of the finest specimens of rugged American manhood. Stuart Henry, in his *Conquering Our Great American Plains,* was not particularly impressed with Hickok's "ruggedness." He wrote of the pistoleer's "Feminine looks and bearing . . . that rather angelic countenance," which were all "quite opposite of the then, rawboned Texas model." Because of his long, ferretlike nose, one hostile writer referred to him as the "human anteater." Others called him the American Cyrano de Bergerac. Hickok reputedly shot one man for having persistently called him Duck Bill.

Hickok was vain. In his early days he strutted

around in an outlandish Zouave uniform—"the very caricature of a frontier scout." As a marshal he usually wore a fringed buckskin outfit, beaded moccasins, and a belt in which were stuck a bowie knife and two six-shooters with their ivory handles facing forward. As a national celebrity he took to wearing frock coats, embroidered vests, plaid capes, and small, stylish hats.

For an opening, he killed unarmed David McCanles, shooting him from behind a window curtain. Later Wild Bill gave his own version of the affair, according to which he had single-handedly killed the notorious McCanles gang of Confederate spies and robbers, no fewer than ten of them, with his trusty rifle, six-shooter, and bowie knife—"Striking savage blows, following the devils up from one side to the other of the room into the corners, striking and slashing until everyone was dead."

Thus the legend of the "Pistol Dead Shot" and the "Knight of the Pistol" was born. In 1871 he became marshal of Abilene, setting up headquarters inside the Alamo Saloon, where he spent most of his time playing poker. Some citizens did not cotton to Wild Bill's "life in the bosom of Abilene's criminal population as one of its steady gamblers." They said he permitted any crime so long as it did not interfere with his own business. Public opinion finally forced him to leave.

In the meantime his legend grew, not without help from the "Knight Chivalric" himself. He boasted to Henry Stanley of having killed "considerably over a hundred men, but not without good cause." The farther away a writer lived, the less he had seen of Wild Bill, the more lyrical he waxed:

Any man who by his own force and fearlessness beats the dark forces of savagery and crime, so

Wild Bill generally won his arguments over cards.

that civilization may be free to take another step forward on her march to progress—is he not the greatest and truest type of the frontiersman? Such a man was Wild Bill.

Those who knew him well did not share these sentiments. The Leavenworth *Times* of July 17, 1869, commented: "If the enthusiastic admirers of this old plainsman could see him on one of his periodical drunks, they would have considerable romance knocked out of them."

Some contemporary westerners found Wild Bill stories merely funny and wondered how the folks back east could swallow such stuff. Eastern ladies were particularly fascinated by tales of Hickok, the Great Lover. Women, in the words of a friend, "fell hard for Bill." It was no wonder that Hickok went into showbiz, cashing in on his reputation by going on stage as well as joining Buffalo Bill's Wild West Show. As an actor he was a failure, a victim of stage fright. On opening night the King of the Pistoleers was struck dumb, unable to utter a single word. Maybe he gagged on the lines he was supposed to speak: "Fear not, fair maid, you are safe at last with Wild Bill, who is ready to risk his life, if need be, in the defense of weak and helpless womanhood." He himself admitted that the show was bad.

How good he was at shooting is a matter of dispute. He was supposed to be able to hit the ace of spades at fifty paces with all six bullets, drive a cork into a bottle at seventy-five yards, and hit spinning silver dollars while racing his horse. But fellow gunmen said that he was a poor shot and painfully slow with his Colt .44. They attributed his successes as a killer to shooting the other fellow when he wasn't looking. By the time a victim merely suspected Wild Bill had it in for him, he was already dead.

Hickok met his fate at Deadwood in 1876. He had come there to gamble and spent most of his time at Nuttall and Mann's saloon playing poker and being polite—and not getting into a single fight.

He was shot by a tinhorn gambler, Jack McCall, who found the King of the Pistoleers sitting in Nuttall and Mann's, playing poker with his back to the door, the first and last time he was caught in that position, holding what has since become known as the "dead man's hand," a pair of black aces and a pair of eights. McCall "drilled a hole neatly through old Bill's cerebellum." The bullet that passed through Hickok's head went on to embed itself in the wrist of his poker partner, Captain Frank Massey. Frank later used to enter saloons with the exultant cry: "Gents, the bullet which killed Wild Bill has come to town!" The doctor who examined Hickok's body later wrote: "I have seen many dead men on the field of battle and in civil life, but Wild Bill was the prettiest corpse I have ever seen."

Wild Bill's death was a calamity for the eastern writers who had made a living out of describing his deeds of derring-do. How were the writers to feed the public's interest? Deadwood, in the throes of a great gold rush, was in the news. Ed Wheeler, a New York brownstone dweller, solved the problem by simply inventing a new gunfighter extraordinary—"Deadwood Dick":

Boston Bill snatched open the door and pulled the struggling woman out onto the hot desert floor.

"Unhand me, foul villain!" she cried, her innocent young face pleading more eloquently than any words.

Boston Bill laughed heartlessly at her tender pleas, and in an instant was galloping away with his fair captive.

"Woe is me!" her aged aunt wailed with tears of grief flowing down her face. "All is lost!"

"Hark!" said the stagecoach driver, turning his ear to the distant hills. "I hear hoofbeats!" Suddenly his face lighted up and he cried: "Fear not, madam, for all is not lost! There is but one man in all the West who rides a great white stallion such as the one that approaches so swiftly! It is Deadwood Dick to the rescue!"

Wheeler ground out Deadwood Dick books, more than sixty of them, until people believed that Deadwood Dick was as real as Buffalo Bill or Sitting Bull. In 1926, the United States celebrated its hundred-fiftieth birthday. Deadwood celebrated "Black Hills Days of '76," glorifying Custer and Wild Bill, who had cashed in their chips half a century before. Buffalo Bill was dead, so were Calamity Jane and the New York author Wheeler. But no record of Deadwood Dick's demise could be found. Might he possibly be alive? A frantic search uncovered not *the* Deadwood Dick, but one elderly Dick Clark, who had lived most of his life in and around Deadwood shoveling manure as a hired farmhand. Well, his name was *Dick,* and he hailed from Deadwood, and he was a nice-looking old geezer, and, yes, for a little bit of the green stuff he would let his hair grow and wear buckskin and stick a "hogleg" in his belt. Deadwood Dick alive! He went to Washington and shook hands with President Coolidge. He posed with tourists for a reasonable fee. He made the rounds of venerable saloons and was treated to countless drinks while spinning his yarn. In time he really believed that he was, indeed, *the* Deadwood Dick.

Most of the mayhem occurring in barrooms was done not by legendary characters who sold their stories to reporters, but by ordinary fellows, neither particularly bad nor good, who got themselves into situations they couldn't back out of. They did what the western he-man code demanded of them, often reluctantly. In most cases they survived. Since there were very many saloons populated by an average of twenty customers on weekdays, drunk and coyoting around for some action, fights were numberless. One man computed that in Nevada alone 402 deaths took place

during the "shooting years." The unsung western heroes' doings make good reading, especially in their accidental oddball ways, unembroidered by pulp writers. It is not from the fights of Holliday, Hardin, or Hickok that one gets the feel of saloon violence.

In Denver, three citizens were drinking tumblers of Red Uprising over a game of poker in a saloon's back room when one of them suddenly keeled over—dead from a heart attack. Afraid of being accused of killing him, his pals arranged the body artfully, resting it on the table as if sleeping off a drunk. They then departed quietly. The bartender later found him and tried to shake him awake. The corpse toppled from his chair and the poor booze-boss was now saddled with the problem of having to explain his death. He quickly shot the dead man through the chest, claiming to have killed him in self-defense. He was immediately exonerated, having found the simplest and most plausible way out of his dilemma.

In Durango, Colorado, a nattily dressed stranger in silk hat, spats, and monocle, smoking a cigarillo, entered a primitive cowhands' whiskey mill with a cocked six-gun in his hand inquiring: "Has anybody anything to say about my clothes?" Nobody had. The dude's nerve was admired. He was treated and he treated in return, having avoided a fight through bluff.

Everything imaginable was used as a weapon during saloon fights—fists, thumbs, feet, boots, spurs, teeth, knees, nails, bung starters, saps, the foot-high variety of cuspidors, bottles, brass knuckles, knives, pistols, six-shooters, rifles, carbines, and shotguns. In Arizona, a lady severely wounded a miner with her hatpin. Fists would do in a pinch. Thom Smith, the fearless and beloved police chief of Abilene, often went around unarmed. He would crowd troublemakers in saloons so closely that they had no chance to draw, whack them good, and then, well pacified, drag them off

"Most of the mayhem was done by ordinary fellows."

to the hoosegow. He was foully murdered by two thugs, shot through the lung, pistol-whipped, and almost decapitated with an ax.

Teeth were used to bite off noses and ears. Michigan and Wisconsin timbermen proved their manhood by biting hunks of wood out of bars. Many bars had rows of half-moon shapes bitten out of the edges of their counters, each neatly labeled in India ink with the biter's name—from which it can be deduced that midwestern bars must have been made of local pine. Drunken loggers would have lost their teeth on a fine western Brunswick-Callander bar made of mahogany or Circassian walnut.

Most corpses on barroom floors were "rich in lead but too badly punctured to hold whiskey." Two punchers from Grey Bull, Wyoming, disgruntled over having been fleeced in a game of three-card monte the night before, argued over who should have the first chance to pour condensed milk over his bowl of oatmeal. Both drew, one a trifle faster than the other. Result: One dead. Verdict: Justifiable self-defense.

In Denver's Murphy's Exchange saloon, known as the Slaughter House because so many men found their deaths inside its barroom, Tom Cady made a lunge with his sword cane at gambler Jim Jordan. Jordan pulled his iron. A shoot-out followed. When the smoke cleared the main opponents were unhurt, but one onlooker, gambler Cliff Sparks, was coughing out his life at the brass rail.

At the last moment, Sparks's closest friend, "Tinhorn Bill" Crooks, rushed forward, tears streaming down his face, crying: "They've killed the dearest pal I ever had!" Sobbing, he pushed

"Everything imaginable was used during saloon fights."

everybody aside, cradled his dead friend in his lap, burying his head on his chest and, still weeping loudly, bit off the $2,500 diamond "headlight" stud from the "bosom of Sparks' biled shirt," and made off in a hurry, wonderfully consoled.

One of the bloodiest shooting scrapes occurred between a Texan named Hugh Anderson and a Kansan, Arthur McCluskey. In 1871 Anderson killed Arthur's brother, policeman Mike McCluskey, in a Newton, Kansas, saloon melee. Leaving nine men dead or wounded, this fracas was known as the Newton General Massacre. It took Arthur two years to catch up with his brother's murderer, but he finally found his man in a Medicine Lodge, Kansas, whiskey mill. Both men agreed to a duel unto death. And that is just what happened. The fight was so long and so brutal that the winner, Anderson, died shortly after McCluskey expired of his fatal wounds. They had first shot each other, then used their knives, and, finally, their teeth and nails.

Women, too, were no strangers to violence. At Eureka, Nevada, during an argument inside the Tiger Saloon "Hog-Eyed Mary" Irwin and "Bulldog Kate" Miller settled an argument with a knife between each other's ribs. At Denver, Madame la Monte felled a waiter with a large, overage, under-done trout. An early San Francisco newspaper reported:

The Cyprian on the Rampage. Rosa Oalaque, the same Spanish maid that slashed John Green across the face, got full of fighting whiskey, donned her warpaint and started out to clean out (the soiled) dovecotes on Bonanza Street, Thanksgiving night. The officers put her in a little bed in jail, where she remains at present.

In Yuma, Arizona, a young Apache woman entered a pulqueria with a large wooden box, walked up to a cavalry sergeant, opened the lid, and let out a large rattler which promptly sank its fangs into the trooper's cheek. Thus she "visited terrible retribution upon her seducer."

Hurdy girls habitually wore derringers in their bodices known as "boob" or "tit" guns. Nymphs *du pavé* had tiny, double-barreled "over-and-under" pistols tied to the inside of their thighs. Known as Wesson's Ladies' Friend, this miniature weapon led to many denouements.

In a Tucson bagnio, an indignant Calamity Jane with an old cap-and-ball opened fire at "greasers" for aspiring to obtain her favors. Her body was for whites only. She also fired four shots into the walls behind Denver's famous Windsor bar, because the bartender had refused to serve whiskey to a lady, and likewise smoked up a Bozeman, Montana, saloon whose owner had served her enough Dakota Dynamite to float a battleship —but who eventually refused her any more drinks "because she had had enough." She claimed to have received her nickname after rescuing an army officer, who was also a lover, from the scalping knives of a Sioux war party—"saving him from a dire calamity." Those who knew her well claimed that she got her name because "gents were stricken by a venereal calamity shortly after making her acquaintance."

The West also had its bona fide female gunfighters and bandidas, some of whom made quite a reputation for themselves. Annie McDougal and Jennie Metcalf, better known as Cattle Annie and Little Britches, while still in their teens had a bootleg operation going, selling moonshine to Osage Indians. They broadened out into cattle rustling and horse stealing, taking time to have their picture taken—Cattle Annie posing with her Winchester, Little Britches in a regular cowboy outfit, with a large cartridge belt and Colt worn at the left hip, its ivory handle facing front. On one occasion they helped the Doolin gang rob a bank.

The Rose of the Cimarron was a sweet girl with an angelic face. She turned bandida through love for her sweetheart George Newcombe, a member of the Dalton-Doolin gang. During an epic shoot-out at Ingalls, Oklahoma, she carried guns and spare ammunition to the bandits while the bullets were flying. It is said that the gallant sheriffs withheld fire while she was scurrying to and fro. She helped her sweetheart escape by having him hang on to her as she galloped off on her fine black mare. She too posed, charmingly wistful and demure, fingering her heavy .45 in a most ladylike way. She eventually married a farmer—some say a blacksmith—and raised a big family.

Pearl Hart was a diminutive brat of a woman in pants, boots, man's shirt, suspenders, a cowboy hat set at a rakish angle, and short dark hair parted on the side. Armed with two Colts, a Winchester, and an old-fashioned buffalo gun, Pearl together with her sweetheart Joe Boot held up the Arizona Globe stage. This little peccadillo made her instantly famous. After her release from prison she starred in a play written about her, reenacting her own experiences as a pistolera:

The drama will embody Pearl's own experience as a stage robber, with all the blood and thunder accompaniments, and the famous Pearl will once again with her trusty Winchester hold up the driver of a western stage, line up the passengers and relieve them of their valuables, while her part-

ner, "Boots," covers the victims with his guns, and takes no chances.

As an actress Pearl was no great success. She faded from view. Twenty-five years later a well-dressed little woman appeared at the Pima County, Arizona, jail and announced: "I am Pearl Hart and I would like to see my old cell." She was given the gala tour, politely said her farewells, and disappeared—for good. It is not to be wondered at that female gunslingers, among them totally fictitious brainchildren of an author's imagination, became the heroines of numerous dime novels.

How many people were actually killed in saloons is, of course, pure guesswork. Jim Marshall,

Some robbers were women in male attire.

who wrote a book about saloons in the 1940s, argued that during three hundred years of drinking in America about ten people a day must have been killed—nationwide—inside drinking places. After all, he argued, in many of the larger cities and camps a man was killed every day, year in, year out, over long periods. By this reasoning he arrives at a nice round quarter-million stiffs lying on sawdust floors. One can arrive at double or at half that number with equal ease, or pick out any number blindfolded for that matter. We shall never know.

While the six-gun still sputtered in the West, a few discerning observers noted that its days were over. As early as 1892 Richard Harding Davis wrote: "The coming of the barb-wire fence and the railroad killed the cowboy as a picturesque element of recklessness and lawlessness. . . . It suppressed him and localized him and limited him to his own range, and made his revolver merely an ornament."

The western writers of the romantic school missed the sound of the festive revolver. The longer it was gone and the safer it became to lift a tumbler of the red essence at the bar, the more they pined for it—and for the craggy he-men who had made the lead fly. Owen White lamented:

Those fine old-timers who used to come to town for a hell of a time, and have it when they got there, who played poker, monte, and faro bank with the far and beautiful North Star as the limit, who took cold unless they carried a six-shooter and a Winchester, who slept better on the ground than they did on a mattress, who "rolled their own" and drank whiskey out of tin dippers have now entirely disappeared from the face of Texas.

In 1911, the age of law and order and electricity, a belated shoot-out took place in that venerable, long-tamed place, the dim bar of Denver's Brown Palace Hotel. It was due to a fault in dead reckoning. Mrs. Isabelle Patterson-Spring, the youngish and beautiful wife of a middle-aged banker, was waiting upstairs for her lover, a certain Herr von Puhl. Unfortunately a second lover, Harold Henwood, also thought he had an appointment with the lady. The lovers met at the bar. Von Puhl taunted Henwood by saying that he was going upstairs "to make love to your sweetheart." Henwood pulled a gun and "made smoke." True to style, he not only killed von Puhl but also an innocent drinking man, George Copeland, and severely wounded another gentleman, Jim Atkinson. It is satisfying to know that Henwood sincerely apologized to these two gentlemen before being overwhelmed by the two bartenders, and that Copeland still had enough life left in him to accept the apology. The mayhem continues to this day, but fatalities are rare.

So in despair I turned into a busy Western
    town,
And hoped to see the gun-fighters a-mowing of
    men down;
But while I loitered on the street to see blood
    by the flagon,
I fell before a green-goods man and then a
    devil wagon.

For Western life ain't wild and woolly now;
There is no daily gunpowder powwow;
There are bunco games galore
And the tourist dude holds the floor.
But Western life ain't wild and woolly now!

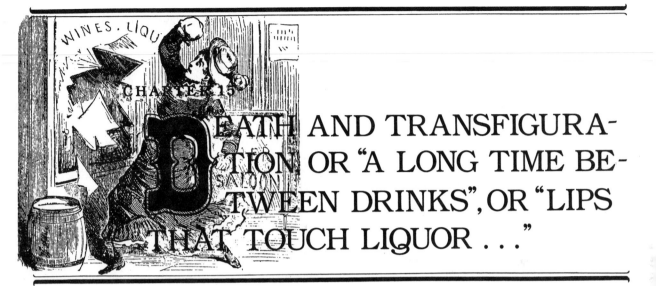

DEATH AND TRANSFIGURA-TION, OR "A LONG TIME BE-TWEEN DRINKS", OR "LIPS THAT TOUCH LIQUOR . . ."

I've been a moonshiner for
    seventeen long years,
I've spent all my money for
    whiskey and beers.
I'll go to some holler, I'll put up
    my still,
I'll make you one gallon for a
    two-dollar bill.

Mother's in the kitchen
Washing out the jugs;
Sister's in the pantry
Bottling the suds;
Father's in the cellar
Mixing up the hops;
Johnny's on the front porch
Watching for the cops.

—Anonymous songs

Prohibition is generally looked upon by westerners as an abomination imposed upon them by sanctimonious easterners, male and female. The thing, they say, was inflicted upon red-blooded drinking men of the prairies and mountains with the help of a meddling, weak-kneed federal government kowtowing to public opinion (eastern), artificially manufactured by Bible-toting, sexless zealots. In reality many western counties and states went dry long before the Noble Experiment was imposed nationwide. Moonshine, on the other hand, has always been localized in the public mind as a phenomenon of the southern highlands. This notion, too, is a false one. Wherever there were Americans, there was also moonshine. Men made their own firewater in colonial times and still do so now, East and West. The trappers, gamblers, cowhands, sodbusters, and gunslingers who populated the early West were in large part native-born southerners, the kind of folks who had crossed the Plains with their portable whiskey stills, kettles, and copper coils, losing no time in setting up their equipment to make fortified high wines and double-rectified corn likker. They brought to the West an old and honorable tradition of home brewing and law defying. Already Ashley's beavermen distilled their own nose paint in the fur traders' forts along the Big Muddy, while other mountain men along the Santa Fe Trail were wetting their whistles with that soul-stirring, scorching concoction known as Old Towse. Mormons had their Utah Valley Tan, Texans their Chock Beer, Montanans their Cowboy White Lightning. Westerners made their own likker, both before, during, and after Prohibition. I know one old cowpuncher who, at this moment, has a fine, gut-warming batch of white lightning on hand, crystal-clear and colorless, made of sugar, yeast, and dried apricots mainly, and maybe one or two other ingredients he won't tell about. Westerners also made their own liquor laws without any help from outsiders.

There were many reasons for the decline and fall of the western saloon, as well as of saloons in general. Partially it was the fault of the saloon keepers, the breweries, and the distillers. Partially it was the times—it was chic to be "anti-saloon." Also to blame was the fact that the old snake ranch had ceased to be a necessity, the universal meeting place and political forum. Progress had brought with it churches, schools, meeting halls, libraries, and a host of other institutions which took over the specialized functions that once had coexisted harmoniously under a saloon's roof. In the words of Jim Marshall:

There have been many institutions with longer lives, but few with more colorful careers and few that had to fight, almost from their inception, such bitter battles for survival. There were nearly always, in most hamlets and cities, more people against saloons than for them, and it was only the sterling character of the noble men who ran them, and the grim determination of their patrons, that kept them in existence.

Many of the old, raucous thirst mills operated, indeed, outside the law and persisted, dinosaur-like, in their unlawfulness far into the new, turn-of-the-century law-and-order days. Contributing to their demise was an immense propaganda war waged against them by the Anti-Saloon League and other temperance societies. At the bottom of it all was the old Puritan abhorrence of everything that could come under the heading of pleasure:

sex, gambling, play acting, dancing, smoking, and, of course, excessive drinking. Even rather innocent pastimes, such as shuffleboard and billiards, were, at some time and place, subject to prohibitive laws. "Anti-drinking" legislation in America was as old as drinking itself. For two hundred years, demon rum and legally enforced abstinence were engaged in a running seesaw battle, with now likker and now water coming out on top—a long drawn-out groin-kicking and eye-gouging fight that is not entirely over yet.

There was also the belief among some that sinful pleasures like liquor and sex were natural—and therefore permissible—for the gentry, but not for common folks or, God forbid, indentured servants, slaves, and Indians, who were too child-like or easily led astray to know what was good for them. In colonial Virginia, captains were strictly forbidden to open their casks or to sell rum to the folks crowding at the pier to greet an arriving vessel. Governor Harvey complained that the whole colony reveled in swinish drunkenness and that half of the Old Dominion's income from tobacco, the all-important cash crop, was spent on drink.

In 1733, the governor of Georgia, General James Oglethorpe, made the first attempt to enforce total prohibition in a part of America. Many of the colony's inhabitants were debtors freed from English jails, and the general thought that cutting them off from liquor would help their chances at a fresh start in the New World. But backwoodsmen, knowing every inch of the streams, rivulets, and swamp labyrinths between tidewater Carolina and Georgia, went into bootlegging with a vengeance. The people, therefore, tippled about twice as much as before Oglethorpe's prohibition. Since everybody, high and low, broke the law, there was no machinery to try and jail them all, and the general had to rescind his ordinances. The first attempt at prohibition in America was a dismal failure.

Elsewhere colonial legislation did not attempt to do away with brandy or rum—the good creature, provided by God to comfort mortal, sinful man. The daily tot of rum was a citizen's birthright exercised in full measure not merely by fine ladies and gentlemen, but also by the parson before and after his sermon. Drinking was fine, drunkenness was not. The inebriated citizen was put in the stocks to be pelted with horse manure and laughed at.

During the 1660s the Massachusetts legislature passed a number of blue laws closing tavern taprooms on the Sabbath, but with the wise proviso that "the faint and the sick could be served their medicinal gill or dram at any day or time." The effect was that people felt poorly on Sundays and had to have their constitution strengthened with a sling or toddy.

In 1708, Connecticut enacted legislation fining drunkards ten shillings for each case of overindul-

Sabbath inspection of the taverns.

gence. Imbibing after 9:00 P.M. was punished by a fine of five shillings. Landlords serving hot waters after hours were mulcted forty shillings and, if failing to pay, put in the stocks. Constables were ordered to enforce the curfew.

The borderline between godly, Christian wine bibbing and getting sinfully drunk had to be defined. The Massachusetts Bay Colony held that drinking more than half a pint of strong waters at one time was going beyond the permissible. It also ruled that drinking steadily "above ye space of half an hour" constituted being unlawfully drunk. Drunkards were fined and whipped behind a cart in early Boston, wore a red "D" around the neck for a month in Connecticut, had their names nailed to the church door in New Hampshire, were forbidden to vote in Plymouth, and put in the stocks at Salem. Virginia required ministers to denounce habitual tipplers by name from the pulpit. Virginia judges who appeared in court drunk—a not infrequent occurrence—were fined five hundred pounds and removed from the bench if they did not mend their ways.

Beginning with the 1770s the word *temperance* was heard more and more frequently. Temperance, mind you, not *abstinence*—not for a long time yet. Nobody had anything to say against wholesome, strength-giving wine or beer, or against the dram swallowed "as preventor of dyspepsia" after a satisfying meal. Undeniably, men and women drank too much in these giddy days of the early republic, and not only lowly folks. Alcoholism was rampant in government and the judiciary. At the end of his second term as President, Thomas Jefferson lamented:

The habit of using ardent spirits by men in public office has often produced more injury to the public service, and more trouble to me, than any other circumstance that has occurred in the internal concerns of the country during my administration. And were I to commence my administration again, with the knowledge which from experience I have acquired, the first question that I would ask with regard to every candidate for office should be, "Is he addicted to the use of ardent spirits?"

Of clergymen it was said that a good Presbyterian never gave up a point of doctrine or a pint of rum. The Reverend Henry Ward Beecher complained that many a parson's "sideboard with the spillings of water, and sugar, and liquor, looked and smelled like the bar of a very active grogshop . . . nullifying the means of Grace." The farmer, too, the "country's backbone," overdid things. The *Farmer's Almanac* of 1812 described this little familiar scene:

"Heigh-ho-hum! Here John, take the jug and run down to Squire Plunket's and get a quart of new rum. Tell him to put it down with the rest and I'll pay him in rye, as I told him. Come, Eunice, hang on the tea-kettle and let us have some sling when John gets back.—Wife, how long before breakfast?" "Alas, husband, where is this to end? Our farm is mortgaged; the mare and colt both attached, last week the oxen were sold; and yesterday the blue heifer was driven away; next goes our grain and at last, I suppose, I must give up my wedding suit, and all for sling! A plague on the shopkeepers—I wish there was not a glass of rum in the universe!"

Universal overindulgence spawned the temperance movement. Its spokesmen, at first, were almost exclusively Protestant ministers. As early as 1780 the General Conference of the Methodist-Episcopalian Church condemned both the making and drinking of distilled spirits. By 1789, Connecticut parsons preached not merely temperance, but at least partial abstinence. In 1812, at Lychfield, Connecticut, the Reverend Lyman Beecher reinforced the impression made by his anti-liquor sermons by distributing to his congregation a little work by Doctor Ben Rush, Physician: *Inquiry into the Effects of Hard Spirits Upon the Human Mind and Body.* Thus a technique of persuasion

was born—scientific and medical, as well as moral.

The temperance movement became a religious crusade. Temperance and Protestantism became inseparable. Together with the emerging anti-slavery movement, they formed a Holy Trinity which gathered momentum. By the 1830s over six thousand branches of the temperance movement were busily spreading the creed. The technique of persuasion was improved upon. Pastors urged members of their congregations to "take the pledge." The first temperance leaders, still imbued with the spirit of revolution, had the utmost respect for a citizen's right *not* to abstain. Their motto was "Moral Suasion." Persuasion, however, was not tame. Devil rum was fought with no holds barred. The Reverend John Pierpont, grandfather of J. P. Morgan, thundered during a Boston temperance conference:

If, I be willingly accessory to my brother's death, by a pistol or cord, the law holds me guilty; but guiltless if I mix his death drink in a cup. The halter is my reward if I bring him his death in a bowl of hemlock; if in a glass of spirits, I am rewarded with his purse.

Martin Luther had once said that in the service of God one must not shy away from a good, strong lie. American clergymen took a cue from him, wildly exaggerating the consequences of getting drunk. The New Hampshire parson Kittredge described to his audiences in minute detail the gruesome, multiform deaths awaiting the wine and whisky bibber: "Some are killed instantly; some die a lingering death; some commit suicide in fits of intoxication; and some are actually burned up." Kittredge preached that drunkards were actually highly combustible. He loved to tell the story of a gin tippler "whose breath caught fire by coming in contact with a lighted candle, and he was consumed!"

The members of one temperance movement

"Moral Suasion" pointed out the evils of demon rum.

called themselves the "Washingtonians." George, they admitted, had been no enemy to the good creature, "but he knew when to stop." Female members called themselves the "Martha Washingtonians," leaders of the "Cold Water Army." Washingtonians employed the technique of the "horrible example." At their lectures they always had the most depraved-looking, raggedy, and diseased drunken bum they could find sitting on the podium to be pointed at repeatedly during the sermon with a spine-chilling "Behold what the imbibing of distilled spirits will do to your mind and body." Thus intimidated, men and women by the thousands signed pledges to "refrain forever from ingesting spirituous and malt liquors, wine or cider," while the choir intoned the Reverend Pierpont's hymn: "Dash the Bowl to the Ground." But the "horrible example" technique fell short of expectations. Americans could not be scared so easily into giving up their booze.

The second- and third-generation preachers of temperance abandoned Moral Suasion for coercion. They pushed for legislation and they got it. In 1816, blue laws were enacted in Indiana forbidding the sale of liquor on Sundays. Local option laws were instituted in Maine in 1829, in Indiana by 1832, in Georgia by 1833; communities from then on could vote themselves wholly or partially dry. Temperance zeal did not leave even the army untouched. In 1833 it had to give up the old, hallowed custom, inherited from the British, that entitled a soldier to his daily tot of rum.

Red-blooded Americans did not take kindly to this interference with their private habits. They formed anti-temperance unions and tried to ridicule their enemies out of existence. They were ingenious in evading the law. In Massachusetts they got around the ordinance by staging educational exhibits, such as displaying curiously striped, deformed, or blind pigs. To see such a freak inside a tent before the tavern cost from four- to sixpence. The paying viewer was given a free and generous tumbler of hot waters. As the law concerned itself only with liquor *sold,* not with liquor given away, the "blind pig" prospered mightily. Thus began the battle between the drys and the wets. As yet the drys focused their attacks upon the wicked individual, not upon the saloon, one reason being that the typical saloon did not come into being until 1850. The dramshop which preceded it came in for its share of criticism, but since it usually was a tavern where the traveling parson or pillar of society found bed and board, his wife a warming pan, and his horse a bag of grain, the criticism was muted.

Oddly enough, the first "whiskey wars" going beyond mere arid exhortations took place during the early 1840s in what was then the Wild West, in Wisconsin and Kansas. Frontier people were not satisfied with mere prayers and suasions. Drunk or sober, they were not the kind who "made their water through the eyes." In Wisconsin the "Great Baraboo Whiskey War" broke out when a poor inebriate found his death inside the ill-famed Brick Tavern. The Reverend Thompson thundered against the widespread sale of liquor in the hamlet of one thousand inhabitants, shouting that he wished "to God the thunderbolts of heaven would shiver the Brick Tavern and its contents, animate and inanimate." He riled up the good women of Baraboo, sending them like a swarm of angry bees against the dens of iniquity. In what later would become standard practice,

they entered the saloons and destroyed the supplies—both in the barrel and in the bottle. Having taken care of Baraboo's whiskey mills, the women transferred their activities to Dodge County at large, devastating the Dan Benjamin Tavern. In 1857 a traveler through Kansas described like goings-on in a town called Quindaro.

As the old tavern evolved into the saloon, the campaign to "scotch the serpent" mounted in intensity. The Temperance Union's propaganda swelled, both in volume and variety. Temperance songs proliferated. A whole anti-alcoholic literature came into being. The "horrifying example" method was intensified. Temperance plays became the rage. In verse and prose, they emphasized the angelic child as victim of depraved, drunken parents. Standard lectures were prepared for preachers who lacked the capacity of making up their own harangues.

Believing that the most potent arguments are those implanted in a child's mind while it is malleable, the drys managed to get pro-temperance material into spelling books used in schools. One touching story depicted the sick temperance girl with the doctor at her bedside, prescribing a dose of brandy. "No brandy for me!" exclaims the little one. "I'll die first! I am a temperance girl!"

In Springfield, Missouri, a lady lecturer told her audience how the temperance cause had saved her marriage: "I slept with a rum barrel for ten years; but now since my husband signed the pledge, I have a man to sleep with—thank God."

To which a local reporter added: "Then all the spinsters laid their hands on their hearts, and said Amen!"

The greatest of all persuaders was an opus called *Ten Nights in a Barroom,* the drys' *Uncle Tom's Cabin.* Originally a book by Timothy Arthur, published in 1854, it described a whole village wiped out by demon rum flowing from a den of iniquity, the Sickle and Sheaf Saloon. In the tale, mothers die from broken hearts, the local loony bin can no longer accommodate the mass of patients, judges are debarred, wealthy men wind up in the poorhouse, young wastrels are murdered, children perish, hopeless sufferers from DTs commit suicide. Hardly anybody within ten miles of the grogshop is left alive. The thing was read aloud in a thousand churches, schools, and meeting halls. The story was also put into vivid and garishly colored slides projected by magic lanterns.

Ten Nights was a smash hit for over fifty years. It was eventually transformed into a musical; one of its songs went in part:

At dawn of day I saw a man
Stand by a grog saloon:
His eyes were sunk, his lips were parched,
O that's the drunkard's doom.

His little son stood by his side,
And to his father said,
"Father, mother lies sick at home
And sister cries for bread."

He rose and staggered to the bar
As oft he'd done before,
And to the landlord smilingly said,
"Just fill me one glass more."

The cup was filled at his command,
He drank of the poisoned bowl,
He drank, while wife and children starved,
And ruined his own soul.

The performance always ended with the admonition: *"Just one drink, one small drink, is all the devil needs!"*

The wets didn't take it lying down. Already during the 1860s Californians parodied the solemnly worded pledge with the "Toper's Soliloquy":

To drink or not to drink, that is the question; whether 'tis nobler to suffer the slings and arrows of outrageous thirst or take up arms against the Temperance League and by besotting frighten them? To get drunk—to sleep it off no more. To get drunk without a headache, and to walk straight when drunk—'tis a consummation devoutly to be wished. To get drunk—to sleep in the street; to sleep! perchance to get "took-up"—ay, there's the rub! And thus the Law doth make sober men of us all; and this, the ruddy hue of brandy, is sicklied o'er with the pale cast of water—to lose the name of DRINK.

Brigham Young voiced this opinion:

You may drink nine cups of strong spiritual drink, and it will not hurt you; but if you drink nine cups of strong tea, see what it will do to you. Let a person that is very thirsty and warm satiate his appetite with cold water, and when he gets through he will perhaps have laid the foundation for death, and may go to an untimely grave, which is frequently done.

Wets had their fun with "Lemonade Lucy," the wife of President Rutherford B. Hayes, who had "dried out" the White House. Malicious men used to say that during Hayes's presidency, "at White House parties the water flowed like champagne." Mark Twain refused to sign his name to a document congratulating Mrs. Hayes for her strong pro-temperance stand, saying: "I have lived a severely moral life. But it would be a mistake for others to try that." While in Virginia City, Nevada, Twain had pronounced the town's water so rich in certain minerals that it had to be neutralized with two fingers of whiskey per glass. The nation's creative people—the writers, editors, artists, and actors—strongly opposed having their drinking legislated. In the words of one St. Louis editor: "No two-fisted writer would want to live anywhere except next door to a saloon."

Drinking men sang: "You'll never miss the liquor til the keg runs dry," "The old man's drunk again," "Everybody works but father," and "Where's my little pitcher of beer?"

They parodied temperance lectures:

The teetotalers were winning—they were better propagandists. *Above:* Ten nights in a barroom. *Below:* The Bottle Imp.

No, no, Eli, my boy, that fust glass of wine has ruined many a yung man. The other nite, I drempt I saw my fav'rite sun adrinken from the floin' bole. My hart yarned for'im an' I strode to'rds 'im. As he razed the wine-glass in the air, I was seezed tragick-like and sez I, "O Rufus, the serpent lurks in that floin' wine. Giv'—O giv' it to your father!" and when he past it to'rds me I quaffed it, serpent an' all, to keep it from my tender sun. He was saved from the tempter, Eli, and turnin' with tears in my eyes I remarkt, "O, my hopeful boy, do anything . . . but don't take that first glass of wine."

"Fear not, father," answered my noble boy. "That first glass o' wine be blowed. Us boys is all a-slingin' in ol' crow whiskey and a-punishin' gin."

But while the drinking men made fun of them, the milk-swilling teetotalers were winning. As George Ade ruefully put it: *The non-drinkers had been organizing for fifty years and the drinkers had no organization whatever.* They had been too busy, drinking." The saloonists were lousy propagandists compared to the bluenoses, possibly because the bluenose took the saloon keeper seriously, an attitude that was not reciprocated.

It has to be admitted that in its days of decadence the saloon became something of a public nuisance and that its defenders did not have much to work with. During its best period, the owners could claim that the saloon was, in a way, a bulwark against universal alcoholism. It was licensed. It operated according to law. It kept women and minors out, thereby preventing over half the population from boozing. And, most important, the average saloon served first-class booze. Even discerning wets found late-period saloons deplorable. George Ade, who loved the old-style thirst parlor was forced to write: "The saloon was the flamboyant and defiant expression of all that was not so good in the booze and beer business. Wherever the saloons were tolerated they multiplied like guinea pigs and behaved much worse."

The main problem was the immense proliferation of saloons. The increase was due not to whiskey, but to beer, which drowned the country in a regular deluge. The ever-increasing mass of European immigrants had created a huge appetite for beer. German brewers, introducing the careful brewing methods of their home country, set themselves the task of satisfying this limitless appetite. They took enormous pride in their products and grew wealthy. As a result, new breweries sprang up like mushrooms in every part of the country, especially in the West. Fierce competition was the result; prices were cut and profits could be maintained only by brewing more beer. In consequence, there had to be more saloons to absorb it. This was bad, but not yet fatal. The saloon's ultimate downfall was caused when the Great English Syndicate went into the American beer and saloon business.

The British Empire was then at the zenith of its financial power. It had invested in the American cattle business, but the great blizzards of the 1880s and the nesters' fences had made this particular venture unprofitable. Watching the huge profits made from beer, they decided to muscle in, buying up more than eighty American breweries. As a result, the drinking business became a cutthroat free-for-all. Since there were not enough saloons to absorb all that booze, the brewers and distillers created them by franchise. By 1900, eight out of ten saloon keepers were no longer their own men, but "tied" to a particular brewery or distillery. At the height of the proliferation, there were close to half a million retail outlets for beer and booze. The national average was one saloon to every 315 persons; this figure, as a contemporary noted, included "babes in arms, young children, invalids, teetotalers, members of the Anti-Saloon League, Sunday-School pupils, bluenoses, persons in prisons or jails, patients in hospitals, and those so aged they haven't the strength to lift a glass of beer!"

The majority of saloons grew exceedingly

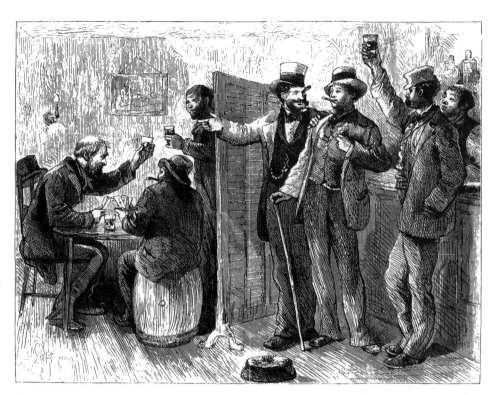

"The majority of saloons grew increasingly dingy."

dingy. The joints of New York's Bowery and Hell's Kitchen were famous for the horrifying quality of their wet goods. In the seventies and eighties drinks were three cents in the lowest dives, whose squalor defied description. No glasses or mugs were in evidence. Tipplers sucked up their fiery refreshments through slender rubber hoses connected to barrels of vile stuff. Planting his pennies down, the customer was allowed to take the end of the hose in his mouth and drink as much as he could without breathing. The moment he stopped for breath, the argus-eyed booze boss yanked the hose from his mouth and nothing but another payment would put it back again. Some tipplers got so adept at taking enormous swallows and holding their breath that they could get gloriously soused on three cents.

Most western drinking places were not as low as the New York and Chicago three-cent joints, but the basic problem was nationwide. Forcing the sale of beer and bourbon became more and more costly. A Chicago saloon owner complained that the brewers had him totally in their clutches, "worse than any loan shark." His place was mortgaged to the brewery for twice its worth. In order to make a living, the man had to open at five in the morning to catch the early factory trade. His bartender's working day averaged fourteen hours, the owner's sixteen. He never got to bed before two in the morning and never slept longer than four—at the most, five—hours. A quart bottle cost him forty cents, and made him more than three times as much, namely $1.50, but this large markup did him no good. It went to pay off the mortgage. Under those circumstances, the saloon owners "had to get away with near-murder in order to annex the needful amount of currency for themselves and their backers."

As the saloons grew worse, the refined, well-heeled drinker withdrew his patronage to sedate private clubs among his own kind. The saloon keeper, therefore, had to scrounge the last penny out of the laboring man, the railroader, miner, cowpuncher, or factory worker. As these did most of their drinking on weekends, he had to remain open on Sunday—his best day. His worst days were Wednesdays and Thursdays, when the working stiff was out of dough. The breweries helped the saloon keepers foster thirst and extract the customer's last cent. Distillers plastered the whole country with billboards and went in for costly magazine advertising and displays. The saloon owners used a variety of come-ons. They gave out "coupons" and "prize numbers" entitling the lucky winner to a free shot. They invented a hundred strategies to encourage treating. They cheerfully cashed payroll checks. They egged on their regulars to spend more than they could afford, putting the pinch on the family budget. It got so bad that the brewers and distillers themselves began to have second thoughts.

Saloon owners broke the law in order to survive, and their bartenders stole them blind for the same reason. Cheating and short-changing became a way of life. In the West, which was strong in dance saloons, where patrons sat down at tables and were served by a waiter or waitress, customers never got the right amount of change back. If they complained, they were pounced upon by the bouncer and thrown out. If they appealed to a policeman, they were laughed at with a "run along, little boy." The saloonists now sold liquor to minors, filled the cans of children with beer to take home, ignored curfews, and mislabeled the whiskey. And worst of all, the brewers and saloon keepers had city governments, judges, and the police in their pockets. Thus the very word "saloon" became synonymous with "evil," ironically so, because when the old terms "road ranch," "tavern,"

and "public house" had fallen into disrepute, the designation "saloon," high-toned and frenchified, had been brought into use expressly to better the drinking place's image.

In June 1893, the Anti-Saloon League was formed in Oberlin, Ohio, with Hiram Price, a five-time Republican congressman from Iowa, as president. This was no soft-treading organization trying to win by gentle persuasion. The League was a hard-hitting outfit whose members believed that the aim hallowed the means; they would go to any length to accomplish their ends, kept tabs on every senator, congressman, and mayor down to the lowliest ward-heeler. They supported anyone who voted dry. If he was lukewarm in the good cause or, God forbid, opposed it, he "was hit over the head with a steeple." Tremendous pressure was brought to bear on lawmakers. The League's methods equaled those of keepers of the worst booze joints. Compared to the Anti-Saloon League, its forerunners—the Temperance Union and the Prohibition Party—had been pikers. The League used the most up-to-date advertising and organizational techniques. It planned and carried out its moves better than the U.S. Army. It was the most politically sophisticated outfit in the country, and most important, it could raise money. Not for the League was the "gradual approach" or the mere enforcing of blue laws; its motto was:

> I stand for prohibition,
> The utter demolition
> Of all this curse of misery and woe;
> Complete extermination,
> Entire annihilation—
> The saloon must go!

The Anti-Saloon League rang the death knell for the old saloon, though for years bar owners were not aware of it.

The Prohibition movement became a women's movement, a mass movement, the main feminist

A little "hatchetation" in Ohio.

movement between 1875 and 1915, taking precedence over the drive for women's suffrage. Women, who had almost no conjugal rights and thus no recourse against a drunken husband, either physically or to control the family funds, considered the saloon the root of many of their troubles.

Even sex was enlisted in the cause. Pamphlets instructed girls in how to keep young men and suitors at arm's length, even if the poor boy had come only to play a game of lawn croquet, and even when his only offense was that he had sipped a single glass of wine at a Christmas dinner:

You may not see me, John, while the breath of alcohol is on your lips. But I shall pray for you, pray to God to deliver you from this evil habit. And, if a year from now, you can say that in that time you have totally abstained, then, John, with the permission of Papa and Mama, you may call on me again.

As a forerunner of the sit-ins and demonstrations of the 1960s and '70s, the militant women of the nineteenth and early twentieth centuries marched upon the saloons, trying to pray and shame them out of existence first, and wrecking them when the nonviolent approach did not get the wished-for results.

> Say, sisters, have you seen the brewer,
> With a bloated, ugly face,
> Pack up his traps and hunt for cover
> Like he meant to leave the place?
> He saw the temp'rance banners waving
> And he started for the sea;
> He left a note behind him saying
> That "this is no place for me."

Wealthy society matrons walked hand-in-hand with shawl-enshrouded wives of miners and bonneted schoolmarms. Fanatic they might have been, radical in their obsession to force their will and moral standards upon an unwilling majority and, especially, on men, but one has to grant them this: unlike modern radicals who skip like grasshoppers from cause to cause, most of them made a long-time commitment, devoting almost their whole lifespan to it. And in the end they won. They wore the men out.

During the "Great Ohio Whiskey War" of the 1870s, more than a hundred ladies marched on Van Pelt's Saloon in New Vienna, attracting a huge crowd. At first Van Pelt defied them with an ax, but suddenly he walked out of his deadfall and announced: "I make a complete surrender, not because of law or force, but to the women who have labored in love. It has reached my heart." Later he said: ". . . I then asked the ministers to please carry out the whiskey. They were terribly willing and out it went. I gathered up the same ax that I had threatened the women with, and drove it as near through those barrels as I could, and out ran the whiskey. Such a shout went up I never heard before, and never will again til I stand before God. The tears ran down their cheeks like a fountain stream."

At the town of Washington Courthouse, also in Ohio, the women besieged Karl Beck's German Beer-Garden. They kept up an uninterrupted day and night vigil, throwing themselves in front of customers who wanted to enter, shining railway spotlights on the place during the hours of darkness. In vain, Karl wailed: "Go vay, vimmins, go home. Shtay at home and tend to your papies; vhat for you wants to come to my peer garten? Dis is de blace to trink peer; ve don't want no brayer-meetings in dis garten." In the end poor Karl broke down, crying: "O, vimmins! I quits, I quits."

The woman who invented saloon smashing was, of course, the one and only Carry Nation. It was perhaps no accident that the Anti-Saloon movement, in the person of Carry, first turned violent in such old Kansas helldorados as Topeka and Wichita, and that the wrath of God descended first upon some of the old whiskey mills that had been the scenes of bloody gun- and fistfights in the trail-driving days. Carry Nation, who dispensed education with a hatchet, had been the wife of a boozer with the capacity of a Goliath, who had "died of the tremors." Possibly it was this fact that awakened in her a near-paranoid hatred of saloons. She decided to save or virtually ruin the "wicked, riotous, rum-soaked, beer-swilled, bedeviled publicans of Kansas." In her own words:

On the 6th of June, 1900, I threw myself face downward at the foot of my bed and told the Lord to use me any way to suppress the dreadful curse of liquor. The next morning, before I awoke, I heard these words very distinctly: "Go to Kiowa, and I'll stand by you."

When Carry started out on her joint-smashing career, she was fifty-four years old, once widowed and about to be divorced. She was almost six feet tall, buxom and muscular, weighing close to 180 pounds. Terrible in her wrath, she required at times the combined efforts of four policemen to subdue her. She had a boxer's beetle-browed, bashed-in face, looking remarkably like J. Edgar Hoover with a bonnet on. She was always severely dressed from neck to ankle in black alpaca, with a high collar and a white bib. Her appearance was forbidding.

She initially went to work on saloons in Kiowa, but her first big job was Carey's in Wichita, one of Kansas' toniest joints. There were about fifty whiskey mills operating at full blast in that town. But she chose Carey's to vent her fury on, probably because it displayed a large painting, "Cleopatra at the Bath," featuring the undraped Egyptian queen against a background of thinly veiled handmaidens and leering eunuchs:

I went into about fourteen places, where men were drinking at bars, the police standing with the others.

I finally came to the "Carey Hotel," next to which was called the Carey Annex or bar. The first thing that struck me was the life-size picture of a naked woman, opposite the mirror.

I went back to the hotel and bound the rod and cane together, then wrapped paper around the top of it. I slept but little that night, spending most of the night in prayer. I wore a large cape. I took the cane and walked down the back stairs the next morning, and out in the alley I picked up as many rocks as I could carry under my cape. I walked into the Carey Barroom, and threw two rocks at the picture; then turned and smashed the mirror that covered almost the entire side of the large room.

This was an understatement. When she first strode into Carey's she had greeted Ed Parker, the booze boss, with a withering: "Good morning, destroyer of men's souls! Shame on you, you rum-soaked ally of Satan!"

"I'm sorry, madam," said Ed, "but we don't serve ladies."

Carry was outraged: "Serve me! Indeed! Do you think I'd drink the hellish poison you've got here? What is that naked woman doing up there?"

"That's only a picture, madam." Ed shrugged his shoulders.

Carry shrieked, "You are a rummy and a law breaker! You should be behind prison bars instead of a saloon bar. Take that filthy thing down and close this murder-mill!"

She not only smashed the huge mirror, worth $1,500, and badly lacerated the painting, but also destroyed a fortune in bottles full of choice whiskey, broke every glass in the place, put to flight two scores of winos, and unnerved poor Ed Parker so badly that he dropped a bottle of prime bonded bourbon. She then swept majestically out of the barroom shouting: "Glory to God! Peace on Earth! Good will to Men!"

This raid made her a nationwide celebrity overnight, but had one result not intended by her. The saloon's owners, Thomas and John Mahan, left the torn painting where it stood, and the place became such an attraction that it could hardly contain the onslaught of eager drinking men. The increased trade more than made good the damage. It was not the only example of Carry's fight against nudity in art. In one place she came face to face with a statue of Diana posed gracefully above a marble fountain. Shocked, she covered her eyes, yelling: "Look! She ain't got a thing on!" Threatening the manager, she continued her harangue: "Look here, my man, you cover up this nasty thing or there'll be some hatchetation around here!"

As a result, Diana was covered with a child's bonnet and dress, but in such a way that part of a shoulder and bosom was wickedly exposed, transforming the chaste goddess into a soliciting *nymphe du pavé*. Again, the joke was on Carry, but ridicule never daunted her. She smashed saloons throughout Kansas and later extended her activities to other states. She soon formed a battalion of like-minded, grim-faced women with pince-nez, high collars, and high-buttoned boots whom she instructed in her technique of hatchetation. This faithful band followed her with axes uplifted, singing her favorite hymn, "Bringing in the Sheaves," or the more lighthearted:

> Sing a song of six joints,
> With bottles full of rye;
> Four and twenty beer kegs,
> Stacked up on the sly.
> When the kegs were opened,
> The beer began to sing,
> "Hurrah for Carry Nation,
> Her work beats anything."

On Carry's cue: "Smash, smash! For the love of Jesus, smash!" they waded in and began their wrecking job. She made money from selling souvenir hatchets; she also published two magazines, the *Smasher's Mail* and the *Hatchet*.

The saloonists did not take Carry lying down. She was on occasion mauled, doused with whiskey, kicked, knocked down, or beaten over the

Carry Nation—a national institution.

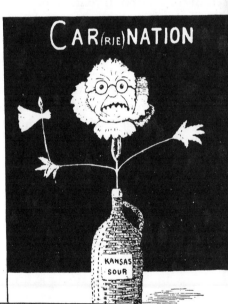

head. One bardog tried to strip her naked. Tipplers put live mice under her skirts and made her a target for rotten eggs. It did not faze her. She thrived on martyrdom. She was thrown into jail again and again, often provoking it by shrieking: "Arrest me! Arrest me!" In prison she would recite the Bible for hours in a thundering voice and revile her jailers loudly as rum-soaked servants of the devil.

The Prohibitionists had at first hailed her as "Madam Caroline Nation, the Great Commander in Chief of God's Hatchet Army." They soon cooled toward her when it dawned upon them that Carry was a comical figure and that the newspapers were making her into a laughingstock.

Saloon owners did well using Carry for their own publicity. They displayed signs reading: "All Nations welcome except Carry!" Many festooned their barrooms with hatchets for decorations. There was a Carry Nation Saloon at Sixteenth and Market Street in St. Louis, a Carry Nation Bar in Leavenworth, Kansas, and a Carrie Nation Saloon in Houston, Texas, which she wrecked. Bartenders John Moriarty and R. T. Willes each invented a Carry Nation Cocktail, both concoctions being frightfully potent. A Carrie Nation Whiskey was hawked in a bottle shaped remarkably like her. The Budweiser brewery people offered her five hundred dollars if she would smash bottles of their beer exclusively. Brewers hired bands to play "Good Morning, Carrie" when she came to town.

Like other saloon celebrities, such as Buffalo Bill, Pawnee Bill, and Wild Bill, she became stagestruck and appeared lecturing between burlesque acts. At Coney Island she starred in a freak show, sharing billing with the Bearded Lady, Lilliputians, and the Siamese Twins.

She wrote two plays, *The War on Drink* and *Hatchetation*, but found nobody to produce them. She did stage a new adaptation of *Ten Nights in a Barroom*, playing the part of the heartbroken mother. A "smashing and hatchetation" scene was written in especially for her. On opening night, she smashed forty-four tumblers and thirty bottles, also chopping up three tables and four chairs. It was, as one reporter said, a "smashing success." Carry Nation died in 1911 without seeing her dream, total coast-to-coast Prohibition, come true. She was, in the parlance of her time, "a card," and something of a joke. But she had added a new dimension in the fight against drinking and played her part in the history of the western saloon.

Besieged from all sides, the old thirst parlor was losing battle after battle. "Slowly, secretly and noiselessly the Murphy [Prohibition] Movement is heading westward!" moaned the Dodge City newspaper, unaware that it had always been there. Kansas went bone dry on March 10, 1881, forbidding the manufacture and sale of intoxicating beverages. It was, of all people, William Barclay (Bat) Masterson who closed down the saloons in which he had quaffed, gambled, fornicated, and occasionally helped tend bar; in, of all places, Dodge City.

If the saloon keepers and distillers had been blind, so also were the drys. Kansas could and should have taught them that Americans' drinking habits could not be changed by legislation. Kansas had voted dry, but drank wet. When, on the fateful day, the clock struck the saloon's doom, the whole state engaged in one truly Homeric drunk while frantic citizens laid in provisions of liquid goods that would last them "through the dry spell." Within hours, blind pigs, underground barrooms, and floating saloons sprang up on the Kaw and Missouri rivers. Just out of reach of Kansas sheriffs, these so-called bum boats and booze rafts sold potent whiskey at two dollars a bottle to Indians, homesteaders, and cowboys. Snooping law-enforcement officers were unceremoniously

Kansas goes dry.

dumped into the river and, if they persisted, killed. The longer Prohibition lasted in Kansas, the worse it got.

Denver, notorious as a city of "gin mills and bagnios" went dry on and off under local option laws. Countermeasures were as prompt in Denver as in Kansas. Nebraska went dry and so did Wyoming. Oklahoma held out fairly long, outlawing booze on November 16, 1907, and, as elsewhere, the wets were prepared. Distillers and retailers sold out their stocks cut-rate: fine bourbon at a dollar a quart, Old Crow at fifty or sixty cents a

pint. At Ponca City, an old bardog set up a sign:

Hush, little saloon, don't you cry;
You'll be a drugstore, by and by.

And, sure enough, the place soon did a land-office business in Hostetter's Bitters and Doctor Fitch's Electric Balsam.

Whiskey and beer consumption in Oklahoma increased to more than twice its former volume under Prohibition. The streets were full of reeling, defiant citizens upholding the free westerner's right to drink what he saw fit. It did not matter. The women's crusade went on to its logical finish. By the time Prohibition became nationwide more than thirty states were already wholly or partially dry. Even so, there were still 177,790 saloons, 1,217 breweries, and 507 distillers in the country, together with tens of thousands of blind pigs and illegal stills.

The Noble Experiment became a reality at 7:05 A.M. on the morning of January 16, 1920, and the last of the old saloons shut down its batwing doors. While the red noses mourned, the bluenoses celebrated, toasting each other in milk or tea. But, on January 17, thousands of "alky cookers" were promptly put into operation, and the unkempt, furtive, shifty-eyed bootlegger took the place of the jolly, red-vested, white-aproned bardog.

There was soon a bootlegger lurking behind every cactus, a still drip-dripping in any sizable clump of cottonwoods, and so much absolutely atrocious rotgut in the whole Southwest "that a man could swim his horse in it clear from the Rio Grande to the Colorado line." In New Mexico, Arizona, and Texas, the leading men were also the leading drinkers. Wise politicians, they used to say that it was easy to make laws but hard to enforce them. In fact, they had neither the manpower nor the money to control those wide-open spaces and rugged mountains, with a thousand-mile-long border.

Other western states dealt with the problem in much the same way. In Denver the place to whet one's whistle was Gahan's on the corner of 15th and Larimer; turned from a saloon into a "restaurant," it stood directly opposite the old city courthouse and the police station. All through Prohibition Gahan's kept its back room open, complete with a well-stocked bar of famous-brand liquors, a watering hole in the desert, serving caravans of politicians, policemen, newspaper reporters, and judges. Under their protective wings, the little fellow could also get his nosepaint without having to worry about raids. Every town of any size throughout the state made sure to have its equivalent of Gahan's Restaurant. Colorado "oozed alcohol from every pore."

In Butte, Montana, a number of saloons kept their swinging doors open from beginning to end of the noble experiment. Washington sent out federal agents at regular intervals to enforce Prohibition in Butte and other parts of Montana. Most of them were bribed, some were never seen again.

One answer to Prohibition was moonshine—White Mule, field whiskey, white lightning, farm whiskey, Blue John, chock beer, Mountain Dew, Utah Valley Tan, Old Towse, Purple Jesus, Sneaky Pete, cow whiskey, and Scorpion Juice. The very word "bootlegger" originated in the West—in western Kansas and the Indian Territory during the 1880s, because when the operator of a pot still went to peddle his stuff, he carried it in pint bottles hidden in his bootlegs. In the wide-open spaces, the bootleggers and their moonshine were unlike the gangsters of Chicago or New York and their stuff. The western moonshiner was a folk hero, a good neighbor, and "a mighty 'commodatin' man."

Moonshining went into men's blood like prospecting or poker. It was an honorable craft. It might be a crime against the far-off big-bellies in Washington, but it did nobody any harm and was a delight to any neighbor who dropped in. That it also put the moonshiner in danger of jail, and occasionally of life and limb, made him a romantic figure. According to a man from the Smoky Mountains:

The little moonshiner . . . fights fair, according to his code, and single-handedly against tremendous odds. He is innocent of graft. There is nothing between him and the whole power of the Federal Government, except his own wits and a well-worn Winchester or muzzle-loader . . . This man is usually a good enough citizen in other ways, of decent standing in his own community, and a right good fellow toward all of the world, save revenue officers.

Some of the stuff westerners concocted was the kind only its makers could love. Texas students had tin washtubs filled with mash set on bricks, with a fire lit beneath. The tub was covered with a horse blanket which caught the rising, condensing fumes. The blanket was then put through a clothes wringer and the precious droplets poured into bottles; and voilà, "Texas Bug Juice" was ready to be quaffed. The operation was simplicity itself, but the product left a lot to be desired. Its most harmless aftereffect was a splitting headache.

Moonshining was not limited to the South.

Bad laws, as a wise man said, make bad liquor. Drugstores sold immense quantities of "Paine's Celery Compound" and "Perry's Pain Killer," which, alcoholic to begin with, could be double-twisted, further improved upon, and miraculously stretched.

Chock beer was fabulously popular throughout the Southwest. It consisted of blackstrap molasses mixed with water, yeast, and corn pone and allowed to sit, ferment, and stink for twenty-one days. It was then strained, bottled, and corked, ready for consumption. Chock beer, also known as Old Hen, was vile stuff, but eagerly sought after because it delivered a fearful kick. Wyoming white lightning, on the other hand, was a noble product, made of dried apricots, sugar, and yeast; "not a bead on it that was not as big as an orange, and not a headache in a wagon load of it." Arizona white mule whiskey was brewed in McKnight Canyon, near Flagstaff, which still "has the world's drunkest chipmunks" feeding on some of the hardened residue left.

Lemon extract was an altogether legal high-power exhilarant held in deep reverence by the citizens of Dallas, Fort Worth, and El Paso. All a thirsty man had to do was get himself a cake of ice, chip a hole in it, and fill it up with the extract. The lemon syrup, within moments, became gooey and hardened, the remaining alcohol could be poured off and made, with some additions, into a soul-satisfying drink.

Prohibition, however, changed drinking habits. For one thing, it made drinking popular and respectable among women. While the pre-Prohibition girl had said, "Lips that touch liquor shall never touch mine," during the Prohibition era, the flat-chested, short-skirted, Charleston-dancing flapper inquired of a prospective date whether he was well provided with inspiring potables and what kind of speakeasy he would take her to. Once it became chic for ladies to have a drink in mixed company, liquor was in and repeal an accomplished fact. The old saloon did not come back with the end of the noble experiment. It had over the years acquired such a reputation for depravity that "saloon" became a dirty word. The swinging doors, too, had grown into symbols of evil. As a result, what came back after repeal was not the old familiar thirst parlor, but bars, cocktail lounges, ye olde tavernes, taprooms, cafés, and clubs. Thus, almost half a century after the end of Prohibition, and after a new generation has forgotten the reason, "saloons" are still legally taboo, except in some vacation spots where the law conveniently closes one eye for the sake of "local color" and the tourist dollar.

A few of the ancient snake ranches have survived. The Buffalo, the Legal Tender, Long Branch, Bucket of Blood, Bull's Head, Red Onion, Red Ram, Number Ten, Stockman, Silver Dollar, Miner's Exchange, Crazy Horse, Kelly's, Andy's, Buckhorn Exchange, Crystal, Moose, Nugget, Antlers, Alamo, Mint, Double Eagle, the Soapy Smith, Seven Gables, Pioneer, Bale of Hay, Windsor, Free Soil, Jerome—maybe three, four dozen in all. A precious few are largely unchanged, except for a television wedged into a corner over the bar, a juke box, and electric light. They are half-deserted and in an advanced stage of gentle decay. Others have gone Williamsburg: more museums than bars, and they are full. Some are ruins now, homes for owls and bats.

And so the cheerful sound of the bung starter is no longer heard in the land, nor the festive revolver, nor the cry of "keno," nor the chorus of drinkers struggling with "Sweet Adeline." The form divine over the backbar has disappeared, and no glitter of diamond shirt studs, brass rails, and spittoons greets the eye. Backsides no longer warm themselves before pot-bellied stoves, the fragrance of sawdust, coal oil, and cheroots has faded, but the ghosts march on.

Epilogue

According to an old tale, a trail-driving boss was sleeping off a jag in an Abilene saloon's upstairs room. All of a sudden, in the wee hours of the night, he was awakened by the loud curses of angry men followed by a fusillade in the barroom below. Rushing down in his long johns, the ramrod found two men bleeding and dying on the floor, and a couple of cowpokes trying to staunch whiskey spilling from a barrel through holes made by stray bullets. Unnerved by the sight, the trail boss asked whether there was anything he could do. "Hell, yes," said one of the cowboys, "give us a hand. If we don't stop them holes all that good liquor will go to waste!"

NOTES
BIBLIOGRAPHY
ACKNOWLEDGMENTS
INDEX

NOTES

Chapter 1

3 Epigraph: *Consolidated Webster Encyclopedia Dictionary* (Chicago: Book Production Industries, Inc., 1954).

6 "Them cute kinds ain't saloons": Author's taped interview with "Keystone" Harvey, Deadwood, South Dakota, 1962.

10 Lincoln as "saloon keeper": His political rivals, including Stephen Douglas, accused Lincoln of keeping a drinking place. Lincoln, in turn, once accused Douglas of being drunk while making a speech. The truth is that Lincoln, in partnership with William F. Berry, for a short time ran a grocery. Since a grocer in the Midwest of that period could not make a living without selling liquor, Lincoln and Berry posted bond to keep a tavern and secured a license to sell alcoholic beverages. Lincoln might have, on occasion, served booze by the bottle, jug, or dipper-full. There is, however, not the slightest evidence that he ever kept a saloon or tended bar in the real sense of the word. At any rate, the grocery store was a failure. See also Bart and Winer, *Homespun America*, p. 354.

11 "Dogville": Lewis, *Wolfville Days*, p. 39.

Chapter 2

12 Epigraph: Old colonial poem quoted by Crawford in *Little Pilgrimages Among New England Inns*, p. 143. "Manhattan, the place where all got drunk": Mentioned by a number of early and modern writers: for example, Kobler, *Ardent Spirits*, p. 37, and Chidsey, *On and Off the Wagon*, p. 5.

13 Colonial inns encouraged building near churches. See Earle, *Stage-Coach and Tavern Days*, p. 13, and the poem on p. 104: "I knew by the pole that's so gracefully crown'd/Beyond the old church, that a tavern was near,/And I said if there's Blackstrap on earth to be found,/A man who had credit might hope for it there." Very striking material on the relationship of church and tavern can be found in Peeke, *America Ebrietatis*, p. 55. "We went therefore into the alehouse": Burr, *Narratives of the Witchcraft Trials*, p. 351. In the words of Cotton Mather: Quoted in Burr, *Narratives of the*

Witchcraft Trials, p. 121; from Cotton Mather, *Memorable Providences*.

14 Thomas Apty wager: Wright, *American Wags and Eccentrics*, p. 588. In the words of George Fontaine: Quoted in Wright, *Everyday Life on the American Frontier*, p. 40; originally in Anne Maury, *Memoirs of a Huguenot Family*, 1853. See also, Branch, *Westward*, p. 44.

16 Description of Parker's Tavern: Nathaniel Hawthorne, *American Notebooks*, as quoted in Marshall, *Swinging Doors*, pp. 46–47.

17 In the words of Timothy Dwight: Marshall, *Swinging Doors*, p. 29.

18 "He is not drunk": Old doggerel, quoted in Carson, *The Social History of Bourbon*, p. 67.

19 "By a sudden stroke": Carson, *Rum and Reform in Old New England*, p. 14. "To keeping ministers": Crawford, *Little Pilgrimages Among New England Inns*, p. 224. Parties of colonial clerics, politicians, soldiers, and tradesmen consumed enormous quantities of hard liquor and other alcoholic beverages as attested by numerous surviving bills. Conversation in taverns: Wright,

American Wags and Eccentrics, pp. 54–55.

20 "We can make liquor": Earle, Stage-Coach and Tavern Days, p. 123.

22 An officer to Governor Clinton: It was not until November 2, 1832, that President Jackson's Secretary of War, Lewis Cass, made obligatory daily rum and spirits ration for American soldiers.

A chaplain sent to Carolina: William Byrd on frontier life in North Carolina 1728. As quoted in Wright, Everyday Life on the American Frontier, p. 42.

23 Bully Dawson's punch recipe: Earle, Stage-Coach and Tavern Days, p. 120; originally in Charles Lamb, Popular Fallacies.

Tangy, scorched taste: We owe an amusing account of flip, and how it tastes, to Alice Morse Earle: "Many a reader of them [old descriptions], inspired by the picture, has heated an iron poker or flip dog and brewed and drunk a mug of flip. I did so not long ago, mixing carefully by a rule for flip recommended and recorded and used by General Putnam—Old Put—in the Revolution. I had the Revolutionary receipt and I had the Revolutionary loggerhead, and I had the old-time ingredients, but alas, I had neither the tastes nor the digestion of my Revolutionary sires, and the indescribable scorched and puckering bitterness of taste and pungency of smell of that rank compound which was flip, will serve for some time in my memory as an antidote for any overweening longing for the good old times." Earle, Stage-Coach and Tavern Days, pp. 113–14.

"And that you may": Two lines of a lengthy poem in Crawford, Little Pilgrimages Among New England Inns, p. 226.

24 Samuel Adams pushed the local

product: Baron, Brewed in America, p. 89.

26 John Adams noted in his diary: Earle, Stage-Coach and Tavern Days, pp. 174–75.

"Strong Halters": Earle, Stage-Coach and Tavern Days, p. 175.

Franklin's drinking song: Kobler, Ardent Spirits, p. 34. This song is often quoted.

The Green Mountain boys were drunk: An eyewitness said that instead of "in the name of the Continental Congress" summons to surrender, Allen really shouted to the British commandant: "Come out, you damn old rat!" John Truslow Adams, The March of Democracy (New York: Scribner's, 1933), p. 108.

27 "They were the centers": Earle, Stage-Coach and Tavern Days, p. 196.

Chapter 3

28 Epigraph: One of various versions. See also Cobb, Red Likker, pp. 21–22.

"Self-reliant, high-tempered": Cobb, Red Likker, p. 21.

29 "Every Boddy took it": Quoted in Dabney, Mountain Spirits, p. 72; originally in Ebenezer Stedman, Bluegrass Craftsman (Lexington: University of Kentucky Press, 1959).

30 "Send us your paupers": From an early St. Paul newspaper, quoted in Le Sueur, North Star Country, p. 19.

31 "Where is your house?": Bart and Winer, Homespun America, p. 24. See also Botkin, ed., A Treasury of Western Folklore, p. 16.

"You'll take the sowbelly": Attributed to Mark Twain. From Botkin, ed., A Treasury of Western Folklore, p. 15.

"May we sleep": Schmitt and Brown, The Settler's West, p. 158.

Brown's Hole: Marshall, Swinging Doors, pp. 48–49.

32 Horace Greeley's description: Horace Greeley, An Overland Journey from New York to San Francisco in the Summer of 1859 (New York: 1860), p. 74.

Chapter 4

37 Epigraph: Anonymous, found by the author in a saloon washroom in 1950.

38 "There is no night in Creede": From a long poem by Cy Warman, editor of the Creede Candle, an early frontier newspaper. Quoted frequently. See, for instance, Robertson and Harris, Soapy Smith, p. 101.

"And there was no longer": Eberhart, Guide to the Colorado Ghost Towns, p. 195.

40 "10 miles": One of many versions of an old homesteader's saying. See variation, Le Sueur, North Star Country, p. 74. See also Dobie, The Flavor of Texas, pp. 15–16.

41 "Dakota Land": Many versions and variations: for example, "Nebraska Land." See Sandburg, American Songbag, p. 280, and Silver, Songs of the American West, p. 234. I quote one of a dozen verses.

The words of James W. Gally: "The Frozen Truth." Quoted in Emrich, ed., The Comstock Bonanza, p. 158.

42 "Dearest Cousin": Dedmon, Fabulous Chicago, p. 11.

"This place is not crossible": Old saying of the Forty-Niners, often quoted. See Davidson, Life in America, p. 246.

"Yes, Sir, this town": St. Paul Pioneer Press. Le Sueur, North Star Country, p. 115.

"There were no women": From Will Henry, *Reckoning at Yankee Flats* (New York: Random House, 1958), p. 71. See Towle, *Vigilante Woman*, p. 94, for a more accessible source.

44 "Just arrived": Dick, *The Sodhouse Frontier*, p. 267.

"A fair sample": From the Wichita *Eagle* (1879–1885). See Dick, *The Sodhouse Frontier*, p. 395.

"At last I was": James Stevens, "Saloon Days," *The American Mercury* 9:43 (July 1927).

46 "I always wanted": "Keystone" Harvey. Author's taped interview, Deadwood, South Dakota, 1962. Shine Philips uses almost the same words in describing the same thing in his book, *Big Spring*, p. 83.

"The railroad": Marshall, *Swinging Doors*, p. 77. See also White, *Texas—An Informal History*, p. 201.

48 "Last evening": *Tombstone Epitaph*, July 23, 1880. In Martin Douglas, *Tombstone's Epitaph* (Albuquerque: University of New Mexico Press, 1951), p. 53.

"A quarrel": Essad Bey, *Geschichten aus dem Kaukasus* (Berlin, 1924).

49 "The 'Klondyke' ": Philips, *Big Spring*, p. 11.

50 "Zoological specimens": The Buckhorn Exchange in Denver, at 1000 Osage Street, is a fine old 1893 edifice with the bar upstairs. It is the prime example of a saloon turned into a museum of natural history. Besides innumerable trophy heads and antlers, there are also a score or so of glass cases lining the walls of the first floor that contain specimens of practically the whole of Rocky Mountain fauna, all neatly and expertly stuffed or prepared, from reptiles to the smaller carnivores. Fine Indian artifacts also abound.

Chapter 5

55 Epigraph: Twain, *Roughing It*, p. 339.

57 "I am not sure": Twain, *Roughing It*, p. 339.

"A red-nosed, jolly fellow": Helper, *Land of Gold*, p. 65.

59 "I never drink behind the bar": Ade, *The Old-Time Saloon*, p. 94.

"What I Know about Saloons": Anonymous, *The Independent* 65, pp. 589–96.

60 "At Nevada": Artemus Ward, *The Works of Artemus Ward* (London: Chatto and Windus, 1865), p. 200.

61 Tom and Jerry: There is a mystery here. Jeremiah Thomas is generally credited with having invented the famous Tom and Jerry cocktail. Nathaniel Hawthorne, however, mentions having a Tom and Jerry in a New England inn as early as 1837. Thomas was born in Connecticut in 1825. It is most unlikely that he concocted his cocktail in early childhood. He traveled west and became San Francisco's number one bartender, a legend in his own time. One must assume that he knew the Tom and Jerry from his earlier days on the East Coast and then unveiled his own, improved version in California. At any rate, he got the credit. According to Jim Marshall (*Swinging Doors*, p. 150), the Tom and Jerry was invented by Professor Jeremiah Thomas in the Planter's Bar in St. Louis, 1853.

62 "This particular barkeep": Marshall, *Swinging Doors*, p. 185.

63 "The notorious killer Slade": Twain, *Roughing It*, pp. 85–86.

64 "William Tilghman, Esq.": Dodge City *Democrat*, April 5, 1884.

German Jewish barkeeper: Julius H. Pratt, "Miner's Sunday in Coloma," *Scribner's Monthly*, 1891, p. 260.

65 Frederic Remington, "A Failure of Justice," a magazine article quoted in Harold McCracken, ed., *Frederic Remington's Own West* (New York: Promontory Press, 1960), p. 129.

John L. Sullivan anecdote: Simmons and Simmons, *On the House*, p. 177.

"There were good and bad": Ellis, *The Life of an Ordinary Woman*, p. 106.

66 "Take pity Miss Fanny": Quoted in Florin, *Ghost Town Eldorado*, p. 95; originally in a local Montana newspaper, the *Cedar Creek Pioneer*.

"My last hope": James Stevens, "Saloon Days," *The American Mercury* 9:43 (July 1927).

Chapter 6

68 Epigraph: by John Copeland, quoted in Dane, *Ghost Town*, p. 233.

"Whiskey has been blamed": Russell, *Trails Plowed Under*, p. 137.

69 "Imagine if you can": Dial, *Saloons of Denver*, p. 30.

"The perfect presentment": Athearn, *Westward the Briton*, p. 92.

"Mostly men": *Ballou's Weekly Magazine*, 1860.

70 "The Dutch and Germans": Ruxton, *In the Old West*, p. 97.

71 Indians were excluded: The writer remembers one old Rosebud Sioux who, back in the 1930s, repeatedly tried to enter a saloon in the hamlet of Carter, South Dakota, now a ghost town. He wanted a drink at the bar just to strike a blow for Native American rights. Each time he was immediately attacked by white, boozing cowboys. Each time he fought

gamely back against overwhelming numbers before being bodily thrown out. He fought forty pitched battles over a period of weeks. When he entered the bar for the forty-first time, the cow punchers owned up that he had earned the right to drink with white men and henceforth he was welcomed into the brotherhood.

72 "When Bill steps off the train": Russell, *Trails Plowed Under*, p. 38.

"Cow men, sheep-men": White, *Lead and Likker*, p. 258.

73 "The cowboy's life": Anonymous, one of four verses. In Thorp, *Songs of the Cowboys*, p. 61.

"An Eastern Drug paper": From *The Gringo and the Greaser*, 1883–1884. Items collected by Peter Hertzog in *The Gringo and Greaser* (Santa Fe: The Press of the Territories, 1964).

74 "There is no limit": Marryat, *Mountains into Molehills*, p. 19.

"Along 17th St.": Dial, *Saloons of Denver*, p. 48; originally in Denver *Rocky Mountain News*, February 2, 1875.

77 "I gave him a tumbler full": Athearn, *Westward the Briton*, p. 74.

78 "Everybody in the place": Marryat, *Mountains into Molehills*, p. 15.

"Who had just enough": Anonymous, "What I Know about Saloons," *The Independent* 65, pp. 589–96.

79 "Approaching the owner": Originally in Fred Hart, *Life in a Mining Town*. Reprinted in Emrich, ed., *The Comstock Bonanza*, an anthology of several western stories, p. 64. See also, "quest for elbow room," in Botkin, ed., *A Treasury of Western Folklore*, p. 16.

"Why does the Westerner spit?": Originally in Rudyard Kipling, *From Sea to Sea*, 1899. Quoted in Athearn, *Westward the Briton*, p. 95.

"The team-hands": James Stevens, "Saloon Days," *The American Mercury* 9:43 (July 1927).

80 "If the defendants": Botkin, ed., *A Treasury of Western Folklore*, pp. 15–16. See also Justice Howard A. Johnson, "Justice in Montana," *The Westerner's Brandbook* 5:3 (Chicago, May 1948), p. 20.

"Part of this winter": Ellis, *The Life of an Ordinary Woman*, p. 195.

81 "Where politicians": Helper, *Land of Gold*, p. 64.

"We find the governor": Helper, *Land of Gold*, pp. 64–65.

82 "Who showed up": Ade, *The Old-Time Saloon*, pp. 105–6.

"Me and a friend": Russell, *Trails Plowed Under*, p. 31.

Chapter 7

84 Epigraph: Origin unknown. Often quoted, this version is from Bravery, *Home Brewing Without Failure*, p. 7.

85 "Panther Piss": Anonymous. The author found this written on a saloon wall in Georgetown, Colorado, in 1964.

86 "Hey! Don't": Charles Edward Russell, *A-Rafting on the Mississippi*, pp. 189–190. See also Botkin, ed., *A Treasury of American Folklore*, p. 51.

87 "And as for Mormon": See Mark Twain on Valley Tan (the "exclusively Mormon refresher"): "Valley Tan is a kind of whisky, or first cousin to it; is of Mormon invention and manufactured only in Utah. Tradition says it is made of (imported) fire and brimstone." *Roughing It*, p. 109.

"In Salt Lake City": Bill Nye,

Bart and Winer, *Homespun America*, p. 628.

"It smells like": From an oft-quoted lecture to Distillers' Code Authority NRA, by Irvin S. Cobb.

88 "Bad men and bad whisky": Martin, *Tombstone's Epitaph*, p. 107.

Mike Fink anecdote: Walter Blairs and Franklin J. Meine, *Half Horse Half Alligator* (Chicago: University of Chicago Press, 1956), pp. 143–44; originally in Lige Shattuck, *Mike Fink: A Legend of the Ohio*, 1848.

89 "If the ocean was whiskey": Popular folksong with many variations. See Downes and Siegmeister, *A Treasury of American Song*, p. 221.

"Whisky is": Aeneas MacDonald, quoted in Fougner, *Along the Wine Trail*, p. 121.

90 "It sloweth age": Aeneas MacDonald, quoted in Fougner, *Along the Wine Trail*, p. 122.

91 "Here's to Corn Likker": Old Tennessee toast and proverb.

"At its best": Dabney, *Mountain Spirits*, p. 19; originally in Jonathan Daniels, *Tarheels, A Portrait of North Carolina* (New York: Dodd, Mead & Co., 1941).

92 "Let me tell you": Cobb, *Red Likker*, pp. 121–25.

93 "It is perfectly colourless": Thomas W. Knox, *The Underground World* (Hartford: The Burr Publishing Co., 1882), p. 769.

94 "Highest and noblest": Kipling, *From Sea to Sea*, 1899. Quoted by Asbury, *The Barbary Coast*, footnote on p. 227.

95 "Oh yes, they boast": Bill Burke, quoted in Emrich, *It's an Old Wild West Custom*, p. 62.

"George Brown's place": Philips, *Big Spring*, p. 86.

96 "It's a burning shame": Anonymous, "What I Know about Saloons," *The Independent* 65, pp. 589–96.

98 "There grows no vine": Henry W. Longfellow, quoted in Fougner, *Along the Wine Trail*, p. 82.

Recipe for trade whiskey: There are innumerable similar recipes. See Mari Sandoz, *The Beaver Men* (New York: Hastings House, 1964), p. 295.

99 "Know ye": Porter and Porter, *Ruxton of the Rockies*, p. 113.

100 "Little spells of fever": Old bottle label.

101 Deadwood freighter: Much-told anecdote. See Agnes Wright Spring, *Cheyenne and Black Hills Stage and Express Routes* (Glendale: Arthur Clark & Co., 1949), p. 177.

"My grandfather": Lewis, *Wolfville Days*, p. 123.

"This, sir, is": Fred Hart anecdote, reprinted in Emrich, ed., *The Comstock Bonanza*, p. 63.

102 "From the time": Marryat, *Mountains into Molehills*, p. 15.

"It has always been": Ellis, *The Life of an Ordinary Woman*, p. 233.

Chapter 8

103 Epigraphs: "Beds, boards": See, among others, Cole, *Stagecoach and Tavern Tales of the Old Northwest*, p. 172. "No more than 5": Sign in Deadwood saloon-hotel.

In 1895: This and the following few incidents are taken mostly from Cole, *Stagecoach and Tavern Tales of the Old Northwest*, pp. 47–48.

104 "Hullo, sir!": Cole, *Stagecoach and Tavern Tales of the Old Northwest*, p. 59.

A western editor: *Solid Muldoon*, 1879–1892.

"For a bed": "Ups and Downs in Leadville," *Scribner's Monthly* 8:6 (October, 1879).

105 "I arrived": Cole, *Stagecoach*

and *Tavern Tales of the Old Northwest*, p. 199.

106 "Travelling": Letter, private collection.

A French aristocrat: Clark, *The Rampaging Frontier*, p. 105.

"Arriving at Sacramento": Masset, *Drifting About*, pp. 124–25.

108 "I have slept": John Ross Browne. Originally "Washoe Revisited," *Harper's Monthly* 9:181. Later collected in J. Ross Browne, *Adventures in Apache Country* (New York: Harper, 1871), p. 364.

Reese River Saloon: Ancient set of rules, printed on blue paper. In author's collection.

109 "Yes! These ruffian miners": Bart and Winer, *Homespun America*, pp. 422–23.

Railroad trains halted: In July 1867 a train from the Kansas UP line was delayed by a gigantic buffalo herd for about forty hours. It advanced sporadically a few hundred yards, only to be stopped again by smaller or larger numbers of animals crossing the track, lying down on the road bed, or massing in front of the engine.

"In the spring of 1869 the train of the Kansas Pacific Railroad was delayed at a point between Forts Harder and Hays, from nine o'clock in the morning until five in the afternoon in consequence of the passage of an immense herd of buffalo across the track." Colonel Henry Inman, *The Old Santa Fe Trail* (New York: Macmillan, 1898), p. 203.

One traveler reported that, in 1869, between Hayes City and Sheridan, his train had to make its way through sixty miles of buffalo.

"When the railroads reached the plains, buffalo met the invaders face to face. Crossing the tracks in masses, they enlightened many an engineer on the matter

of bisontine right of way." Tom McHugh, *The Time of the Buffalo* (New York: Knopf, 1972), p. 6.

Chicago tavern menu: Dedmon, *Fabulous Chicago*, p. 48.

110 "Accomodations of all kinds": Cole, *Stagecoach and Tavern Tales of the Old Northwest*, p. 176.

"The coffee": Parker, *Gold in the Black Hills*, p. 145.

112 "We are now ready": Helper, *Land of Gold*, p. 168.

"In respect": J. Browne, *Washoe Revisited* (New York: Harper & Brothers, 1871). A Mark Twain story tells about a dinner he had with a friend in a California mining camp. Though the eatery was run by a Frenchman, who supposedly knew how to cook, Twain reported, "Had Hell-Fire soup and the old regular beans and dishwater. The Frenchman has 4 kinds of soup which he furnishes to customers only on great occasions. They are popularly known among the boarders as 'Hellfire,' 'General Debility,' 'Insanity,' and 'Sudden Death,' but it is not possible to describe them." Quoted in Ivan Benson, *Mark Twain's Western Years* (New York: Russell & Russell, 1966).

"Bill's chef": Russell, *Trails Plowed Under*, p. 39.

"They breakfast": Masset, *Drifting About*, p. 255.

113 "It was no unusual thing": Nadeau, *Ghost Towns and Mining Camps of California*, p. 81.

Oyster cocktail: Simmons and Simmons, *On the House*, p. 179.

"Talking about food": Abbott and Smith, *We Pointed Them North*, p. 219.

"Casey's tabble dote": By Eugene Field. From a collection, *Red Hoss Mountain*. Reprinted in Dallas, *No More Than Five in a Bed*, p. 3.

114 Occidental Saloon menu: Waters, *The Earp Brothers of Tombstone*, pp. 93–94.

115 "A discreet waiter": Athearn, *Westward the Briton*, p. 29.

116 "The aristocratic sardine": Ade, *The Old-Time Saloon*, pp. 45-46.

118 "Hunger will overcome": Ade, *The Old-Time Saloon*, p. 36.
"Whenever I was": Author's taped interview.

Chapter 9

119 Epigraph: "Preacher McCabe." Often quoted western anecdote. "When I hear." Widely quoted saying, attributed to Abraham Lincoln.

120 "We had little": Rev Peter Cartwright. From Peter Cartwright, *Autobiography of a Backwoods Preacher*, edited by William Strickland (New York: 1856), preface, p. 7.

122 "You talk of": Circuit-riding preacher, Ralph Riley. Quoted by Emrich, *It's an Old Wild West Custom*, p. 148.

124 "Preaching in this room": Nelson, *Wyoming and Its Big Horn Basin*, p. 24.
"I will place": Nelson, *Wyoming and Its Big Horn Basin*, p. 24.
"The ace reminds us": Brown, *Calabazas*, p. 83.

125 "Hear what the great herd book": From a manuscript in the New Mexico State Library, Santa Fe.
"When this man": White, *Lead and Likker*, pp. 87-88.

126 Close and Patterson's saloon: Las Vegas, New Mexico, *Optic*.
"You sinners": Calamity Jane, from a pamphlet issued by Deadwood Chamber of Commerce, 1974.
Brother Magath: James W. Gally, "Spirits," quoted in Emrich, ed., *Comstock Bonanza*, pp. 152-57.
The first sermon in Bismarck:

Dick, *The Sodhouse Frontier*, p. 333.

127 "The preacher": William Devere, "Tramp Poet of the West," reprinted in *Jim Marshall's New Pianner* (New York: M. Witmark & Sons, 1897), pp. 62-63.

128 "The games were going": Streeter, *The Kaw*, pp. 153-54.
"At night, sounds": George Douglas Brewerton, "Incidents of Travel in New Mexico," *Harper's Monthly* (1854), pp. 586-91.
An Irish priest: Jackson, *Anybody's Gold*, p. 83.

129 "The friends": Newspaper item, Laramie, Wyoming, *Boomerang*, 1884.
"A tenderfoot": David F. Day, in his newspaper the *Solid Muldoon*, reprinted in Greever, *The Bonanza West, 1848-1900*, p. 181.

130 "Shoot-'em-up-Jake": Ruth, *Touring the Old West*, p. 136.
"Here lies Charlotte": From *The Solid Muldoon*. See Ruth, *Touring the Old West*, p. 137.

Chapter 10

131 Epigraphs: "Gents, this Honorable Court": Roy Bean, in Botkin, ed.: *A Treasury of American Folklore*, p. 135.
"Your fine": Botkin, ed., *A Treasury of American Folklore*, pp. 123-24.

132 Judge Slaughter's justice: Ellis, *The Life of an Ordinary Woman*, pp. 24-25.
Judge David Irvin story: Cole, *Stagecoach and Tavern Tales of the Old Northwest*, pp. 271-72.
The Honorable Henry Jacques: Cole, *Stagecoach and Tavern Tales of the Old Northwest*, pp. 271-72.

133 Adam Smith stories: Cole, *Stagecoach and Tavern Tales of the Old Northwest*, pp. 273-76.

Judge Stephen J. Field's justice: Jackson, *Anybody's Gold*, p. 76.
Major R. C. Barry's rulings: Greever, *The Bonanza West, 1848-1900*, p. 276. Also in Jackson, *Anybody's Gold*.

134 "H.P. Barber": Wells and Peterson, *The '49ers*, p. 206.
Downieville boot thief anecdote: Jackson, *Anybody's Gold*, p. 419.

135 Perform marriages: Judge Roy Bean began his marriage ceremonies with this customary introduction: "Faller citizens, this here man and this here woman want to get hitched in the legal bond of wedlock. If any galoot knows anything to block the game let him toot his bazoo or else keep his jaw shet now and forever more. Grab yer fins. . . ." Le Sueur, *North Star Country*, p. 120.
The first trial in Montana: Greever, *The Bonanza West, 1848-1900*, p. 226.
"Judge": *The Gringo and the Greaser* 1:14.
McCook incident: Described in the Klondike *Nugget,* during the week of April 9, 1899.

136 "The marshal": Dodge city newspaper story, reprinted in Miller and Snell, *Great Gunfighters of the Kansas Cowtowns*, p. 171.
"He was born": Quoted in Finger, *Frontier Ballads*, pp. 133-36.
"At Langtry, Texas": Originally in a San Francisco newspaper, the *Wave*, 1899. Reprinted in Botkin, ed., *A Treasury of American Folklore*, pp. 120-21.

138 Carlos Robles trial: Originally in Ruel McDaniel, *Vinegarroon* (Kingsport, Tenn.: Southern Publishers, 1936). Reprinted in Botkin, ed., *A Treasury of American Folklore*, pp. 135-36.
"Then a-down": Finger, *Frontier Ballads*, pp. 133-36.
"One of the jurors": Martin, *Tombstone's Epitaph*, p. 23.

139 Cook County courthouse:
Figures for early courthouses
from Gard, *Rawhide Texas*,
pp. 170–71.

140 "1st Resolved": Jackson,
Anybody's Gold, p. 91. Also in
Shinn, *Mining Camps*, p. 237.
"Thou shalt have": Jackson,
Anybody's Gold, p. 95.

Chapter 11

141 Epigraph: Lomax and Lomax,
*Cowboy Songs and Other Frontier
Ballads*, p. 415.

142 Mining king John McKay:
Among the sources for McKay's
grasshopper wager is Ethel Van
Vick Tomes, *Comstock* (New
York: Ballantine Books, 1973).
There are also several
contemporary Virginia City
newspaper accounts.

143 Two professional gamblers:
Beetown anecdote from Cole,
*Stagecoach and Tavern Tales of the
Old Northwest*, p. 316.
"Such a sight": Cole, *Stagecoach
and Tavern Tales of the Old
Northwest*, pp. 326–27.
"Public gambling": *Harper's
Monthly*, 1857. See also Duffus,
The Santa Fe Trail, p. 165:
"Tables for gambling
surrounded the square, and
continually occupied the
attentions of the crowds. . . . I
never saw any people so
infatuated with the passion of
gaming. Women of rank were
betting at the faro bank and dice
tables. They frequently lost all
their money; then followed the
jewelry from their fingers, arms,
and ears, then . . . the sash
edged with gold which they
wear over their shoulders was
staked and lost. . . . The
demons of chance and avarice
seemed to possess them all."

144 "When a town": Martin,
Tombstone's Epitaph, p. 107.

145 "Gambling in Cheyenne": From
a series of articles by Mrs. Frank
Leslie describing an overland
journey by train, from Chicago
to San Francisco. *Leslie's
Illustrated Weekly*, October 13,
1877.

149 "I met my brother": Devol,
*Twenty Years a Gambler on the
Mississippi*, p. 14.

150 Charlie Utter "always
appeared": *New Mexico Historical
Review* 40:1 (1965), pp. 31–32.
"The traditional gambler": "Ups
and Downs in Leadville,"
Scribner's Monthly 18:6 (1879),
p. 823.

152 Holliday supposedly killed: The
number of men killed by
Holliday ranges from fifteen to
thirty-eight according to what
book or biography one reads.
The author could find only
sixteen fairly well-authenticated
victims. Lorenzo D. Walters
(*Tombstone's Yesterdays* [Tucson,
Arizona, 1928]), who was still
able to interview men who had
known the living Doc Holliday,
put him down for twenty-three
men killed.

153 "Doc was a dentist": Myers, *Doc
Holliday*, p. 207.
"Of course, a kyard sharp":
Lewis, *Wolfville Days*, p. 76.
"They are the curse": William
Perkins, quoted in Margo,
Taming the Forty-Niner, p. 36.

154 Nobody ever took a census: For
number of gamblers in Kansas
cowtowns, see Streeter, *The Kaw*,
p. 152. For Chicago see Wilson,
Chicago and Its Cesspools, p. 89.
For San Francisco see Asbury,
The Barbary Coast, p. 19.
Lansquenet: A card game
invented by German
sixteenth-century
"Landsknechts" [free lances,
i.e., mercenaries]. Landsknecht,
in due time, became the French
lansquenet. The game resembled
the more popular faro.

155 "I then paid a visit": Margo,
Taming the Forty-Niner,
pp. 50–51.

157 "Come down!": For gambler's
spiel, see Wells and Peterson,
The '49ers, p. 169.
"Come on up": Parker, *Gold in
the Black Hills*, p. 153; originally
in Zack T. Sutley, *The Last
Frontier* (New York: Macmillan,
1930).
An eleven-year-old bucking the
tiger: "Miner's Sunday in
Coloma," *Harper's Monthly*,
1891, pp. 262–64.

158 The biggest poker match:
Asbury, *Sucker's Progress*,
pp. 347–49.

161 A story, supposedly true: First
mentioned in John Lillard, *Poker
Stories* (New York, 1896). Retold
by Asbury, *Sucker's Progress*,
pp. 28–29. Also in Parkhill, *The
Wildest of the West*, p. 73.

162 "Here you are, gentlemen":
Richardson, *Travels Beyond the
Mississippi*, p. 187.

163 "Now, gentlemen": Soapy
Smith's spiel appeared originally
in *Rocky Mountain News*, July
1889, and is widely quoted. See,
for example, Parkhill, *The Wildest
of the West*, p. xviii.
"All men that bet": Devol,
*Twenty Years a Gambler on the
Mississippi*, pp. 282–83.
"WARNING!": This and similar
warnings were posted during the
1880s in a number of western
towns, particularly in Colorado.
See Robertson and Harris, *Soapy
Smith*, p. 183.

Chapter 12

166 Epigraphs: Bella Union
Advertisement. Asbury, *The
Barbary Coast*, pp. 130–31.
"There is a cat": 1884, Bodie,
California, newspaper item.
"For Western life": Thorp, *Songs
of the Cowboys*, pp. 160–61.

"A surprising MONSTER": New York *Mercury*, 1739.

Execution in Cambridge: Earle, *Stage-Coach and Tavern Days*, p. 218.

167 "He always brought": Cole, *Stagecoach and Tavern Tales of the Old Northwest*, p. 256.

A respected citizen: Story drawn from Cole, *Stagecoach and Tavern Tales of the Old Northwest*, p. 256.

168 "Tremendous grizzly bear" and poster: From Helper, *Land of Gold*, pp. 116–30.

"There will be RARE SPORT": Clark, *The Rampaging Frontier*, p. 110.

169 Danny O'Brien's saloon: Asbury, *The Barbary Coast*, p. 118.

"A wildcat": Bodie *Evening Miner*, June 1880.

"Bodie has a chicken cock": Bodie *Evening Miner*, January 21, 1884.

Whitman-Hanley match: Miller and Snell, *Great Gunfighters of the Kansas Cowtowns*, pp. 18–19. Originally in the Dodge City *Times*, June 16, 1877.

170 Acceptance and Challenge: Martin, *Tombstone's Epitaph*, p. 113.

"Saturday, March 15, 1884": The Bodie *Evening Miner*, March 14 or 15, 1884.

"All the elite": From an article in the *Montezuma Millrun*, September 30, 1882.

171 *"Indecent exhibition"*: From the *Daily Alta California*, 1852. Quoted in Beebe and Clegg, *The American West*, chapter 5.

172 "AT THE BELLA UNION": Asbury, *The Barbary Coast*, pp. 130–32.

"Shortly after midnight": Arizona *Star*, 1881.

173 "Anvil Chorus": Willison, *Here They Dug the Gold*, p. 98.

"At last the orchestra": Dial, *Saloons of Denver*, p. 30.

"He comes!": Dedmon, *Fabulous Chicago*, p. 170.

174 "I went to the theatre": Oscar Wilde, in Willison, *Here They Dug the Gold*, p. 176.

"Wilde stumbled on": Willison, *Here They Dug the Gold*, p. 176.

177 "The auditorium": From a series of articles by Mrs. Frank Leslie for *Leslie's Illustrated Weekly*, October 13, 1877.

178 "One jumps": Margo, *Taming the Forty-Niner*, p. 181.

"The Spider Dance": Margo, *Taming the Forty-Niner*, p. 182.

179 "Her exhibitions": Margo, *Taming the Forty-Niner*, p. 174.

"Adah had top billing": Mark Twain was enraptured by the Menken's performance. In the words of Bernard Falk, Adah's foremost biographer: "Quarrying a rude vein of local journalism, Mark Twain, the moment his eyes glimpsed the astonishing vision, fell under Menken's spell. In Dante Gabriel Rossetti's memorable phrase, 'she was a stunner!' What should impress his youthful imagination more than this strange woman, who united rare intelligence and most glamorous personality, with ravishing loveliness of an order rarely witnessed in those parts? . . . To speak her praises in the Virginia City *Enterprise* became the humorist's solemn and chivalrous duty. His championship of the actress extended to the boycott of a manager who caused her offense. A final expression of his admiration was to nominate her his *Egeria*." From *The Naked Lady or Storm over Adah* (London: Hutchinson & Co., Ltd.), pp. 67–68.

"At exactly 8:31": Editor-publisher Ed How in the Kansas *Globe*, March 21, 1881.

Chapter 13

182 Epigraphs: "Mattie Silks and Fanny Ford": Anonymous, many variations.

"The average man": Mark Twain, quoted by Beer, *The Mauve Decade*, p. 41.

183 "Eureka!": Margo, *Taming the Forty-Niner*, p. 143.

184 "But these were *only*": Dodge City *Times*, week of July 18–25, 1877.

185 "In no part of the world": Originally in Hittel, *A History of the City of San Francisco*, reprinted in Margo, *Taming the Forty-Niner*, p. 237.

"Apropos, how *can* women": Clappe, *The Shirley Letters*, Tenth Letter, p. 11.

"I was working": Ellis, *The Life of an Ordinary Woman*, pp. 36–37.

187 "An individual": John Day, in *The Solid Muldoon*. Day had nothing but contempt for small-breasted women. Commenting on ladies at a ball at the Beaumont Hotel in Ouray, he wrote: "They were all sizes from ginger-snaps up." *Denver Brandbook* (Denver: The Westerners, Denver Posse, 1953), p. 179, and Chauncy Thomas, "Ouray, the Opal of America," *Colorado Magazine* 9 (1934), pp. 17–22.

188 "When you are single": Old cowboy song. Branch, *The Cowboy and His Interpreters*, p. 172.

"I was horse-tied": Hendricks, *The Bad Men of the West*, p. 154.

189 Pretty waiter girls: Samuel Bowles in *Our New West* (1869) noted this advertisement from an Austin, Nevada, newspaper: "Mammoth Lager Beer Saloon, in the basement corner Main and Virginia Streets, Austin, Nevada. Choice liquors, wines, lager beer and cigars, served by pretty girls, who understand their business and attend to it.

Votaries of Bacchus, Gambrinus, Venus or Cupid can spend an evening agreeably at the Mammoth Saloon."

192 "Let us describe": Dimsdale, *The Vigilantes of Montana*, pp. 9–10.

194 "Pickin' up buffler bones": Lewis, ed., *Oklahoma*, p. 249.

"I never had no skirt": Author's taped interview, Truth or Consequences, N.M., 1964.

"Oh, Cowboy Annie": 1880s song, quoted in Abbott (Teddy Blue) and Smith, *We Pointed Them North*, p. 229.

195 "AN UNFORTUNATE MADE HAPPY": Dodge City *Kansas Cowboy*, August 27, 1884.

196 "A nice-looking girl": Wyman, *Nothing But Prairie and Sky*, p. 81.

"I walked up": Jesse Benton, *Cow by the Tail* (Boston: Houghton-Mifflin, 1943), p. 56. Also quoted in Parkhill, *The Wildest of the West*, p. 216.

Strict rules of comportment: Dial, *Saloons of Denver*, p. 35.

"We give the precise": Asbury, *The Barbary Coast*, pp. 100–1.

"The concert saloons": Wilson, *Chicago and Its Cesspools*, p. 166.

197 "Eyes of a preacher": Nineteenth-century writers were considerably more frank about sex, prostitution, and venereal diseases than supposed. Doctors and patent medicines were advertised in family newspapers and magazines. Madames also advertised openly. The well-known cowboy song "The Streets of Laredo" was originally sung this way: "Had she but told me when she sicked me,/Had she but told me of it in time,/I would have got doctored with pills and with mercury,/But now I'm laid low in the time of my prime."

The Cowboy Artist, Charles Russell, put it in a series of four watercolors: "Just a little sunshine,/Just a little rain,/Just

a little pleasure,/Just a little pain."

The third picture in the series shows a cowboy being undressed by a prostitute; the last picture shows him on the range, hopping around in pain, holding his crotch.

198 "Who shot Maggie": From a publicity pamphlet handed out by the famous refurbished Bucket of Blood Saloon, Virginia City, Nevada.

"Pull up your skirts": Towle, *Vigilante Woman*, p. 140.

"I believe": *Western Wilds*, p. 41.

"BOUND TO A HORSE'S BACK": Item in the Cheyenne *Democratic Leader*, July 18, 1884.

"We learn that on Friday": "The Territorial Press of New Mexico," *New Mexico Historical Review*, p. 177. Originally in the Grant County *Herald*, Silver City, N.M., 1879.

199 "One of the chief evils": Mrs. Nathaniel Collins, "Cattle Queen of Montana." Towle, *Vigilante Woman*, p. 51.

"They were easily recognizable": Smith, *Rocky Mountain Mining Camps*, p. 230.

BEST HOUSE IN TOWN!": See Dallas, *No More Than Five in a Bed*, p. 84.

"Brass checks": Inscriptions from brass checks in author's collection. For more on the subject, see Mazzulla and Mazzulla, *Brass Checks and Red Lights*, a booklet with the following poem on the inside cover: "Oh, the lust for mountain gold dust/Brought us lusty mountin men,/Who through lust for mountin' women,/Quickly lost their gold again."—E.L. Some of the old parlor house brass checks are currently being reproduced for the tourist trade by a firm in El Paso.

201 Red light district: Deadwood

claims to have been the birthplace of the name "cat house" for bordello. According to several writers, a Deadwood freighter by the name of Phatty Thompson discovered a sudden fad, among the shady ladies, for cats as pets. Thompson proposed to furnish them. He bought an entire cartload of felines, at twenty-five cents a piece, selling them, according to their condition, color, etc., at a good profit to the numerous inmates of Deadwood's houses of ill repute, which from then on were known as cat houses. The story is mentioned in Greever, *The Bonanza West, 1848–1900*, p. 314.

"Beautiful Bibulous Babylon": Originally in Wright, *Dodge City—Cowboy's Capital*. Quoted in Parkhill, *The Wildest of the West*, p. 223.

"The Barbary Coast": Benjamin Estelle Lloyd, *Lights and Shadows of San Francisco* (San Francisco, 1876) and Asbury, *The Barbary Coast*, p. 101.

"A fallen angel was arrested": Martin, *Tombstone's Epitaph*, p. 28.

"Take back the ring": Popular nineteenth-century ballad with several variations. See, for instance, White, *Texas—An Informal History*, p. 189.

202 "These modern girls": Willison, *Here They Dug the Gold*, p. 180.

"My Lulu, she's a dandy": Sandburg, *American Songbag*, p. 378.

203 "Sometimes when I see": Philips, *Big Spring*, p. 96.

"If there have been": Advertisement in the Deadwood *Pioneer*, 1880s, on the "Black Hills Pioneer," author's collection.

"Every saloon": Ellis, *The Life of an Ordinary Woman*, p. 257.

204 "That the calamity": Beebe,

"Like a Wolf in the Fold," in
Bedroom Companion, pp. 55–56.
"And the women": Dane, *Ghost
Town*, p. 250.
"Yes, times": Philips, *Big Spring*,
p. 95.
"Well, it was the way": Abbott
(Teddy Blue)and Smith, *We
Pointed Them North*, pp. 189–90.

Chapter 14

205 Epigraphs: "He shot a greaser":
From "Billy the Kid," an old
cowboy song, Lomax and
Lomax, *Cowboy Songs and Other
Frontier Ballads*, p. 140. See also
Riegel, *America Moves West*,
p. 543.
"Whiskey en women en poker":
Thorp, *Songs of the Cowboys*,
pp. 6–7.
"I always carried a gun": Abbott
(Teddy Blue) and Smith, *We
Pointed Them North*, p. 211.

206 "A'm raised in a swamp" and "I
got two rows of nipples":
Traditional brags, anonymous.
See Botkin, ed., *A Treasury of
American Folklore*, pp. 59, 67.

207 "Oh Lord, we pray Thee":
Often quoted. See Vestal, *Queen
of the Cowtowns*, p. 30.

208 "Why thar's more": John Filson,
"The Adventures of Colonel
Daniel Boon," in *The Discovery
and Settlement of Kentucke*
(Wilmington, 1784). There are
many reprints.

209 "Discharging his rifle":
Originally in Emerson Bennett,
The Prairie Flower (1849). Quoted
by Steckmesser in *The Western
Hero in History and Legend*, p. 37.

210 "For the matter of a week":
Lewis, *Wolfville Days*, pp. 7–15.

211 "Oh a man there lives": Clark,
ed., *Cowboy Songs*, p. 69. Also in
Lomax and Lomax, *Cowboy Songs
and Other Frontier Ballads*,
p. 139.

212 "The stars of a new heaven":
Hough, *The Way West*, p. 72.
"Well, replied the citizen":
William A. Baille-Grohman,
Camps in the Rockies (New York:
Scribner's, 1882), p. 4.
"Witness this sweet ancient
weapon": Hough, *The Way West*,
p. 11.

213 Hawken rifle: It has been
doubted by some gun
aficionados that any
muzzle-loading rifle that
westerners used before the Civil
War was able to "stop a buffalo
in its tracks." There are,
however, numerous accounts
that a well-placed shot, and the
emphasis is on "well-placed," by
a plains rifle, specifically a
Hawken, did just that. The
Hawken brothers themselves
had confidence that their
weapon could stop a bison and
touted their product as a
"buffalo gun."
Carl P. Russell, in *Firearms,
Traps, and Tools of the Mountain
Men* (New York: Knopf, 1967),
p. 94, says, "The advent of the
'Plains' rifle was momentous in
the history of mountain-man
armament. . . . Its big caliber,
heavy charges, and slow twist of
rifling resulted in . . . great
smashing power. . . . The
capacity of the rifle could be
increased greatly through the
use of the 'double charge,' yet
such loading was not
accompanied by impractible side
effects."
Twenty-four rounds: So a
number of devotees of the old
cap and ball dragoon pistol say.
Perhaps as a stunt, this rate of
fire might have been achieved.
The author, who is not an
authority, somehow doubts it:
imagine a madly galloping rider,
closely pursued, fumbling for
those two extra cylinders.

215 Phil Coe—Wild Bill Hickok gun
battle: The Abilene *Chronicle*,

October 12, 1871, describes the
fight: "When he [Hickok]
reached the Alamo saloon, in
front of which the crowd had
gathered, he was confronted by
Coe, who said that he had fired
the shot at a dog. Coe had his
revolver in his hand, as had also
other parties in the crowd. As
quick as thought the Marshal
drew two revolvers and both
men fired simultaneously."

216 "There was a fellow": Abbott
(Teddy Blue) and Smith *We
Pointed Them North*, p. 219.

217 "Some ranch outfits": Philips,
Big Spring, p. 94.

218 "To rise up": Gene Rhodes.
Quoted in the *Denver Brandbook*
(Denver: The Westerners,
Denver Posse, 1950),
p. 151.

219 The average western badman:
Brown, *Calabazas*, pp. 25–26.
"It would be": Brown, *Calabazas*,
p. 26.
The great esteem: Mark Twain
commented on the western
badmen and American worship
of violence: "If an unknown
individual arrived, they did not
inquire if he was capable,
honest, industrious, but had he
killed his man? If he had not, he
gravitated to his natural and
proper position, that of a man
of small consequence; if he had,
the cordiality of his reception
was graduated according to the
number of his dead. It was
tedious work struggling up to a
position of influence with
bloodless hands; but when a
man came with the blood of half
a dozen men on his soul, his
worth was recognized at once
and his acquaintance sought."
Roughing It, p. 339.

220 "I'd shot him": Miller and Snell,
*Great Gunfighters of the Kansas
Cowtowns*, pp. 444–45.

221 "There they lay": White, *Texas—
An Informal History*,
p. 175.

222 "BAT'S BULLETS": Originally in

the Kansas City, Missouri, *Journal* November 15, 1881. Quoted in full in Miller and Snell, *Great Gunfighters of the Kansas Cowtowns*, pp. 287–89.

224 "Striking savage blows": George Ward Nichols, "Wild Bill," *Harper's Magazine*, February 1867, pp. 273–85.

"Any man who": Connelley, *Wild Bill and His Era*, p. 7.

225 "Boston Bill": From Edward Wheeler's *Deadwood Dick*, a series of nineteenth-century dime novels. See also Huffaker, *Profiles of the American West*, p. 60.

227 "Tom Cady made a lunge": This story, originally in a Denver newspaper, is often quoted. For instance, see Robertson and Harris, *Soapy Smith*, p. 95.

228 "The Cyprian on the Rampage": The *Daily Alta California*, 1852. Quoted in Beebe and Clegg, *The American West*, n.p.

229 "The drama will embody": Miller, *Arizona Calvacade*, p. 257. See also "Pearl Hart—An Arizona Episode," *Cosmopolitan* 27 (1899), pp. 673–77.

230 "The coming of the barb-wire fence": Richard Harding Davis, *The West from a Car Window* (New York: Harper Brothers, 1892), pp. 135–48.

"Those fine old-timers": White, *Them Was the Days*, pp. 47–48.

"So in despair": Thorp, *Songs of the Cowboys*, pp. 160–61.

Chapter 15

231 Epigraphs: "I've been a moonshiner": Old song, "The Kentucky Moonshiner," from Downes and Siegmeister, *A Treasury of American Song*, p. 218.

"Mother's in the kitchen": anonymous poem. Quoted in Kobler, *Ardent Spirits*, p. 238.

232 "There have been many institutions": Marshall, *Swinging Doors*, p. 14.

233 "The habit of using": Kobler, *Ardent Spirits*, p. 33.

234 "Heigh-ho-hum": From the "Farmer's Calendar, 1812." See Lyman Kittredge, *The Old Farmer's Almanach* (Cambridge: Harvard University Press, 1920), pp. 272–73.

"If, I be willingly accessary": Reverend John Pierpont, in Carson, *Rum and Reform in Old New England*, p. 13.

Parson Kittredge described: From a lecture of the Reverend Jonathan Kittredge of Lyme, New Hampshire. See Carson, *The Social History of Bourbon*, p. 65.

236 "I slept with a rum barrel": Originally in the Springfield, Missouri, *Advertiser*, April 6, 1847. See Carson, *The Social History of Bourbon*, p. 176.

237 "Toper's Soliloquy": Jackson, *Anybody's Gold*, p. 252.

"You may drink": Brigham Young, quoted in Bart and Winer, *Homespun America*, p. 341.

239 "No, no, Eli, my boy": Originally in Melvin Landon, *Eli Perkins at Large* (1911). See also

Bart and Winer, *Homespun America*, pp. 500–1.

"The non-drinkers": Ade, *The Old-Time Saloon*, p. 26.

"The saloon was": Ade, *The Old-Time Saloon*, p. 136.

240 The joints of New York: For drinking habits in the Bowery and Hell's Kitchen, see Asbury, *The Gangs of New York*.

241 "I stand for prohibition": Temperance song quoted in Chidsey, *On and Off the Wagon*, p. 38.

242 "You may not see me": White, "Lips that touch liquor," *Collier's*, March 6, 1926. See also, Kellner, *Moonshine*, pp. 72–73.

"Say, sisters": Old Temperance pamphlet, author's collection.

243 "I make a complete surrender": Kobler, *Ardent Spirits*, p. 121.

"Go vay, vimmins": Kobler, *Ardent Spirits*, p. 120.

"On the 6th of June": Nation, *The Use and the Need for the Life of Carry Nation*, p. 65.

"I went into": Nation, *The Use and the Need for the Life of Carry Nation*, p. 90.

244 "Good Morning": Asbury, *Carry Nation*, p. 102.

"Look, she ain't": Asbury, *Carry Nation*, p. 239.

"Sing a song": Asbury, *Carry Nation* p. 240.

Carrie Nation: Her name is correctly spelled "Carry." Spellings are reproduced here as originally used.

248 "The little moonshiner": Kephart, *Our Southern Highlanders*, p. 127.

BIBLIOGRAPHY

Periodicals and Newspapers

The American Mercury. New York, 1920s. H. L. Mencken, Editor.
Black Hills Pioneer. Deadwood South Dakota, 1870s.
Boomerang. Laramie, Wyoming.
Collier's Magazine. New York, 1920–1932.
Cosmopolitan. New York, Volume 27, 1899.
Daily Alta California. San Francisco, 1852.
Evening Miner. Bodie, California, 1880s.
The Gringo and the Greaser. Manzano, New Mexico, 1870s. Charles Kusz, Editor.
Harper's Monthly. New York, 1857.
The Independent. New York, 1908.
Leslie's Illustrated Weekly. 1877, 1891.
New Mexico Historical Review. Santa Fe, New Mexico, 1952–1976.
Rocky Mountain News. Denver, Colorado.
Scribner's Monthly. New York, 1879.
The Solid Muldoon. Ouray, Colorado, 1879–1892. John S. Day, Editor.
Times. Dodge City, Kansas, 1877.

Abbott, E. C. (Teddy Blue), and Smith, Helena Huntingdon. *We Pointed Them North.* New York: Farrar & Rinehart, 1939; Norman: University of Oklahoma Press, 1954.
Adams, Ramon F. *Cowboy Lingo.* Boston: Houghton Mifflin, 1936.

Ade, George. *The Old-Time Saloon.* New York: Ray Long & Richard Smith, Inc., 1931.
Albert, Herman W. *Odyssey of a Desert Prospector.* Norman: University of Oklahoma Press, 1967.
Asbury, Herbert. *The Barbary Coast.* New York: Alfred A. Knopf, 1933.
——. *The Bonvivant's Companion.* New York: Alfred A. Knopf, 1928.
——. *Carry Nation.* New York: Alfred A. Knopf, 1929.
——. *The French Quarter.* New York: Garden City Publishers, 1938.
——. *The Gangs of New York.* New York: Alfred A. Knopf, 1929.
——. *Gem of the Prairie.* New York: Alfred A. Knopf, 1940.
——. *Sucker's Progress.* New York: Dodd, Mead & Co. 1938.
Athearn, Robert G. *Westward the Briton.* New York: Scribner's, 1953.

Baron, Stanley. *Brewed in America.* Boston: Little, Brown & Co., 1962.
Bart, Wallace Brockway, and Winer, Keith, eds. *Homespun America.* New York: Simon & Schuster, 1958.
Bayard, Taylor. *Eldorado.* 2 vols. New York: Putnam's, 1850.
Beebe, Lucius. "Like a Wolf in the Fold." In *The Bedroom Companion.* New York: Farrar & Rinehart, 1935.
——, and Clegg, Charles. *The American West.* New York: Dutton, 1955.
——, and Clegg, Charles. *Legends of the Comstock Lode.* Salinas, Calif.: Hardy (El Camino Press), 1951.
Beer, Thomas. *The Mauve Decade.* New York: Alfred A. Knopf, 1936.
Bennett, Estelline. *Old Deadwood Days.* New York: Scribner's, 1935.
Borthwick, J. D. *Three Years in California.* Edinburgh, 1857.
Botkin, B. A., ed. *A Treasury of American Folklore.* New York: Little & Ives, 1944.
——. *A Treasury of Western Folklore.* New York: Crown Publishing Co., 1951.
Bowles, Samuel. *Across the Continent.* Springfield, Mass., 1866.
——. *Our New West.* Springfield, Mass., 1869.
Branch, Douglas. *The Cowboy and His Interpreters.* New York: Cooper Square Publishers, 1961.
——. *Westward.* New York: D. Appleton & Co., 1930.
Bravery, H. E. *Home Brewing Without Failure.* New York: Crown Publishers, 1957.
Breakenridge, William M. *Helldorado.* Boston: Houghton Mifflin, 1928.
Brockett, L. P. *Our Western Empire.* Philadelphia: Bradley, 1881.
Brown, Dee. *The Gentle Tamers.* New York: Putnam's, 1958.
Brown, James Cabell. *Calabazas.* San Francisco: Valleau & Peterson, 1892.

Brown, John Hull. *Early American Beverages.* New York: Bonanza Books, 1966.

Brown, Mark, and Felton, W. R. *The Frontier Years.* New York: Henry Holt, 1955.

Brown, Robert L. *Saloons of the American West.* Denver: Sundance Books, 1978.

Bruce, John. *Gaudy Century.* New York: Random House, 1948.

Burns, Walter Noble. *The Saga of Billy the Kid.* New York: Garden City Publishers, 1925.

———. *Tombstone.* New York: Doubleday, 1951.

Burr, George Lincoln. *Narratives of the Witchcraft Trials.* New York: Barnes & Noble, 1946.

Cain, Ella M. *The Story of Bodie.* San Francisco: Fearon Press, 1956.

Calvertson, V. F.: *The Awakening of America.* New York: John Day, 1939.

Campbell, Mrs. Helen. *Darkness and Daylight in New York.* Hartford, Conn.: Hartford Publishing Co., 1896.

Carr, Jess. *The Second Oldest Profession.* Englewood Cliffs, N.J.: Prentice-Hall, 1972.

Carson, Gerald. *Rum and Reform in Old New England.* Sturbridge, Mass: Old Sturbridge, Inc., 1966.

———. *The Social History of Bourbon.* New York: Dodd, Mead & Co., 1963; Englewood Cliffs, N.J.: Prentice-Hall, 1972.

Casey, Robert J. *The Black Hills.* New York: Bobbs-Merrill, 1949.

Chidsey, Donald Barr. *On and Off the Wagon.* New York: Cowles, 1969.

Chisholm, Joe. *Brewery Gulch.* New York: Naylor Co., 1949.

Clappe, Amelia K. *The Shirley Letters.* Edited by Carl E. Wheat. San Francisco, Calif.: The Pioneer Magazine, 1851–52; New York: Alfred A. Knopf, 1949.

Clark, Kenneth, ed. *Cowboy Songs.* New York: Paull Pioneer Music Corporation.

Clark, Thomas D. *The Rampaging Frontier.* New York: Bobbs-Merrill, 1956.

Cleaveland, Agnes Morley. *Satan's Paradise.* Boston: Houghton-Mifflin, 1952.

Cobb, Irvin S. *Red Likker.* New York: Cosmopolitan Book Co., 1929.

Coffey, Thomas M. *The Long Thirst.* New York: Norton, 1975.

Cole, Harry Ellsworth. *Stagecoach and Tavern Tales of the Old Northwest.* Cleveland, Ohio: Arthur Clark & Co., 1930.

Connelley, William E. *Wild Bill and His Era.* New York: Pioneer Press, 1933.

Couch, Jacqueline Grannell. *The Golden Girls of Market Street.* Fort Collins, Colo.: The Old Army Press, 1974.

Crawford, Mary Caroline. *Little Pilgrimages Among New England Inns.* Boston: L. C. Page & Co., 1897.

Dabney, Joseph Earl. *Mountain Spirits.* New York: Scribner's, 1974.

Dale, Edward Everett. *Cow Country.* Norman: University of Oklahoma Press, 1942/1965.

Dallas, Sandra. *No More Than Five in a Bed.* Norman: University of Oklahoma Press, 1967.

Dane, Ezra G. *Ghost Town.* New York: Tudor Publishing Co., 1948.

Davidson, Marshall B. *Life in America.* Boston: Houghton-Mifflin, 1951.

Davis, Clyde Brion. *The Arkansas.* Self-published, 1892.

Debo, Angie. *Prairie City.* New York: Alfred A. Knopf, 1944.

Dedmon, Emmett. *Fabulous Chicago.* New York: Random House, 1953.

Devol, George H. *Twenty Years a Gambler on the Mississippi.* Self-published, 1892.

Dial, Scott. *Saloons of Denver.* Fort Collins, Colo.: The Old Army Press, 1973.

Dick, Everett. *The Sodhouse Frontier.* Lincoln, Neb·· The Johnson Publishing Co., 1954.

———. *The Story of the Frontier.* New York: Tudor Publishing Co., 1941.

Dimsdale, Thomas. *The Vigilantes of Montana.* Norman: University of Oklahoma Press, 1953 (reprint of nineteenth-century edition).

Dobie, Frank. *The Flavor of Texas.* Dallas: Dealey and Lowe, 1936.

Dorset, Phyllis Flanders. *The New Eldorado.* New York: Macmillan, 1970.

Downes, Olin, and Siegmeister, Eli. *A Treasury of American Song.* New York: Howell, Soskin & Co., 1940.

Downie, William Major. *Hunting for Gold.* San Francisco, 1893.

Duffus, R. L. *The Santa Fe Trail.* New York: Longman's, Green Co., 1930.

Durham, Philip, ed. *Seth Jones* by Edward Ellis, and *Deadwood Dick* by Edward L. Wheeler. *Critique of Dime Novels.* New York: Odyssey Press, 1960.

Earle, Alice Morse. *Stage-Coach and Tavern Days.* New York: Macmillan, 1900.

Eberhart, Perry. *Guide to the Colorado Ghost Towns.* Denver: Sage Books, 1959.

Edwards, J. B. *Early Days in Abilene.* Abilene, Kansas, 1946.

Einstein, Izzy. *Prohibition Agent No. 1* New York: Frederick A. Stoke Co., 1932.

Ellis, Anne. *The Life of an Ordinary Woman.* Boston: Houghton-Mifflin, 1932.

Emrich, Duncan. *The Comstock Bonanza.* New York: Vanguard, 1950.

———. *It's an Old Wild West Custom.* New York: Vanguard, 1949.

Faulk, Odie B. *Tombstone—Myth and Reality.* New York: Oxford University Press, 1972.

Finger, C. J. *Frontier Ballads.* New York: Doubleday, 1927.

Florin, Lambert. *Ghost Town Eldorado.* Seattle, Wash.: Superior Publishing Co., 1968.

Fougner, G. Selmer. *Along the Wine Trail.* Boston: The Stratford Co., 1935.

Franklin, James Lewis. *Born Sober.* Norman: University of Oklahoma Press, 1971.

Gard, Wayne. *Rawhide Texas.* Norman: University of Oklahoma Press, 1965.

Garrard, Lewis H. *Wah-to-Yah and the Taos Trail.* Palo Alto, Calif.: American West Publishing Co., 1968 (reprint from 1851 edition, one of several).

Gladstone, T. H. *The Englishman in Kansas.* Lincoln: University of Nebraska Press, 1971 (reprint from 1857 edition).

Glasscock, C. B. *A Golden Highway.* Garden City, N.Y.: Doubleday, 1948.

Greenway, John. *Folklore of the Great West.* Palo Alto, Calif.: American West Publishing Co., 1969.

Greever, William S. *The Bonanza West, 1848–1900.* Norman: University of Oklahoma Press, 1963.

Griffin, Buckley S. *Offbeat History.* Cleveland, Ohio: World Publishing Co., 1967.

Haney, Hood L. *Pioneer Living in Texas.* New York: Vantage Press, 1970.

Hardin, John Wesley. *The Life of John Wesley Hardin—Written by Himself.* Texas, 1896; Norman: University of Oklahoma Press, 1961.

Harris, Charles W., and Rainey, Buck. *The Cowboy: Six-Shooters, Songs and Sex.* Norman: University of Oklahoma Press, 1975.

Heller, Herbert L. *Sourdough Sagas.* Cleveland, Ohio: World Publishing Co., 1967.

Helper, Hinton. *Land of Gold.* Baltimore, 1855; Indianapolis: Bobbs-Merrill Co., 1948.

Hendricks, George D. *The Bad Men of the West.* New York: Naylor Co., 1942.

Hittel, John S. *A History of the City of San Francisco.* San Francisco: A. L. Bancroft & Co., 1878.

Holdredge, Helen. *Woman in Black.* New York: Putnam's, 1955.

Horan, James D. *Across the Cimarron.* New York: Crown Publishing Co., 1956.

———. *The Great American West.* New York: Crown Publishing Co., 1959.

Hough, Emerson. *The Way West,* first of a trilogy in *Frontier Omnibus.* New York: Grosset & Dunlap, 1907.

Howard, Robert West. *This Is the West.* New York: Rand McNally, 1957.

Huffaker, Clair. *Profiles of the American West.* New York: Pocket Books, 1976.

Hutchens, John K.: *One Man's Montana.* Philadelphia: Lippincott, 1964.

Jackson, Joseph Henry. *Anybody's Gold.* New York: Appleton-Century Co., 1941.

———. *Bad Company.* New York: Harcourt-Brace, 1939/1949.

Johnson, J. H. *The Open Book.* Kansas City, 1927.

Jordan, Philip. *Frontier Law and Order.* Lincoln: University of Nebraska Press, 1970.

Kellner, Esther: *Moonshine.* New York: Bobbs-Merrill, 1971.

Kennon, Bob, and Adams, Ramon F. *From the Pecos to the Powder.* Norman: University of Oklahoma Press, 1965.

Kephart, Horace. *Our Southern Highlanders.* New York: Macmillan, 1913, 1922, 1949.

Kobler, John. *Ardent Spirits.* New York: Putnam's, 1973.

Lee, Mabel Barbee. *Cripple Creek Days.* New York: Doubleday, 1958.

Lemmon, Ed. *Boss Cowman.* Lincoln: University of Nebraska Press, 1969.

Le Sueur, Meridel. *North Star Country.* New York: Bookfind Club, 1945.

Lewis, Alfred Henry. *Wolfville Days.* New York: Grosset & Dunlap, 1902.

Lewis, Oscar, ed. *Oklahoma.* Norman: University of Oklahoma Press, 1941.

Lewis, Oscar. *Sea Routes to the Goldfields.* New York: Alfred A. Knopf, 1949.

Lomax, John A., and Lomax, Alan. *Cowboy Songs and Other Frontier Ballads.* New York: Macmillan, 1938.

Lyon, Peter. *The Wild, Wild West.* New York: Funk & Wagnalls, 1969.

Margo, Elisabeth. *Taming the Forty-Niner.* New York: Rinehart & Co., 1955.

Marryat, Frank. *Mountains into Molehills.* 1855. Facsimile reprint, Lippincott, 1962. Other reprints.

Marshall, James (Jim). *Swinging Doors.* Seattle: Frank McCaffrey, 1949.

Martin, Douglas D. *Tombstone's Epitaph.* Albuquerque: University of New Mexico Press, 1951.

Masset, Steven. *Drifting About.* New York: Carlton, 1863.

Mazzula, Fred, and Mazzula, Jo. *Brass Checks and Red Lights.* Self-published, Denver, 1966.

McCoffey, Thomas. *The Long Thirst.* New York: Norton, 1975.

McCoy, Joseph. *Historic Sketches of the Cattle Trade.* Kansas City, 1874.

Miller, Joseph. *Arizona Cavalcade.* New York: Hastings House, 1962.

Miller, Nyle H., and Snell, Joseph W. *The Cowboy Reader.* Lincoln: University of Nebraska Press, 1963/1967.

———. *Great Gunfighters of the Kansas Cowtowns.* Lincoln: University of Nebraska Press, 1963.

Morris, Lloyd. *Incredible New York.* New York: Random House, 1951.

Myers, John Myers: *Doc Holliday.* Lincoln: University of Nebraska Press, 1955.

———. *The Westerners.* Englewood Cliffs, N.J.: Prentice-Hall, 1969.

Nadeau, Remi. *Ghost Towns and Mining Camps of California.* Los Angeles: Ritchie Press, 1965.

Nation, Carry A. *The Use and the Need for the Life of Carry Nation, Written by Herself.* Topeka, Kansas: Steves & Sons, 1905.

Nelson, John Young. *Fifty Years on the*

Trail. Norman: University of Oklahoma Press, 1963.

———. *Wyoming and Its Big Horn Basin.* San Diego: Dick Nelson, 1957.

Nunis, Doyle B., Jr. *The Golden Frontier.* Austin: University of Texas Press, 1962.

O'Kieffe, Charlie. *Western Story.* Norman: University of Oklahoma Press, 1960.

Paine, Ralph D. *The Greater America.* New York: The Outing Publishing Co., 1906.

Parker, Watson. *Gold in the Black Hills.* Norman: University of Oklahoma Press, 1966.

Parkhill, Forbes. *The Wildest of the West.* Denver: Sage Books, 1951/1957.

Peattie, Roderick. *The Black Hills.* New York: Vanguard, 1952.

Peeke, Hewson L. *America Ebrietatis.* New York: Hacker Art Books, 1970.

Philips, Shine. *Big Spring.* Englewood Cliffs, N.J.: Prentice-Hall, 1944.

Porter, Clyde, and Porter, Mae Reed. *Ruxton of the Rockies.* Norman: University of Oklahoma Press, 1950.

Raine, James Watt. *The Land of Saddlebags.* New York: Home Missions, 1924.

Raine, William McLeod. *Guns of the Frontier.* Boston: Houghton-Mifflin, 1940.

Reeves, Ira L. *Ol' Rum River.* Chicago: Thomas S. Rockwell Co., 1931.

Richardson, Albert. *Travels Beyond the Mississippi.* Hartford, Conn.: The American Publishing Co. 1867.

Rickards, Colin. *Bowlerhats and Stetsons.* Palo Alto, Calif.: R and E Research Associates.

Riegel, Robert E. *America Moves West.* New York: Henry Holt, 1930.

Robertson, Frank G., and Harris, Beth Kay. *Soapy Smith.* New York: Hastings House, 1961.

Rollins, Philip Ashton. *The Cow-boy.* New York: Scribner's, 1922.

Ross, Nancy Wilson. *Westward the Women.* New York: Alfred A. Knopf, 1944.

Royce, Sarah. *Frontier Lady.* New Haven, Conn.: Yale University Press, 1932.

Russell, Charles. *Trails Plowed Under.* New York: Doubleday, 1927.

Ruth, Kent. *Touring the Old West.* Brattleboro, Vt.: Stephen Greene Press, 1971.

Ruxton, George Frederick. *In the Old West.* New York: Macmillan, 1915.

Sandburg, Carl. *American Songbag.* New York: Harcourt Brace, 1927.

Schmitt, Martin F., and Brown, Dee. *The Settler's West.* New York: Scribner's, 1955.

Schoberlin, Melvin. *Candles to Footlights.* Denver, Colo.: Old West Publishing Co., 1941.

Shinn, Charles Howard. *Mining Camps.* New York: Harper & Row, 1965.

Silver, Irving. *Songs of the American West.* New York: Macmillan, 1967.

Simmons, Matty, and Simmons, Don. *On the House.* New York: Coward McCann, 1955.

Smith, Duane. *Rocky Mountain Mining Camps.* Bloomington: Indiana University Press, 1967.

Smith, Henry Nash. *Virgin Land.* New York: Vintage, 1950.

Sonnichsen, C. L. *Cowboys and Cattle Kings.* Norman: University of Oklahoma Press, 1950.

———. *Roy Bean.* Greenwich, Conn.: Devin Adair Co., 1953.

Steckmesser, Kent Ladd. *The Western Hero in History and Legend.* Norman: University of Oklahoma Press, 1965.

Stillwell, Hart. "Farewell Peacemaker." In *The Best of the True West.* New York: Julian Messner, Inc., 1964.

Streeter, Floyd Benjamin. *The Kaw.* New York: Farrar & Rinehart, 1941.

———. *Prairie Trails and Cowtowns.*

Boston: Chapman and Grimes, 1936.

Taylor, Bayard. *Eldorado.* New York: Putnam's, 1850.

Thayer, William M. *Marvels of the New West.* Norwich, Conn.: Henry Bill Publishing Co., 1891.

Thomas, Lowell, Jr. *The Trail of '98.* New York: Duell, Sloan & Pearce, 1962.

Thompson, Toby. *Saloon.* New York: Grossman Publishers, 1976.

Thorp, Howard. *Songs of the Cowboys.* Boston: Houghton-Mifflin, 1908/1921.

Tinkle, Edward, and Maxwell, Allen. *The Cowboy Reader.* New York: Longman Greene, 1959.

Towle, Virginia Rowe. *Vigilante Woman.* South Brunswick, N.J.: Barnes & Co., 1966.

Twain, Mark. *Roughing It.* Hartford, Conn.: The American Publishing Co., 1872.

Van Rensselaer, Mrs. Schuyler. *History of the City of New York.* New York: Macmillan, 1909.

Vestal, Stanley. *Queen of the Cowtowns.* New York: Harper & Row, 1952.

Waters, Frank. *The Earp Brothers of Tombstone.* New York: Clarkson Potter, 1960.

Wellman, Paul I. *A Dynasty of Western Outlaws.* New York: Doubleday, 1961.

———. *The Trampling Herd.* New York: Doubleday, 1951.

Wells, Evelyn, and Peterson, Harry C. *The '49ers.* New York: Doubleday, 1949.

White, Owen P. *Lead and Likker.* New York: Minton, Balch & Co., 1932.

———. *Texas—An Informal History.* New York: Putnam's, 1945.

———. *Them Was the Days.* New York: Minton, Balch & Co., 1925.

Willison, George F. *Here They Dug the Gold.* London: Reader's Union, 1952.

Wilson, Samuel Paynter. *Chicago and Its Cesspools.* Chicago, 1909.

WPA Writers' Project. *Copper Camp.*

Bibliography

New York: Hastings House, 1943.
Wright, Louis B. *Everyday Life on the American Frontier*. New York: Putnam's, 1968.
Wright, Richardson. *American Wags and Eccentrics*. Philadelphia:

Lippincott, 1939; New York: Frederic Ungar, 1965.
Wright, Robert. *Dodge City—Cowboy's Capital*. New York: Ray Long and Richard R. Smith, Inc., 1931.
Wyman, Walker D. *Nothing But Prairie*

and Sky. Norman: University of Oklahoma Press, 1954.

Zamonski, Stanley. *The Fifty-Niners*. Denver: Sage Books, 1961.

ACKNOWLEDGMENTS

Grateful acknowledgment is made to the following for permission to reprint previously published material:
Gale Research Company: Excerpts from *The Old-Time Saloon* by George Ade; originally published by Ray Long & Richard R. Smith, 1931; republished by Gale Research Co., 1975. Excerpts from *Stagecoach and Tavern Tales of the Old Northwest* by Harry Ellsworth Cole; originally published by Arthur Clark Co., 1930; republished by Gale Research Co., 1972.
Houghton-Mifflin Company: Excerpts from *The Life of an Ordinary Woman* by Anne Ellis; copyright renewed 1957 by Neita Carey and Earl E. Ellis; reprinted by permission of Houghton Mifflin Co.
Jack Russell and Nancy Russell: Excerpts from *Trails Plowed Under* by Charles Russell; copyright 1927 by Charles Russell, copyright renewed 1955 by Jack Russell and Nancy Russell.
Grateful acknowledgment is made to the following museums and historical societies for the use of their pictorial material: *Collier's Magazine,* the Colorado Historical Society, the Denver Public Library, The Thomas Gilcrease Institute of American History and Art, the Kansas State Historical Society, the Museum of New Mexico, and the Raton Museum, N.M.

The illustrations in this book have been made available by the institutions and people listed below. Many thanks is due the curators of these collections for making them available for public use. The illustrations are listed with abbreviated titles, and the page on which they occur is given in parentheses. All the illustrations not listed here are in the author's collection, which consists of many prints from old books and line cuts in great quantity from *Leslie's, The Police Gazette,* and especially *Harper's.*

HERBERT ASBURY, THE BONVIVANT'S COMPANION,

Jeremiah Thomas (62)

HERBERT ASBURY, CARRY NATION

Cartoon Carrie Nation (245)
The Hatchet emblem (245)

COLLIER'S MAGAZINE

The Bung-Starter (66)

COLORADO HISTORICAL SOCIETY

Gold Hill, Colorado (40)
The National Saloon (43)
Creede canvas saloon (43)
Teller House (45)
The Pioneer Club (47)
The Rifle Saloon (47)
The Teller House Bar (52)
"Face on the Barroom Floor" (53)
The Navarre in Denver (75)
The Denver Exchange (84)

"Whiskey was the stuff" (89)
Boot Hill, Dodge City (128)
The Palace Theatre (176)
Tabor Grand, inside (181)

DENVER PUBLIC LIBRARY

St. Elmo, Colorado (10)
The Pioneer Club (51)
The Tollgate Saloon (58)
Andy Nelson's Place (58)
The Pioneer Club (77)
"I guess there's not . . ." (117)
Trial scene (139)
Doc Holliday (151)
Madame Mustache (156)
Gambling at the Pioneer Club (165)
Cripple Creek Saloon (193)
"Fallen angels" (200)

RICHARD ERDOES

The Tiffany Room (7)
False-front saloon in Crested Butte (39)
Player piano (50)
"Saturday night art" (52)
Fairplay, Colorado, 1975 (130)
Saloon doors in Texas town (251)

THE FITCH COLLECTION

Hands of a barroom fighter (210)
"The majority of saloons" (240)
Kansas goes dry (247)

THE THOMAS GILCREASE INSTITUTE OF HISTORY AND ART

Strong Cup (31)
The Barkeep (56)
Circuit Rider (123)

Acknowledgments

Pioneer Mother (184)
Dance Hall Girl (200)

KANSAS STATE HISTORICAL SOCIETY

Carry Nation poster (245)

LIBRARY OF CONGRESS

The Sour Mash Express (93)
Oscar Wilde (173)
A Cheyenne concert saloon (177)
Sarah Bernhardt (180)
"Dance-House" (191)

A Fandango house (197)
"Eye-gouging, groin-kneeing" (208)
"Gunmen did not always observe"
    (218)
A women's liquor raid (242)

MOVIE STAR NEWS

The Spoilers (5)

MUSEUM OF NEW MEXICO

Tom Anderson's Place (39)
Old Town, Albuquerque (67)

Making Old Towse (86)
Gambling Saloon in Santa Fe (144)
La Tules (155)
Billy the Kid (220)

NEW YORK PUBLIC LIBRARY

Taverns provided food (111)
The Jersey Lilly (137)
The Menken as Mazeppa (179)

RATON MUSEUM

Last drink (83)

INDEX

Abilene, Kans., Alamo saloon in, 46, 148, 199, 215, 224
absinthe, 70, 94
actors, in western theaters, 174–5
Adams, John, 26
Adams, Samuel, 24, 27
Ade, George, 82, 118, 217, 239
Alaska, 9; hurdy-gurdy houses in, 192
alcoholic remedies and cure-alls, 19, 99–100, 250
Allison, Clay, 219, 221
American Revolution, role of taverns in, 24–7
"anti-drinking" legislation, 232–3, 235–6; see also dry states; Prohibition
Anti-Saloon League, 241; propaganda of, 232
applejack, 21
art and artists, 50–3

Baptists, 121
Barcelo, Gertrude (La Tules), 155
"barrelhouse," 44, 87–8
barroom fixtures, 48–50; transportation of, 35–6, 46–8
Barry, Major R. C., 133–4
bartenders: in colonial taverns, 17; as mixologists, 60–2; reputations of, 57–60, 65–7; shooting of, 63; typical appearance of, 56–7; varied backgrounds of, 64; in western saloons, 55–67; women as, 17, 65; see also saloon keepers; tavern keepers
Bean, Roy, 55, 94, 136–8
bearbaiting, 168–9

Beecher, Henry Ward, 234
beer, 24, 61, 95–6, 239; as medicine, 100; served in beer gardens, 95; see also breweries
Bernhardt, Sarah, 179–80
Billy the Kid, 8, 189, 219–20
blacks, in saloons, 70, 71
blizzards of 1880s, 41, 74
"bloomers," 185–6
Blue, Teddy, 113, 204
blue laws, 233, 235
boardwalk, 45–6
boat bars (paddle wheelers), 32, 64
"boilermaker and his helper," 94–5
Bonney, William, see Billy the Kid
Boone, Daniel, 208–9
bootleggers, 248
Boston, Mass.: colonial taverns in, 14, 27; tavern keepers in, 17; taverns as Revolutionary headquarters in, 24, 26
bourbon (red likker), 29, 61, 87, 89, 92; origin of, 90, 92; price of, 101
boxing matches, in saloons, 169–70
brandy, 22; see also Pisco brandy
Breen's, San Francisco, 48
breweries: colonial, 24; German, 95, 239; increase in number of, 82, 239; saloon keepers and, 239, 241
Brown's Hole, 31–2
Brunswick bars, 48
Budweiser brewery, advertising by, 50, 246
buffalo, 109
Buffalo Bill, 76, 209; Wild West Show of, 5, 225
Butte, Mont., 38; "boilermakers" in, 94; Prohibition in, 248

cactus beer (tiswin), 98
Calamity Jane, 210, 228
California wines, 96–8
Campbellites, 121
Carson, Kit, 209–10
Catawba wine, 98
Catholic missionaries, 121
cattle trail drives, 56, 148; eliminated by railroads, 74, 114
caudle, 20
Central City, Colo., Teller House in, 51, 53
champagne, price of, 101
Cherokee Bill, 189
Cheyenne, Wyo.: gambling in, 145; theater saloon in, 177
Chicago, Ill., 9; barroom equipment made in, 48; dancing saloons in, 196–7; gamblers in, 154; restaurant meals in, 109–10
Chinese saloon customers, 70; in Denver race riot, 71
Chock Beer, 232, 250
chop suey, invention of, 113
churches: colonial taverns and, 13; saloons as, 119, 123–8; see also clergymen; preachers
cider, 21
Cincinnati Whiskey, 88
clergymen: colonial, 13; drinking by, 19, 99, 128, 234; as reformers, 196; in temperance movement, 202, 234; see also preachers
Cobb, Irvin S., 28, 91, 92
cocktails, see mixed drinks
Cody, William F., see Buffalo Bill
coffee, 110, 111
Cole House, Boston, 14, 15

colonial drinks and drinking habits, 12–14, 18–24; anti-drinking legislation and, 232–3; distilling and, 14, 21; *see also* taverns, colonial
Colorado mining settlements, *see* mining settlements and towns
Colt, Sam, 213, 214
Comstock gold mines, 64
"concert saloons," 190; *see also* variety and concert saloons
cordials, 20
corn whiskey, 91–2
courthouses, 139; saloons as, 131–40
cowboys: in dance saloons, 192, 194; era of, 6; as gamblers, 148, 149, 159; as gunfighters, 210–11, 215, 216, 230; riding horses into saloons, 217–18; in saloons, 56, 72–3, 76, 101; women and, 183–4, 186, 188; as workers, 74
cowtowns: gambling saloons in, 149, 154; hurdy-gurdy houses in, 189; price of whiskey in, 100; after railroads, 74; saloons in, 56, 74, 82; theater in, 175
Creede, Colo.: Ford's Exchange saloon, 88, 127, 129, 199; saloons in, 38
Crockett, Davy, 10, 86, 209
"Custer's Last Stand," 50–1

dances, 167, 170–1; in hurdy-gurdy houses, 191–2
dancing saloons, 189–202; short-changing customers in, 241
Daniels, Jonathan, 91
Deadwood, S. Dak.: Bella Union, 175; Hickok's death in, 225; saloons in, 38
Deadwood Dick, 209, 225–6
Dean, Julia, 174
death, *see* funerals; violent deaths
Denver, Colo.: actors in, 175; Bagnio saloon, 65; Brown Palace, 48, 49, 57, 199, 230; Criterion saloon, 63; drinks served in, 93, 94; dry laws in, 247; Elephant Corral, 145, 199; ethnic saloons in, 70; Gahan's, 76, 488; growth of, 42; race riot in, 71; "respectable" ladies in, 201; saloons in, 36, 48, 69, 74–6; Taos Lightning in, 59, 85; variety and concert saloons in, 173, 178
Devol, George, 149, 162, 163

distillers: colonial, 14, 21; saloons and, 82, 239, 241
Dodge City, Kans.: gambling in, 154; Masterson as marshal of, 222, 246; Oasis saloon, 64; prostitution in, 201, 202; reputation of, 207; theater in, 175; Varieties saloon, 54, 64, 148–9
dogfights, in saloons, 169
Dougherty, John, 158–9
drinking habits and customs: anti-drinking legislation and, 232–3, 235–6, 246; of colonists, 12–14, 18–19; of pioneers, 29–30; under Prohibition, 250; of westerners, 71–4, 76–80, 101–2; *see also* treating, in saloons
drinks: colonial, 20–4; western, 84–98; *see also* hot drinks; iced drinks; mixed drinks; whiskey
drummers (traveling salesmen), 81
dry states, 4, 246–8
Dubles, Emanuel, 135
Dumont, Eleanor, 155–6

Earp, Wyatt, 64, 184, 210, 215, 216, 223; Doc Holliday and, 113, 153
Ellis, Anne, 65, 80, 102, 185–6, 203
El Paso, Tex.: Pass Brandy from, 87; saloons in, 35, 46, 72
entertainments, 166–71; in variety and concert saloons, 171–8
Erickson's saloon, Portland, 48

"Face on the Barroom Floor," 53
"false fronts," 37
"fandango" saloons, 44, 190
faro, 159–61; expressions from, 164
Field, Stephen J., 133
Filson, John, 208, 209
firewater, 98, 231
flip, 23
floating saloons, 32, 64
food, served in saloons, 109–15; as "free lunch," 115–18
Ford, Robert, 88, 127, 129, 199
Foy, Eddie, 153–4, 178
Franklin, Benjamin, 9, 24, 26; taverns named after, 27
Fraunces Tavern, New York, 18, 26
frontier: short life of, 6; social equality of, 20
frontiersmen: attitudes of, 30–1; entertainments of, 167–8; frontierswomen and, 186; heroic image of, 208–9; as tough and

wild, 69; weapons of, 211–12; *see also* mountain men; pioneers
funerals, 129; and epitaphs, 130

Gahan's Restaurant, Denver, 76, 248
gamblers: amateur, 157–9; female, 154–7; professional, 149–54
gambling and games, 141–2, 159–61; cheating devices for, 163–4; expressions and superstitions of, 164; tricks and, 161–3
gambling saloons, 141–9; end of, 165
"Gospel Sharks," 121–2
Great Whiskey Rebellion, 90
Greeley, Horace, 32, 173
gunfighters: as badmen and "kids," 219; guns and, 211–15; as legends, 205–10; marksmanship of, 215–16; saloon fights and, 226–30; shooting in fun by, 216–18

Hall, Bessie, 65
Hancock, John, 9, 24; taverns named after, 14, 27
Hand, Dora, 198
hangings, as entertainment, 166
Hardin, John Wesley, 210, 221–2
Hargraves, Dick, 150
Hart, Pearl, 229
Harvey House, Topeka, 114
Hawthorne, Nathaniel, 16
Hayes, Mrs. Rutherford B., 237
"hells on wheels," 44, 145
Helper, Hinton, 57, 81, 92, 168
Henry, Patrick, 26
Hickok, Wild Bill, 189, 209, 210, 215–16, 223–5; as marshal of Abilene, 148, 224
Holliday, John Henry ("Doc"), 64, 113, 151–3, 210, 216, 219; and Big Nose Kate, 195, 198
"honky-tonks," 189–90
horses and horsemen: at colonial taverns, 17–18; in saloons, 217–18; at western saloons, 46
Hostetter's Bitters, 99, 247
hot drinks, 23
hotel-saloons, 103–8; *see also* road ranches
Houston, Sam, 10
Hudson, Henry, 12
hurdy-gurdy houses, 189–202

iced drinks, 61
Indians, 4–5; betting games of, 141–2; drinking by, 12, 13; drinks

of, 98; excluded from saloons, 71;
  weapons used against, 213
Irish: in Denver saloons, 70; liquor
  consumption of, 102
Irvin, David, 132
Irving, Washington, 209
Italian saloons, in Denver, 70
Ivers, "Poker Alice," 156–7

Jefferson, Thomas, 9, 24, 27, 98, 233
journalists, saloons and, 75–7
judges: jurors and, 138–9; in saloon
  courtrooms, 131–8
juleps, 94
Jules, Simone, 154–5

Kansas: antebellum hatred in, 55–6;
  as dry state, 246–7; early saloons
  in, 32–4, 36; *see also* cowtowns
Kentucky: origin of bourbon in, 90,
  92; pioneer settlers in, 28–9
Key, Francis Scott, 27
"kids," as western badmen, 219
Kipling, Rudyard, 79, 94

Langtry, Tex., Jersey Lilly saloon,
  137–8
Leadville, Colo.: beer gardens in, 95;
  gambling saloon in, 148;
  hurdy-gurdy houses in, 197; road
  ranch in, 105; saloons in, 37;
  Tabor Opera House, 180–1;
  temperance movement in, 202;
  Oscar Wilde in, 173–4
Lee, Browney, 153
Lincoln, Abraham, 10
liquor, *see* drinks; whiskey
liquor consumption, *see* drinking
  habits and customs
liquor laws, *see* "anti-drinking"
  legislation
Longworth, Nicholas, 98

MacDonald, Aeneas, 89
Manathan, 20
Marryat, Frank, 74, 77, 102
Marshall, Jim, 229–30, 232
Masterson, Bat, 6, 64, 69, 126, 150;
  as Dodge City marshal, 222, 246;
  as gunfighter, 210, 213–14, 216,
  222–3
Masterson, George, 64, 148–9
Mather, Cotton, 13, 19, 78
McCook, James Church, 135
McDougal, Annie, 228–9
McKay, John, 142

McSorley's, New York, 6, 204
medicines, *see* patent medicines
Menken, Adah Isaacs, 179
mescal, 98
Metcalf, Jennie, 228–9
metheglin, 20
Methodists, 120–1
miners: "company saloons" for, 44;
  drinking by, 102; entertainments
  of, 168, 171; as exploited workers,
  73; as gamblers, 143, 159; women
  and, 183, 186–8
mining settlements and towns:
  conditions in, 38–40, 73; gambling
  saloons in, 148; hurdy-gurdy
  houses in, 189; names of, 11, 201,
  207; price of whiskey in, 100;
  saloons in, 37–8; social affairs in,
  170–1
mixed drinks: in colonial taverns, 16;
  in western saloons, 61, 76, 94
Monongahela rye, 90
Montez, Lola, 178
moonshine, 231, 248–50
Mormon Whiskey (Valley Tan), 87,
  231
mountain men, 4, 31–2, 211, 213
Murat, Count Henry, 63–4

Nation, Carry, 243–6
New England, colonial: drinking in,
  13, 20, 21, 24; *see also* taverns
New Mexico: gambling in, 143–4;
  vineyards in, 96
New Orleans, La., 9; "barrelhouse"
  in, 87–8; "honky-tonks" and
  "concert saloons" in, 190
Newton General Massacre, 228
New York, N.Y.: dingy saloons in,
  240; Fraunces Tavern, 18, 26;
  McSorley's, 6, 204; White Horse
  Tavern and Stadt-Herberg, 15–16
Nichol, Duncan, 93

Ohio: pioneer settlers in, 28;
  women's anti-saloon marches in,
  243
Ohio River vineyards, 98
Old Towse, *see* Taos Lightning
opera houses, 180–1; variety saloons
  as, 175
oyster cocktail, origin of, 113

paddle wheeler bars, 32, 64
paintings, in saloons, 50–3
Pass Brandy, 87

patent medicines, 19, 99–100, 250
Penn, William, 24
Perkins, William, 153, 155, 183
Philadelphia, Penn.: drinking in, 14;
  Franklin in, 26; Jefferson in, 27;
  liquor prices in, 24
Pierpont, John, 234, 235
pioneers, 28–31; religious apathy of,
  119; weapons of, 211–12; whiskey
  made by, 90; *see also* frontiersmen;
  westerners
Pisco brandy, 93–4
Plains Indians, 4–5
poker, 143, 158–9, 161
politicians, in saloons, 81–2
Portland, Oreg., Erickson's saloon in,
  48
prairie settlements: conditions in,
  40–1; saloons in, 38
preachers, 120–9, 130, 202; *see also*
  churches; clergymen
Presbyterians, 121
"pretty waiter" saloons, 44, 190
Prohibition (Volstead Act), 6, 22, 60,
  118, 148–50; moonshine and, 231,
  232, 248–50
Prohibition movement: achievements
  of, 246–8; Carry Nation and,
  243–6; as feminist cause, 241–3;
  preachers as leaders of, 130; *see
  also* "anti-drinking" legislation;
  temperance movement
pulque, 98–9
punch, 22–3
Putnam, General Israel, 27

race prejudice, 70–1
railroad: development of West and,
  73–4, 114; saloon equipment
  delivered by, 46; saloons on, 44,
  145
religion: westerners' attitudes toward,
  119–20, 122; *see also* churches;
  clergymen
Remington, Frederic, 65
restaurants, saloons as, 109–18
Revere, Paul, 26
road ranches, 31, 32–4, 103–9
roads, 42, 103
Rose of the Cimarron, 229
rum, 21–2
Russell, Charles, 53, 68, 71–2, 82,
  87, 112
rye whiskey, 61, 87, 89;
  Monongahela, 90; price of, 101

St. Louis, Mo., 9; saloons in, 70
saloon buildings: interiors of, 46–50;
  typical classic, 36, 37
saloon era, short life of, 4, 6, 56
saloon keepers: deterioration of
  saloons and, 239–41; distilleries
  and, 60, 82, 239; *see also*
  bartenders
saloons: number of, 37–8;
  proliferation of, 60, 82, 239
San Francisco, Calif.: Bella Union,
  147, 154, 172, 178; Breen's, 48;
  drinks and drinking in, 92–3, 102;
  early saloons in, 35, 36, 56; El
  Dorado, 147; first theater in, 174;
  gambling saloons in, 145–7, 154;
  hurdy-gurdy houses in, 190, 192,
  196; mixed population of, 69–70;
  oyster cocktail and chop suey
  invented in, 113; prostitution in,
  201; variety saloons in, 171–2;
  women drinking in, 71, 202
Santa Fe, N. Mex.: gambling in, 143;
  La Fonda, 54
"Sazerac," 94
Shawn O'Farrel ("boilermaker"),
  94–5
Shelby Lemonade, 87
signs, in saloons, 53–4
Silverton, Colo.: Imperial saloon,
  46–8; saloons in, 38
Slade, 63, 198
Smith, Adam, 133
Smith, John, 208
social equality: in early taverns,
  19–20; stratification and, 74–6; in
  western saloons, 74
soldiers, in saloons, 61, 81, 102
Sons of Liberty, 24–6
sports, western, 170
stagecoaches, 17–18
Stamp Act, 24, 90
Stevens, James, 44, 66, 79
Sullivan, John L., 65, 203

Tabor Opera House, Leadville,
  180–1
Taos Lightning (Old Towse), 32, 59,
  85–6, 231; price of, 101
tavern keepers: colonial, 17–18; early
  western, 55, 109; female, 17;
  punches made by, 22–3; *see also*
  bartenders
taverns, colonial, 14–20; churches
  and, 13; discussions in, 19; drinks
  served in, 20–4; gambling in, 143;

mingling in, 19–20; names of, 15,
  27; as precursors of western
  saloons, 16, 27; as Revolutionary
  headquarters, 24–7; stagecoaches
  at, 17–18
taverns, early midwestern: as
  courtrooms, 132–3; gambling in,
  143; as restaurants, 109–10;
  weddings in, 167–8; *see also* road
  ranches
Teller House, Central City, 51, 53
temperance movement, 233–9;
  clergymen as leaders of, 130, 202,
  234–5; propaganda of, 232
Tennessee: pioneer settlers of, 28–9;
  Sipping Whiskey made in, 90
Ten Nights in a Barroom, 236–7, 246
Texas: early courthouses in, 139;
  pioneer judges of, 132, 134–5,
  136–8
Texas Rangers, 213, 215
theater saloons: actors appearing in,
  174–5; descriptions of, 177–8;
  drama in, 174–6; variety saloon
  shows and, 171–3
Thomas, Jeremiah, 61, 147
Thompson, Ben, 220–1
Thompson, Will, 57
Thorpe, Captain John, 12
Tilghman, Bill, 64
tiswin (Apache cactus beer), 98
tobacco, sold in saloons, 111–12
toddies, 23, 94
Tombstone, Ariz.: Bird Cage variety
  saloon, 172; Golden Eagle
  Brewery, 95; Occidental saloon,
  114; Oriental saloon, 48
trade whiskey (firewater), 98, 231
travel, on early frontier, 103–4
traveling salesmen, 81
treating, in saloons, 16, 59, 77–8
trials, in saloons, 131–9
Twain, Mark, 57, 102, 112, 237

Uncle Tom's Cabin, 170, 175, 176
Utter, Charlie, 150

variety and concert saloons, 171–8;
  songs in, 201
Vassar, Matthew, 24
Vestal, Madame, 155
violent deaths: in hurdy-gurdy
  houses, 198; in saloons, 205, 206,
  226, 229–30
Virginia, colonial: drinking in, 14, 20,
  24, 26

Virginia City, Nev.: Crystal saloon,
  49; drinks served in, 93; food and
  service in, 115; as ghost town, 165;
  "Jones Canvas Hotel," 144–5;
  Mark Twain's binge in, 102
Virginie, Mademoiselle, 155

Ward, Artemus, 102, 173
Washington, George, 9, 26; as
  example to temperance movement
  members, 235; taverns named
  after, 27
weapons, of westerners, 212–15
Webster, Daniel, 10, 24
weddings, in taverns, 167–8
West: definitions of, 9; effects of
  railroads in, 73–4, 114
westerners: attitudes of, 28; diet of,
  114–15; drinking habits and
  customs of, 71–4, 76–80, 101–2;
  exaggeration by, 150, 206; as
  gamblers, 142, 150; as gregarious,
  68; heroic gunfighters, 205–10;
  marksmanship of, 215–16; religious
  attitudes of, 119–20, 122;
  respectability of, 165; table
  manners of, 112–13; of varied
  nationalities and races, 69–70; *see
  also* cowboys; frontiersmen; miners;
  mountain men
whiskey: excise tax on, 90; made by
  pioneers, 90; medicinal uses of,
  29–30, 99–100; origin of, 89; price
  of, 100–1; western concoctions
  and, 84–9; as western drink, 29,
  61, 87, 89, 91, 101–2; western
  varieties of, 91–2; *see also* bourbon;
  corn whiskey; rye whiskey
whiskey peddlers, 32
"whiskey wars," 236, 242
White, Owen P., 72, 230
white lightning, 232, 250
Wichita, Kans.: drama in, 175–6;
  Carry Nation in, 243–4; Rowdy
  Kate's saloon in, 65
Wilde, Oscar, 173–4, 181
Willard, Francis, 15
wines, western, 96–8
Wolcott, Edward O., 158
women: as anti-saloon crusaders, 82,
  165, 184, 241–3; barroom
  paintings of, 51–3; as bartenders,
  17, 65; cordials drunk by, 20;
  gambling and, 153, 154–7, 165; in
  hurdy-gurdy houses, 189–99;
  pioneer settlements, 29, 40;

women (*continued*)
  preachers' attitudes toward, 202;
  Prohibition and, 250; as
  prostitutes, 199–201; in road

ranches and taverns, 108–9, 113;
  role in the West of, 182–7; in
  saloon fights, 228–9; in saloons, 6,
  71, 182, 202–4

Wooton, "Uncle Dick," 59, 85
Wyman, "Pap," 148

Young, Brigham, 171